GANGSTA YOGA
with a dog

A HOUSEBROKEN collection by Steve Watkins

**Andrews McMeel
Publishing**

Kansas City

For information, write Andrews McMeel Publishing, an Andrews McMeel Universal company, 4520 Main Street, Kansas City, Missouri 64111.

05 06 07 08 09 BBG 10 9 8 7 6 5 4 3 2 1

ISBN-13: 978-0-7407-5454-8
ISBN-10: 0-7407-5454-8

Library of Congress Control Number: 2005925667

www.andrewsmcmeel.com

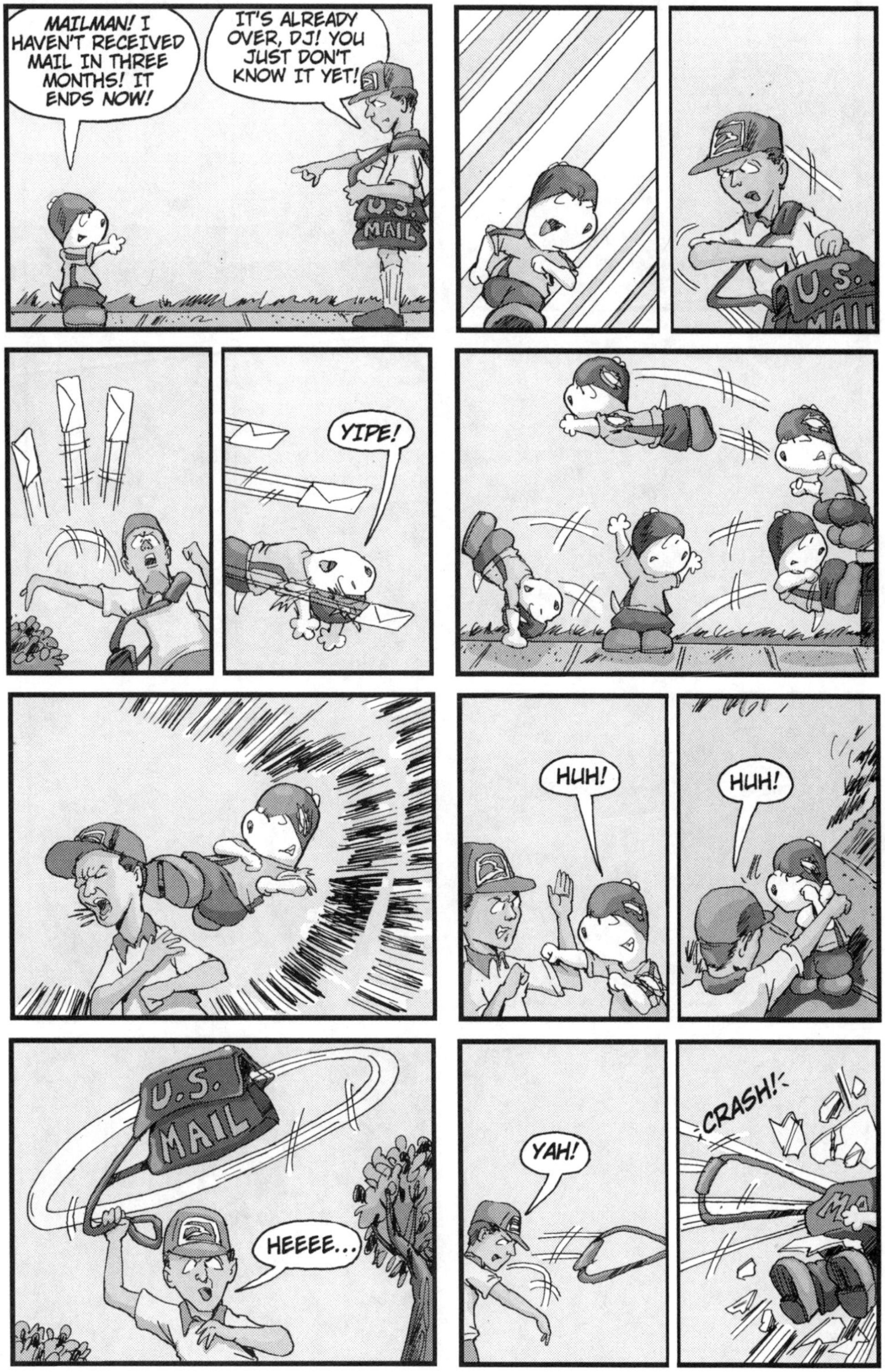

MAILMAN! I HAVEN'T RECEIVED MAIL IN THREE MONTHS! IT ENDS NOW!
IT'S ALREADY OVER, DJ! YOU JUST DON'T KNOW IT YET!
U.S. MAIL
YIPE!
HUH!
HUH!
U.S. MAIL
HEEEE...
YAH!
CRASH!

'SUP!
WHAP!
WHEW! I'M GLAD THAT'S OVER!
RUMBLE!

YOU DIDN'T THINK IT WOULD BE THAT EASY, DID YOU?
YEAH, I KINDA DID.

See how it ends in the animated webisode "Fists of Furry"

now online at www.myhousebroken.com

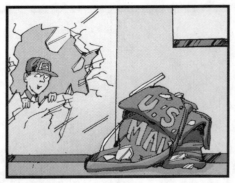

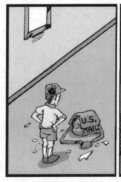

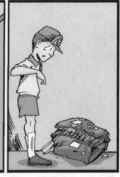

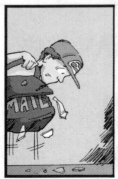

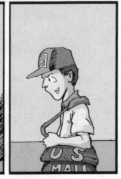

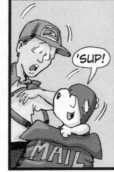

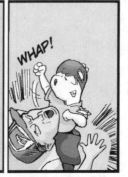

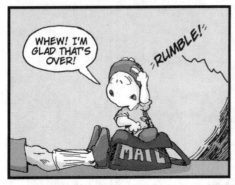

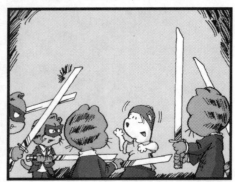

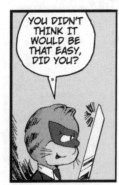

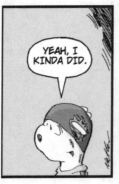

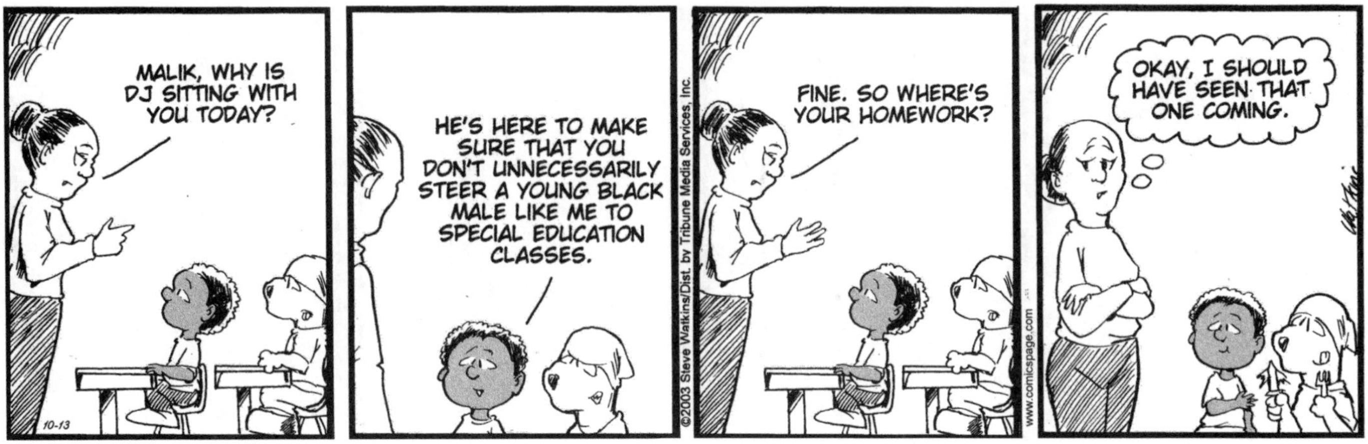
10-13
MALIK, WHY IS DJ SITTING WITH YOU TODAY?
HE'S HERE TO MAKE SURE THAT YOU DON'T UNNECESSARILY STEER A YOUNG BLACK MALE LIKE ME TO SPECIAL EDUCATION CLASSES.
©2003 Steve Watkins/Dist. by Tribune Media Services, Inc.
FINE. SO WHERE'S YOUR HOMEWORK?
www.comicspage.com
OKAY, I SHOULD HAVE SEEN THAT ONE COMING.

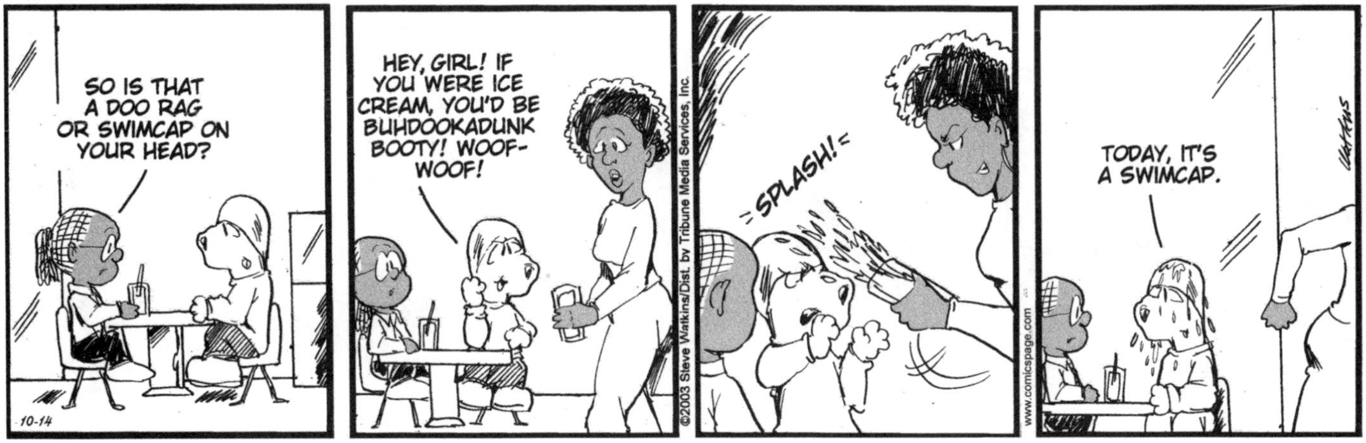
10-14
SO IS THAT A DOO RAG OR SWIMCAP ON YOUR HEAD?
HEY, GIRL! IF YOU WERE ICE CREAM, YOU'D BE BUHDOOKADUNK BOOTY! WOOF-WOOF!
©2003 Steve Watkins/Dist. by Tribune Media Services, Inc.
SPLASH!
www.comicspage.com
TODAY, IT'S A SWIMCAP.

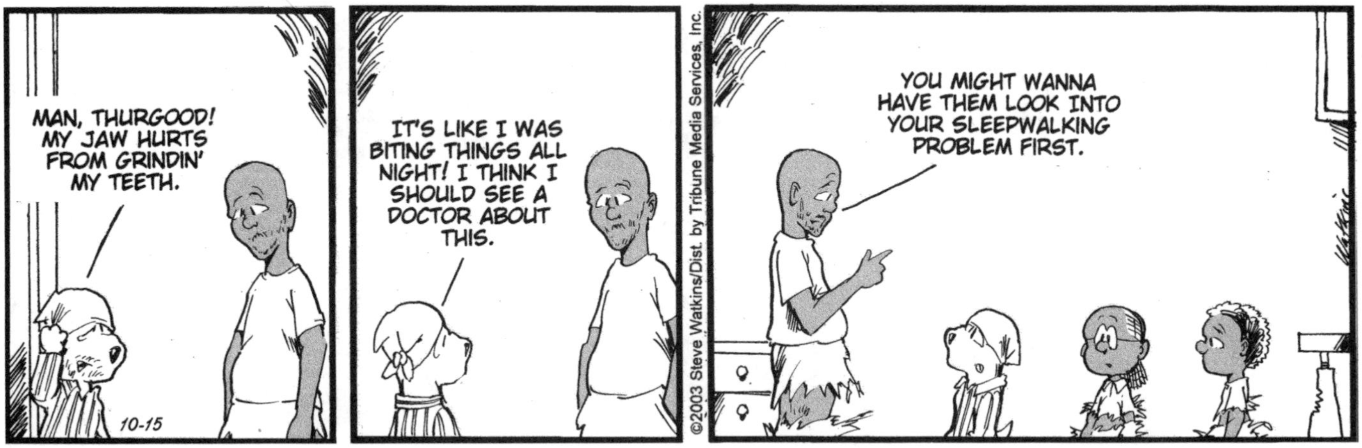
10-15
MAN, THURGOOD! MY JAW HURTS FROM GRINDIN' MY TEETH.
IT'S LIKE I WAS BITING THINGS ALL NIGHT! I THINK I SHOULD SEE A DOCTOR ABOUT THIS.
©2003 Steve Watkins/Dist. by Tribune Media Services, Inc.
YOU MIGHT WANNA HAVE THEM LOOK INTO YOUR SLEEPWALKING PROBLEM FIRST.

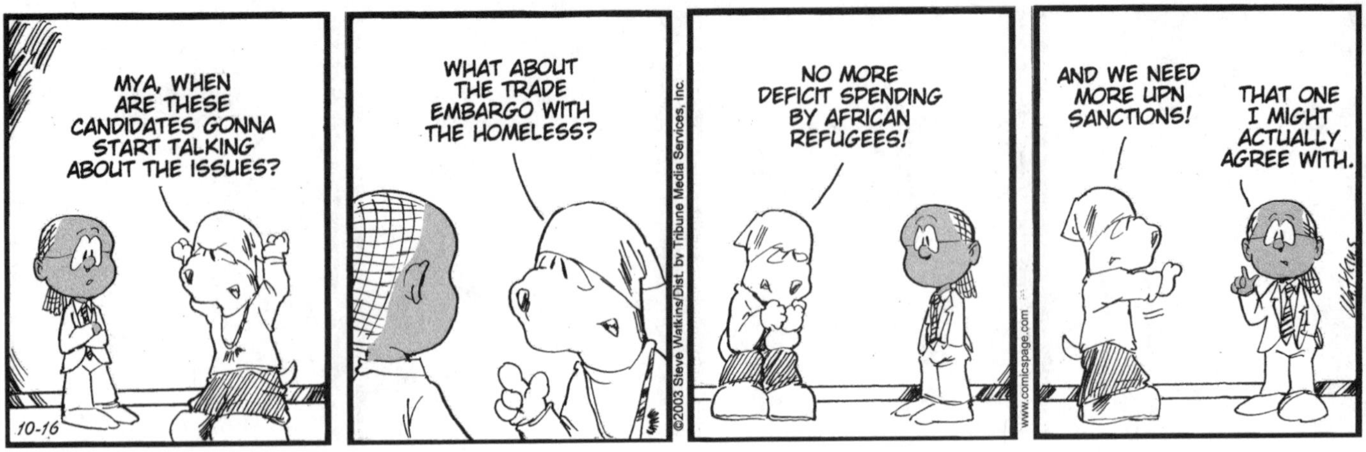
MYA, WHEN ARE THESE CANDIDATES GONNA START TALKING ABOUT THE ISSUES?
10-16
WHAT ABOUT THE TRADE EMBARGO WITH THE HOMELESS?
©2003 Steve Watkins/Dist. by Tribune Media Services, Inc.
NO MORE DEFICIT SPENDING BY AFRICAN REFUGEES!
www.comicspage.com
AND WE NEED MORE UPN SANCTIONS!
THAT ONE I MIGHT ACTUALLY AGREE WITH.

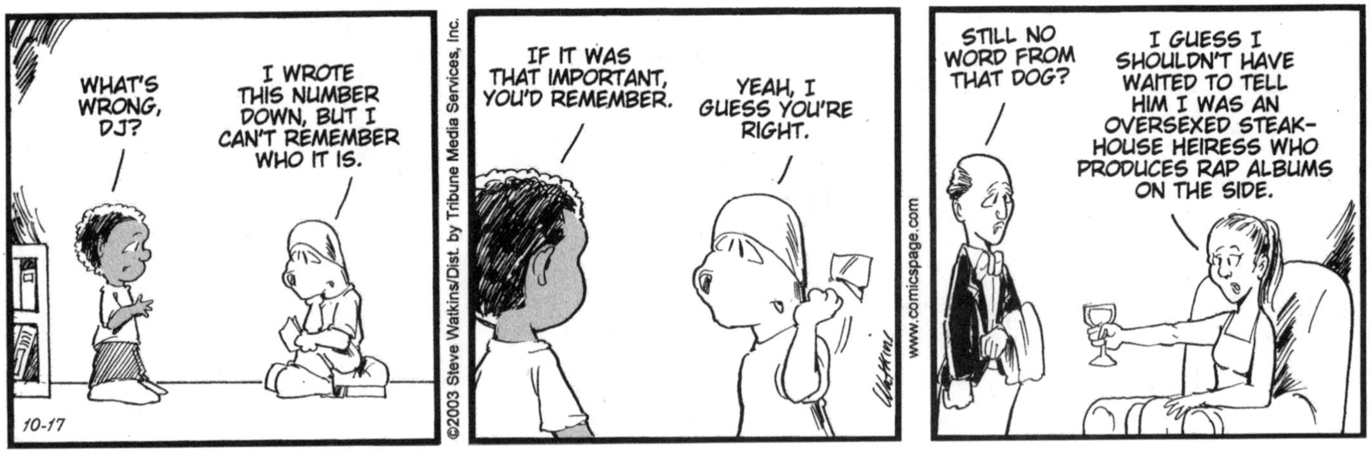
WHAT'S WRONG, DJ?
I WROTE THIS NUMBER DOWN, BUT I CAN'T REMEMBER WHO IT IS.
10-17
©2003 Steve Watkins/Dist. by Tribune Media Services, Inc.
IF IT WAS THAT IMPORTANT, YOU'D REMEMBER.
YEAH, I GUESS YOU'RE RIGHT.
www.comicspage.com
STILL NO WORD FROM THAT DOG?
I GUESS I SHOULDN'T HAVE WAITED TO TELL HIM I WAS AN OVERSEXED STEAK-HOUSE HEIRESS WHO PRODUCES RAP ALBUMS ON THE SIDE.

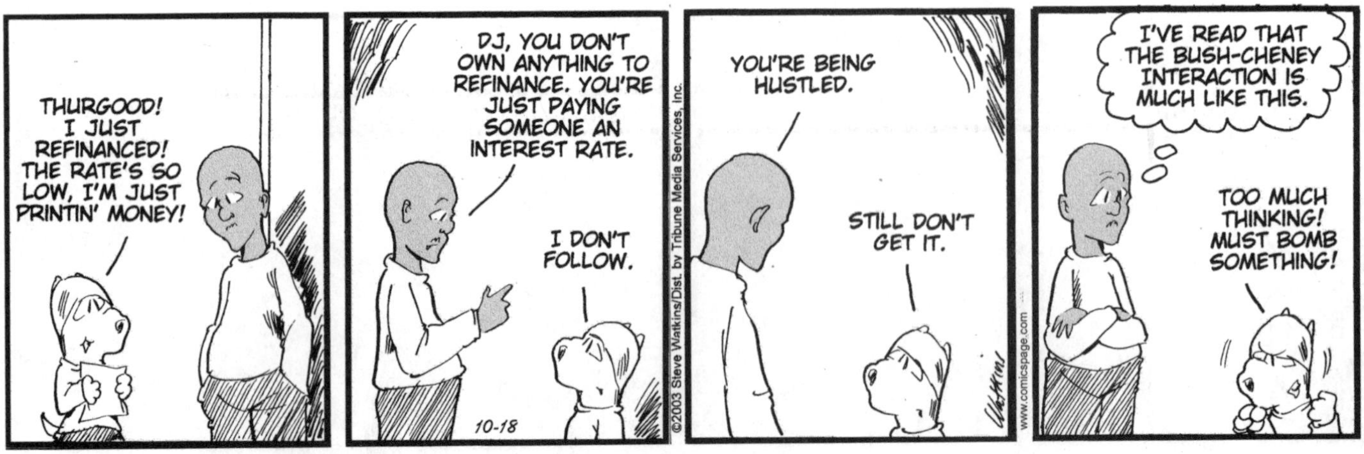
THURGOOD! I JUST REFINANCED! THE RATE'S SO LOW, I'M JUST PRINTIN' MONEY!
DJ, YOU DON'T OWN ANYTHING TO REFINANCE. YOU'RE JUST PAYING SOMEONE AN INTEREST RATE.
I DON'T FOLLOW.
10-18
©2003 Steve Watkins/Dist. by Tribune Media Services, Inc.
YOU'RE BEING HUSTLED.
STILL DON'T GET IT.
www.comicspage.com
I'VE READ THAT THE BUSH-CHENEY INTERACTION IS MUCH LIKE THIS.
TOO MUCH THINKING! MUST BOMB SOMETHING!

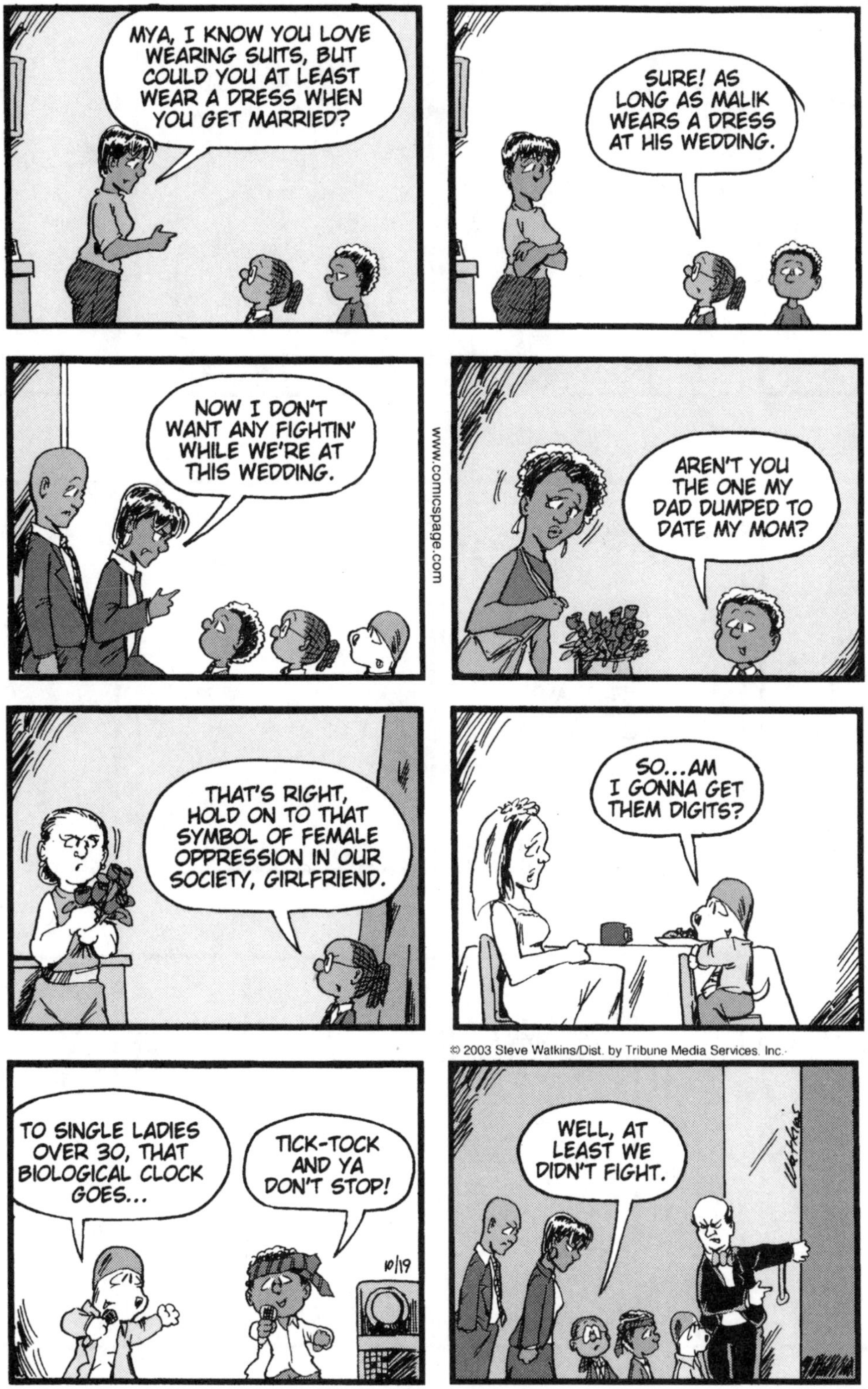
MYA, I KNOW YOU LOVE WEARING SUITS, BUT COULD YOU AT LEAST WEAR A DRESS WHEN YOU GET MARRIED?
SURE! AS LONG AS MALIK WEARS A DRESS AT HIS WEDDING.
NOW I DON'T WANT ANY FIGHTIN' WHILE WE'RE AT THIS WEDDING.
AREN'T YOU THE ONE MY DAD DUMPED TO DATE MY MOM?
THAT'S RIGHT, HOLD ON TO THAT SYMBOL OF FEMALE OPPRESSION IN OUR SOCIETY, GIRLFRIEND.
SO...AM I GONNA GET THEM DIGITS?
TO SINGLE LADIES OVER 30, THAT BIOLOGICAL CLOCK GOES...
TICK-TOCK AND YA DON'T STOP!
10/19
WELL, AT LEAST WE DIDN'T FIGHT.

www.comicspage.com

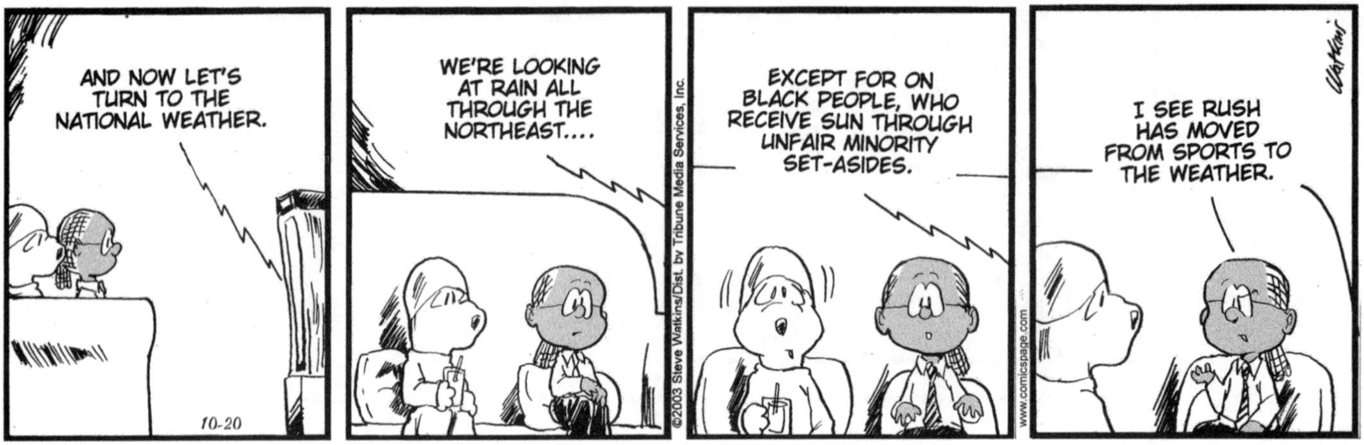
AND NOW LET'S TURN TO THE NATIONAL WEATHER.
10-20
WE'RE LOOKING AT RAIN ALL THROUGH THE NORTHEAST....
©2003 Steve Watkins/Dist. by Tribune Media Services, Inc.
EXCEPT FOR ON BLACK PEOPLE, WHO RECEIVE SUN THROUGH UNFAIR MINORITY SET-ASIDES.
www.comicspage.com
Watkins
I SEE RUSH HAS MOVED FROM SPORTS TO THE WEATHER.

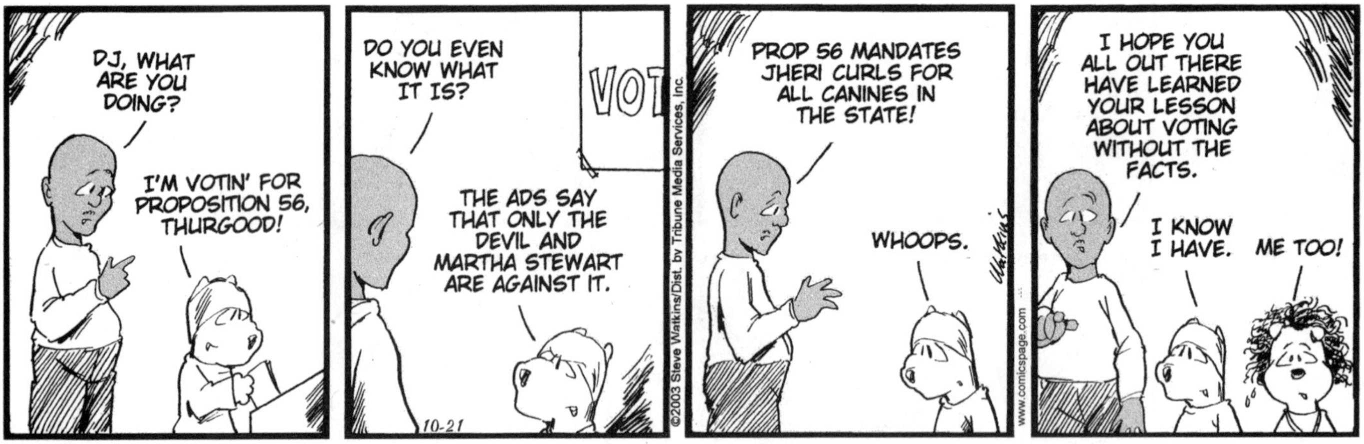
DJ, WHAT ARE YOU DOING?
I'M VOTIN' FOR PROPOSITION 56, THURGOOD!
DO YOU EVEN KNOW WHAT IT IS?
VOT
THE ADS SAY THAT ONLY THE DEVIL AND MARTHA STEWART ARE AGAINST IT.
10-21
©2003 Steve Watkins/Dist. by Tribune Media Services, Inc.
PROP 56 MANDATES JHERI CURLS FOR ALL CANINES IN THE STATE!
WHOOPS.
Watkins
www.comicspage.com
I HOPE YOU ALL OUT THERE HAVE LEARNED YOUR LESSON ABOUT VOTING WITHOUT THE FACTS.
I KNOW I HAVE.
ME TOO!

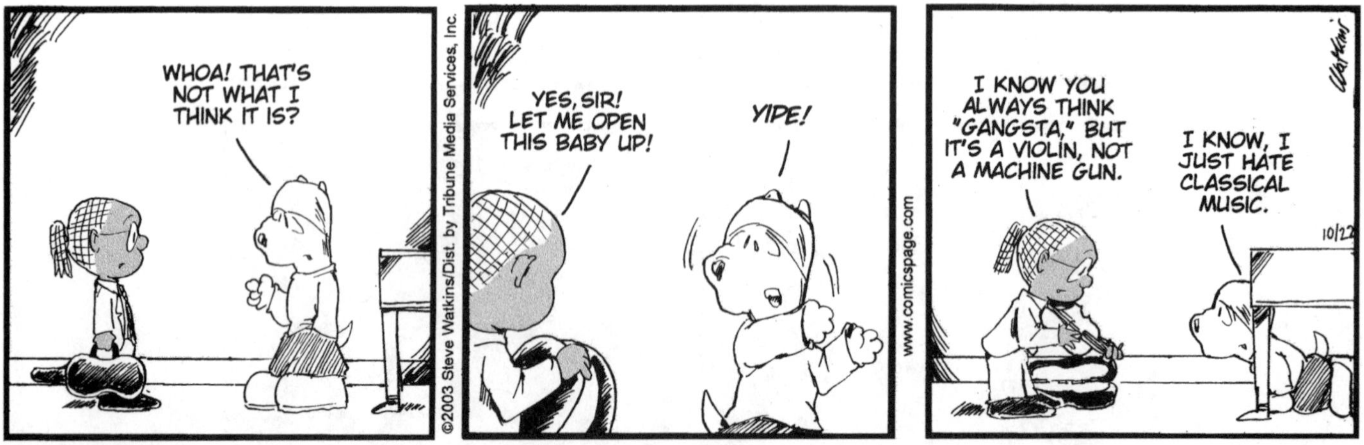
WHOA! THAT'S NOT WHAT I THINK IT IS?
©2003 Steve Watkins/Dist. by Tribune Media Services, Inc.
YES, SIR! LET ME OPEN THIS BABY UP!
YIPE!
www.comicspage.com
Watkins
I KNOW YOU ALWAYS THINK "GANGSTA," BUT IT'S A VIOLIN, NOT A MACHINE GUN.
I KNOW, I JUST HATE CLASSICAL MUSIC.
10/22

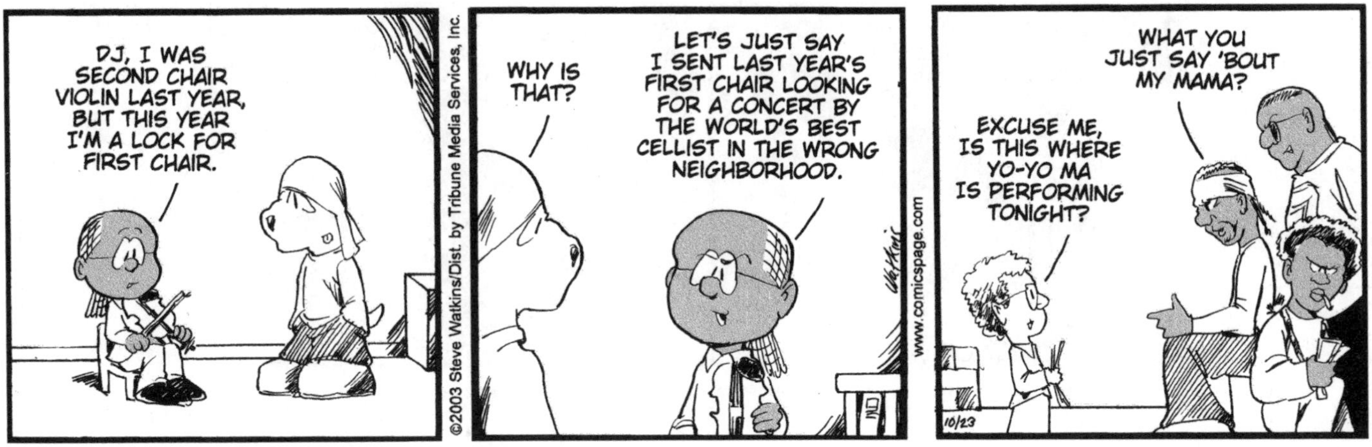
DJ, I WAS SECOND CHAIR VIOLIN LAST YEAR, BUT THIS YEAR I'M A LOCK FOR FIRST CHAIR.
©2003 Steve Watkins/Dist. by Tribune Media Services, Inc.
WHY IS THAT?
LET'S JUST SAY I SENT LAST YEAR'S FIRST CHAIR LOOKING FOR A CONCERT BY THE WORLD'S BEST CELLIST IN THE WRONG NEIGHBORHOOD.
www.comicspage.com
EXCUSE ME, IS THIS WHERE YO-YO MA IS PERFORMING TONIGHT?
WHAT YOU JUST SAY 'BOUT MY MAMA?
10/23

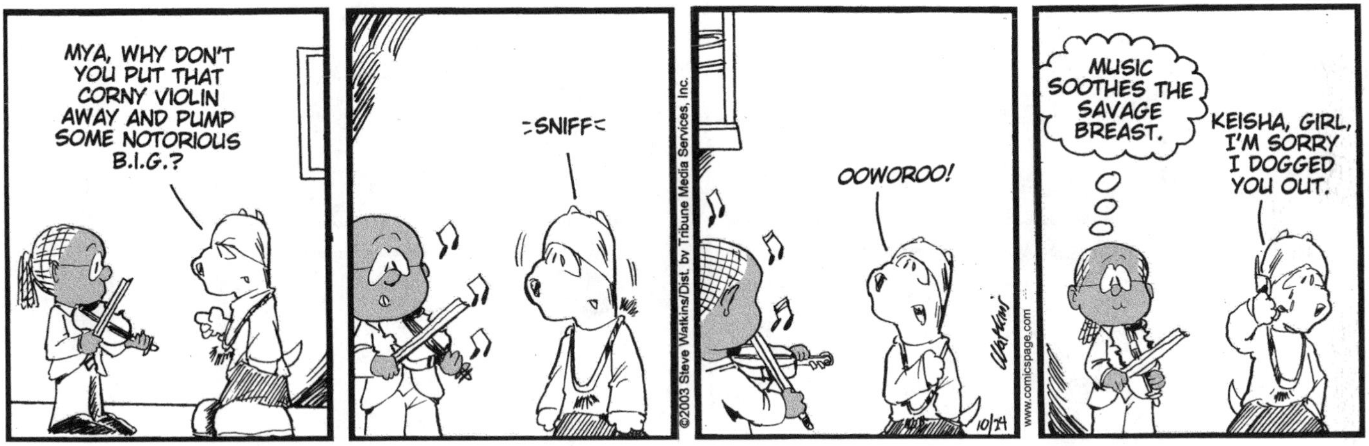
MYA, WHY DON'T YOU PUT THAT CORNY VIOLIN AWAY AND PUMP SOME NOTORIOUS B.I.G.?
=SNIFF=
©2003 Steve Watkins/Dist. by Tribune Media Services, Inc.
OOWOROO!
10/24
www.comicspage.com
MUSIC SOOTHES THE SAVAGE BREAST.
KEISHA, GIRL, I'M SORRY I DOGGED YOU OUT.

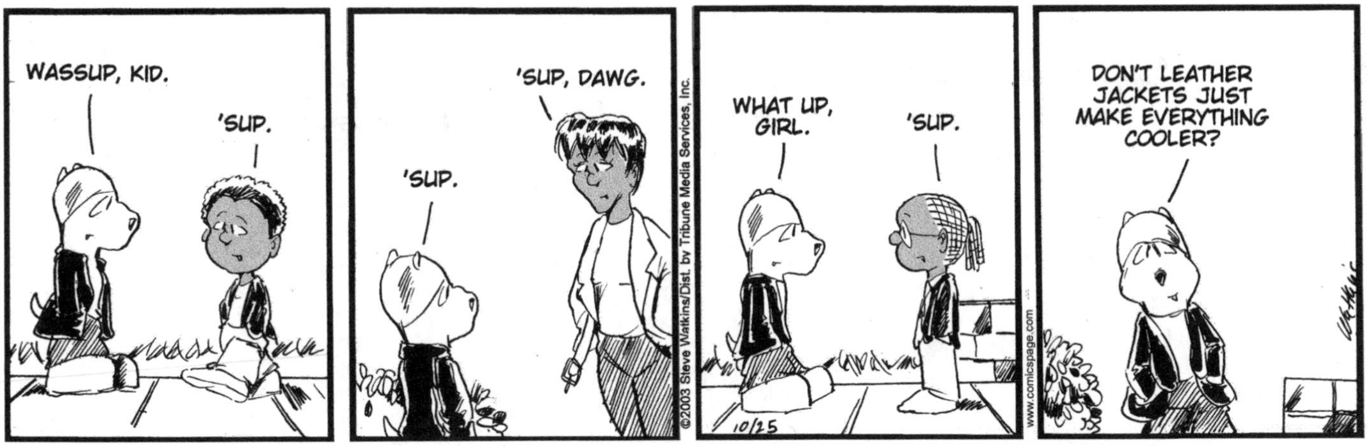
WASSUP, KID.
'SUP.
'SUP.
'SUP, DAWG.
©2003 Steve Watkins/Dist. by Tribune Media Services, Inc.
WHAT UP, GIRL.
'SUP.
10/25
www.comicspage.com
DON'T LEATHER JACKETS JUST MAKE EVERYTHING COOLER?

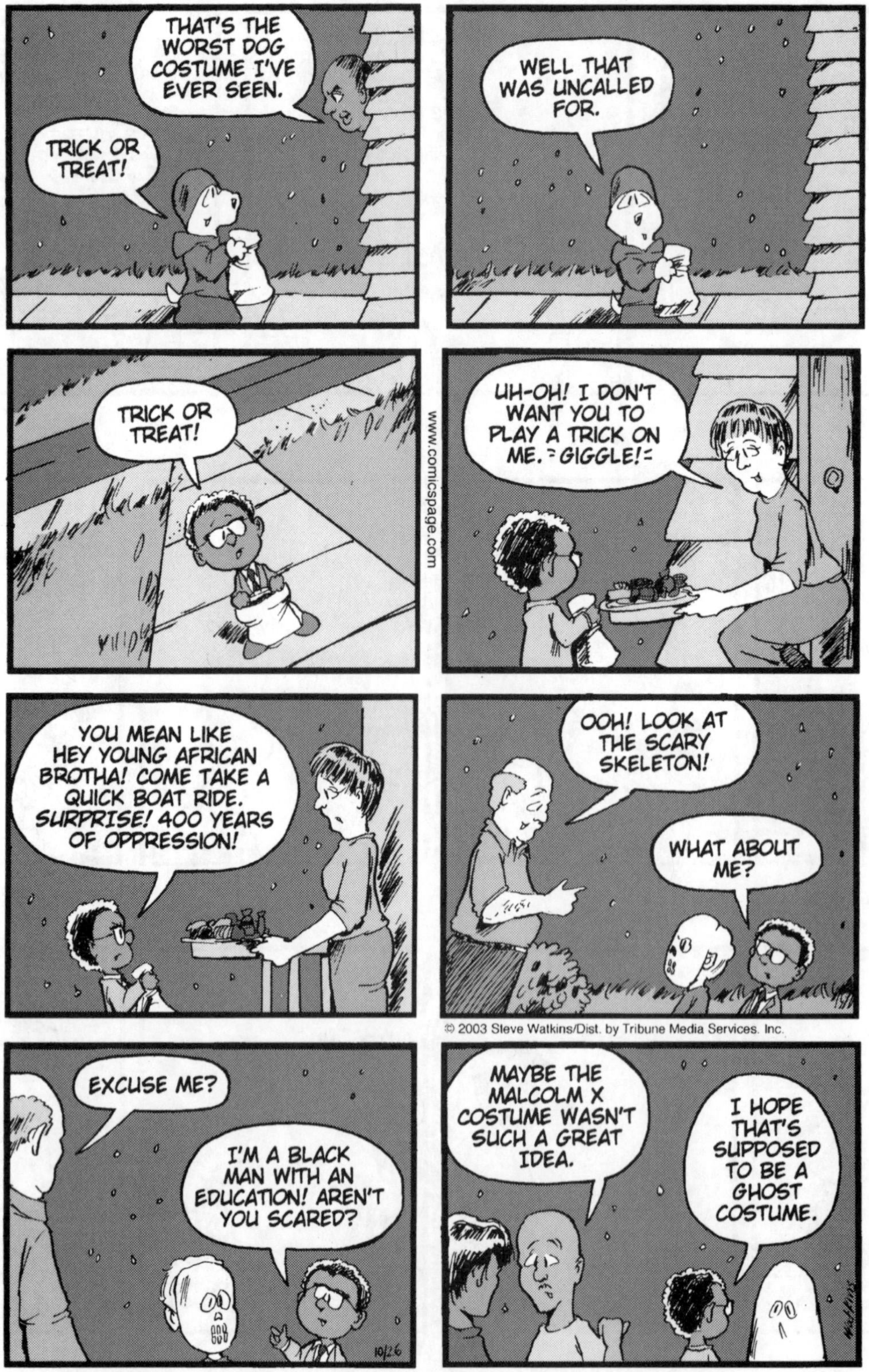

TRICK OR TREAT!
THAT'S THE WORST DOG COSTUME I'VE EVER SEEN.
WELL THAT WAS UNCALLED FOR.
TRICK OR TREAT!
UH-OH! I DON'T WANT YOU TO PLAY A TRICK ON ME. =GIGGLE!=
YOU MEAN LIKE HEY YOUNG AFRICAN BROTHA! COME TAKE A QUICK BOAT RIDE. SURPRISE! 400 YEARS OF OPPRESSION!
OOH! LOOK AT THE SCARY SKELETON!
WHAT ABOUT ME?
EXCUSE ME?
I'M A BLACK MAN WITH AN EDUCATION! AREN'T YOU SCARED?
MAYBE THE MALCOLM X COSTUME WASN'T SUCH A GREAT IDEA.
I HOPE THAT'S SUPPOSED TO BE A GHOST COSTUME.
www.comicspage.com
10/26

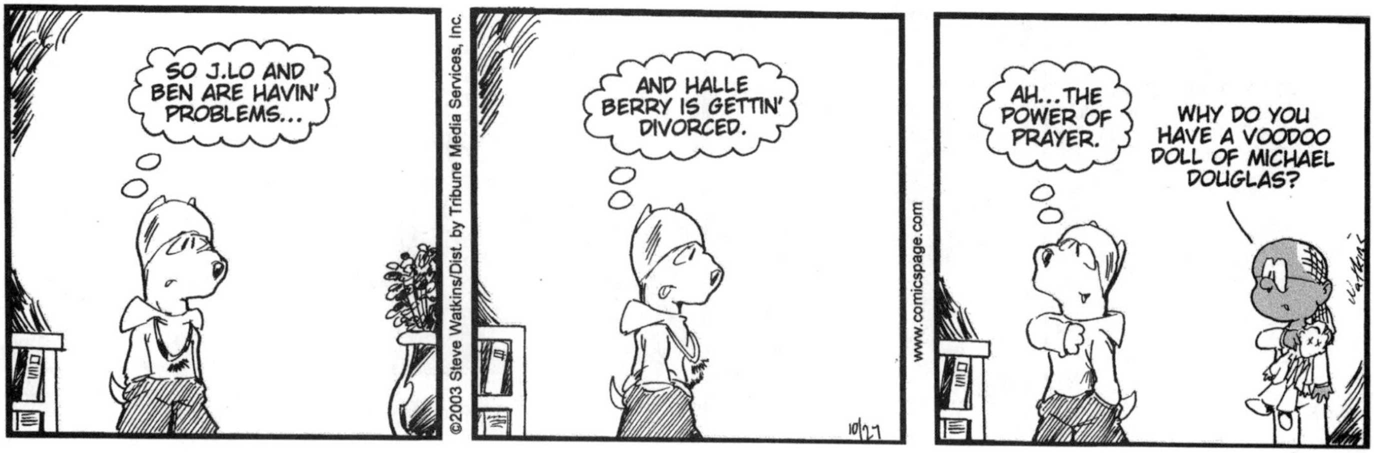
SO J.LO AND BEN ARE HAVIN' PROBLEMS...
©2003 Steve Watkins/Dist. by Tribune Media Services, Inc.
AND HALLE BERRY IS GETTIN' DIVORCED.
www.comicspage.com
AH...THE POWER OF PRAYER.
WHY DO YOU HAVE A VOODOO DOLL OF MICHAEL DOUGLAS?

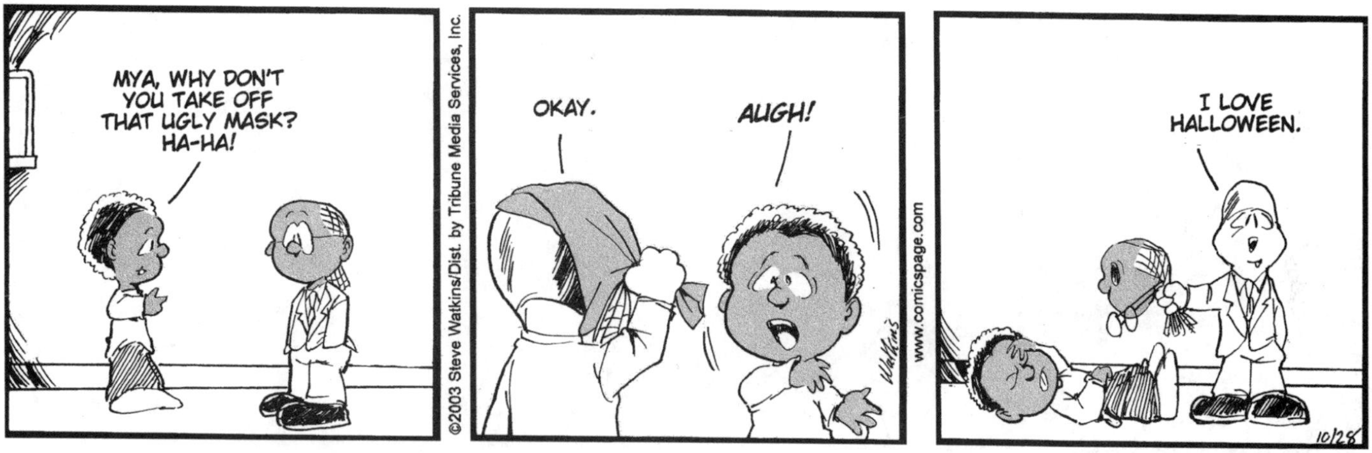
MYA, WHY DON'T YOU TAKE OFF THAT UGLY MASK? HA-HA!
©2003 Steve Watkins/Dist. by Tribune Media Services, Inc.
OKAY.
AUGH!
www.comicspage.com
I LOVE HALLOWEEN.

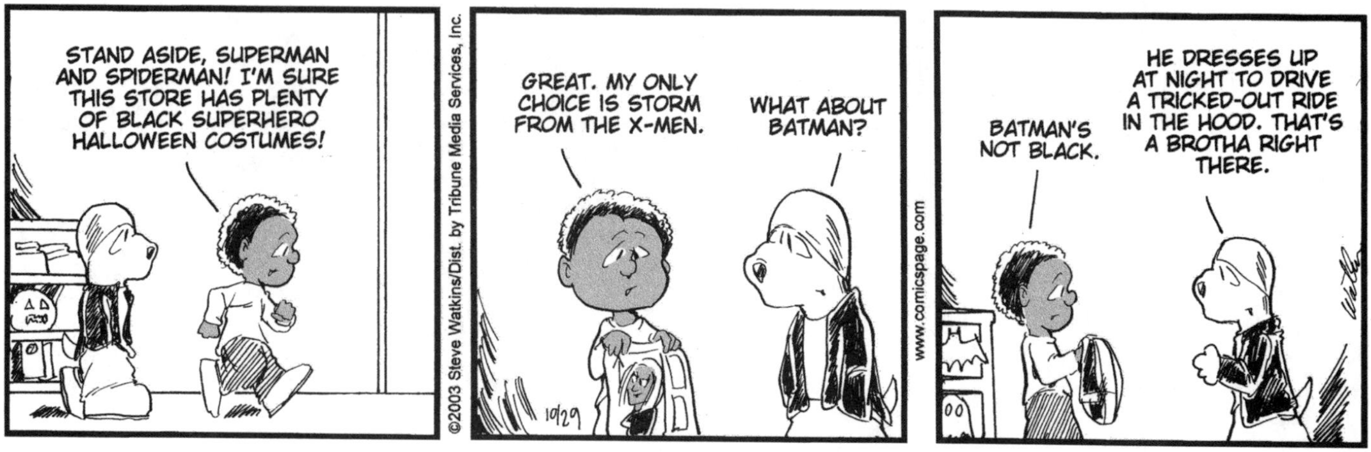
STAND ASIDE, SUPERMAN AND SPIDERMAN! I'M SURE THIS STORE HAS PLENTY OF BLACK SUPERHERO HALLOWEEN COSTUMES!
©2003 Steve Watkins/Dist. by Tribune Media Services, Inc.
GREAT. MY ONLY CHOICE IS STORM FROM THE X-MEN.
WHAT ABOUT BATMAN?
www.comicspage.com
BATMAN'S NOT BLACK.
HE DRESSES UP AT NIGHT TO DRIVE A TRICKED-OUT RIDE IN THE HOOD. THAT'S A BROTHA RIGHT THERE.

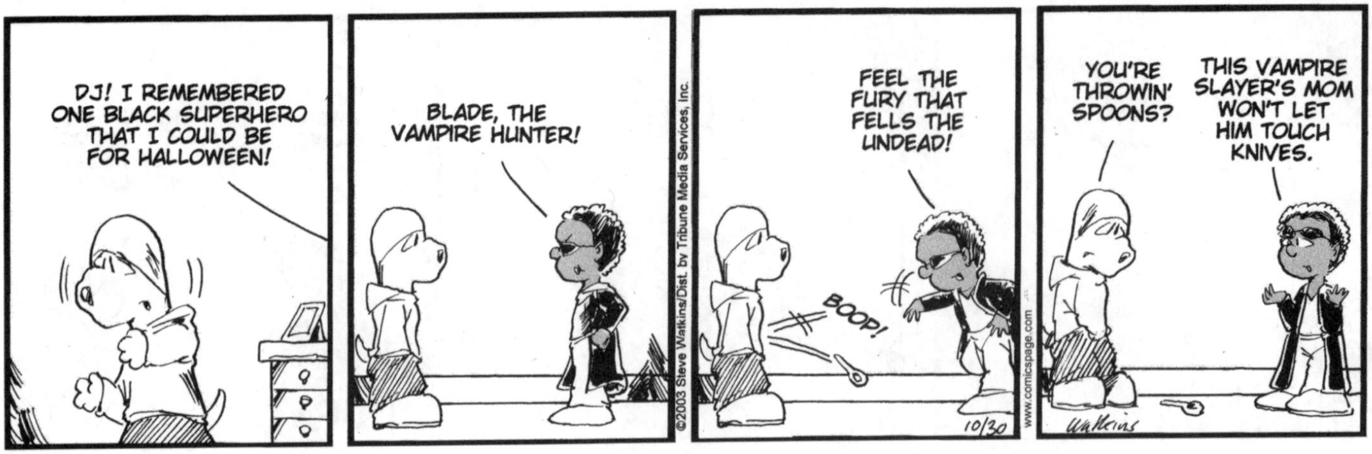
DJ! I REMEMBERED ONE BLACK SUPERHERO THAT I COULD BE FOR HALLOWEEN!
BLADE, THE VAMPIRE HUNTER!
FEEL THE FURY THAT FELLS THE UNDEAD!
BOOP!
YOU'RE THROWIN' SPOONS?
THIS VAMPIRE SLAYER'S MOM WON'T LET HIM TOUCH KNIVES.
©2003 Steve Watkins/Dist. by Tribune Media Services, Inc.
www.comicspage.com
10/30
Watkins

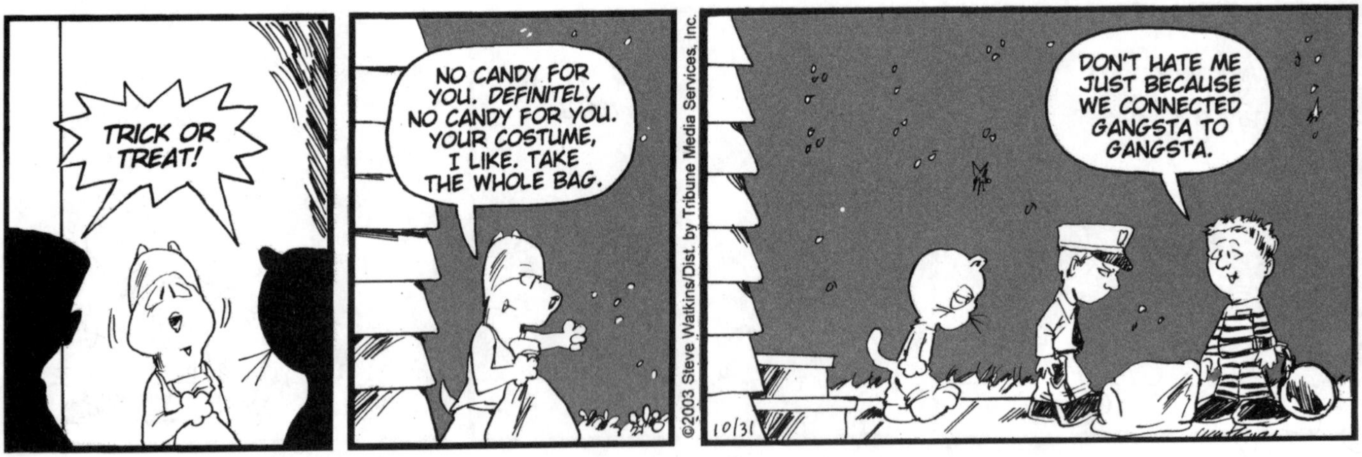
TRICK OR TREAT!
NO CANDY FOR YOU. DEFINITELY NO CANDY FOR YOU. YOUR COSTUME, I LIKE. TAKE THE WHOLE BAG.
DON'T HATE ME JUST BECAUSE WE CONNECTED GANGSTA TO GANGSTA.
©2003 Steve Watkins/Dist. by Tribune Media Services, Inc.
10/31

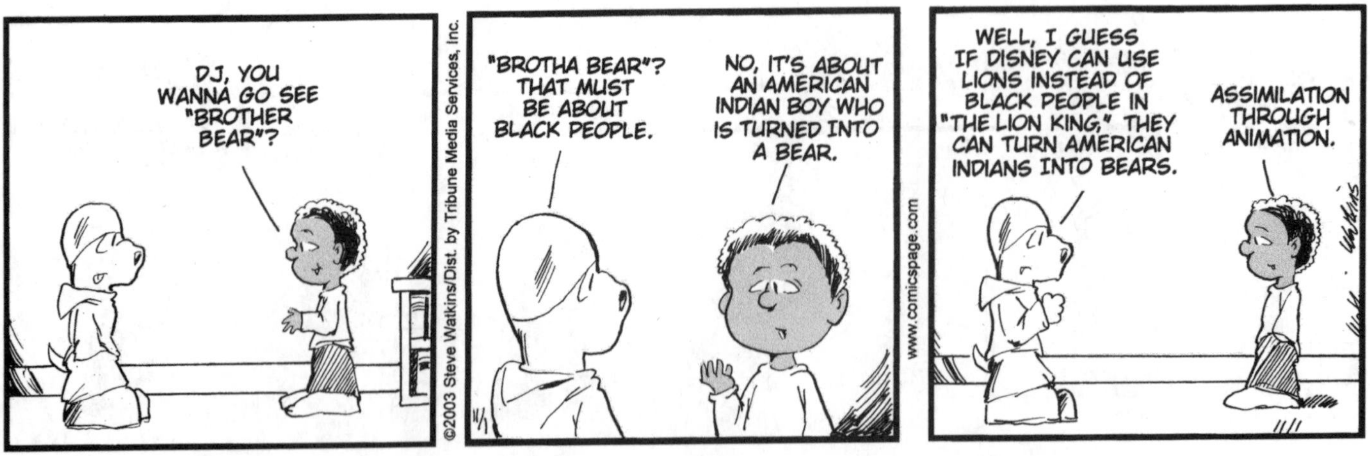
DJ, YOU WANNA GO SEE "BROTHER BEAR"?
"BROTHA BEAR"? THAT MUST BE ABOUT BLACK PEOPLE.
NO, IT'S ABOUT AN AMERICAN INDIAN BOY WHO IS TURNED INTO A BEAR.
WELL, I GUESS IF DISNEY CAN USE LIONS INSTEAD OF BLACK PEOPLE IN "THE LION KING," THEY CAN TURN AMERICAN INDIANS INTO BEARS.
ASSIMILATION THROUGH ANIMATION.
©2003 Steve Watkins/Dist. by Tribune Media Services, Inc.
www.comicspage.com
11/1
Watkins

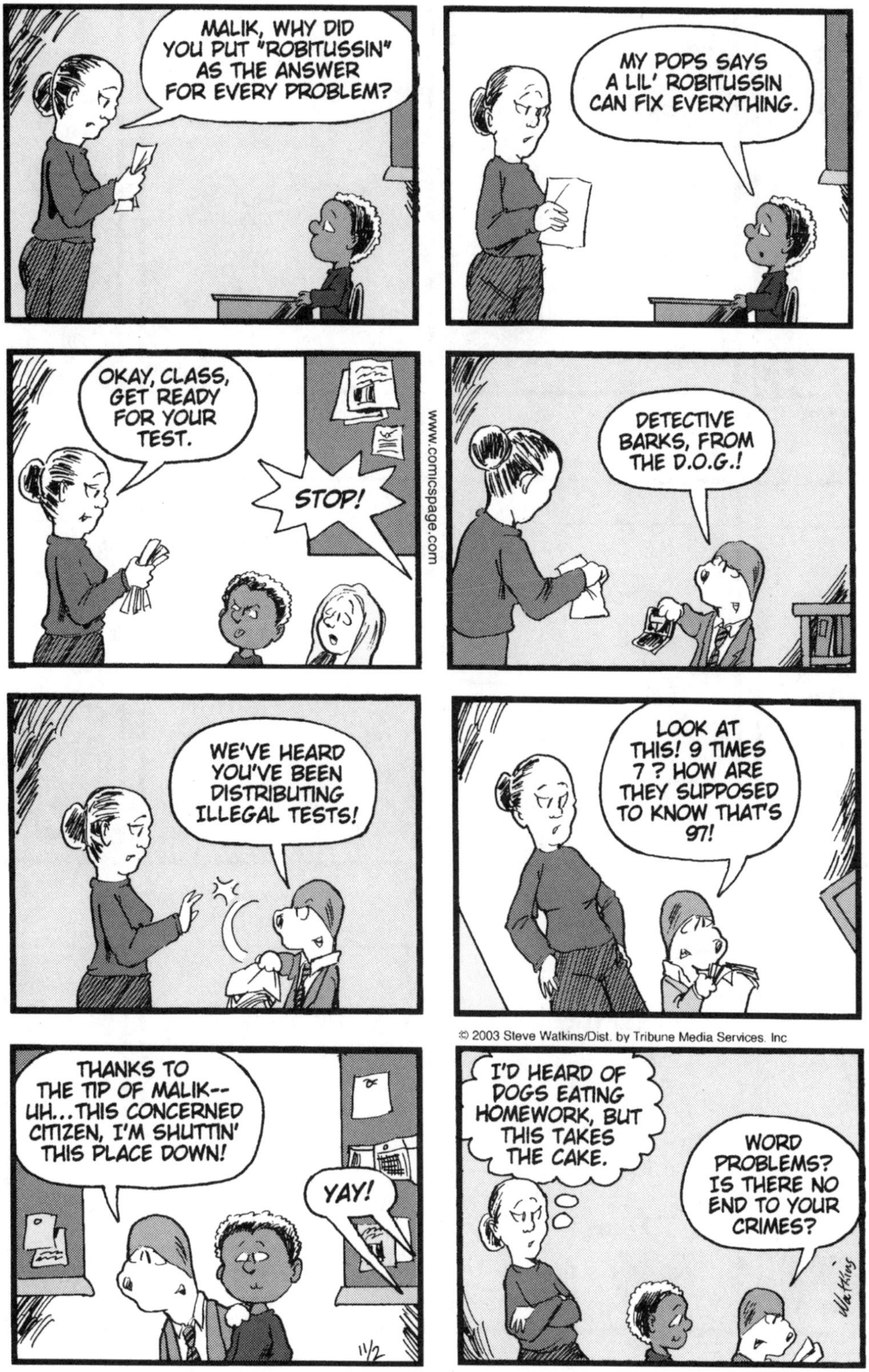
MALIK, WHY DID YOU PUT "ROBITUSSIN" AS THE ANSWER FOR EVERY PROBLEM?
MY POPS SAYS A LIL' ROBITUSSIN CAN FIX EVERYTHING.
OKAY, CLASS, GET READY FOR YOUR TEST.
STOP!
www.comicspage.com
DETECTIVE BARKS, FROM THE D.O.G.!
WE'VE HEARD YOU'VE BEEN DISTRIBUTING ILLEGAL TESTS!
LOOK AT THIS! 9 TIMES 7 ? HOW ARE THEY SUPPOSED TO KNOW THAT'S 97!
THANKS TO THE TIP OF MALIK-- UH...THIS CONCERNED CITIZEN, I'M SHUTTIN' THIS PLACE DOWN!
YAY!
11/2
I'D HEARD OF DOGS EATING HOMEWORK, BUT THIS TAKES THE CAKE.
WORD PROBLEMS? IS THERE NO END TO YOUR CRIMES?
Watkins

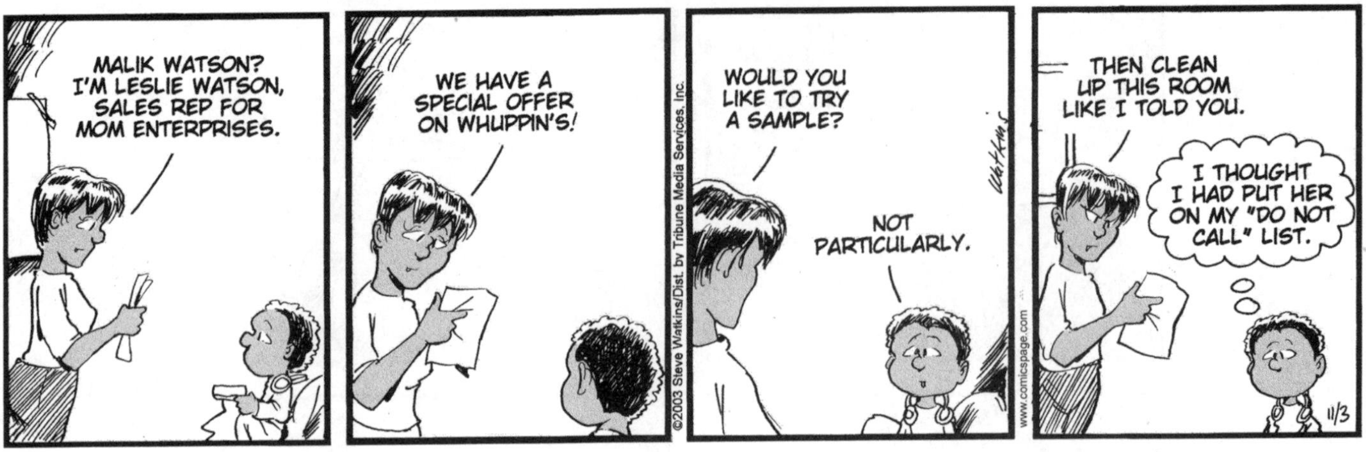
MALIK WATSON? I'M LESLIE WATSON, SALES REP FOR MOM ENTERPRISES.
WE HAVE A SPECIAL OFFER ON WHUPPIN'S!
©2003 Steve Watkins/Dist. by Tribune Media Services, Inc.
WOULD YOU LIKE TO TRY A SAMPLE?
NOT PARTICULARLY.
THEN CLEAN UP THIS ROOM LIKE I TOLD YOU.
I THOUGHT I HAD PUT HER ON MY "DO NOT CALL" LIST.
www.comicspage.com
11/3

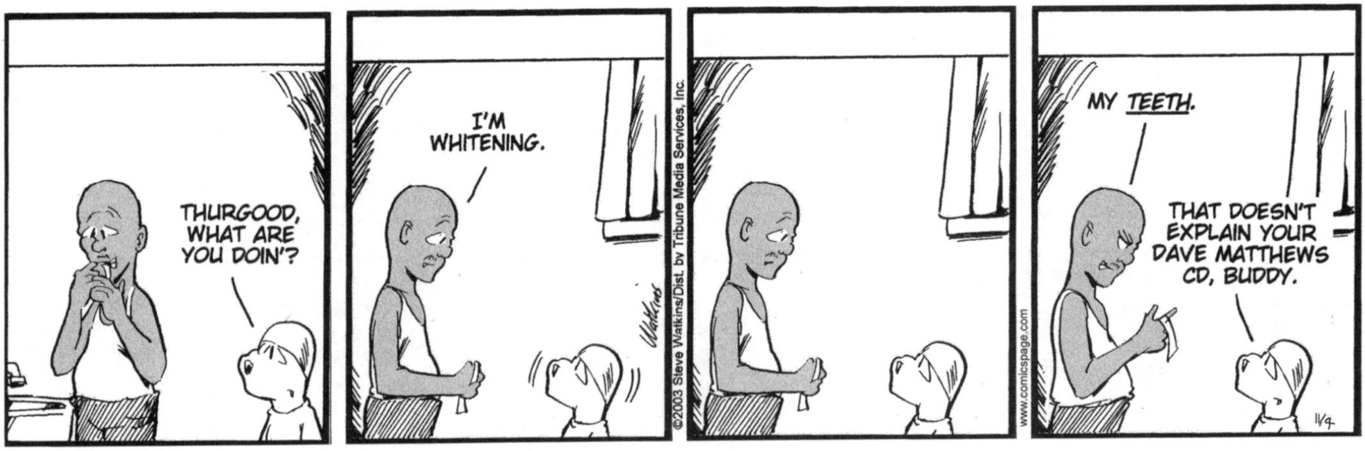
THURGOOD, WHAT ARE YOU DOIN'?
I'M WHITENING.
©2003 Steve Watkins/Dist. by Tribune Media Services, Inc.
MY TEETH.
THAT DOESN'T EXPLAIN YOUR DAVE MATTHEWS CD, BUDDY.
www.comicspage.com
11/4

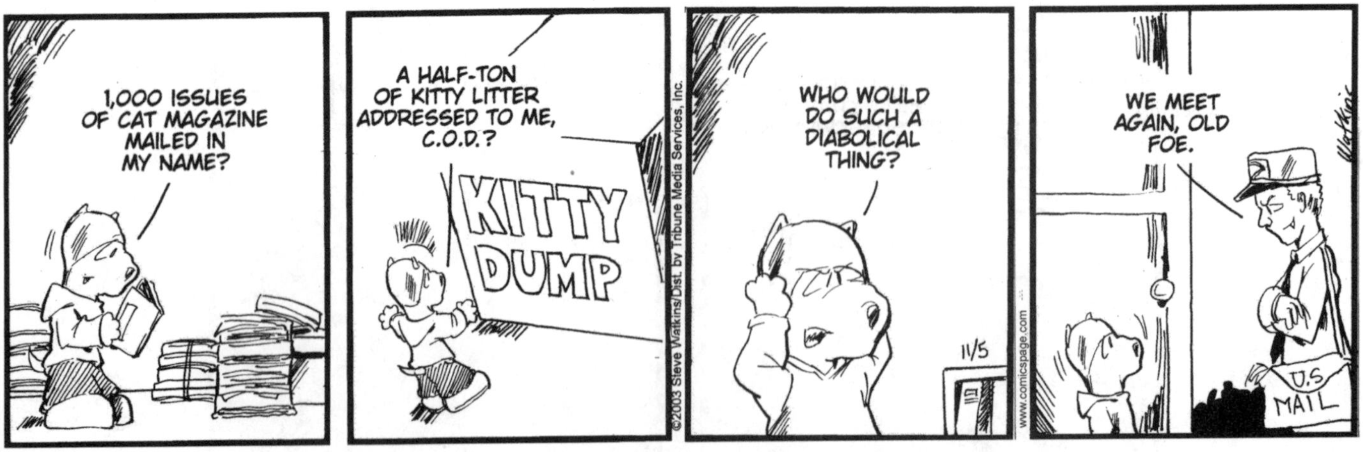
1,000 ISSUES OF CAT MAGAZINE MAILED IN MY NAME?
A HALF-TON OF KITTY LITTER ADDRESSED TO ME, C.O.D.?
KITTY DUMP
©2003 Steve Watkins/Dist. by Tribune Media Services, Inc.
WHO WOULD DO SUCH A DIABOLICAL THING?
11/5
www.comicspage.com
WE MEET AGAIN, OLD FOE.
U.S MAIL

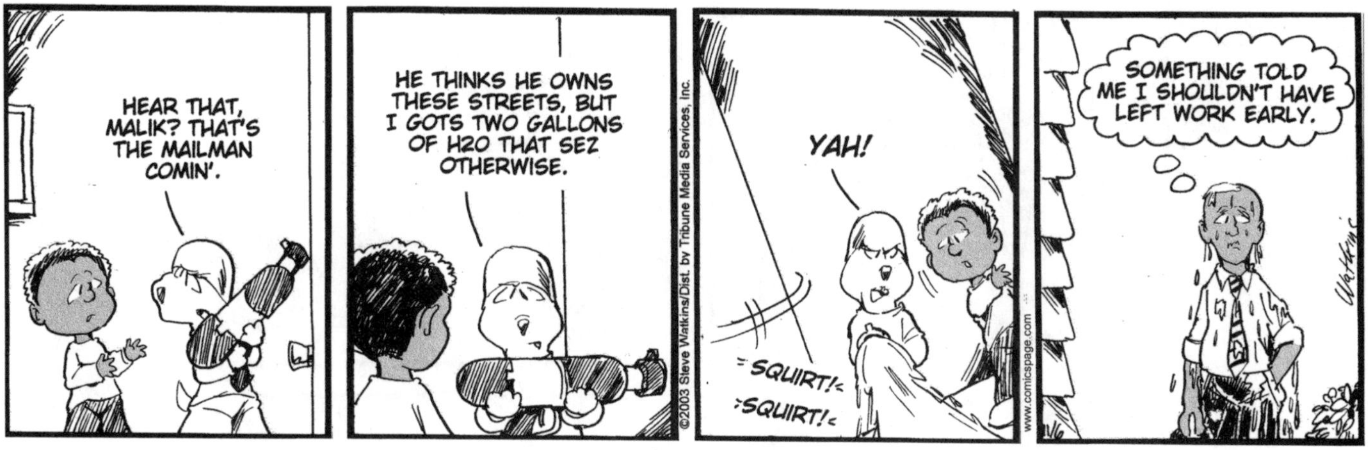
HEAR THAT, MALIK? THAT'S THE MAILMAN COMIN'.
HE THINKS HE OWNS THESE STREETS, BUT I GOTS TWO GALLONS OF H2O THAT SEZ OTHERWISE.
©2003 Steve Watkins/Dist. by Tribune Media Services, Inc.
YAH!
SQUIRT!
SQUIRT!
www.comicspage.com
SOMETHING TOLD ME I SHOULDN'T HAVE LEFT WORK EARLY.
Watkins

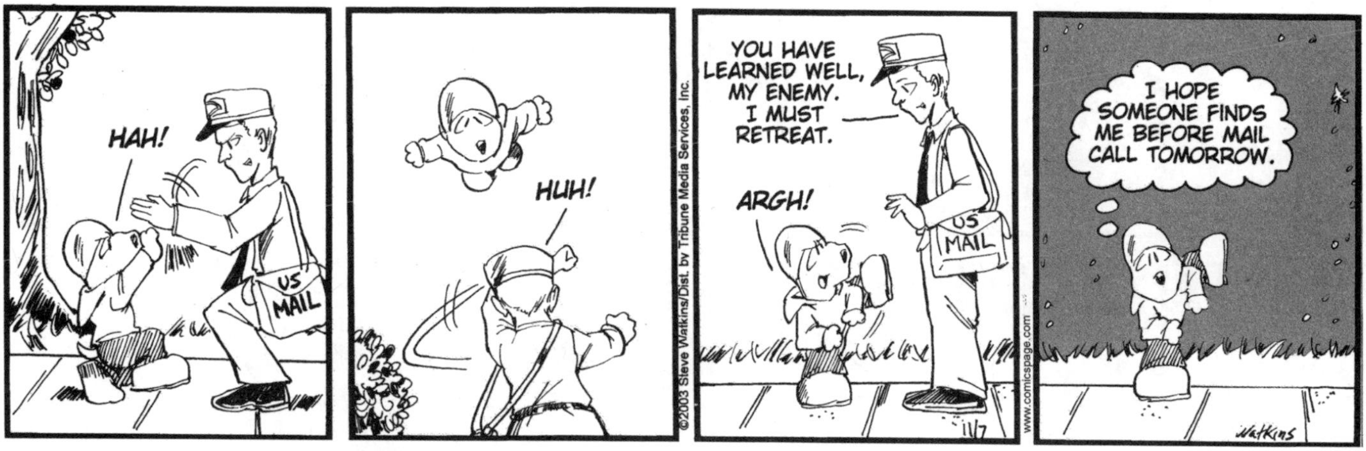
HAH!
US MAIL
HUH!
©2003 Steve Watkins/Dist. by Tribune Media Services, Inc.
YOU HAVE LEARNED WELL, MY ENEMY. I MUST RETREAT.
ARGH!
US MAIL
11/7
www.comicspage.com
I HOPE SOMEONE FINDS ME BEFORE MAIL CALL TOMORROW.
Watkins

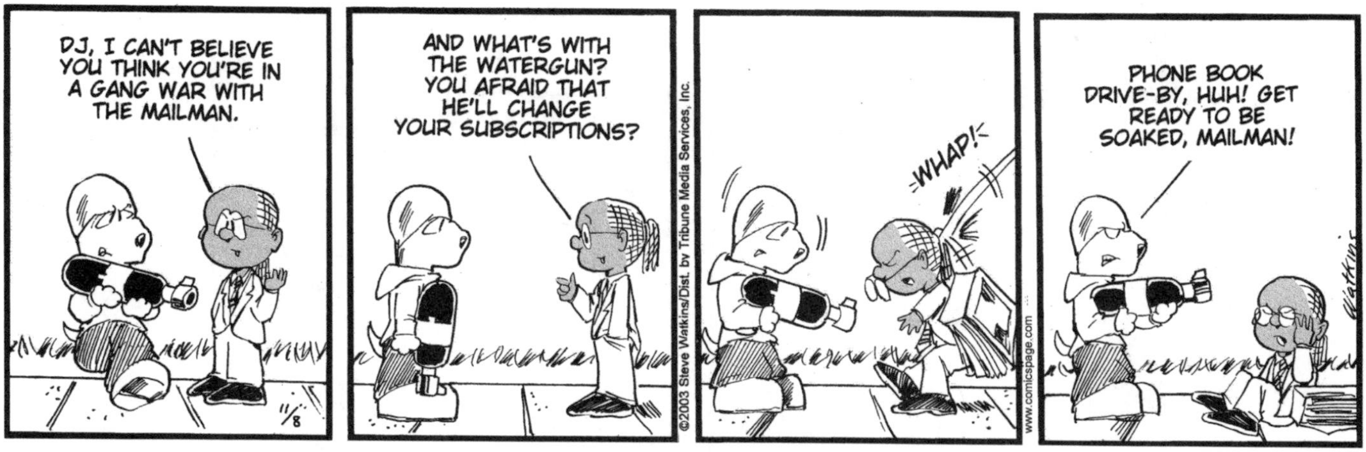
DJ, I CAN'T BELIEVE YOU THINK YOU'RE IN A GANG WAR WITH THE MAILMAN.
11/8
AND WHAT'S WITH THE WATERGUN? YOU AFRAID THAT HE'LL CHANGE YOUR SUBSCRIPTIONS?
©2003 Steve Watkins/Dist. by Tribune Media Services, Inc.
WHAP!
www.comicspage.com
PHONE BOOK DRIVE-BY, HUH! GET READY TO BE SOAKED, MAILMAN!
Watkins

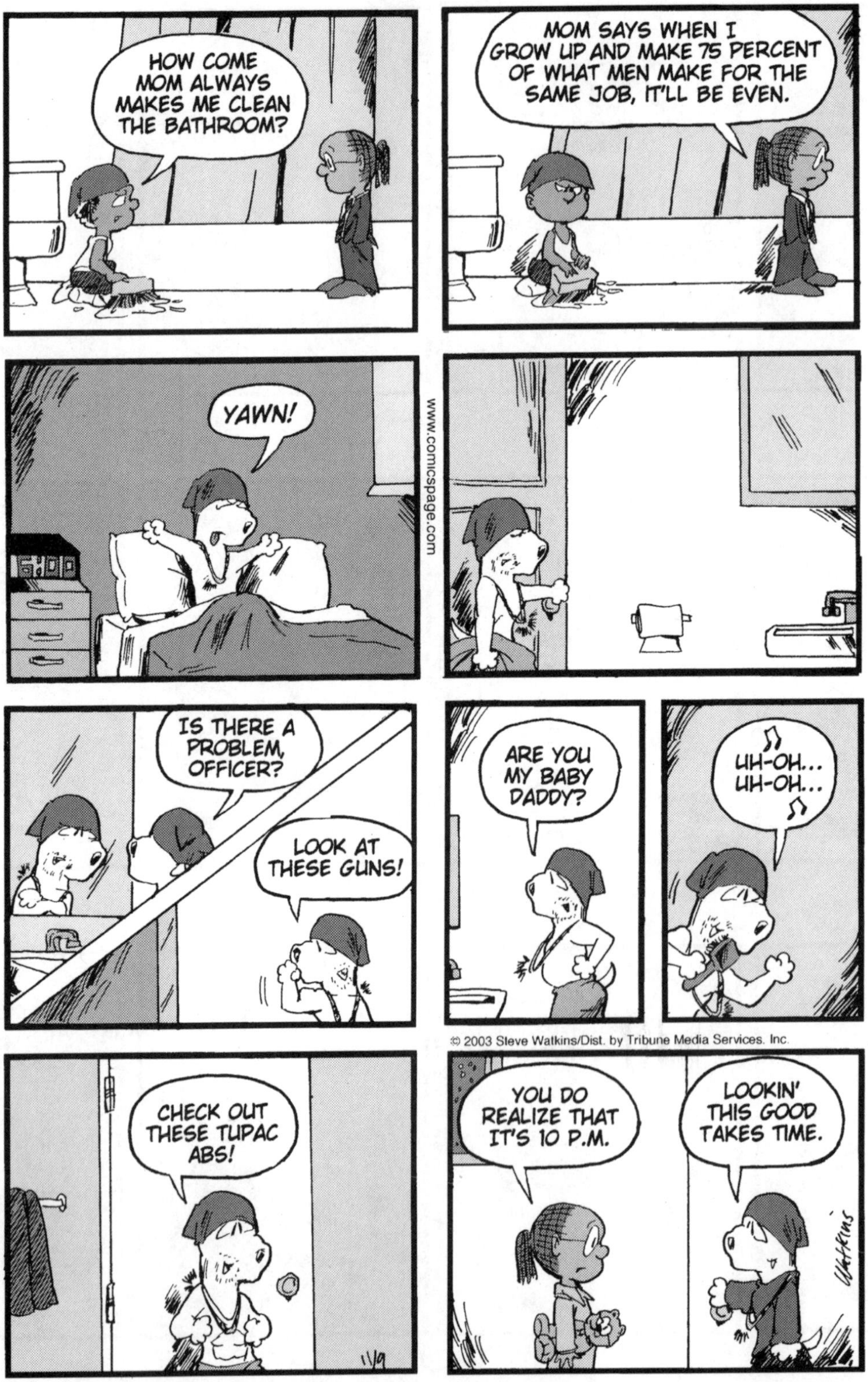
HOW COME MOM ALWAYS MAKES ME CLEAN THE BATHROOM?
MOM SAYS WHEN I GROW UP AND MAKE 75 PERCENT OF WHAT MEN MAKE FOR THE SAME JOB, IT'LL BE EVEN.
YAWN!
IS THERE A PROBLEM, OFFICER?
LOOK AT THESE GUNS!
ARE YOU MY BABY DADDY?
UH-OH... UH-OH...
CHECK OUT THESE TUPAC ABS!
YOU DO REALIZE THAT IT'S 10 P.M.
LOOKIN' THIS GOOD TAKES TIME.
WATKINS

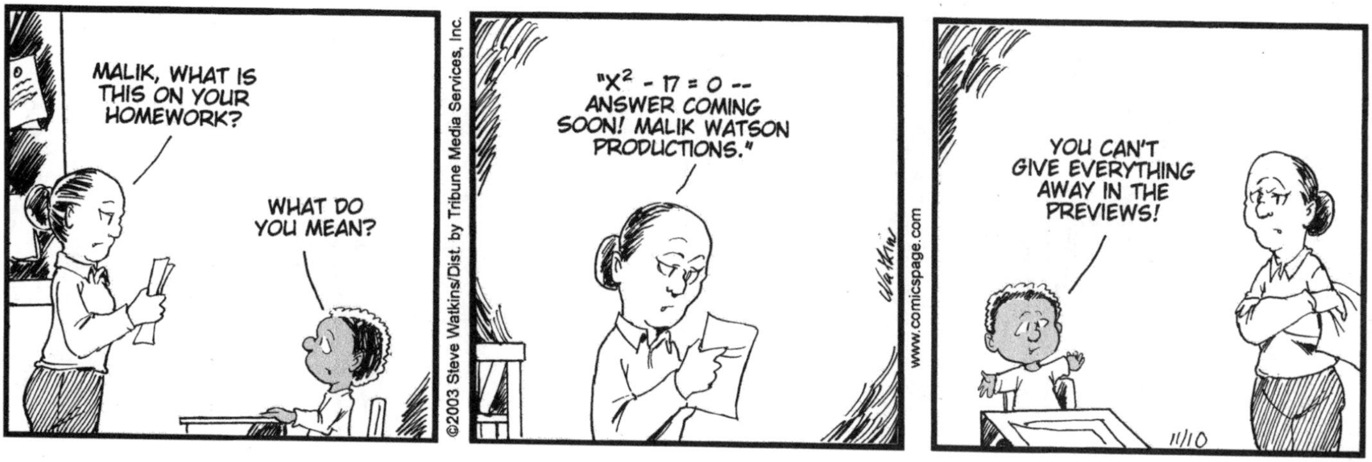
MALIK, WHAT IS THIS ON YOUR HOMEWORK?
WHAT DO YOU MEAN?
©2003 Steve Watkins/Dist. by Tribune Media Services, Inc.
"X^2 - 17 = 0 -- ANSWER COMING SOON! MALIK WATSON PRODUCTIONS."
www.comicspage.com
YOU CAN'T GIVE EVERYTHING AWAY IN THE PREVIEWS!
11/10

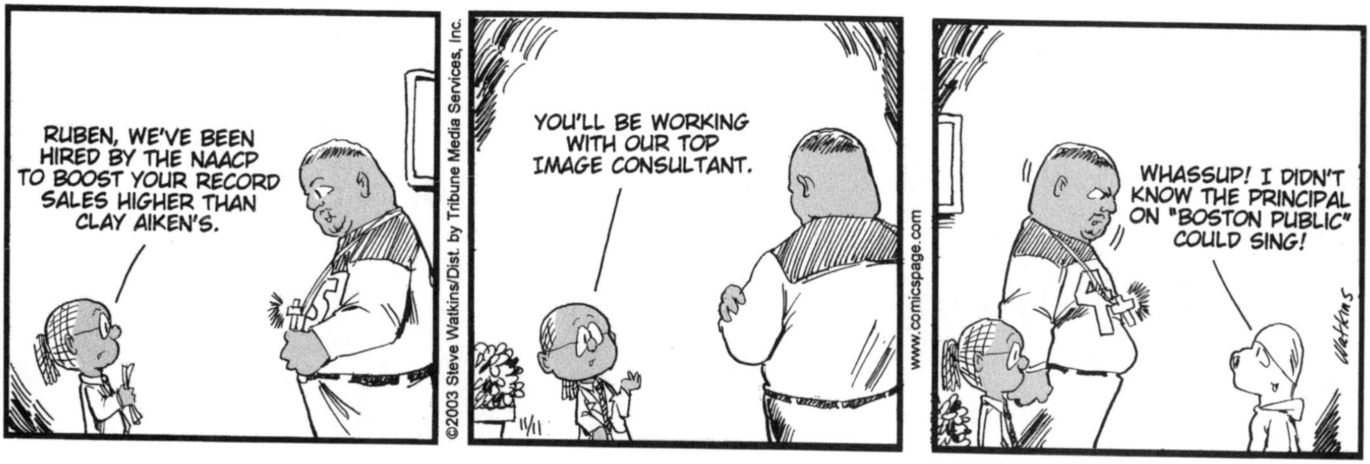
RUBEN, WE'VE BEEN HIRED BY THE NAACP TO BOOST YOUR RECORD SALES HIGHER THAN CLAY AIKEN'S.
©2003 Steve Watkins/Dist. by Tribune Media Services, Inc.
YOU'LL BE WORKING WITH OUR TOP IMAGE CONSULTANT.
11/11
www.comicspage.com
WHASSUP! I DIDN'T KNOW THE PRINCIPAL ON "BOSTON PUBLIC" COULD SING!
Watkins

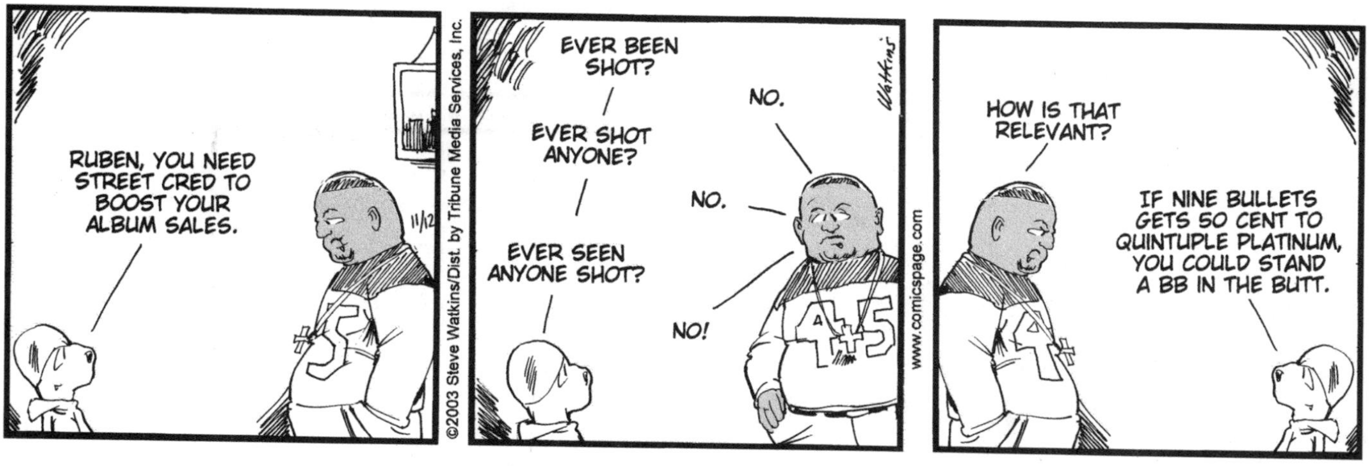
RUBEN, YOU NEED STREET CRED TO BOOST YOUR ALBUM SALES.
11/12
©2003 Steve Watkins/Dist. by Tribune Media Services, Inc.
EVER BEEN SHOT?
NO.
EVER SHOT ANYONE?
NO.
EVER SEEN ANYONE SHOT?
NO!
Watkins
www.comicspage.com
HOW IS THAT RELEVANT?
IF NINE BULLETS GETS 50 CENT TO QUINTUPLE PLATINUM, YOU COULD STAND A BB IN THE BUTT.

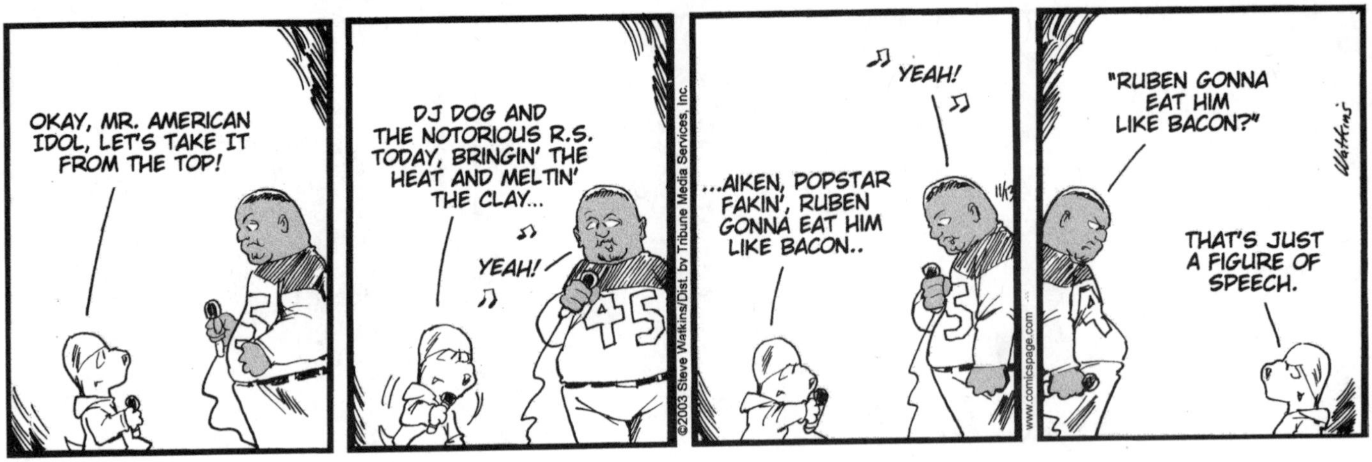
OKAY, MR. AMERICAN IDOL, LET'S TAKE IT FROM THE TOP!
DJ DOG AND THE NOTORIOUS R.S. TODAY, BRINGIN' THE HEAT AND MELTIN' THE CLAY...
YEAH!
45
©2003 Steve Watkins/Dist. by Tribune Media Services, Inc.
YEAH!
...AIKEN, POPSTAR FAKIN', RUBEN GONNA EAT HIM LIKE BACON..
11/13
www.comicspage.com
"RUBEN GONNA EAT HIM LIKE BACON?"
THAT'S JUST A FIGURE OF SPEECH.
Watkins

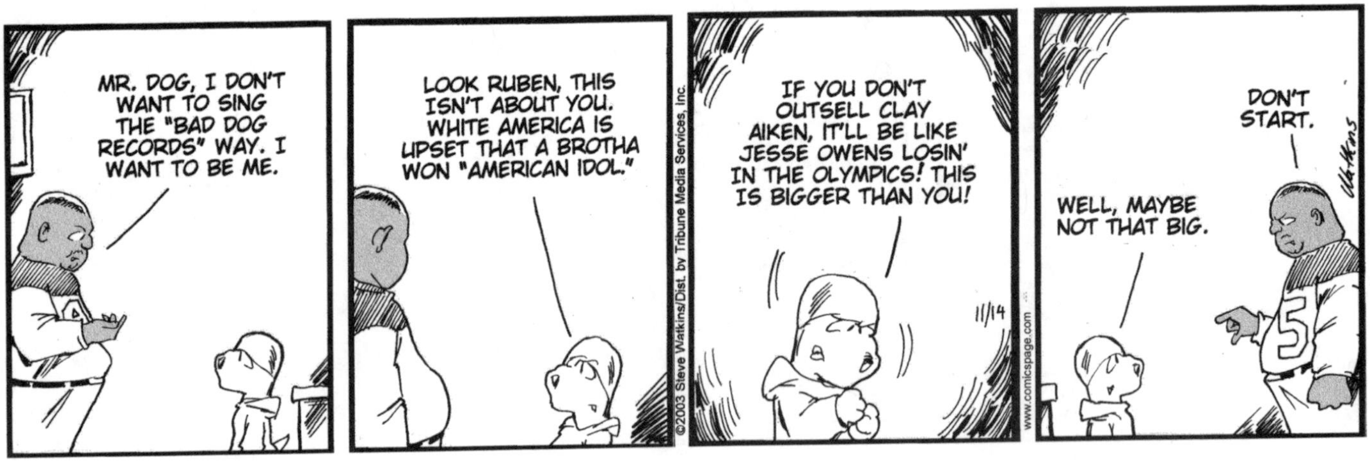
MR. DOG, I DON'T WANT TO SING THE "BAD DOG RECORDS" WAY. I WANT TO BE ME.
LOOK RUBEN, THIS ISN'T ABOUT YOU. WHITE AMERICA IS UPSET THAT A BROTHA WON "AMERICAN IDOL."
©2003 Steve Watkins/Dist. by Tribune Media Services, Inc.
IF YOU DON'T OUTSELL CLAY AIKEN, IT'LL BE LIKE JESSE OWENS LOSIN' IN THE OLYMPICS! THIS IS BIGGER THAN YOU!
11/14
www.comicspage.com
WELL, MAYBE NOT THAT BIG.
DON'T START.
Watkins

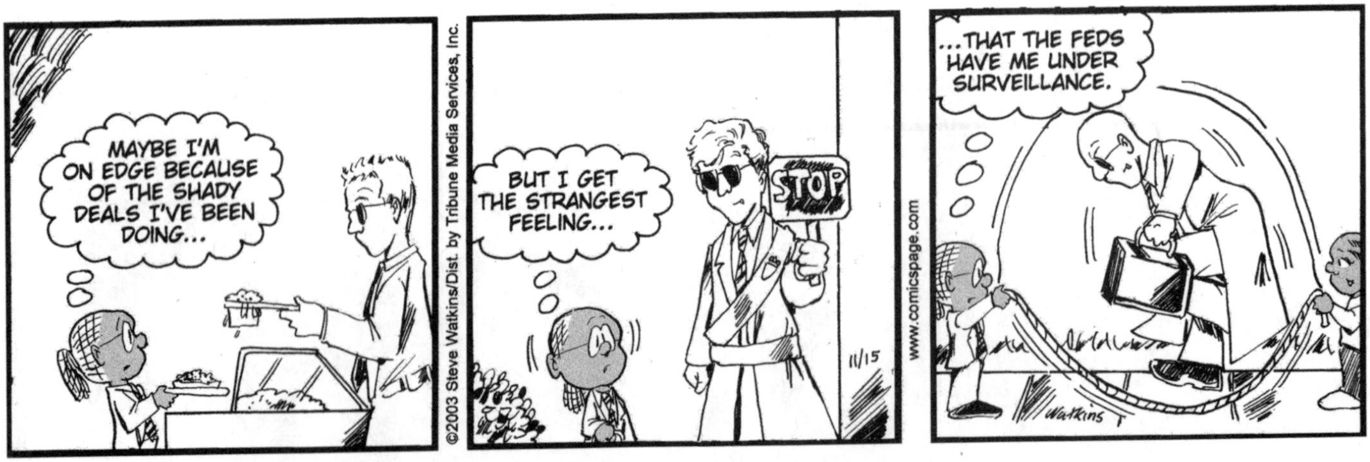
MAYBE I'M ON EDGE BECAUSE OF THE SHADY DEALS I'VE BEEN DOING...
©2003 Steve Watkins/Dist. by Tribune Media Services, Inc.
BUT I GET THE STRANGEST FEELING...
STOP
11/15
www.comicspage.com
...THAT THE FEDS HAVE ME UNDER SURVEILLANCE.
Watkins

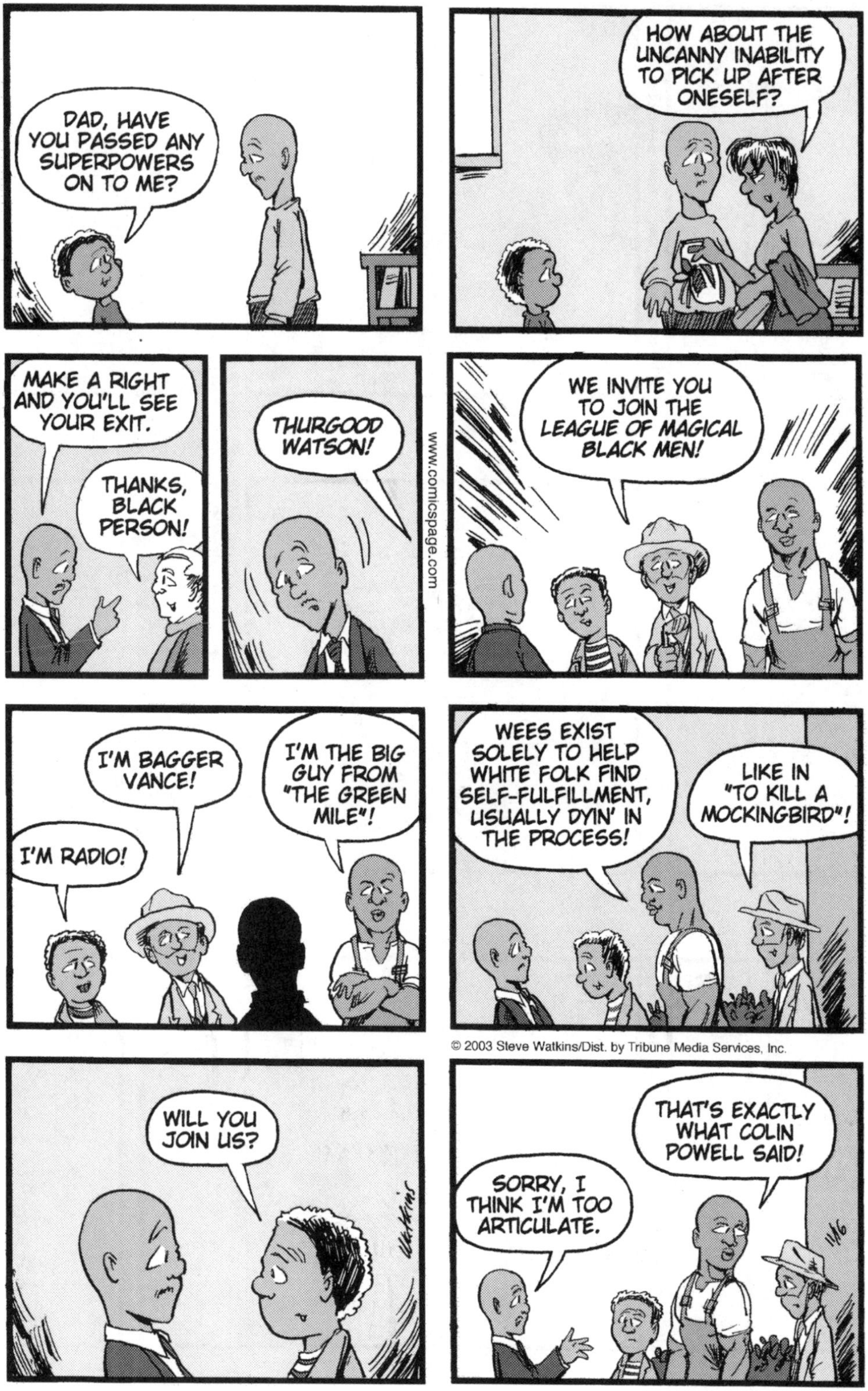
DAD, HAVE YOU PASSED ANY SUPERPOWERS ON TO ME?
HOW ABOUT THE UNCANNY INABILITY TO PICK UP AFTER ONESELF?
MAKE A RIGHT AND YOU'LL SEE YOUR EXIT.
THANKS, BLACK PERSON!
THURGOOD WATSON!
WE INVITE YOU TO JOIN THE LEAGUE OF MAGICAL BLACK MEN!
I'M RADIO!
I'M BAGGER VANCE!
I'M THE BIG GUY FROM "THE GREEN MILE"!
WEES EXIST SOLELY TO HELP WHITE FOLK FIND SELF-FULFILLMENT, USUALLY DYIN' IN THE PROCESS!
LIKE IN "TO KILL A MOCKINGBIRD"!
WILL YOU JOIN US?
SORRY, I THINK I'M TOO ARTICULATE.
THAT'S EXACTLY WHAT COLIN POWELL SAID!
WATKINS
11/16

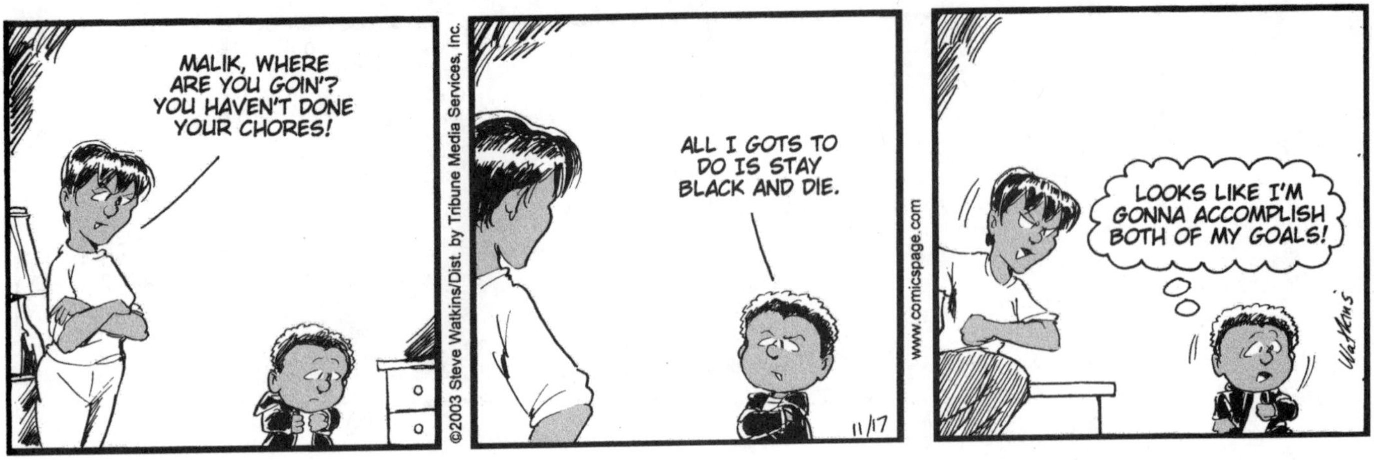
MALIK, WHERE ARE YOU GOIN'? YOU HAVEN'T DONE YOUR CHORES!
ALL I GOTS TO DO IS STAY BLACK AND DIE.
LOOKS LIKE I'M GONNA ACCOMPLISH BOTH OF MY GOALS!

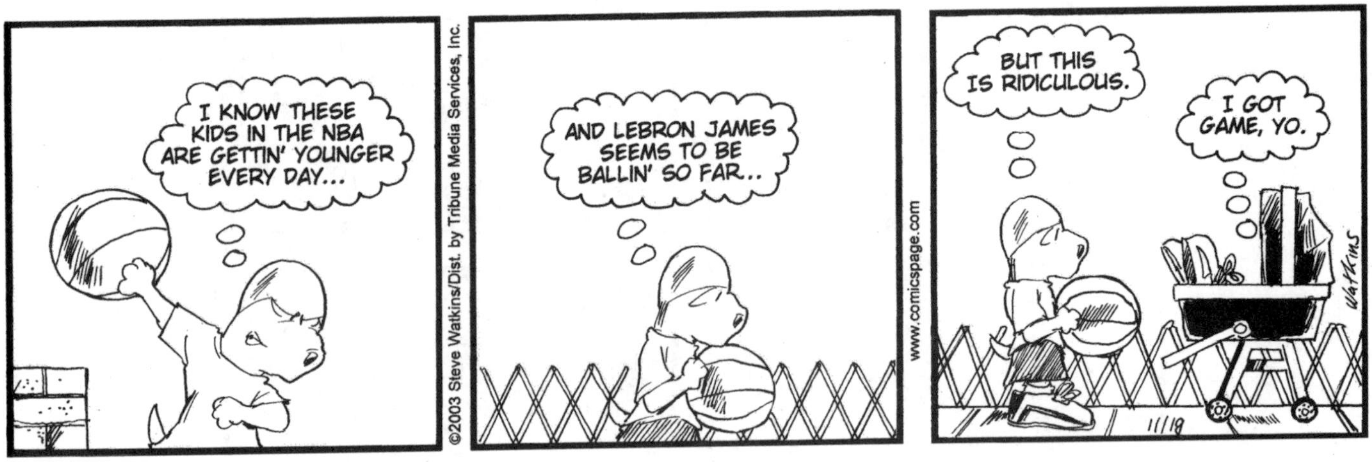
I KNOW THESE KIDS IN THE NBA ARE GETTIN' YOUNGER EVERY DAY...
AND LEBRON JAMES SEEMS TO BE BALLIN' SO FAR...
BUT THIS IS RIDICULOUS.
I GOT GAME, YO.

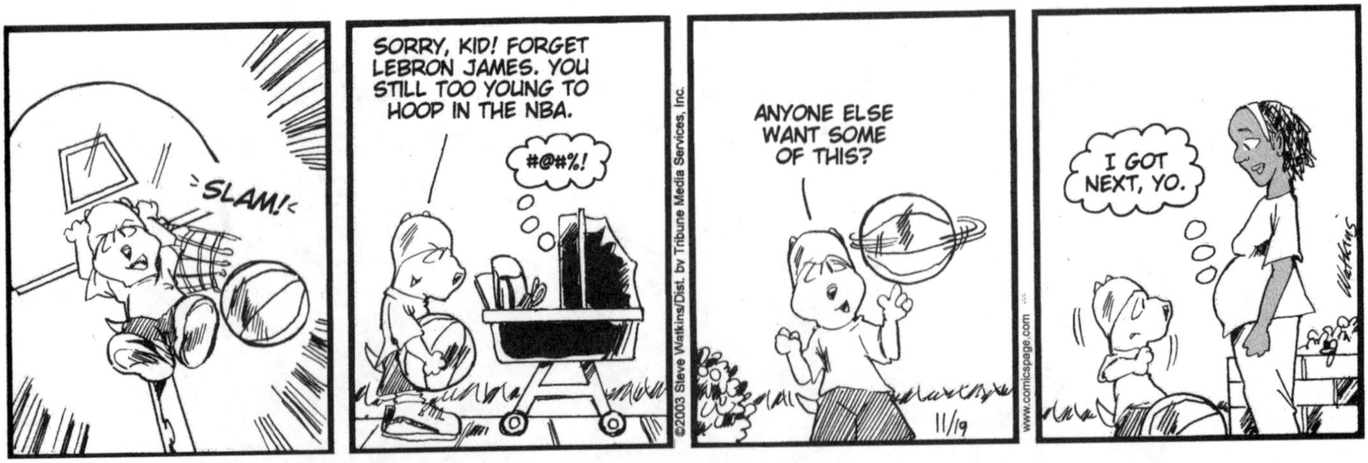
SLAM!
SORRY, KID! FORGET LEBRON JAMES. YOU STILL TOO YOUNG TO HOOP IN THE NBA.
#@#%!
ANYONE ELSE WANT SOME OF THIS?
I GOT NEXT, YO.

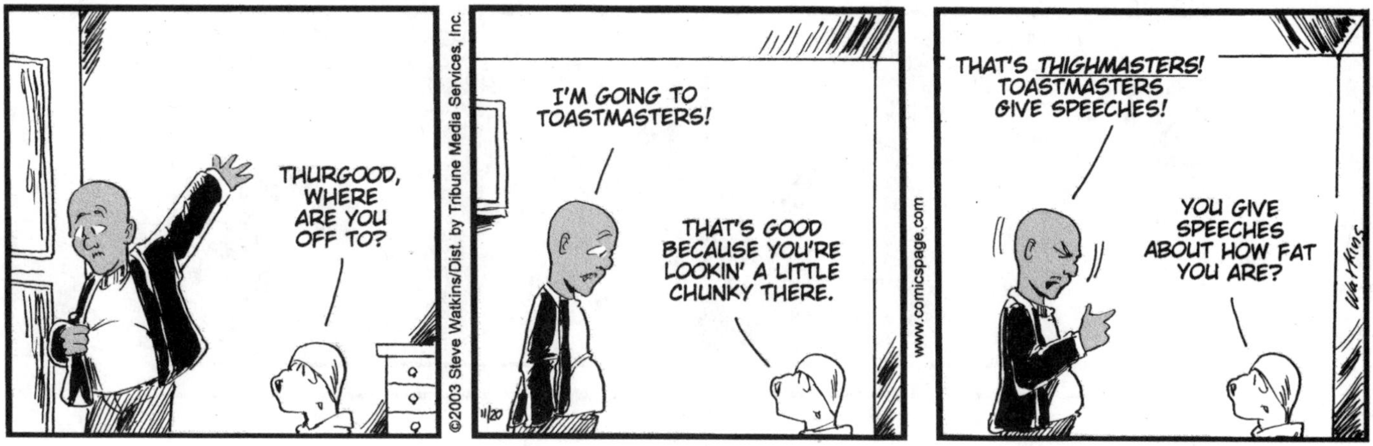
THURGOOD, WHERE ARE YOU OFF TO?
©2003 Steve Watkins/Dist. by Tribune Media Services, Inc.
I'M GOING TO TOASTMASTERS!
THAT'S GOOD BECAUSE YOU'RE LOOKIN' A LITTLE CHUNKY THERE.
11/20
www.comicspage.com
THAT'S THIGHMASTERS! TOASTMASTERS GIVE SPEECHES!
YOU GIVE SPEECHES ABOUT HOW FAT YOU ARE?
Watkins

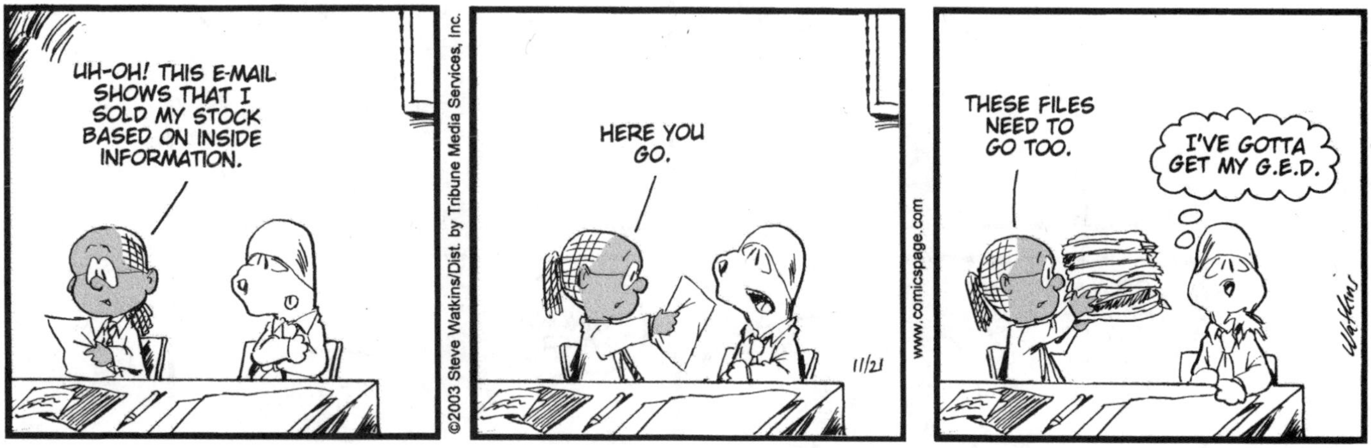
UH-OH! THIS E-MAIL SHOWS THAT I SOLD MY STOCK BASED ON INSIDE INFORMATION.
©2003 Steve Watkins/Dist. by Tribune Media Services, Inc.
HERE YOU GO.
11/21
www.comicspage.com
THESE FILES NEED TO GO TOO.
I'VE GOTTA GET MY G.E.D.
Watkins

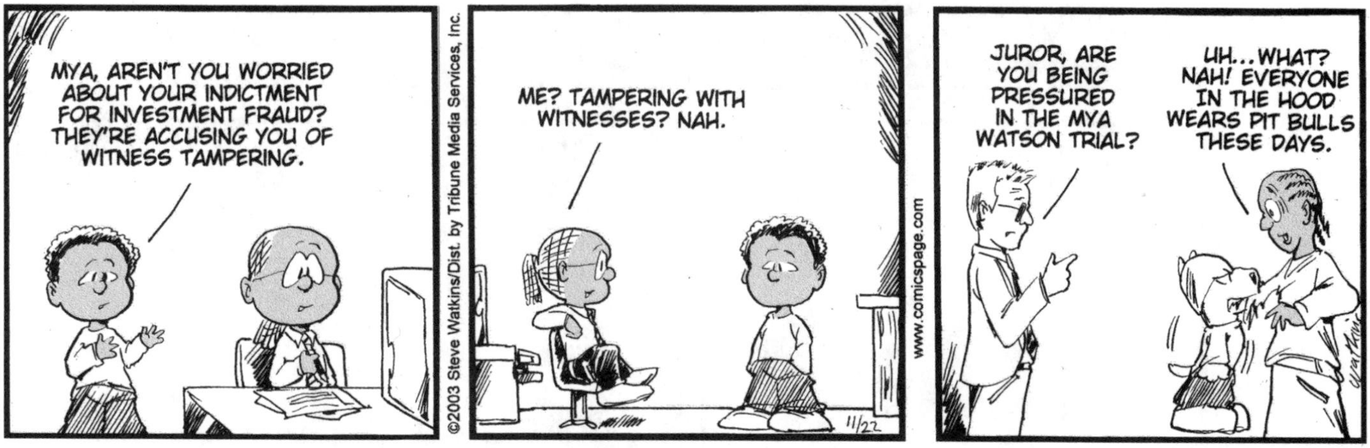
MYA, AREN'T YOU WORRIED ABOUT YOUR INDICTMENT FOR INVESTMENT FRAUD? THEY'RE ACCUSING YOU OF WITNESS TAMPERING.
©2003 Steve Watkins/Dist. by Tribune Media Services, Inc.
ME? TAMPERING WITH WITNESSES? NAH.
11/22
www.comicspage.com
JUROR, ARE YOU BEING PRESSURED IN THE MYA WATSON TRIAL?
UH...WHAT? NAH! EVERYONE IN THE HOOD WEARS PIT BULLS THESE DAYS.
Watkins

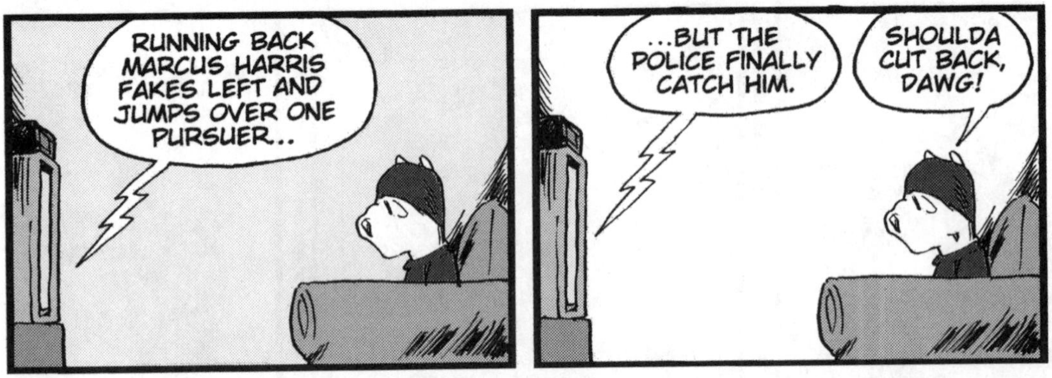
RUNNING BACK MARCUS HARRIS FAKES LEFT AND JUMPS OVER ONE PURSUER...
...BUT THE POLICE FINALLY CATCH HIM.
SHOULDA CUT BACK, DAWG!

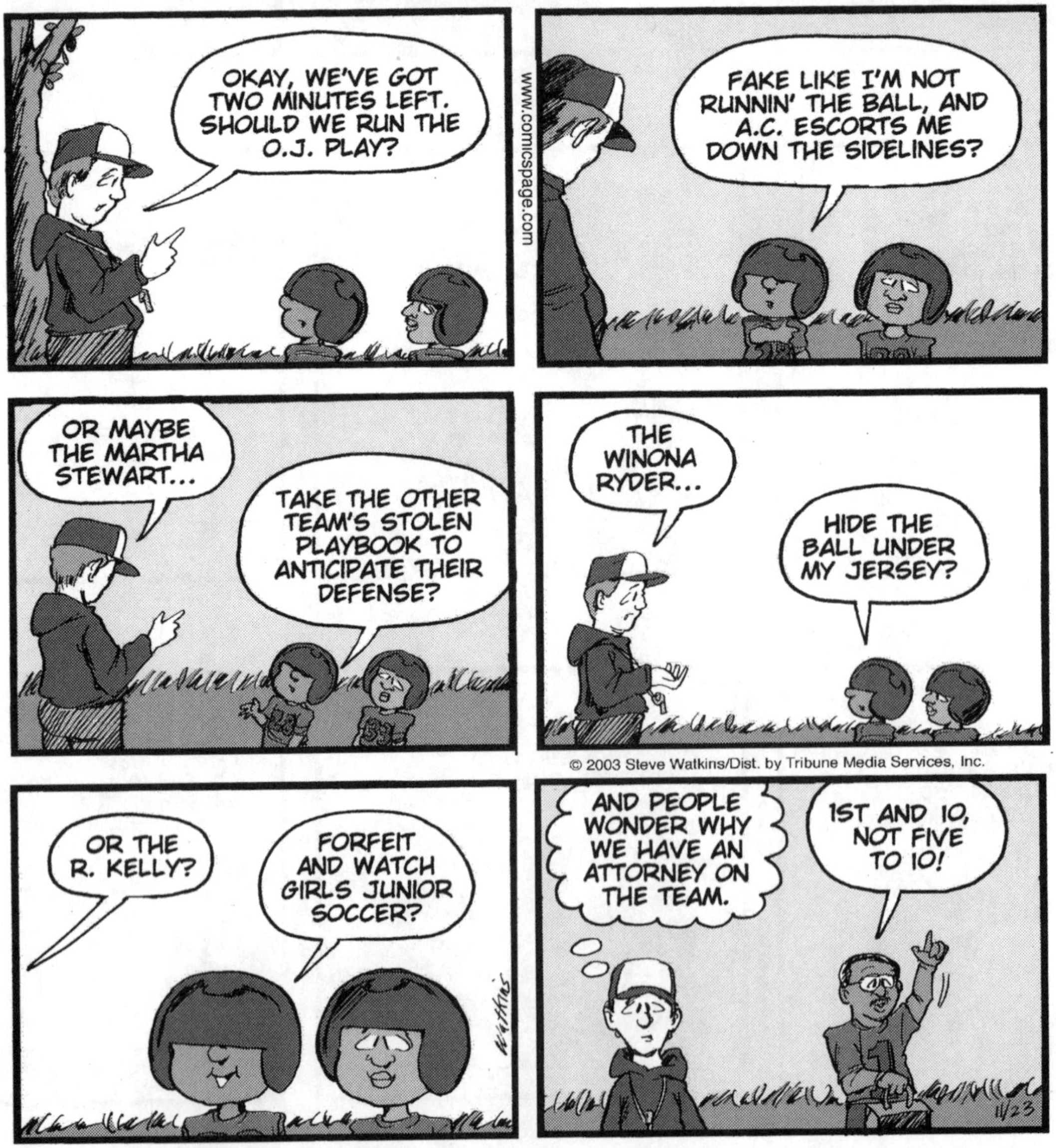
OKAY, WE'VE GOT TWO MINUTES LEFT. SHOULD WE RUN THE O.J. PLAY?
www.comicspage.com
FAKE LIKE I'M NOT RUNNIN' THE BALL, AND A.C. ESCORTS ME DOWN THE SIDELINES?
OR MAYBE THE MARTHA STEWART...
TAKE THE OTHER TEAM'S STOLEN PLAYBOOK TO ANTICIPATE THEIR DEFENSE?
THE WINONA RYDER...
HIDE THE BALL UNDER MY JERSEY?
© 2003 Steve Watkins/Dist. by Tribune Media Services, Inc.
OR THE R. KELLY?
FORFEIT AND WATCH GIRLS JUNIOR SOCCER?
AND PEOPLE WONDER WHY WE HAVE AN ATTORNEY ON THE TEAM.
1ST AND 10, NOT FIVE TO 10!
Watkins
11/23

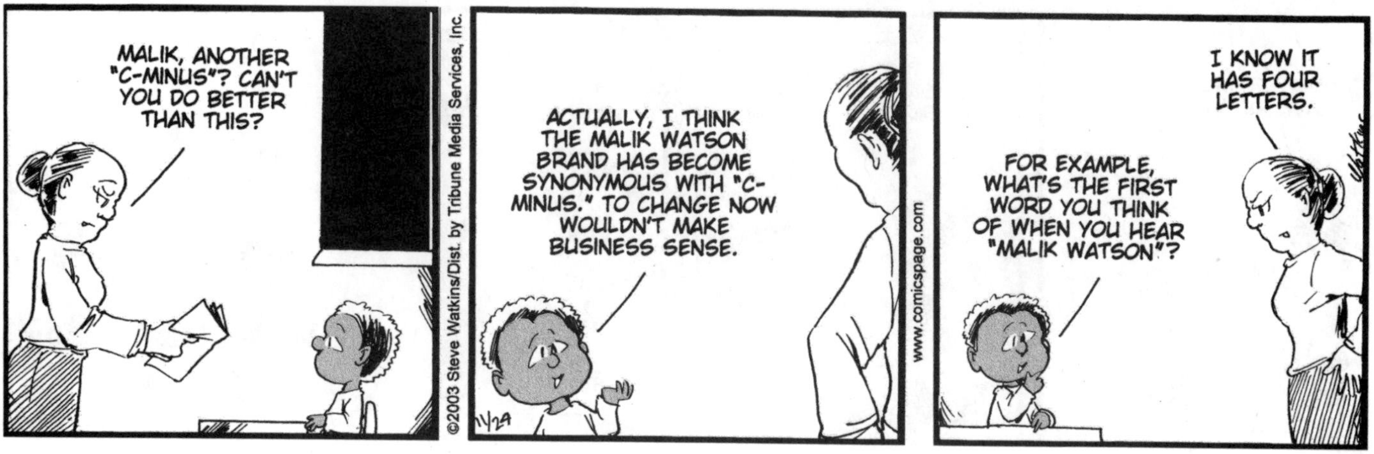
MALIK, ANOTHER "C-MINUS"? CAN'T YOU DO BETTER THAN THIS?
©2003 Steve Watkins/Dist. by Tribune Media Services, Inc.
ACTUALLY, I THINK THE MALIK WATSON BRAND HAS BECOME SYNONYMOUS WITH "C-MINUS." TO CHANGE NOW WOULDN'T MAKE BUSINESS SENSE.
11/24
www.comicspage.com
FOR EXAMPLE, WHAT'S THE FIRST WORD YOU THINK OF WHEN YOU HEAR "MALIK WATSON"?
I KNOW IT HAS FOUR LETTERS.

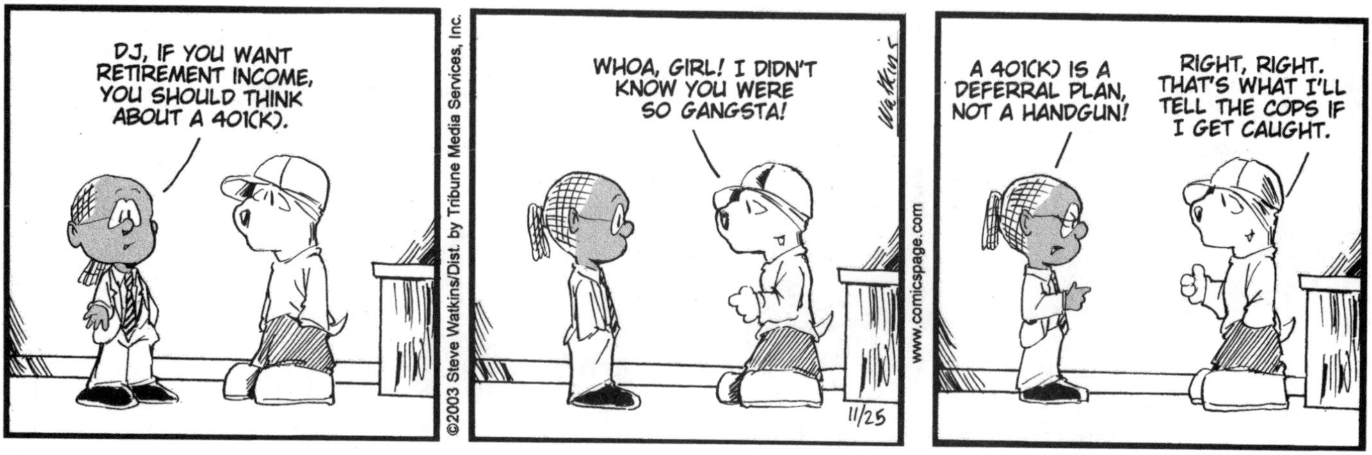
DJ, IF YOU WANT RETIREMENT INCOME, YOU SHOULD THINK ABOUT A 401(K).
©2003 Steve Watkins/Dist. by Tribune Media Services, Inc.
WHOA, GIRL! I DIDN'T KNOW YOU WERE SO GANGSTA!
11/25
www.comicspage.com
A 401(K) IS A DEFERRAL PLAN, NOT A HANDGUN!
RIGHT, RIGHT. THAT'S WHAT I'LL TELL THE COPS IF I GET CAUGHT.

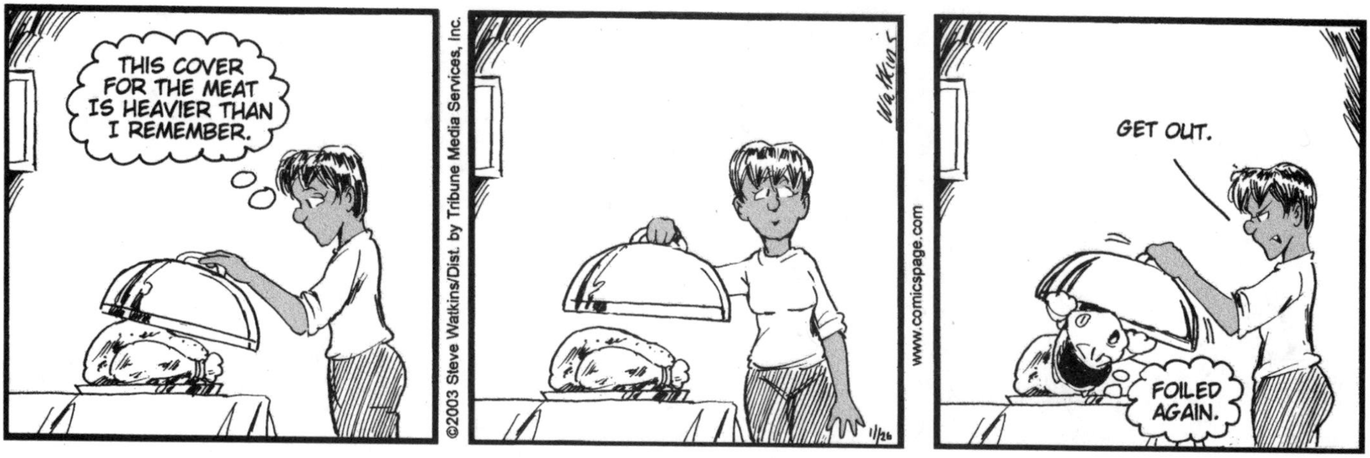
THIS COVER FOR THE MEAT IS HEAVIER THAN I REMEMBER.
©2003 Steve Watkins/Dist. by Tribune Media Services, Inc.
11/26
www.comicspage.com
GET OUT.
FOILED AGAIN.

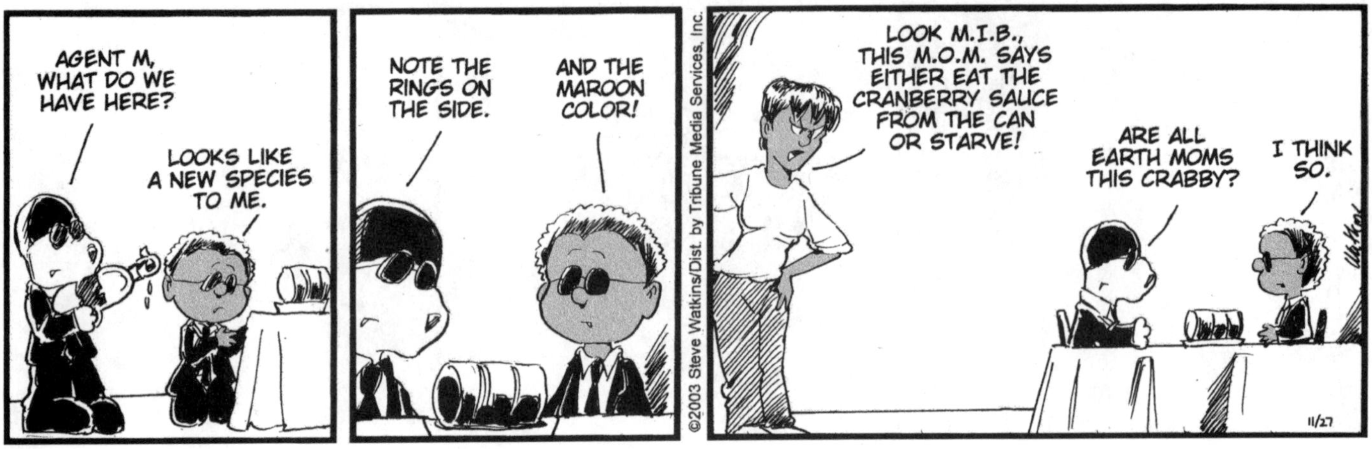
AGENT M, WHAT DO WE HAVE HERE?
LOOKS LIKE A NEW SPECIES TO ME.
NOTE THE RINGS ON THE SIDE.
AND THE MAROON COLOR!
©2003 Steve Watkins/Dist. by Tribune Media Services, Inc.
LOOK M.I.B., THIS M.O.M. SAYS EITHER EAT THE CRANBERRY SAUCE FROM THE CAN OR STARVE!
ARE ALL EARTH MOMS THIS CRABBY?
I THINK SO.
11/27

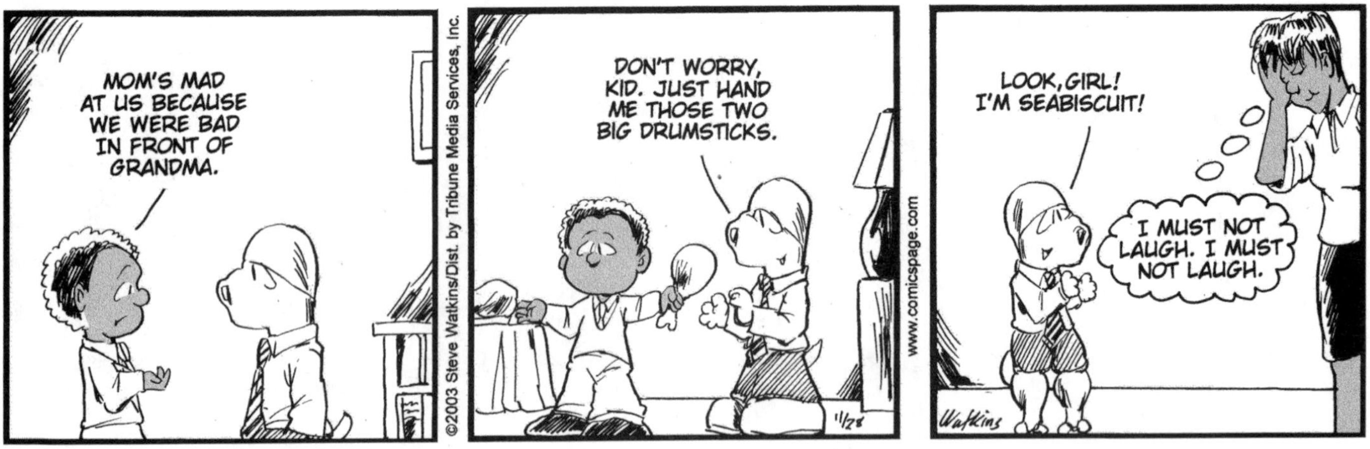
MOM'S MAD AT US BECAUSE WE WERE BAD IN FRONT OF GRANDMA.
©2003 Steve Watkins/Dist. by Tribune Media Services, Inc.
DON'T WORRY, KID. JUST HAND ME THOSE TWO BIG DRUMSTICKS.
11/28
www.comicspage.com
LOOK, GIRL! I'M SEABISCUIT!
I MUST NOT LAUGH. I MUST NOT LAUGH.
Watkins

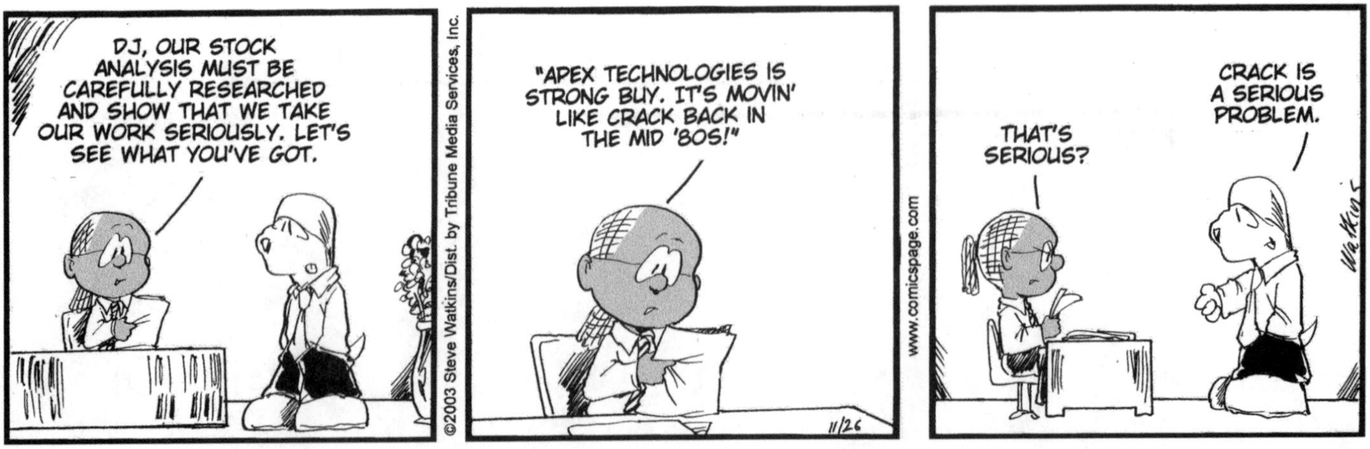
DJ, OUR STOCK ANALYSIS MUST BE CAREFULLY RESEARCHED AND SHOW THAT WE TAKE OUR WORK SERIOUSLY. LET'S SEE WHAT YOU'VE GOT.
©2003 Steve Watkins/Dist. by Tribune Media Services, Inc.
"APEX TECHNOLOGIES IS STRONG BUY. IT'S MOVIN' LIKE CRACK BACK IN THE MID '80S!"
11/26
www.comicspage.com
THAT'S SERIOUS?
CRACK IS A SERIOUS PROBLEM.

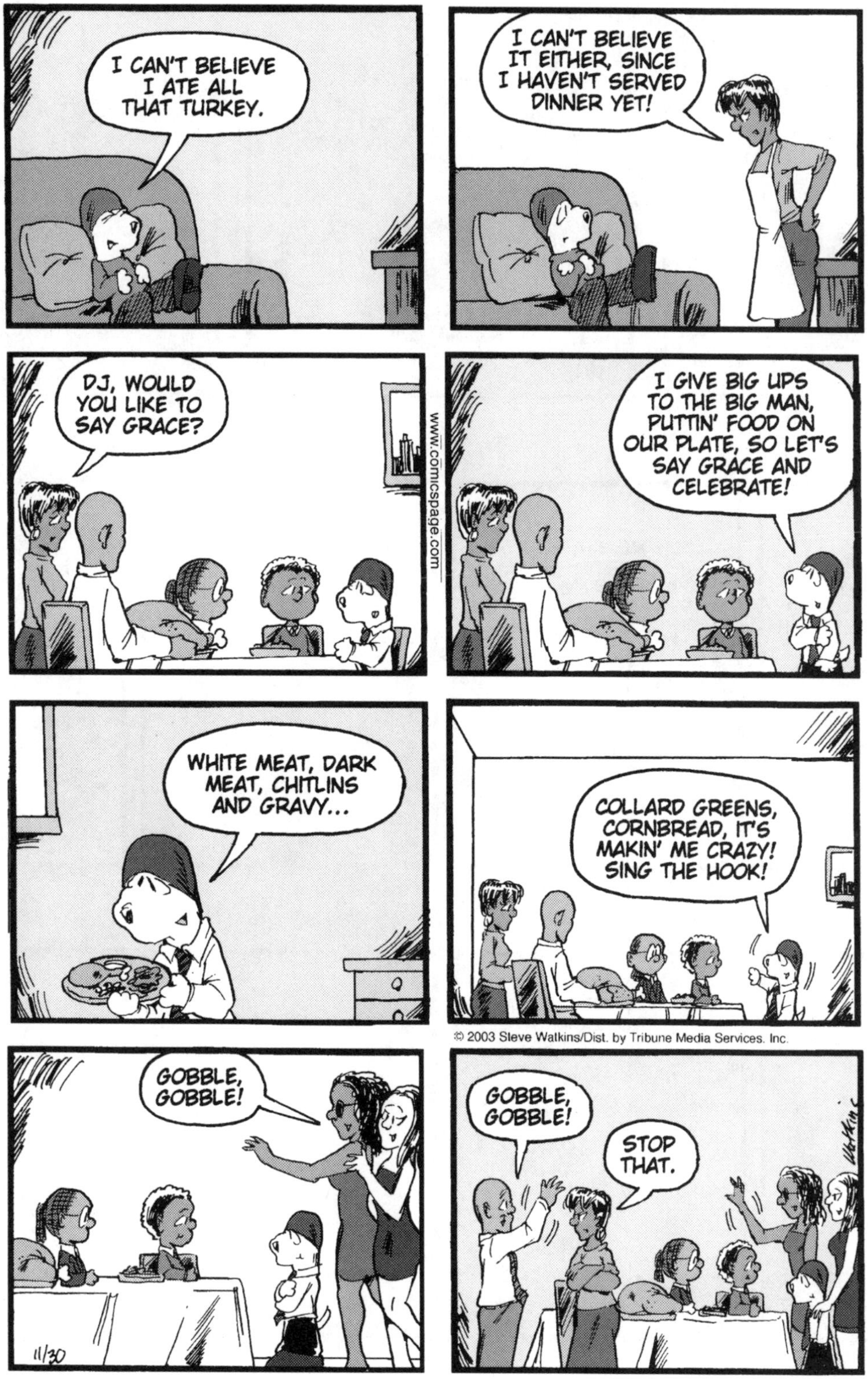
I CAN'T BELIEVE I ATE ALL THAT TURKEY.
I CAN'T BELIEVE IT EITHER, SINCE I HAVEN'T SERVED DINNER YET!
DJ, WOULD YOU LIKE TO SAY GRACE?
www.comicspage.com
I GIVE BIG UPS TO THE BIG MAN, PUTTIN' FOOD ON OUR PLATE, SO LET'S SAY GRACE AND CELEBRATE!
WHITE MEAT, DARK MEAT, CHITLINS AND GRAVY...
COLLARD GREENS, CORNBREAD, IT'S MAKIN' ME CRAZY! SING THE HOOK!
GOBBLE, GOBBLE!
11/30
GOBBLE, GOBBLE!
STOP THAT.

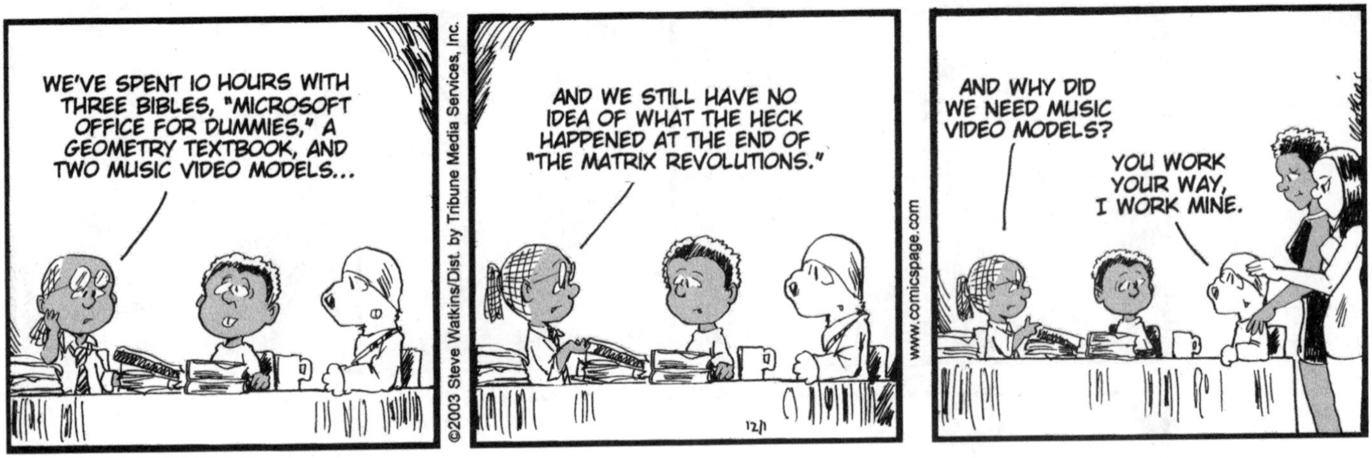
WE'VE SPENT 10 HOURS WITH THREE BIBLES, "MICROSOFT OFFICE FOR DUMMIES," A GEOMETRY TEXTBOOK, AND TWO MUSIC VIDEO MODELS...
©2003 Steve Watkins/Dist. by Tribune Media Services, Inc.
AND WE STILL HAVE NO IDEA OF WHAT THE HECK HAPPENED AT THE END OF "THE MATRIX REVOLUTIONS."
12/1
www.comicspage.com
AND WHY DID WE NEED MUSIC VIDEO MODELS?
YOU WORK YOUR WAY, I WORK MINE.

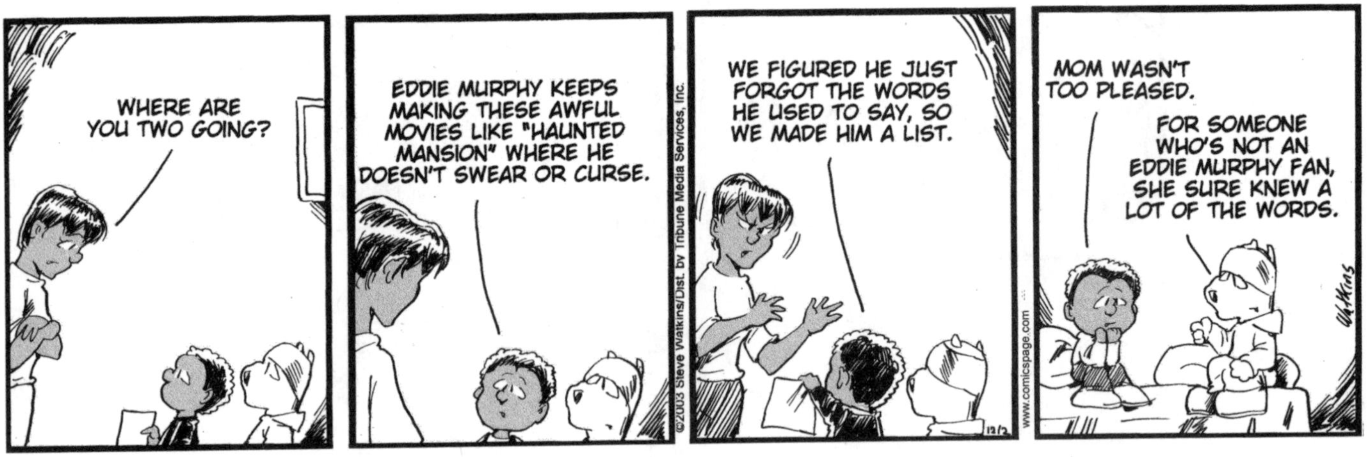
WHERE ARE YOU TWO GOING?
EDDIE MURPHY KEEPS MAKING THESE AWFUL MOVIES LIKE "HAUNTED MANSION" WHERE HE DOESN'T SWEAR OR CURSE.
©2003 Steve Watkins/Dist. by Tribune Media Services, Inc.
WE FIGURED HE JUST FORGOT THE WORDS HE USED TO SAY, SO WE MADE HIM A LIST.
12/2
www.comicspage.com
MOM WASN'T TOO PLEASED.
FOR SOMEONE WHO'S NOT AN EDDIE MURPHY FAN, SHE SURE KNEW A LOT OF THE WORDS.
WATKINS

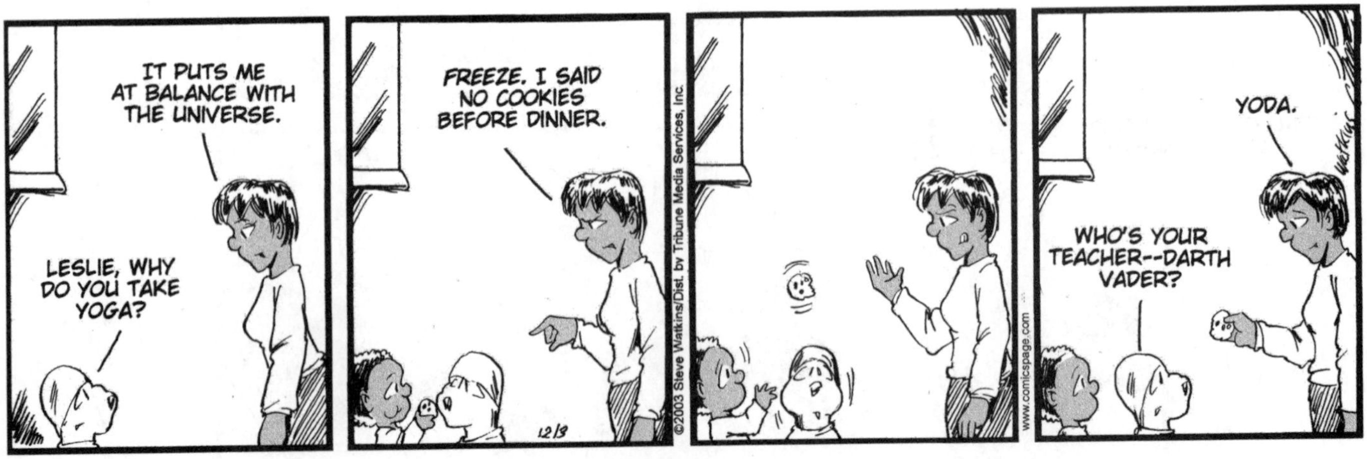
LESLIE, WHY DO YOU TAKE YOGA?
IT PUTS ME AT BALANCE WITH THE UNIVERSE.
FREEZE. I SAID NO COOKIES BEFORE DINNER.
12/3
©2003 Steve Watkins/Dist. by Tribune Media Services, Inc.
www.comicspage.com
WHO'S YOUR TEACHER--DARTH VADER?
YODA.
WATKINS

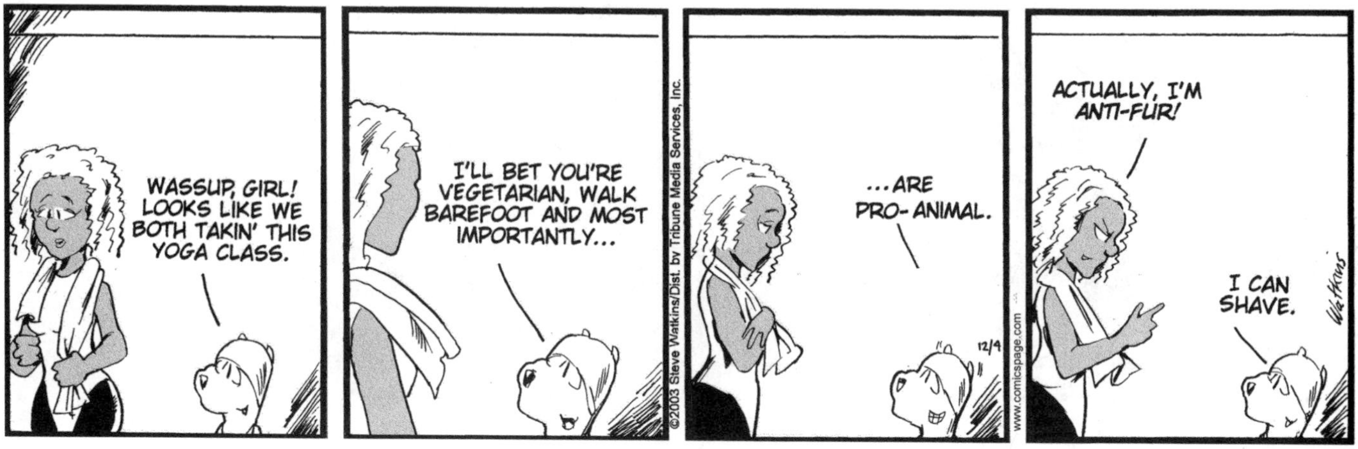
WASSUP, GIRL! LOOKS LIKE WE BOTH TAKIN' THIS YOGA CLASS.
I'LL BET YOU'RE VEGETARIAN, WALK BAREFOOT AND MOST IMPORTANTLY...
©2003 Steve Watkins/Dist. by Tribune Media Services, Inc.
...ARE PRO-ANIMAL.
12/4
www.comicspage.com
ACTUALLY, I'M ANTI-FUR!
I CAN SHAVE.

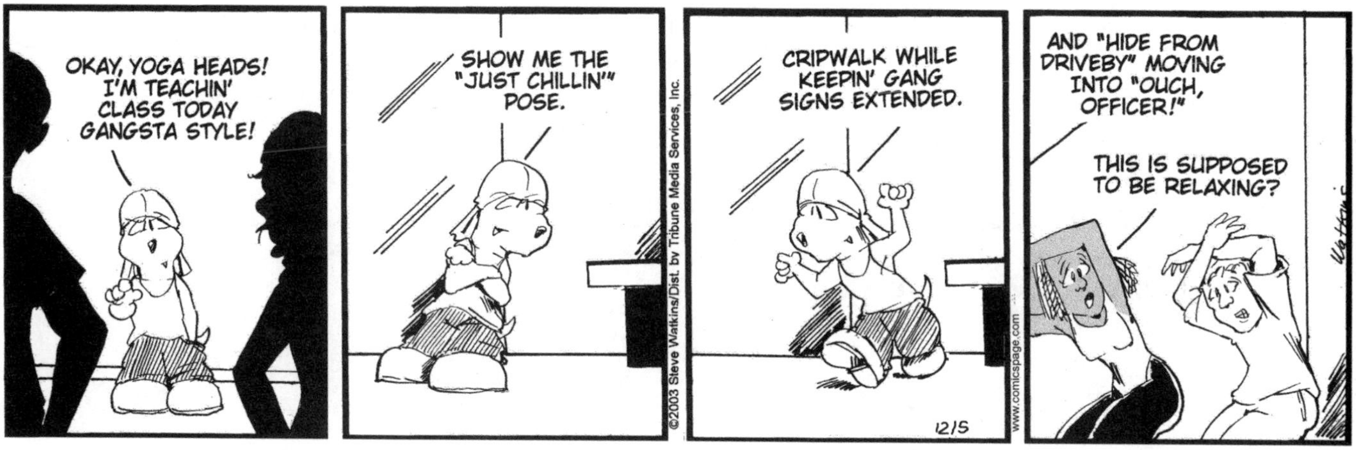
OKAY, YOGA HEADS! I'M TEACHIN' CLASS TODAY GANGSTA STYLE!
SHOW ME THE "JUST CHILLIN'" POSE.
©2003 Steve Watkins/Dist. by Tribune Media Services, Inc.
CRIPWALK WHILE KEEPIN' GANG SIGNS EXTENDED.
12/5
www.comicspage.com
AND "HIDE FROM DRIVEBY" MOVING INTO "OUCH, OFFICER!"
THIS IS SUPPOSED TO BE RELAXING?

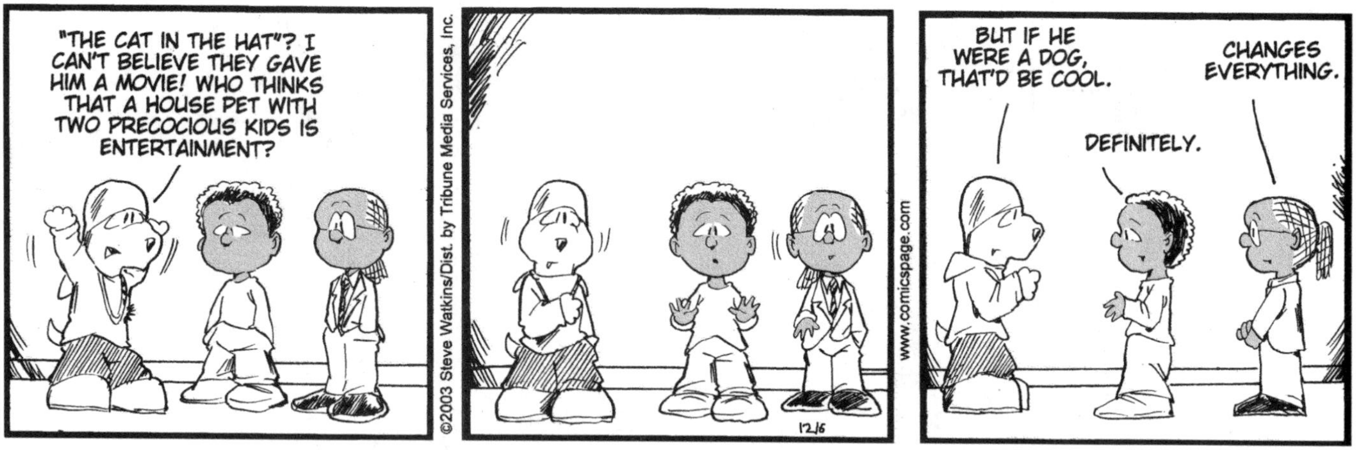
"THE CAT IN THE HAT"? I CAN'T BELIEVE THEY GAVE HIM A MOVIE! WHO THINKS THAT A HOUSE PET WITH TWO PRECOCIOUS KIDS IS ENTERTAINMENT?
©2003 Steve Watkins/Dist. by Tribune Media Services, Inc.
12/6
www.comicspage.com
BUT IF HE WERE A DOG, THAT'D BE COOL.
DEFINITELY.
CHANGES EVERYTHING.

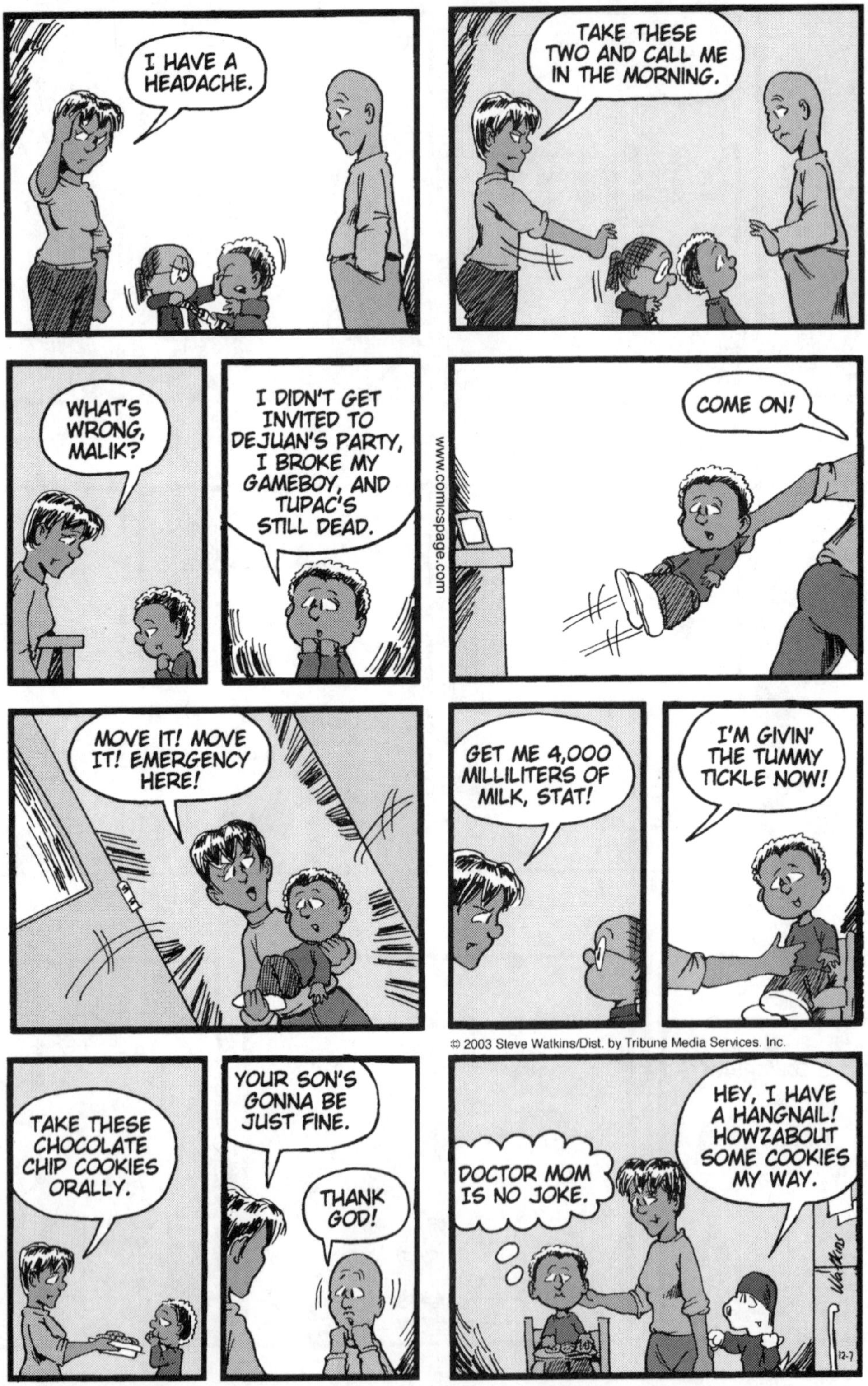
I HAVE A HEADACHE.
TAKE THESE TWO AND CALL ME IN THE MORNING.
WHAT'S WRONG, MALIK?
I DIDN'T GET INVITED TO DEJUAN'S PARTY, I BROKE MY GAMEBOY, AND TUPAC'S STILL DEAD.
www.comicspage.com
COME ON!
MOVE IT! MOVE IT! EMERGENCY HERE!
GET ME 4,000 MILLILITERS OF MILK, STAT!
I'M GIVIN' THE TUMMY TICKLE NOW!
© 2003 Steve Watkins/Dist. by Tribune Media Services. Inc.
TAKE THESE CHOCOLATE CHIP COOKIES ORALLY.
YOUR SON'S GONNA BE JUST FINE.
THANK GOD!
DOCTOR MOM IS NO JOKE.
HEY, I HAVE A HANGNAIL! HOWZABOUT SOME COOKIES MY WAY.
Watkins
12-7

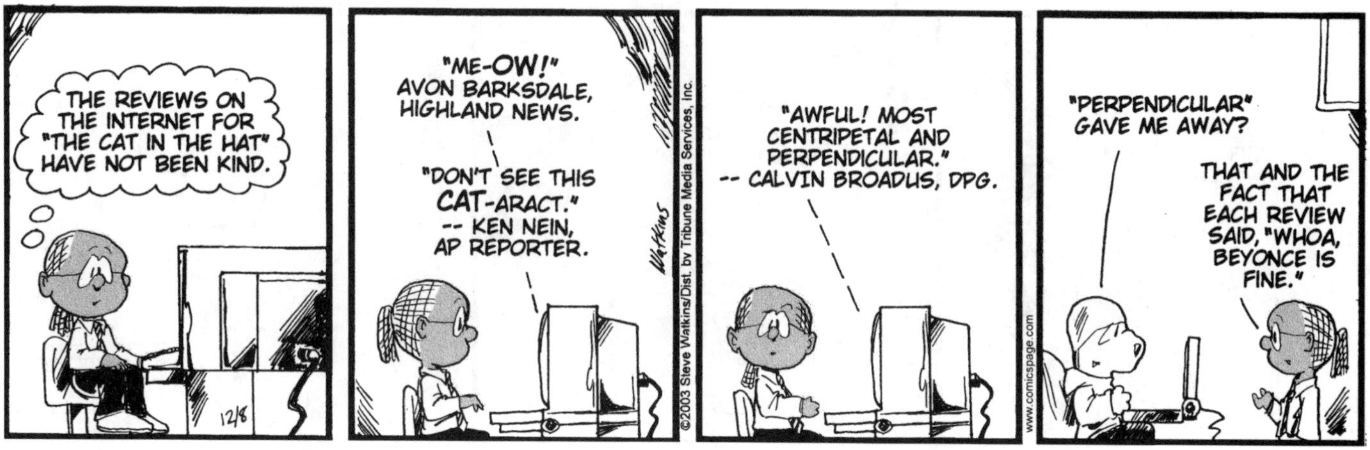
THE REVIEWS ON THE INTERNET FOR "THE CAT IN THE HAT" HAVE NOT BEEN KIND.
12/8
"ME-OW!" AVON BARKSDALE, HIGHLAND NEWS.
"DON'T SEE THIS CAT-ARACT." -- KEN NEIN, AP REPORTER.
Watkins
©2003 Steve Watkins/Dist. by Tribune Media Services, Inc.
"AWFUL! MOST CENTRIPETAL AND PERPENDICULAR." -- CALVIN BROADUS, DPG.
www.comicspage.com
"PERPENDICULAR" GAVE ME AWAY?
THAT AND THE FACT THAT EACH REVIEW SAID, "WHOA, BEYONCE IS FINE."

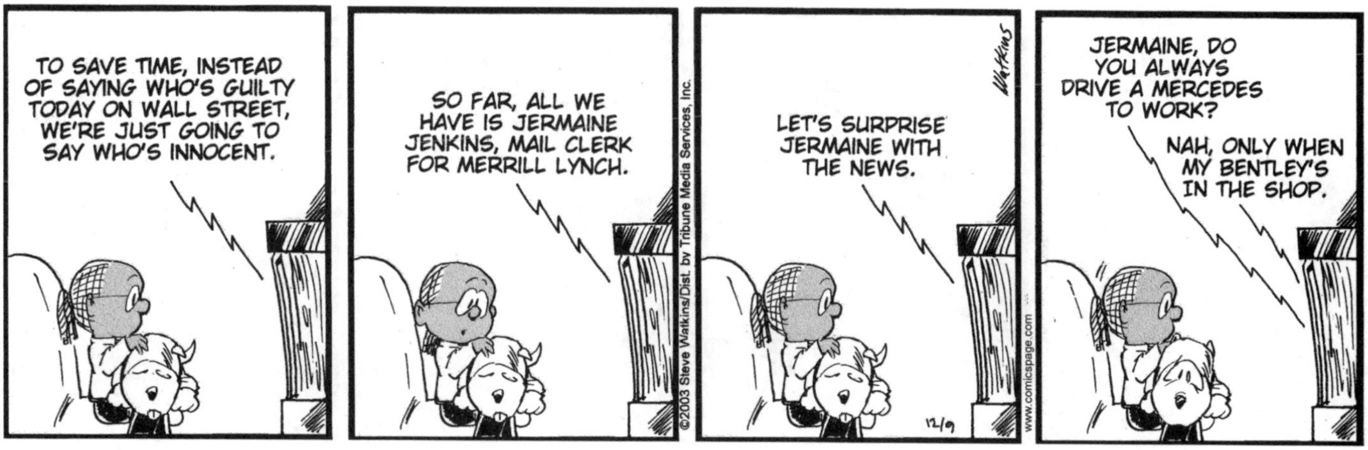
TO SAVE TIME, INSTEAD OF SAYING WHO'S GUILTY TODAY ON WALL STREET, WE'RE JUST GOING TO SAY WHO'S INNOCENT.
SO FAR, ALL WE HAVE IS JERMAINE JENKINS, MAIL CLERK FOR MERRILL LYNCH.
©2003 Steve Watkins/Dist. by Tribune Media Services, Inc.
Watkins
LET'S SURPRISE JERMAINE WITH THE NEWS.
12/9
www.comicspage.com
JERMAINE, DO YOU ALWAYS DRIVE A MERCEDES TO WORK?
NAH, ONLY WHEN MY BENTLEY'S IN THE SHOP.

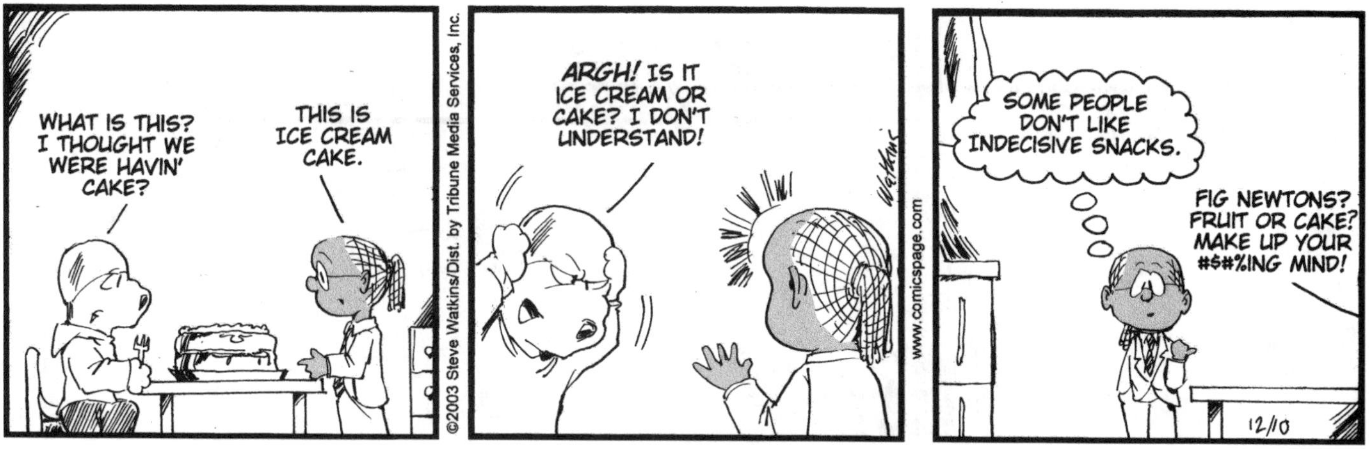
WHAT IS THIS? I THOUGHT WE WERE HAVIN' CAKE?
THIS IS ICE CREAM CAKE.
©2003 Steve Watkins/Dist. by Tribune Media Services, Inc.
ARGH! IS IT ICE CREAM OR CAKE? I DON'T UNDERSTAND!
Watkins
www.comicspage.com
SOME PEOPLE DON'T LIKE INDECISIVE SNACKS.
FIG NEWTONS? FRUIT OR CAKE? MAKE UP YOUR #$#%ING MIND!
12/10

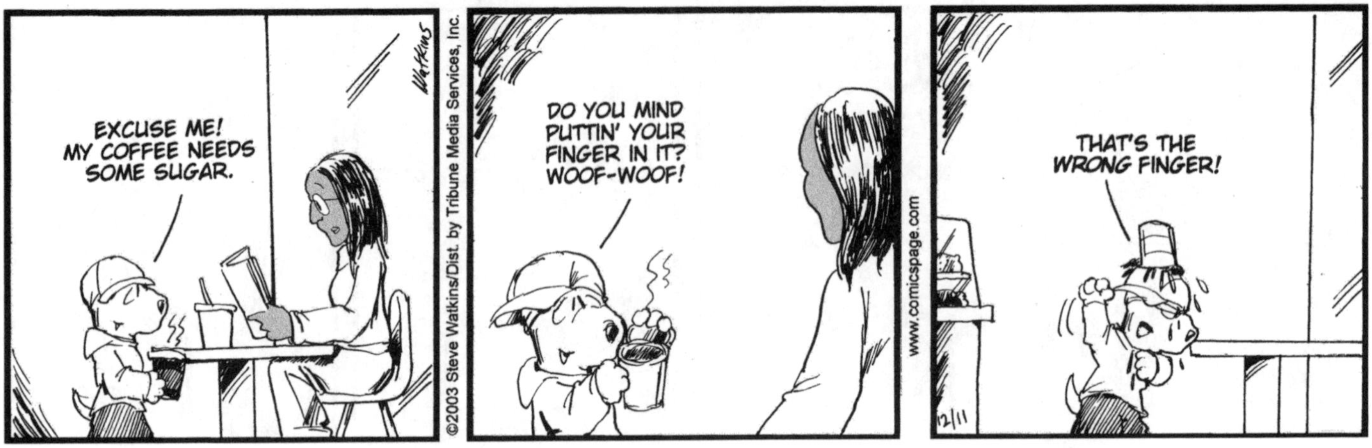
Watkins
EXCUSE ME! MY COFFEE NEEDS SOME SUGAR.
©2003 Steve Watkins/Dist. by Tribune Media Services, Inc.
DO YOU MIND PUTTIN' YOUR FINGER IN IT? WOOF-WOOF!
www.comicspage.com
THAT'S THE WRONG FINGER!
12/11

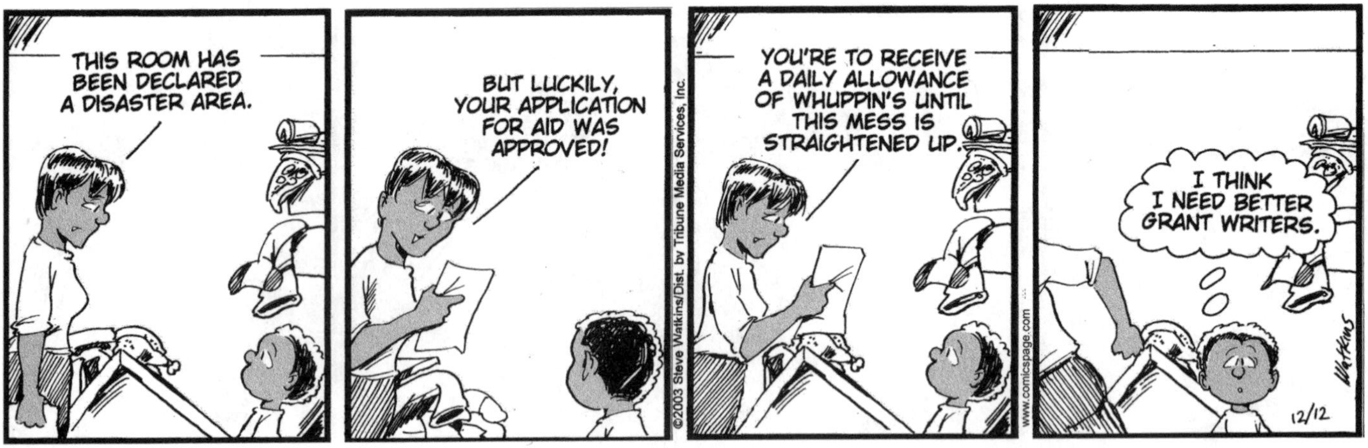
THIS ROOM HAS BEEN DECLARED A DISASTER AREA.
BUT LUCKILY, YOUR APPLICATION FOR AID WAS APPROVED!
©2003 Steve Watkins/Dist. by Tribune Media Services, Inc.
YOU'RE TO RECEIVE A DAILY ALLOWANCE OF WHUPPIN'S UNTIL THIS MESS IS STRAIGHTENED UP.
www.comicspage.com
I THINK I NEED BETTER GRANT WRITERS.
Watkins
12/12

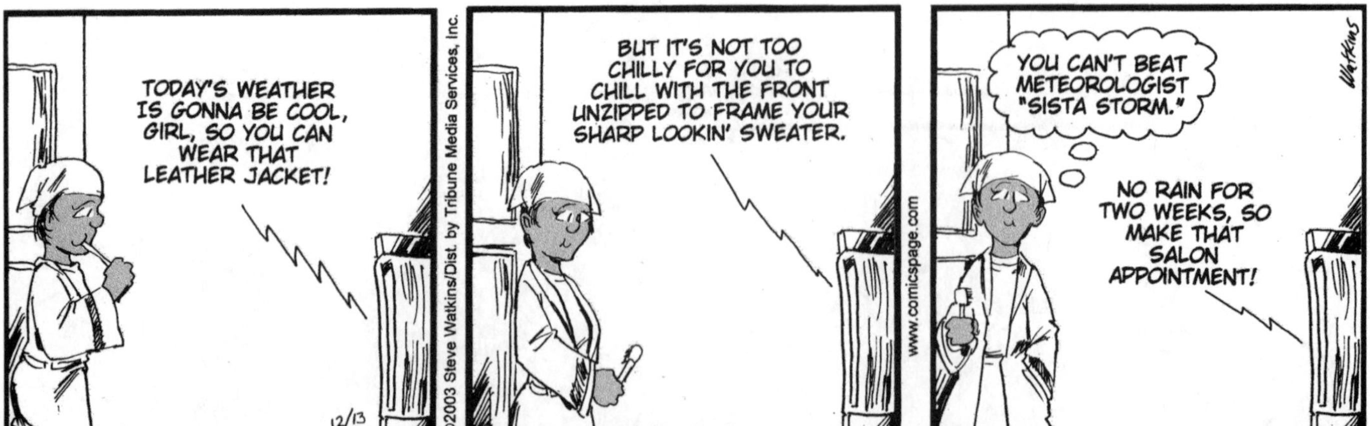
TODAY'S WEATHER IS GONNA BE COOL, GIRL, SO YOU CAN WEAR THAT LEATHER JACKET!
12/13
©2003 Steve Watkins/Dist. by Tribune Media Services, Inc.
BUT IT'S NOT TOO CHILLY FOR YOU TO CHILL WITH THE FRONT UNZIPPED TO FRAME YOUR SHARP LOOKIN' SWEATER.
www.comicspage.com
YOU CAN'T BEAT METEOROLOGIST "SISTA STORM."
NO RAIN FOR TWO WEEKS, SO MAKE THAT SALON APPOINTMENT!
Watkins

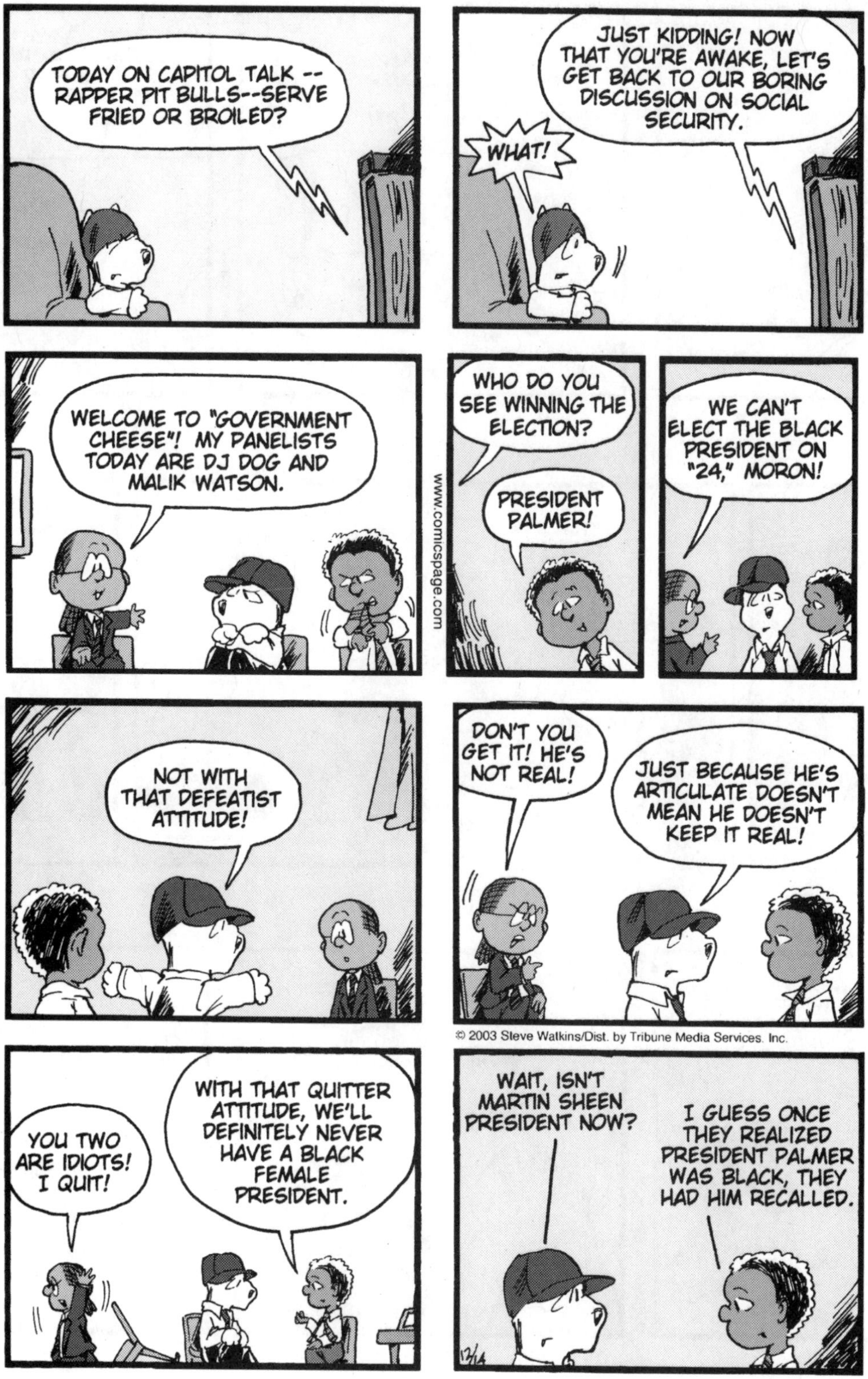
TODAY ON CAPITOL TALK -- RAPPER PIT BULLS--SERVE FRIED OR BROILED?
JUST KIDDING! NOW THAT YOU'RE AWAKE, LET'S GET BACK TO OUR BORING DISCUSSION ON SOCIAL SECURITY.
WHAT!
WELCOME TO "GOVERNMENT CHEESE"! MY PANELISTS TODAY ARE DJ DOG AND MALIK WATSON.
www.comicspage.com
WHO DO YOU SEE WINNING THE ELECTION?
PRESIDENT PALMER!
WE CAN'T ELECT THE BLACK PRESIDENT ON "24," MORON!
NOT WITH THAT DEFEATIST ATTITUDE!
DON'T YOU GET IT! HE'S NOT REAL!
JUST BECAUSE HE'S ARTICULATE DOESN'T MEAN HE DOESN'T KEEP IT REAL!
© 2003 Steve Watkins/Dist. by Tribune Media Services, Inc.
YOU TWO ARE IDIOTS! I QUIT!
WITH THAT QUITTER ATTITUDE, WE'LL DEFINITELY NEVER HAVE A BLACK FEMALE PRESIDENT.
WAIT, ISN'T MARTIN SHEEN PRESIDENT NOW?
I GUESS ONCE THEY REALIZED PRESIDENT PALMER WAS BLACK, THEY HAD HIM RECALLED.
12/14

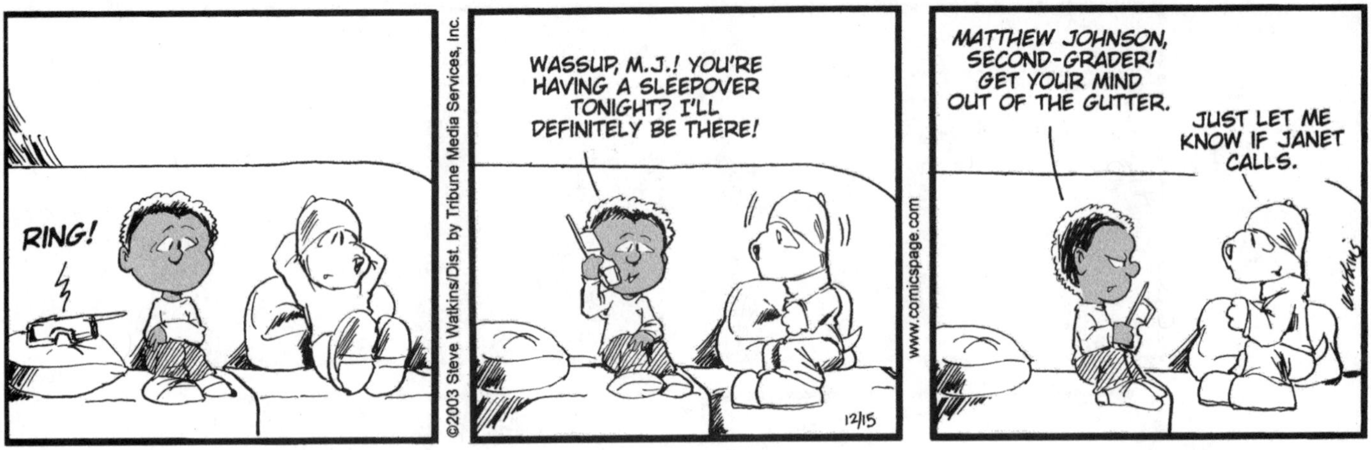
RING!
WASSUP, M.J.! YOU'RE HAVING A SLEEPOVER TONIGHT? I'LL DEFINITELY BE THERE!
MATTHEW JOHNSON, SECOND-GRADER! GET YOUR MIND OUT OF THE GUTTER.
JUST LET ME KNOW IF JANET CALLS.
12/15
Watkins

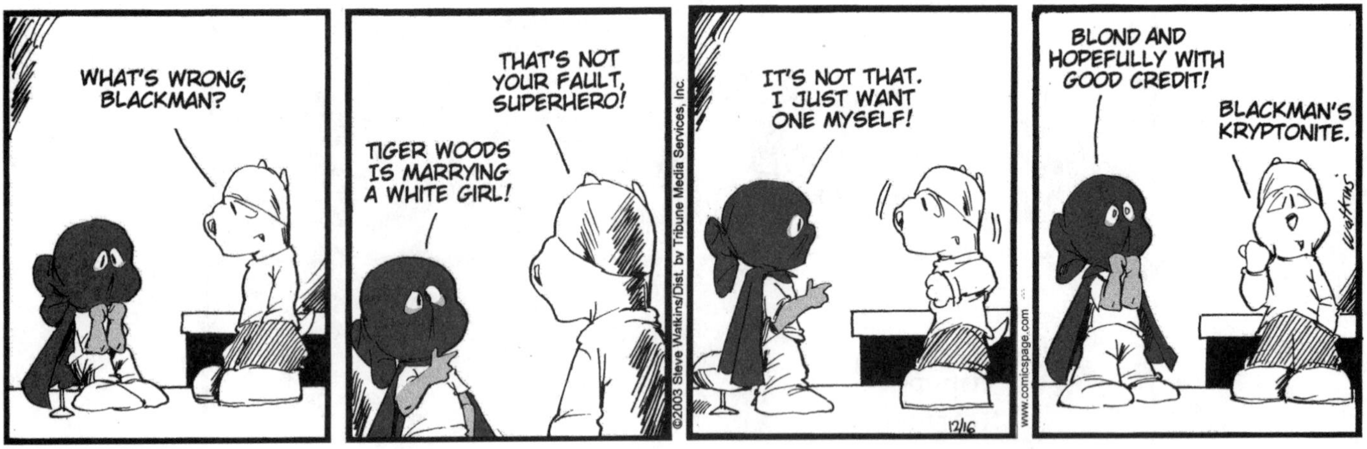
WHAT'S WRONG, BLACKMAN?
TIGER WOODS IS MARRYING A WHITE GIRL!
THAT'S NOT YOUR FAULT, SUPERHERO!
IT'S NOT THAT. I JUST WANT ONE MYSELF!
BLOND AND HOPEFULLY WITH GOOD CREDIT!
BLACKMAN'S KRYPTONITE.
12/16
Watkins

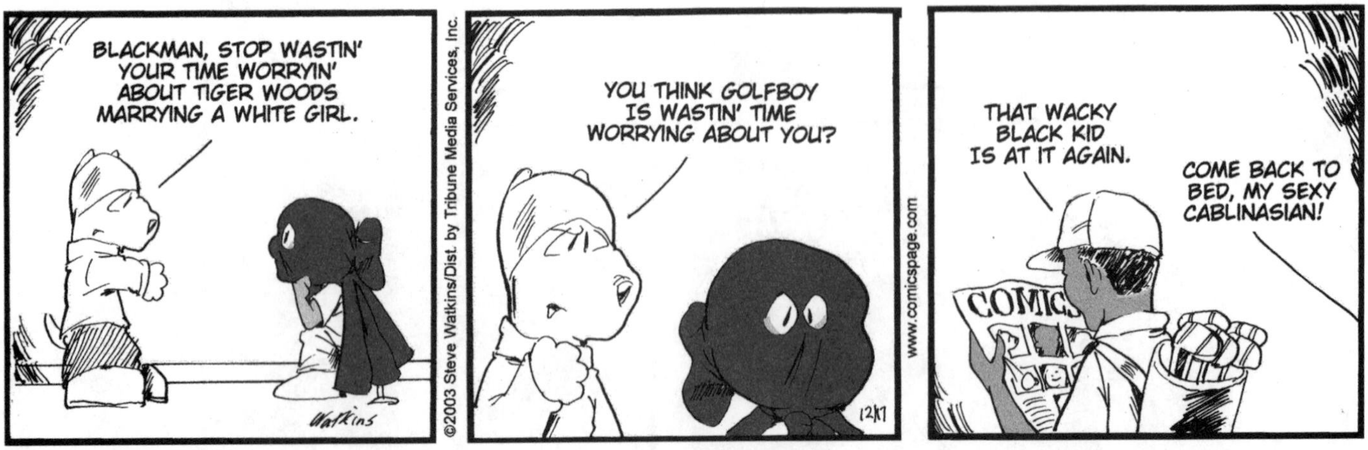
BLACKMAN, STOP WASTIN' YOUR TIME WORRYIN' ABOUT TIGER WOODS MARRYING A WHITE GIRL.
Watkins
YOU THINK GOLFBOY IS WASTIN' TIME WORRYING ABOUT YOU?
12/17
THAT WACKY BLACK KID IS AT IT AGAIN.
COMICS
COME BACK TO BED, MY SEXY CABLINASIAN!

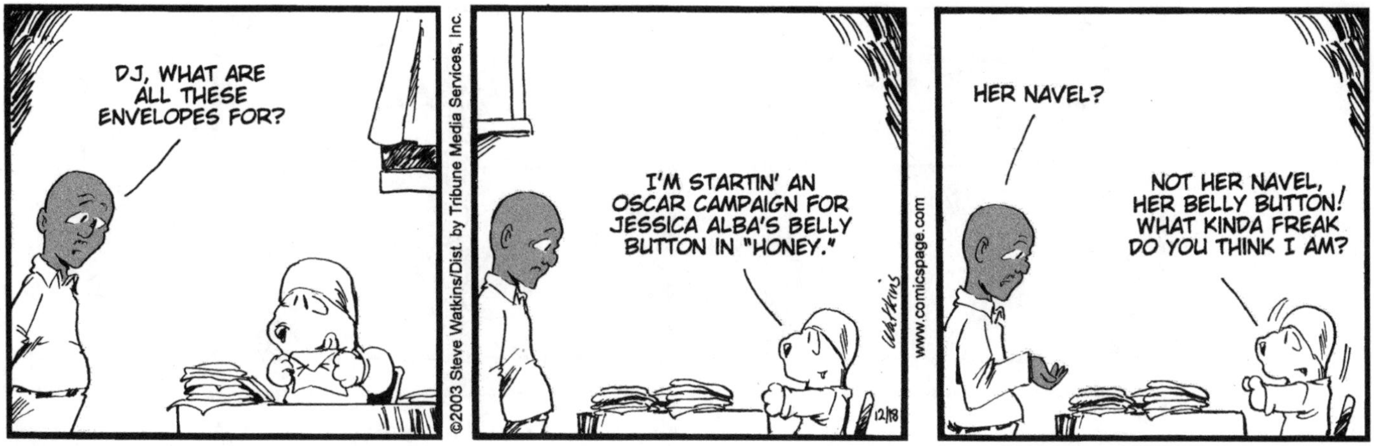
DJ, WHAT ARE ALL THESE ENVELOPES FOR?
©2003 Steve Watkins/Dist. by Tribune Media Services, Inc.
I'M STARTIN' AN OSCAR CAMPAIGN FOR JESSICA ALBA'S BELLY BUTTON IN "HONEY."
Watkins
12/18
www.comicspage.com
HER NAVEL?
NOT HER NAVEL, HER BELLY BUTTON! WHAT KINDA FREAK DO YOU THINK I AM?

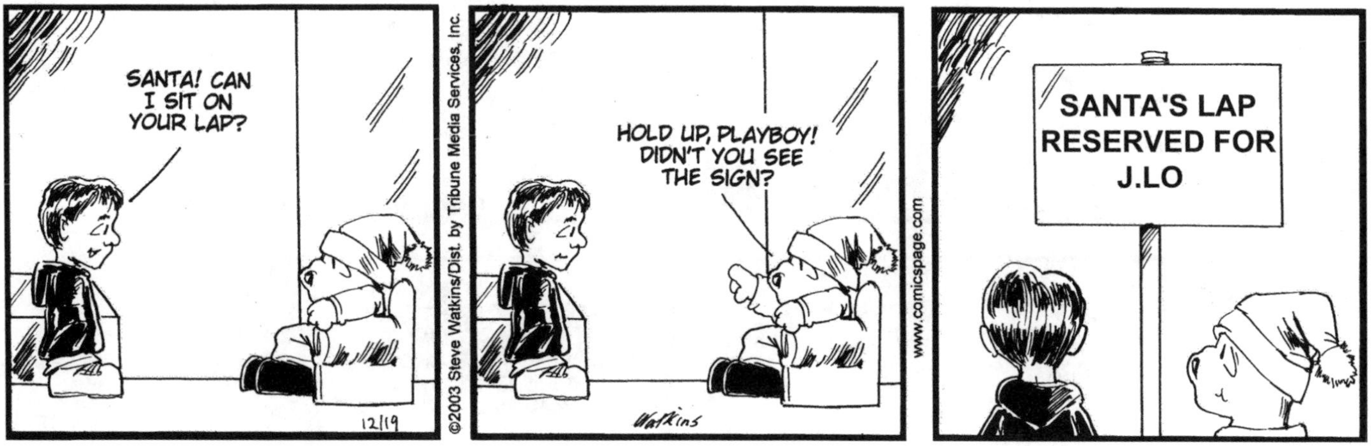
SANTA! CAN I SIT ON YOUR LAP?
12/19
©2003 Steve Watkins/Dist. by Tribune Media Services, Inc.
HOLD UP, PLAYBOY! DIDN'T YOU SEE THE SIGN?
Watkins
www.comicspage.com
SANTA'S LAP RESERVED FOR J.LO

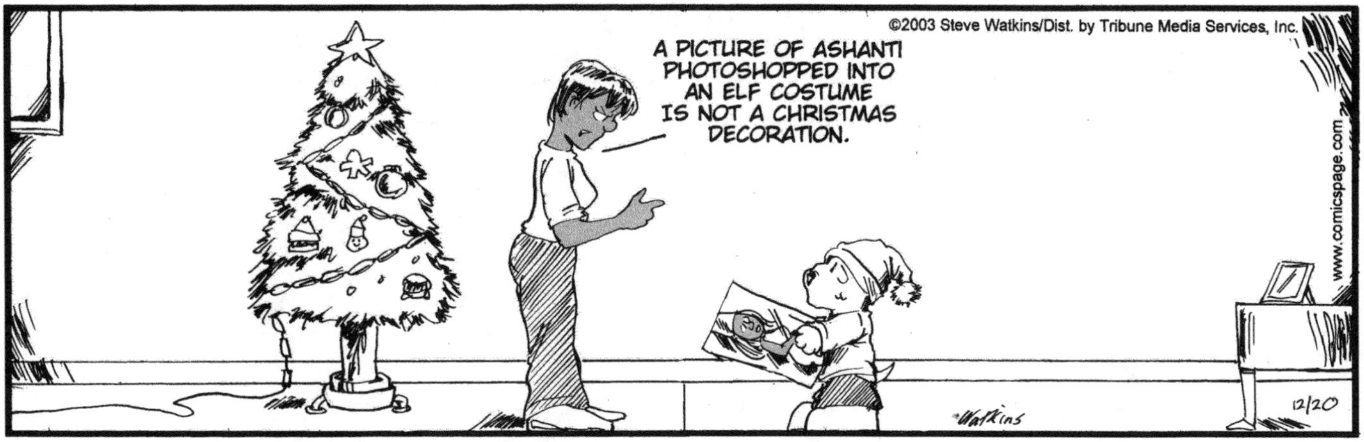
©2003 Steve Watkins/Dist. by Tribune Media Services, Inc.
A PICTURE OF ASHANTI PHOTOSHOPPED INTO AN ELF COSTUME IS NOT A CHRISTMAS DECORATION.
www.comicspage.com
Watkins
12/20

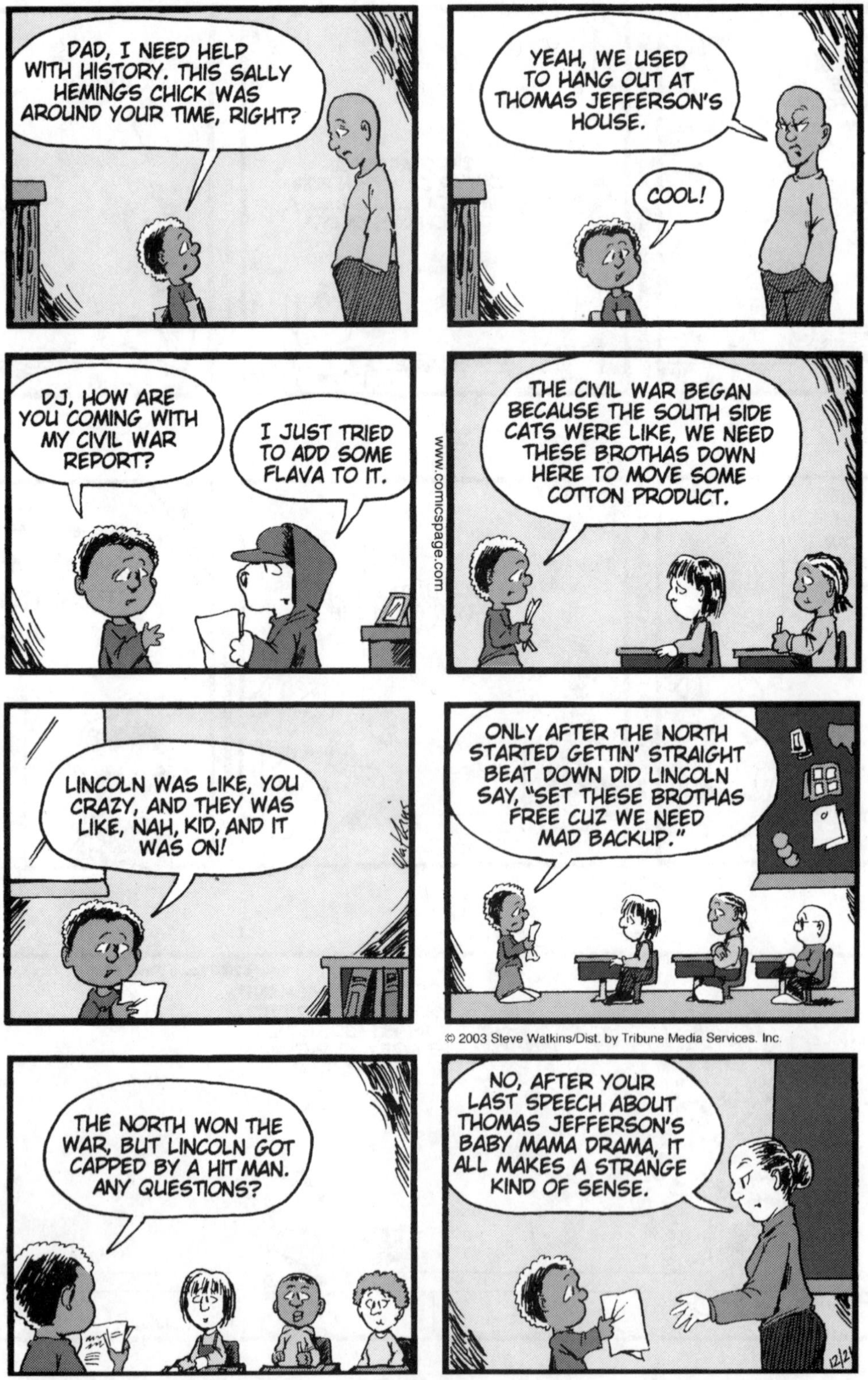

DAD, I NEED HELP WITH HISTORY. THIS SALLY HEMINGS CHICK WAS AROUND YOUR TIME, RIGHT?
YEAH, WE USED TO HANG OUT AT THOMAS JEFFERSON'S HOUSE.
COOL!
DJ, HOW ARE YOU COMING WITH MY CIVIL WAR REPORT?
I JUST TRIED TO ADD SOME FLAVA TO IT.
www.comicspage.com
THE CIVIL WAR BEGAN BECAUSE THE SOUTH SIDE CATS WERE LIKE, WE NEED THESE BROTHAS DOWN HERE TO MOVE SOME COTTON PRODUCT.
LINCOLN WAS LIKE, YOU CRAZY, AND THEY WAS LIKE, NAH, KID, AND IT WAS ON!
ONLY AFTER THE NORTH STARTED GETTIN' STRAIGHT BEAT DOWN DID LINCOLN SAY, "SET THESE BROTHAS FREE CUZ WE NEED MAD BACKUP."
THE NORTH WON THE WAR, BUT LINCOLN GOT CAPPED BY A HIT MAN. ANY QUESTIONS?
NO, AFTER YOUR LAST SPEECH ABOUT THOMAS JEFFERSON'S BABY MAMA DRAMA, IT ALL MAKES A STRANGE KIND OF SENSE.

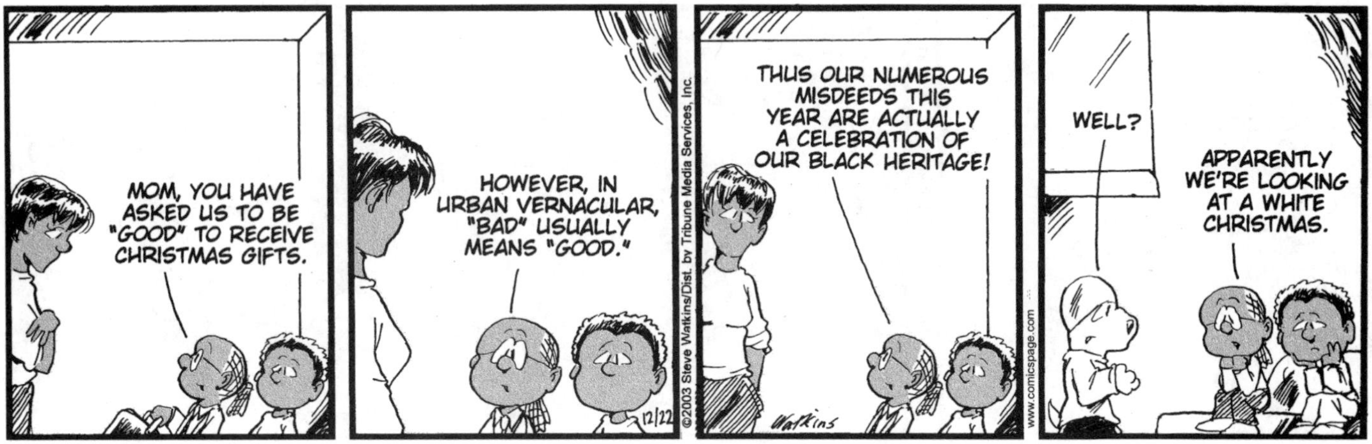
MOM, YOU HAVE ASKED US TO BE "GOOD" TO RECEIVE CHRISTMAS GIFTS.
HOWEVER, IN URBAN VERNACULAR, "BAD" USUALLY MEANS "GOOD."
12/22
©2003 Steve Watkins/Dist. by Tribune Media Services, Inc.
THUS OUR NUMEROUS MISDEEDS THIS YEAR ARE ACTUALLY A CELEBRATION OF OUR BLACK HERITAGE!
Watkins
www.comicspage.com
WELL?
APPARENTLY WE'RE LOOKING AT A WHITE CHRISTMAS.

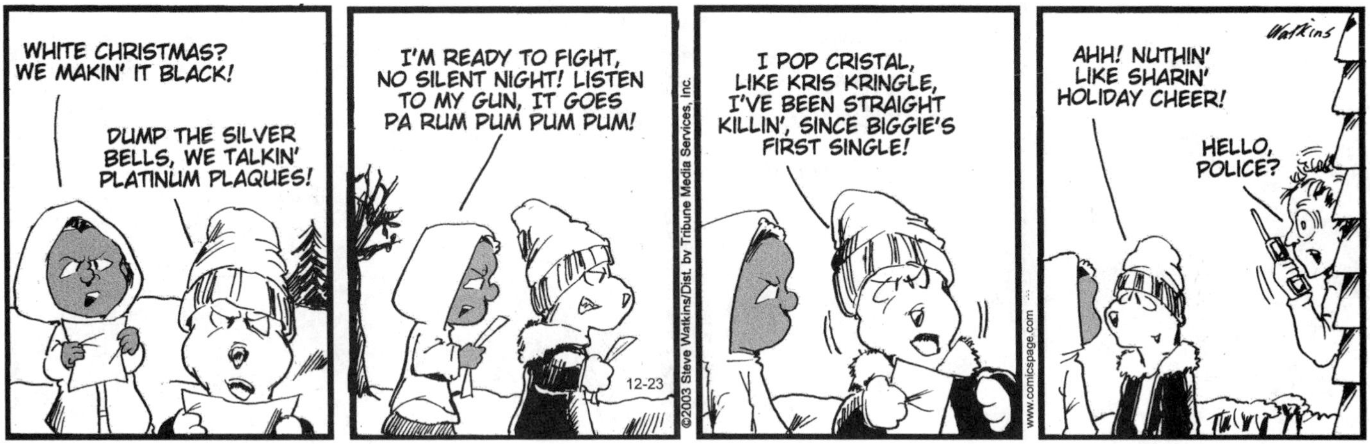
WHITE CHRISTMAS? WE MAKIN' IT BLACK!
DUMP THE SILVER BELLS, WE TALKIN' PLATINUM PLAQUES!
I'M READY TO FIGHT, NO SILENT NIGHT! LISTEN TO MY GUN, IT GOES PA RUM PUM PUM PUM!
12-23
©2003 Steve Watkins/Dist. by Tribune Media Services, Inc.
I POP CRISTAL, LIKE KRIS KRINGLE, I'VE BEEN STRAIGHT KILLIN', SINCE BIGGIE'S FIRST SINGLE!
www.comicspage.com
Watkins
AHH! NUTHIN' LIKE SHARIN' HOLIDAY CHEER!
HELLO, POLICE?

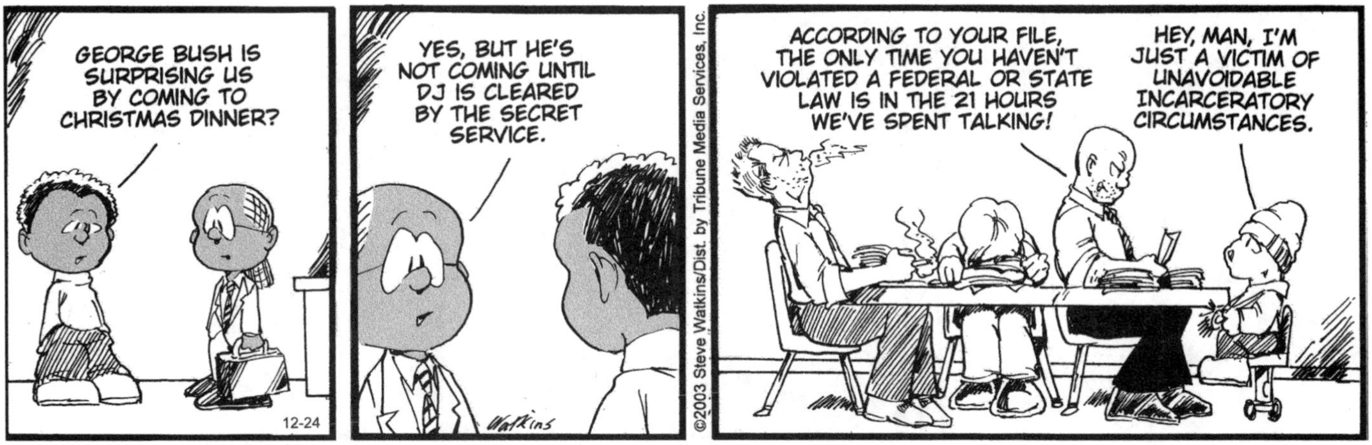
GEORGE BUSH IS SURPRISING US BY COMING TO CHRISTMAS DINNER?
12-24
YES, BUT HE'S NOT COMING UNTIL DJ IS CLEARED BY THE SECRET SERVICE.
Watkins
©2003 Steve Watkins/Dist. by Tribune Media Services, Inc.
ACCORDING TO YOUR FILE, THE ONLY TIME YOU HAVEN'T VIOLATED A FEDERAL OR STATE LAW IS IN THE 21 HOURS WE'VE SPENT TALKING!
HEY, MAN, I'M JUST A VICTIM OF UNAVOIDABLE INCARCERATORY CIRCUMSTANCES.

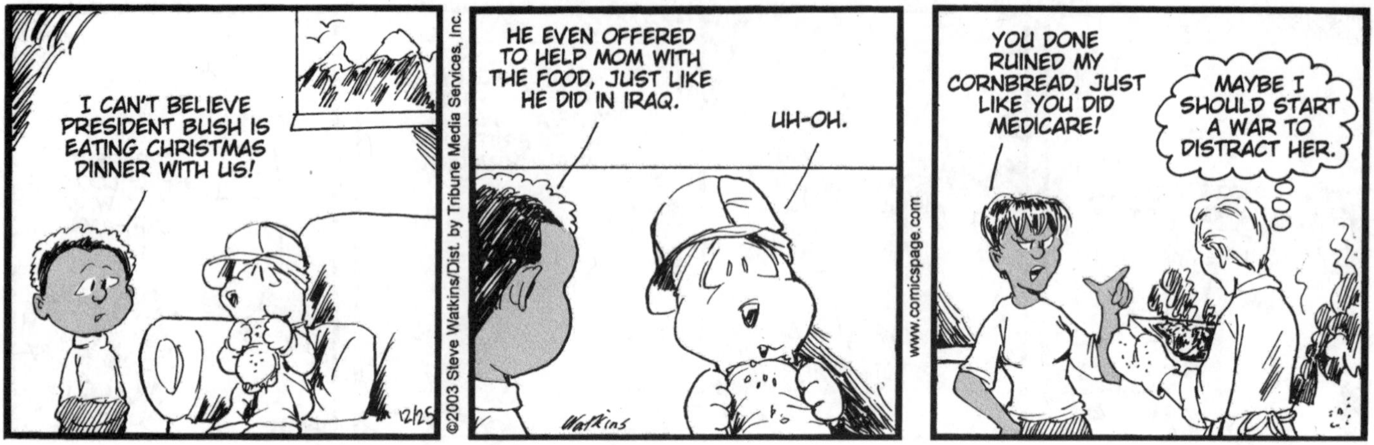
I CAN'T BELIEVE PRESIDENT BUSH IS EATING CHRISTMAS DINNER WITH US!
12/25
©2003 Steve Watkins/Dist. by Tribune Media Services, Inc.
HE EVEN OFFERED TO HELP MOM WITH THE FOOD, JUST LIKE HE DID IN IRAQ.
UH-OH.
Watkins
www.comicspage.com
YOU DONE RUINED MY CORNBREAD, JUST LIKE YOU DID MEDICARE!
MAYBE I SHOULD START A WAR TO DISTRACT HER.

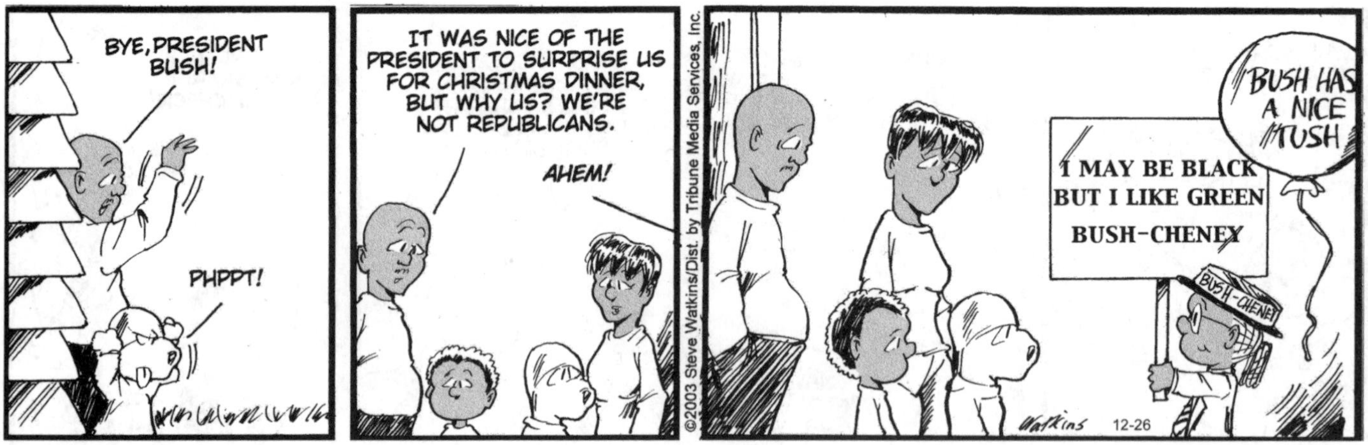
BYE, PRESIDENT BUSH!
PHPPT!
IT WAS NICE OF THE PRESIDENT TO SURPRISE US FOR CHRISTMAS DINNER, BUT WHY US? WE'RE NOT REPUBLICANS.
AHEM!
©2003 Steve Watkins/Dist. by Tribune Media Services, Inc.
BUSH HAS A NICE TUSH
I MAY BE BLACK BUT I LIKE GREEN
BUSH-CHENEY
BUSH-CHENEY
Watkins
12-26

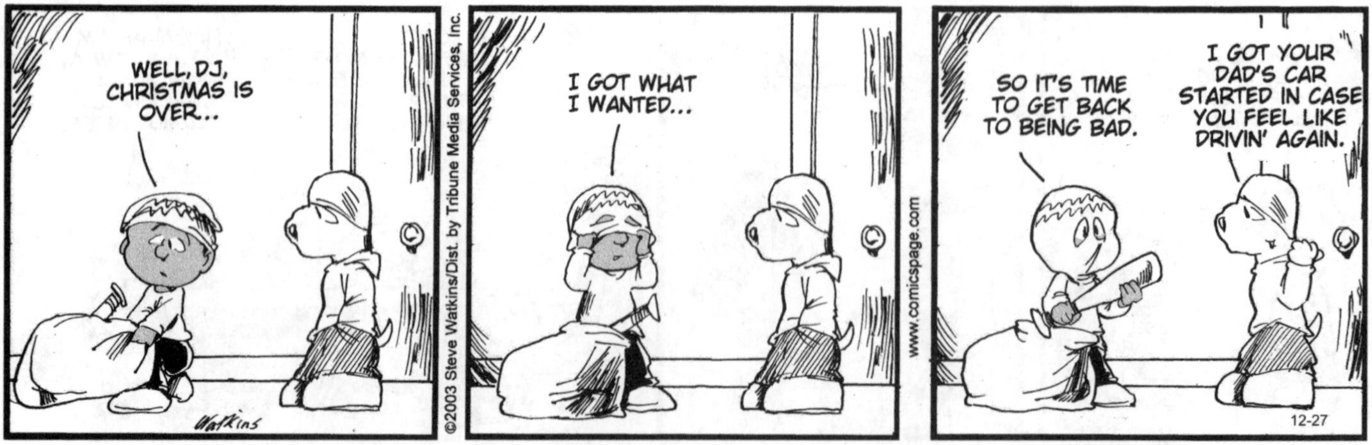
WELL, DJ, CHRISTMAS IS OVER...
Watkins
©2003 Steve Watkins/Dist. by Tribune Media Services, Inc.
I GOT WHAT I WANTED...
www.comicspage.com
SO IT'S TIME TO GET BACK TO BEING BAD.
I GOT YOUR DAD'S CAR STARTED IN CASE YOU FEEL LIKE DRIVIN' AGAIN.
12-27

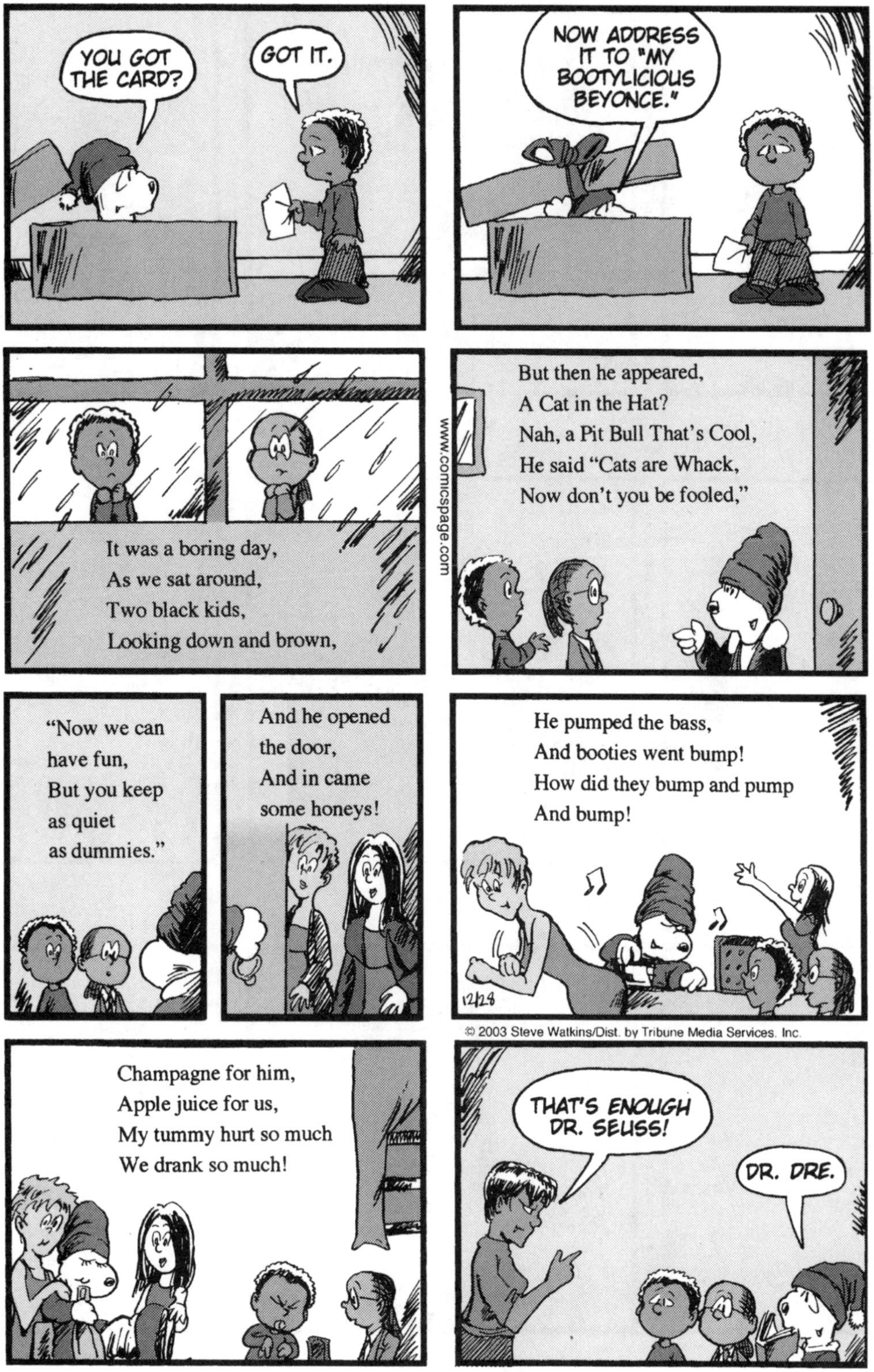

YOU GOT THE CARD?
GOT IT.
NOW ADDRESS IT TO "MY BOOTYLICIOUS BEYONCE."
It was a boring day,
As we sat around,
Two black kids,
Looking down and brown,
www.comicspage.com
But then he appeared,
A Cat in the Hat?
Nah, a Pit Bull That's Cool,
He said "Cats are Whack,
Now don't you be fooled,"
"Now we can have fun,
But you keep as quiet as dummies."
And he opened the door,
And in came some honeys!
He pumped the bass,
And booties went bump!
How did they bump and pump
And bump!
12/28
© 2003 Steve Watkins/Dist. by Tribune Media Services, Inc.
Champagne for him,
Apple juice for us,
My tummy hurt so much
We drank so much!
THAT'S ENOUGH DR. SEUSS!
DR. DRE.

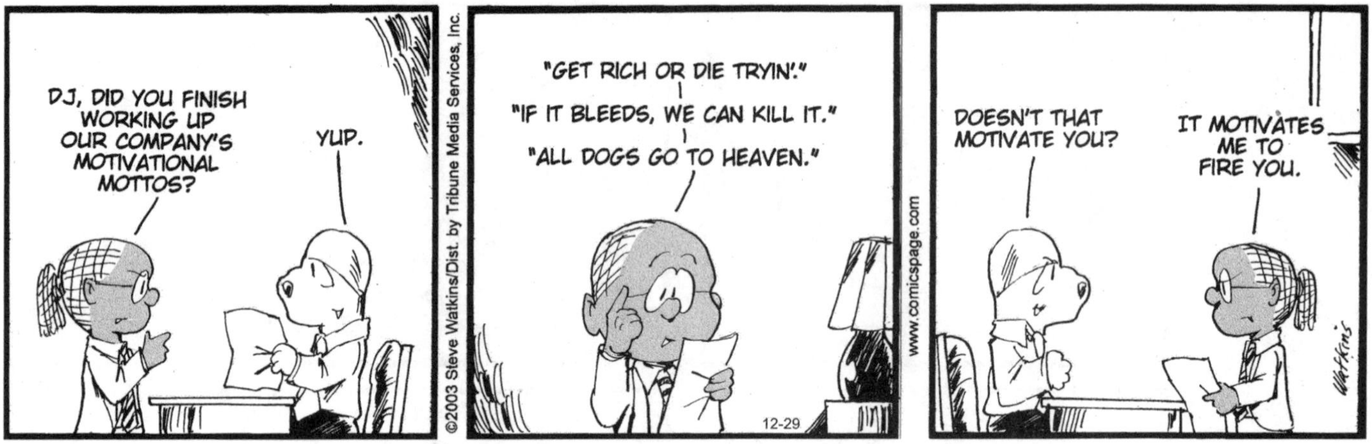
DJ, DID YOU FINISH WORKING UP OUR COMPANY'S MOTIVATIONAL MOTTOS?
YUP.
©2003 Steve Watkins/Dist. by Tribune Media Services, Inc.
"GET RICH OR DIE TRYIN'."
"IF IT BLEEDS, WE CAN KILL IT."
"ALL DOGS GO TO HEAVEN."
12-29
www.comicspage.com
DOESN'T THAT MOTIVATE YOU?
IT MOTIVATES ME TO FIRE YOU.
Watkins

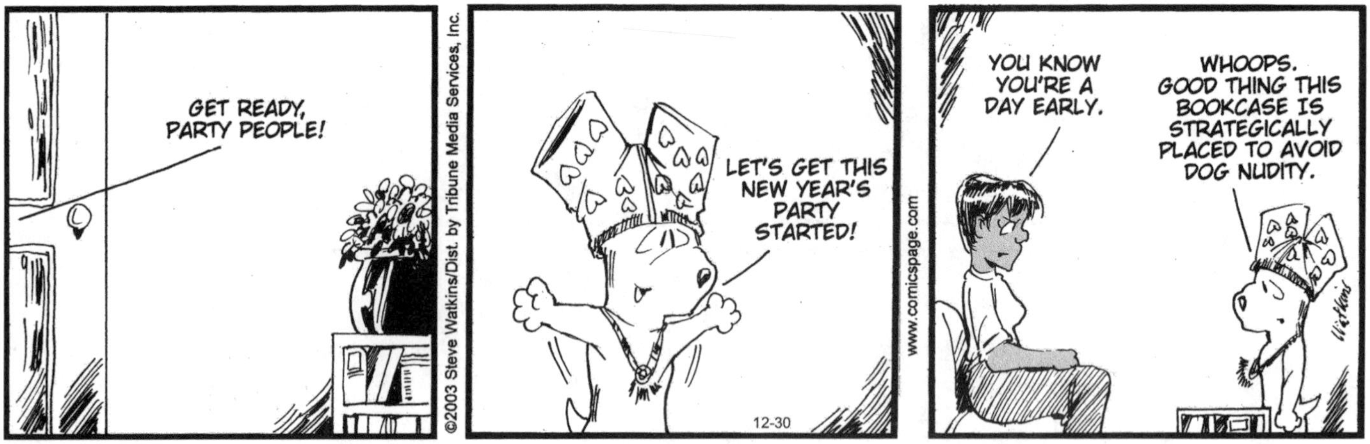
GET READY, PARTY PEOPLE!
©2003 Steve Watkins/Dist. by Tribune Media Services, Inc.
LET'S GET THIS NEW YEAR'S PARTY STARTED!
12-30
www.comicspage.com
YOU KNOW YOU'RE A DAY EARLY.
WHOOPS. GOOD THING THIS BOOKCASE IS STRATEGICALLY PLACED TO AVOID DOG NUDITY.
Watkins

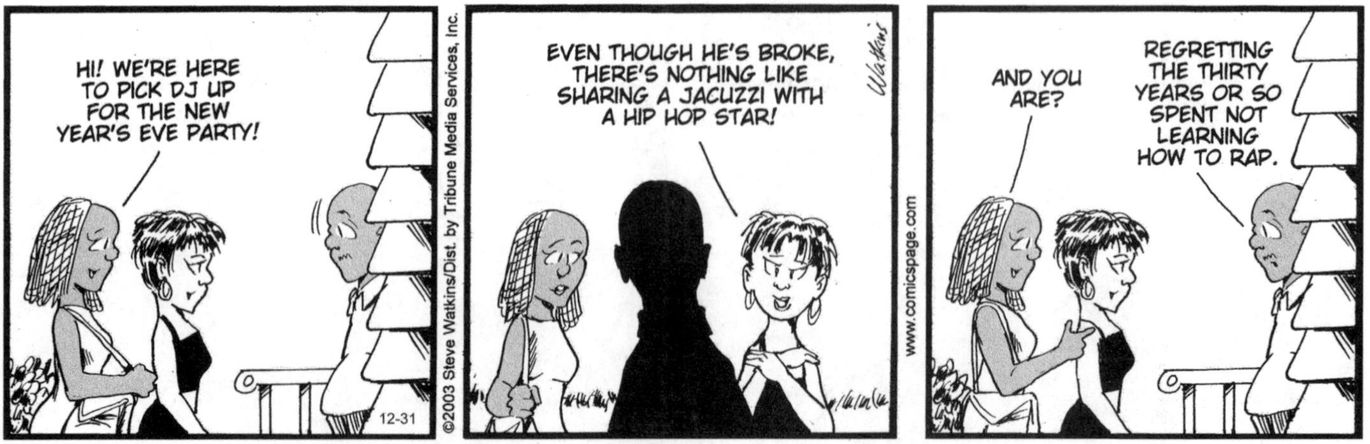
HI! WE'RE HERE TO PICK DJ UP FOR THE NEW YEAR'S EVE PARTY!
12-31
©2003 Steve Watkins/Dist. by Tribune Media Services, Inc.
EVEN THOUGH HE'S BROKE, THERE'S NOTHING LIKE SHARING A JACUZZI WITH A HIP HOP STAR!
Watkins
www.comicspage.com
AND YOU ARE?
REGRETTING THE THIRTY YEARS OR SO SPENT NOT LEARNING HOW TO RAP.

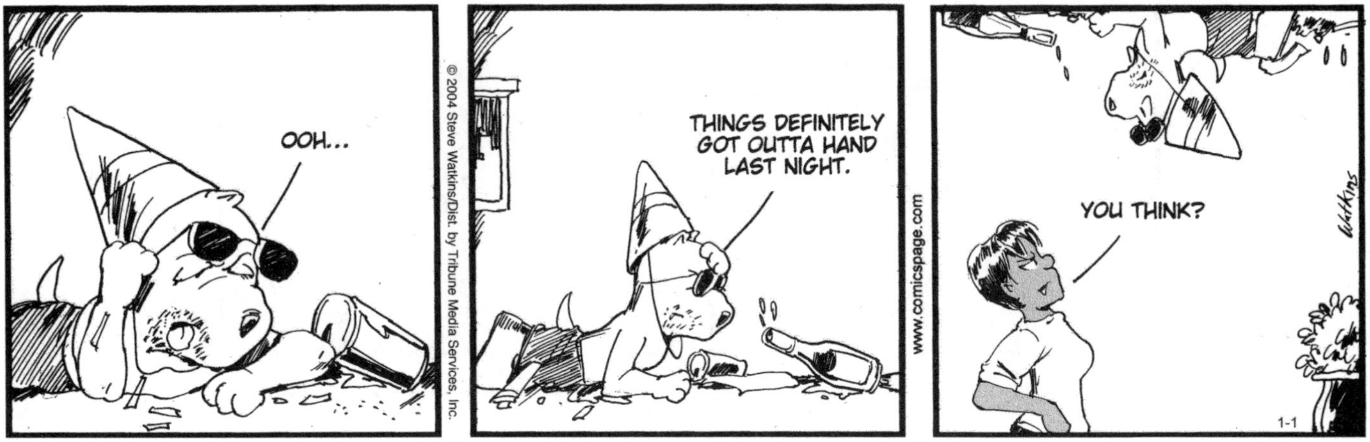
OOH...
© 2004 Steve Watkins/Dist. by Tribune Media Services, Inc.
THINGS DEFINITELY GOT OUTTA HAND LAST NIGHT.
www.comicspage.com
YOU THINK?
Watkins
1-1

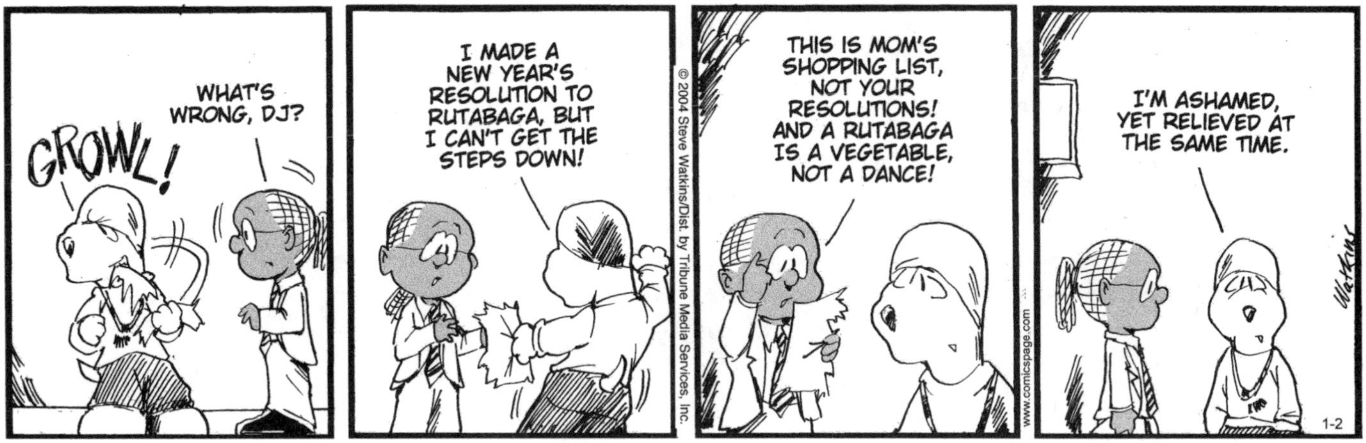
GROWL!
WHAT'S WRONG, DJ?
I MADE A NEW YEAR'S RESOLUTION TO RUTABAGA, BUT I CAN'T GET THE STEPS DOWN!
© 2004 Steve Watkins/Dist. by Tribune Media Services, Inc.
THIS IS MOM'S SHOPPING LIST, NOT YOUR RESOLUTIONS! AND A RUTABAGA IS A VEGETABLE, NOT A DANCE!
www.comicspage.com
I'M ASHAMED, YET RELIEVED AT THE SAME TIME.
Watkins
1-2

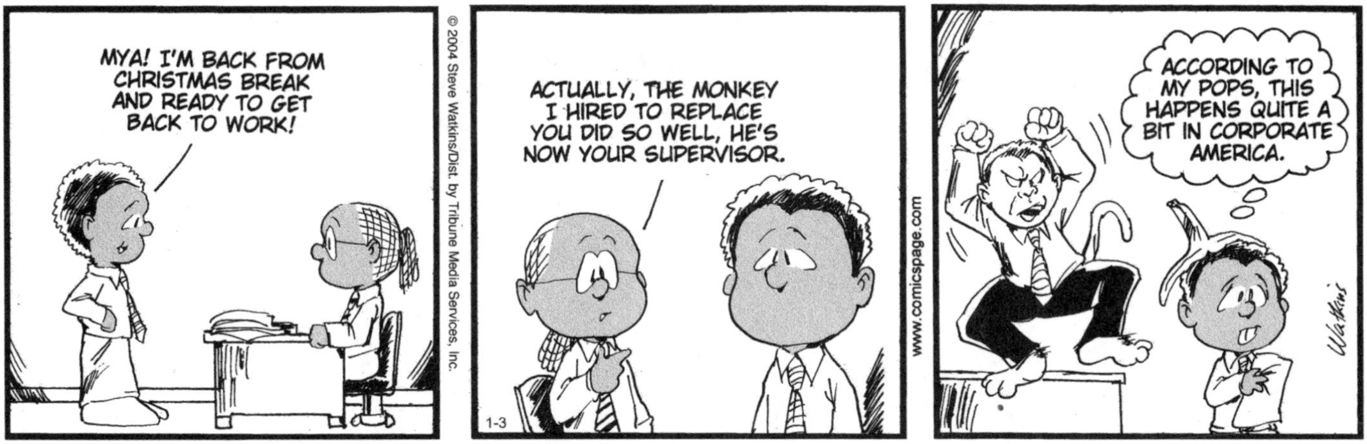
MYA! I'M BACK FROM CHRISTMAS BREAK AND READY TO GET BACK TO WORK!
© 2004 Steve Watkins/Dist. by Tribune Media Services, Inc.
ACTUALLY, THE MONKEY I HIRED TO REPLACE YOU DID SO WELL, HE'S NOW YOUR SUPERVISOR.
1-3
www.comicspage.com
ACCORDING TO MY POPS, THIS HAPPENS QUITE A BIT IN CORPORATE AMERICA.
Watkins

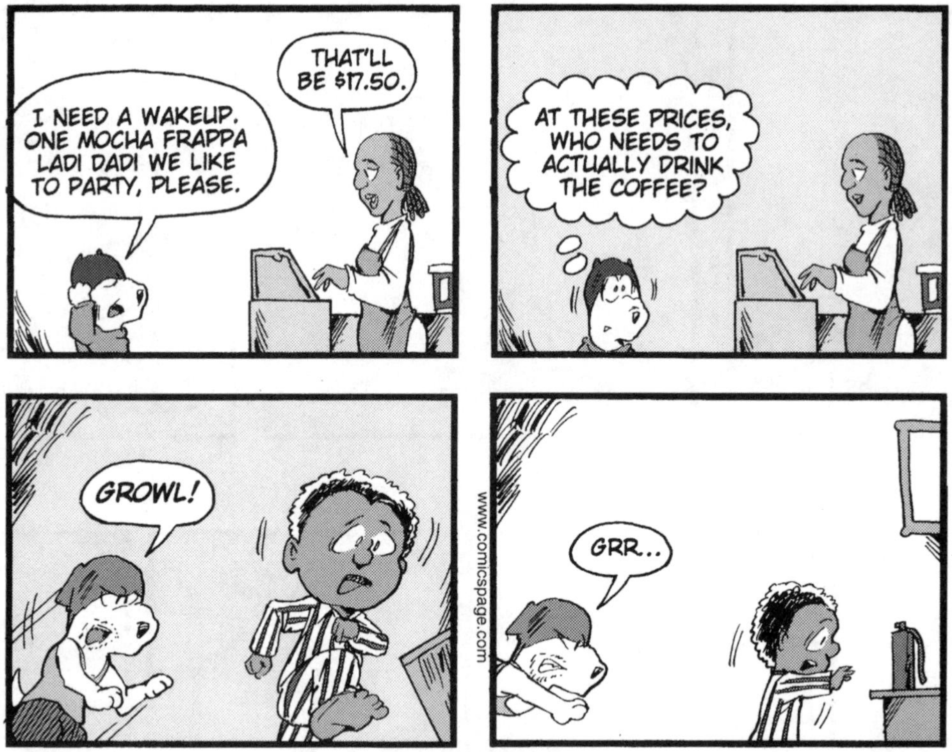
I NEED A WAKEUP. ONE MOCHA FRAPPA LADI DADI WE LIKE TO PARTY, PLEASE.
THAT'LL BE $17.50.
AT THESE PRICES, WHO NEEDS TO ACTUALLY DRINK THE COFFEE?
GROWL!
GRR...
www.comicspage.com

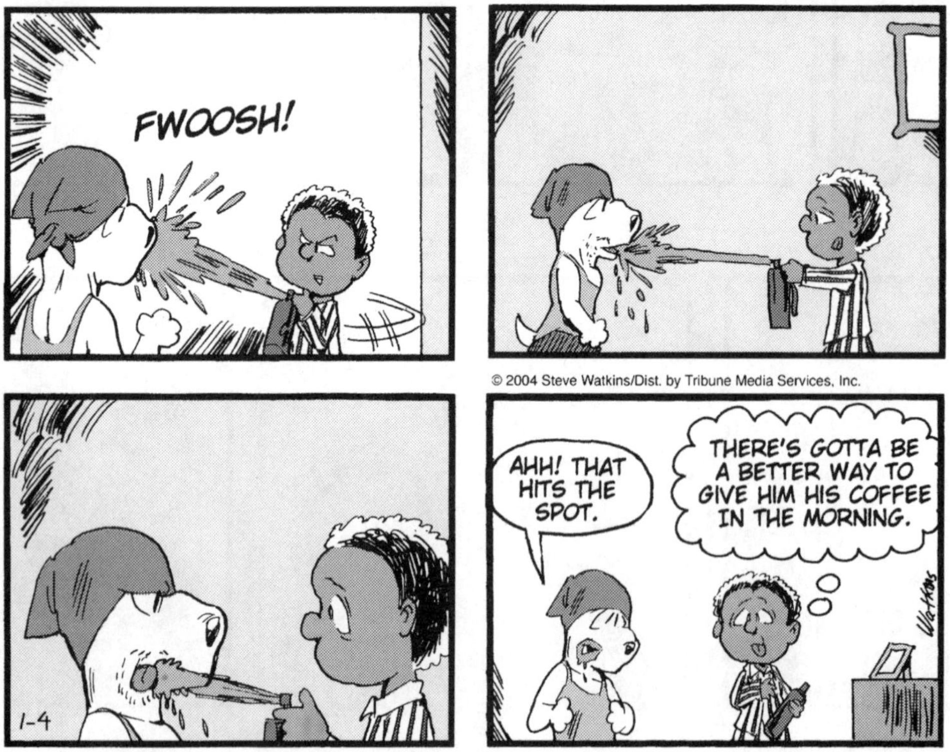
FWOOSH!
1-4
AHH! THAT HITS THE SPOT.
THERE'S GOTTA BE A BETTER WAY TO GIVE HIM HIS COFFEE IN THE MORNING.

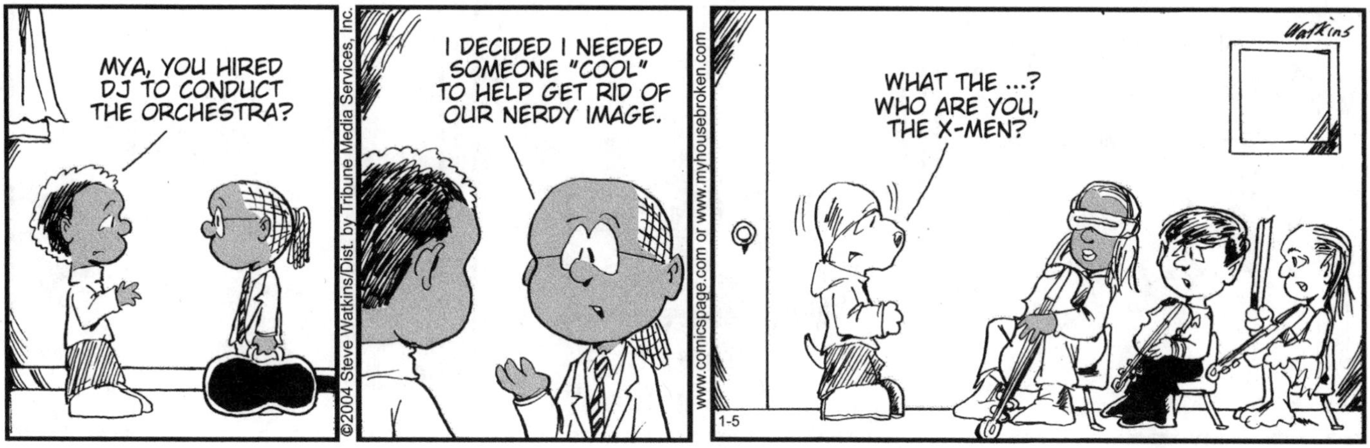
MYA, YOU HIRED DJ TO CONDUCT THE ORCHESTRA?
©2004 Steve Watkins/Dist. by Tribune Media Services, Inc.
I DECIDED I NEEDED SOMEONE "COOL" TO HELP GET RID OF OUR NERDY IMAGE.
www.comicspage.com or www.myhousebroken.com
1-5
Watkins
WHAT THE ...? WHO ARE YOU, THE X-MEN?

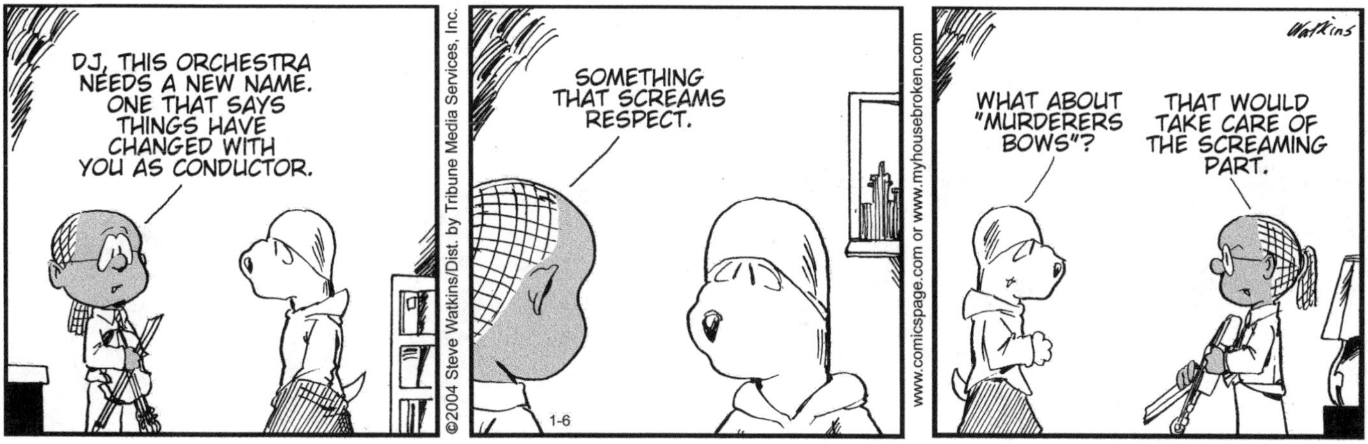
DJ, THIS ORCHESTRA NEEDS A NEW NAME. ONE THAT SAYS THINGS HAVE CHANGED WITH YOU AS CONDUCTOR.
©2004 Steve Watkins/Dist. by Tribune Media Services, Inc.
SOMETHING THAT SCREAMS RESPECT.
1-6
www.comicspage.com or www.myhousebroken.com
Watkins
WHAT ABOUT "MURDERERS BOWS"?
THAT WOULD TAKE CARE OF THE SCREAMING PART.

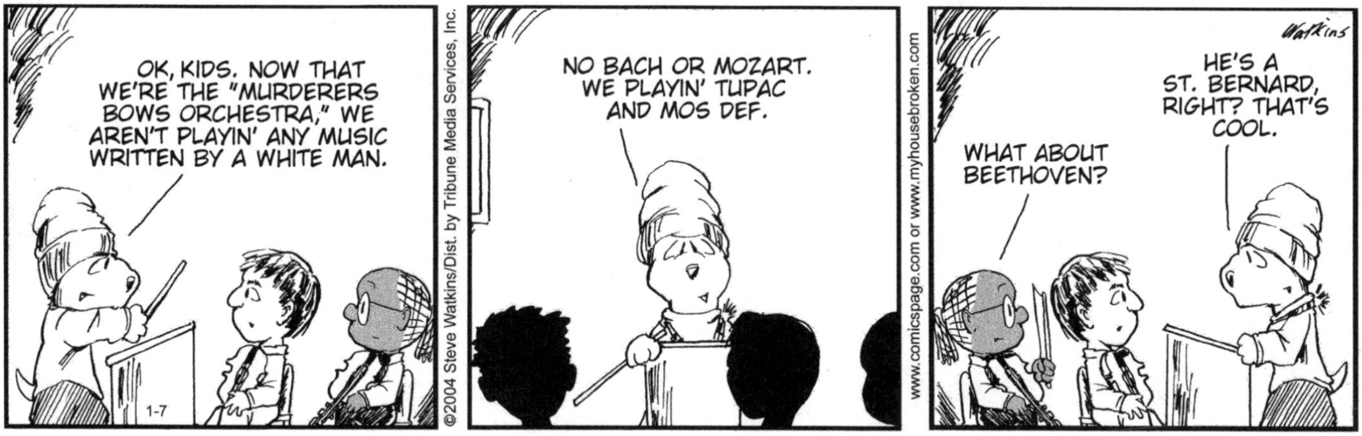
OK, KIDS. NOW THAT WE'RE THE "MURDERERS BOWS ORCHESTRA," WE AREN'T PLAYIN' ANY MUSIC WRITTEN BY A WHITE MAN.
1-7
©2004 Steve Watkins/Dist. by Tribune Media Services, Inc.
NO BACH OR MOZART. WE PLAYIN' TUPAC AND MOS DEF.
www.comicspage.com or www.myhousebroken.com
Watkins
WHAT ABOUT BEETHOVEN?
HE'S A ST. BERNARD, RIGHT? THAT'S COOL.

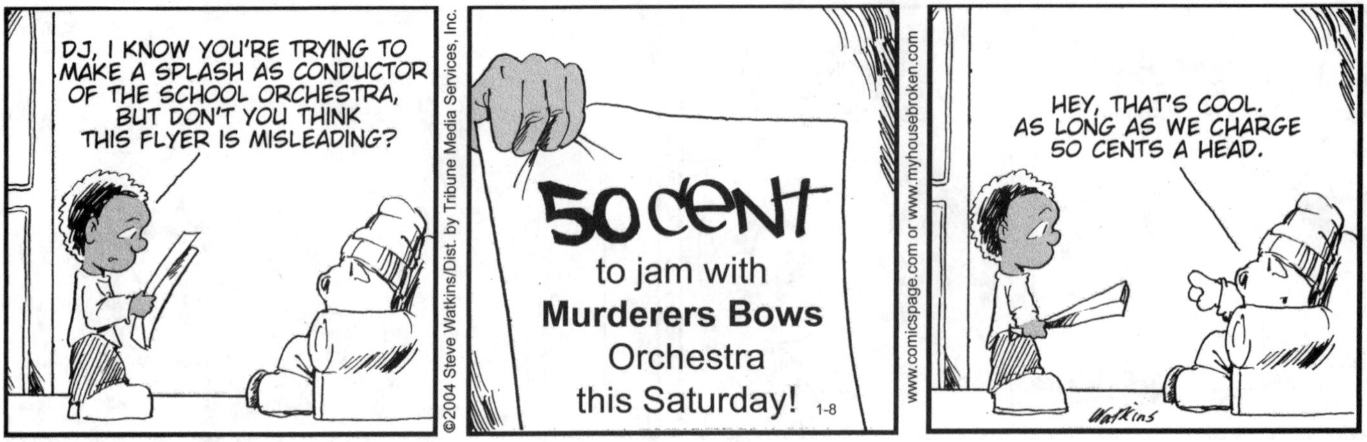
DJ, I KNOW YOU'RE TRYING TO MAKE A SPLASH AS CONDUCTOR OF THE SCHOOL ORCHESTRA, BUT DON'T YOU THINK THIS FLYER IS MISLEADING?
50 cent
to jam with
Murderers Bows
Orchestra
this Saturday!
1-8
©2004 Steve Watkins/Dist. by Tribune Media Services, Inc.
www.comicspage.com or www.myhousebroken.com
HEY, THAT'S COOL. AS LONG AS WE CHARGE 50 CENTS A HEAD.
Watkins

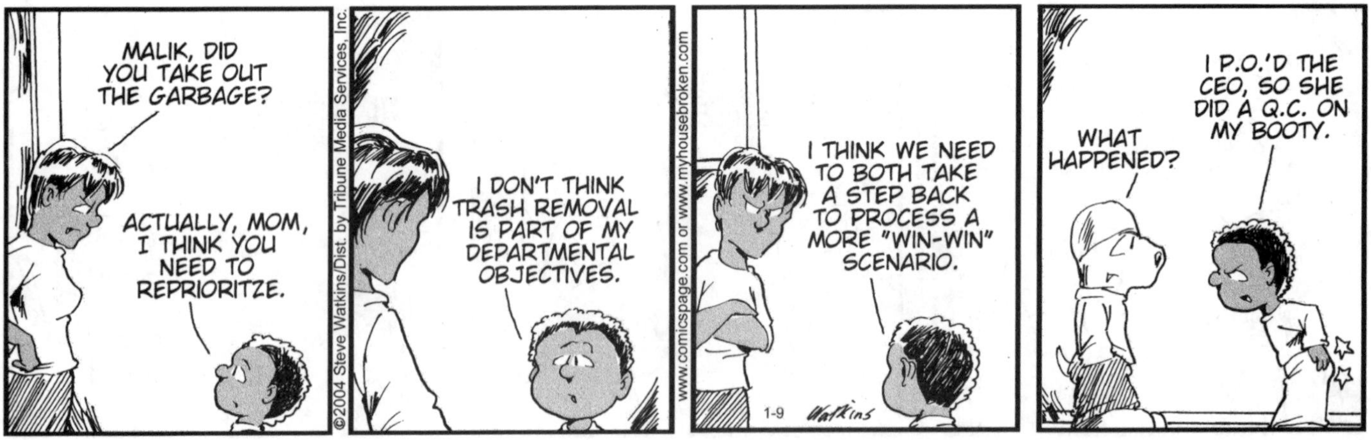
MALIK, DID YOU TAKE OUT THE GARBAGE?
ACTUALLY, MOM, I THINK YOU NEED TO REPRIORITZE.
©2004 Steve Watkins/Dist. by Tribune Media Services, Inc.
I DON'T THINK TRASH REMOVAL IS PART OF MY DEPARTMENTAL OBJECTIVES.
www.comicspage.com or www.myhousebroken.com
I THINK WE NEED TO BOTH TAKE A STEP BACK TO PROCESS A MORE "WIN-WIN" SCENARIO.
1-9
Watkins
WHAT HAPPENED?
I P.O.'D THE CEO, SO SHE DID A Q.C. ON MY BOOTY.

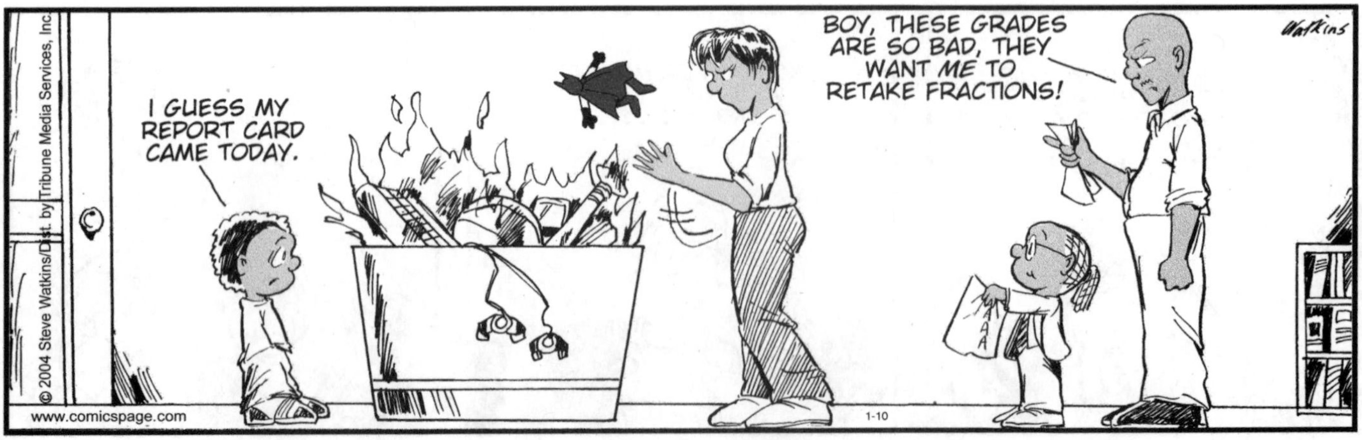
© 2004 Steve Watkins/Dist. by Tribune Media Services, Inc.
I GUESS MY REPORT CARD CAME TODAY.
BOY, THESE GRADES ARE SO BAD, THEY WANT *ME* TO RETAKE FRACTIONS!
Watkins
www.comicspage.com
1-10

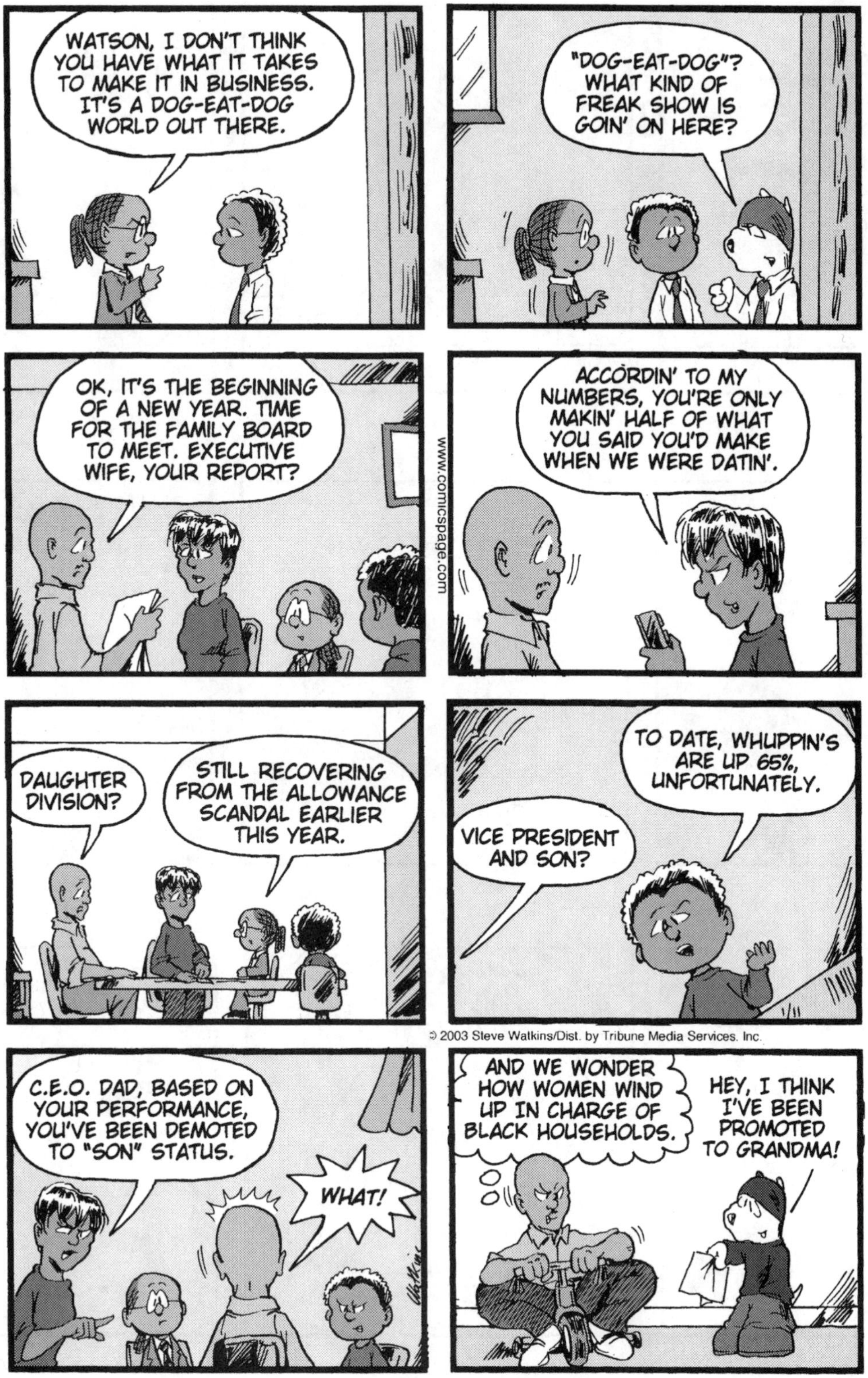

WATSON, I DON'T THINK YOU HAVE WHAT IT TAKES TO MAKE IT IN BUSINESS. IT'S A DOG-EAT-DOG WORLD OUT THERE.
"DOG-EAT-DOG"? WHAT KIND OF FREAK SHOW IS GOIN' ON HERE?
OK, IT'S THE BEGINNING OF A NEW YEAR. TIME FOR THE FAMILY BOARD TO MEET. EXECUTIVE WIFE, YOUR REPORT?
ACCORDIN' TO MY NUMBERS, YOU'RE ONLY MAKIN' HALF OF WHAT YOU SAID YOU'D MAKE WHEN WE WERE DATIN'.
www.comicspage.com
DAUGHTER DIVISION?
STILL RECOVERING FROM THE ALLOWANCE SCANDAL EARLIER THIS YEAR.
VICE PRESIDENT AND SON?
TO DATE, WHUPPIN'S ARE UP 65%, UNFORTUNATELY.
© 2003 Steve Watkins/Dist. by Tribune Media Services, Inc.
C.E.O. DAD, BASED ON YOUR PERFORMANCE, YOU'VE BEEN DEMOTED TO "SON" STATUS.
WHAT!
AND WE WONDER HOW WOMEN WIND UP IN CHARGE OF BLACK HOUSEHOLDS.
HEY, I THINK I'VE BEEN PROMOTED TO GRANDMA!

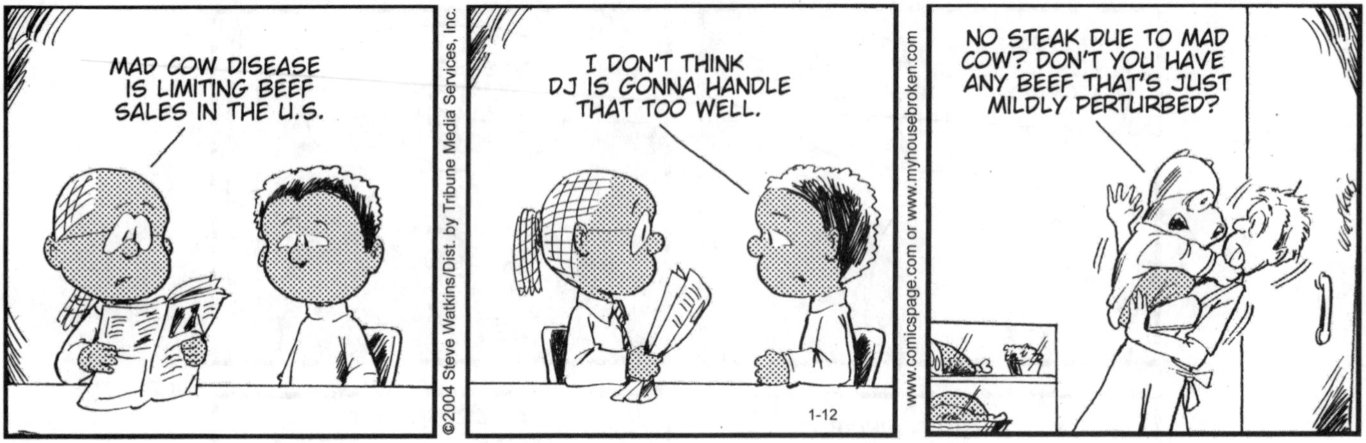
MAD COW DISEASE IS LIMITING BEEF SALES IN THE U.S.
©2004 Steve Watkins/Dist. by Tribune Media Services, Inc.
I DON'T THINK DJ IS GONNA HANDLE THAT TOO WELL.
1-12
www.comicspage.com or www.myhousebroken.com
NO STEAK DUE TO MAD COW? DON'T YOU HAVE ANY BEEF THAT'S JUST MILDLY PERTURBED?

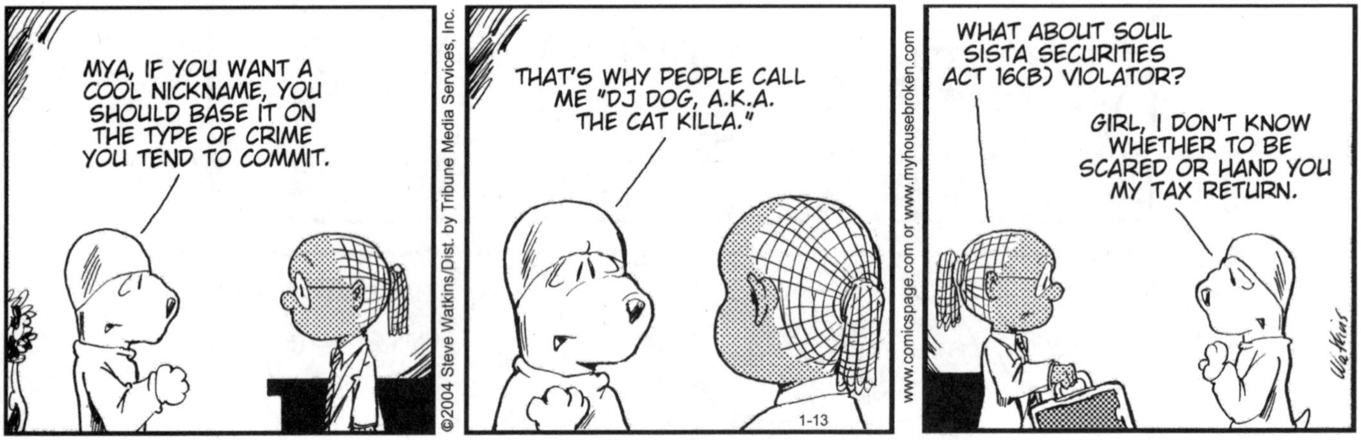
MYA, IF YOU WANT A COOL NICKNAME, YOU SHOULD BASE IT ON THE TYPE OF CRIME YOU TEND TO COMMIT.
©2004 Steve Watkins/Dist. by Tribune Media Services, Inc.
THAT'S WHY PEOPLE CALL ME "DJ DOG, A.K.A. THE CAT KILLA."
1-13
www.comicspage.com or www.myhousebroken.com
WHAT ABOUT SOUL SISTA SECURITIES ACT 16(B) VIOLATOR?
GIRL, I DON'T KNOW WHETHER TO BE SCARED OR HAND YOU MY TAX RETURN.

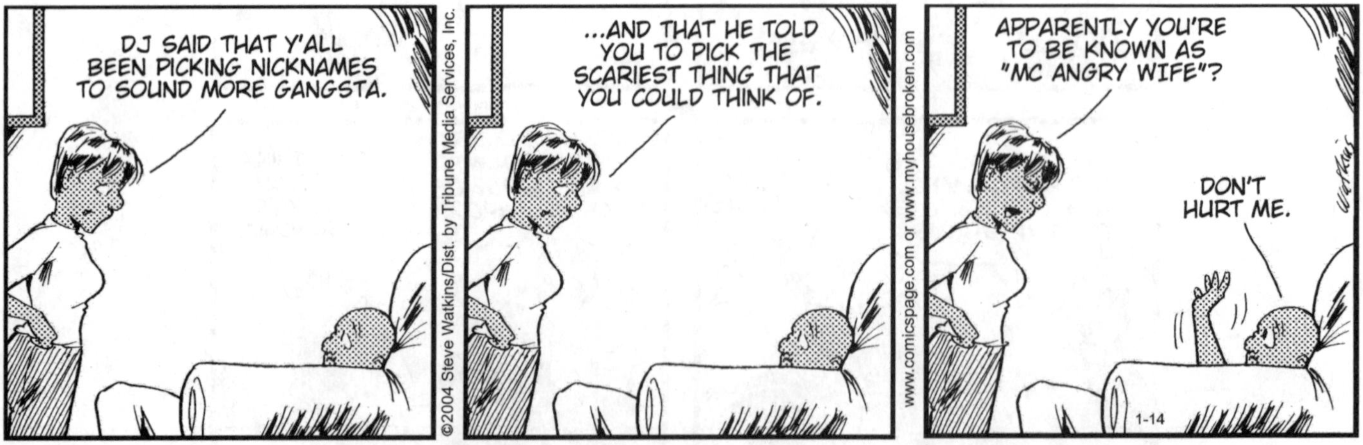
DJ SAID THAT Y'ALL BEEN PICKING NICKNAMES TO SOUND MORE GANGSTA.
©2004 Steve Watkins/Dist. by Tribune Media Services, Inc.
...AND THAT HE TOLD YOU TO PICK THE SCARIEST THING THAT YOU COULD THINK OF.
www.comicspage.com or www.myhousebroken.com
APPARENTLY YOU'RE TO BE KNOWN AS "MC ANGRY WIFE"?
DON'T HURT ME.
1-14

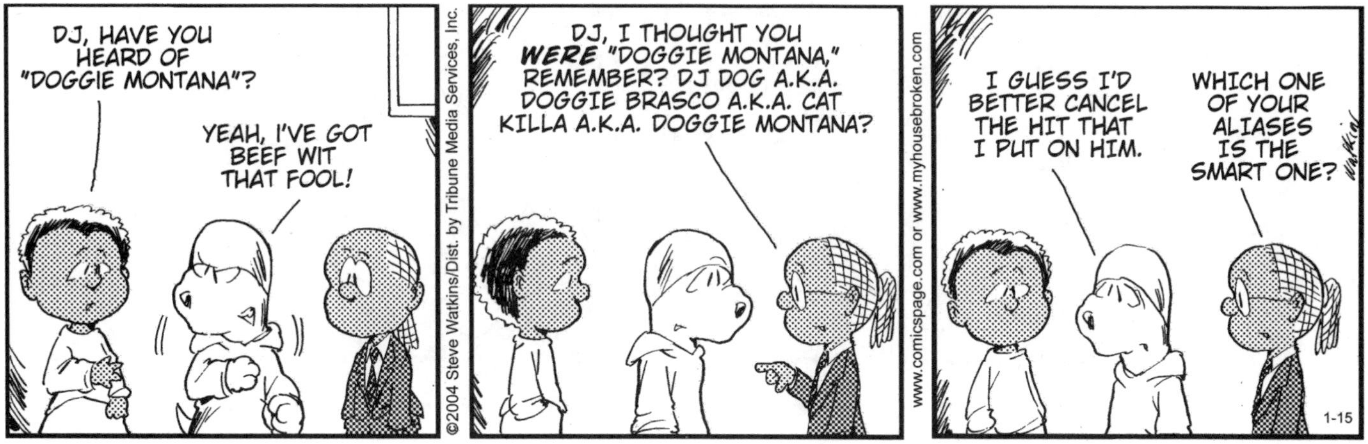
DJ, HAVE YOU HEARD OF "DOGGIE MONTANA"?
YEAH, I'VE GOT BEEF WIT THAT FOOL!
DJ, I THOUGHT YOU *WERE* "DOGGIE MONTANA," REMEMBER? DJ DOG A.K.A. DOGGIE BRASCO A.K.A. CAT KILLA A.K.A. DOGGIE MONTANA?
I GUESS I'D BETTER CANCEL THE HIT THAT I PUT ON HIM.
WHICH ONE OF YOUR ALIASES IS THE SMART ONE?
1-15

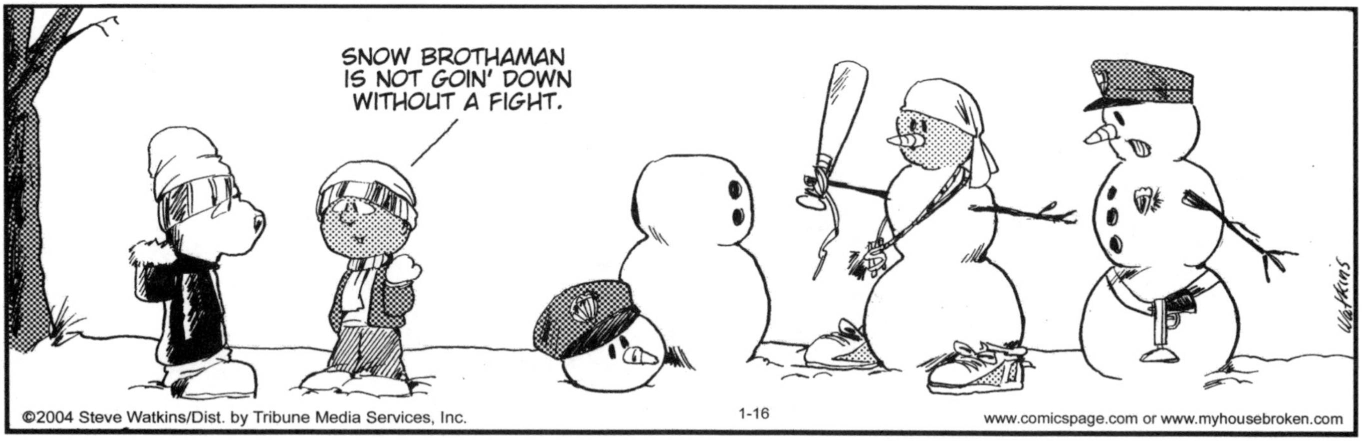
SNOW BROTHAMAN IS NOT GOIN' DOWN WITHOUT A FIGHT.
1-16

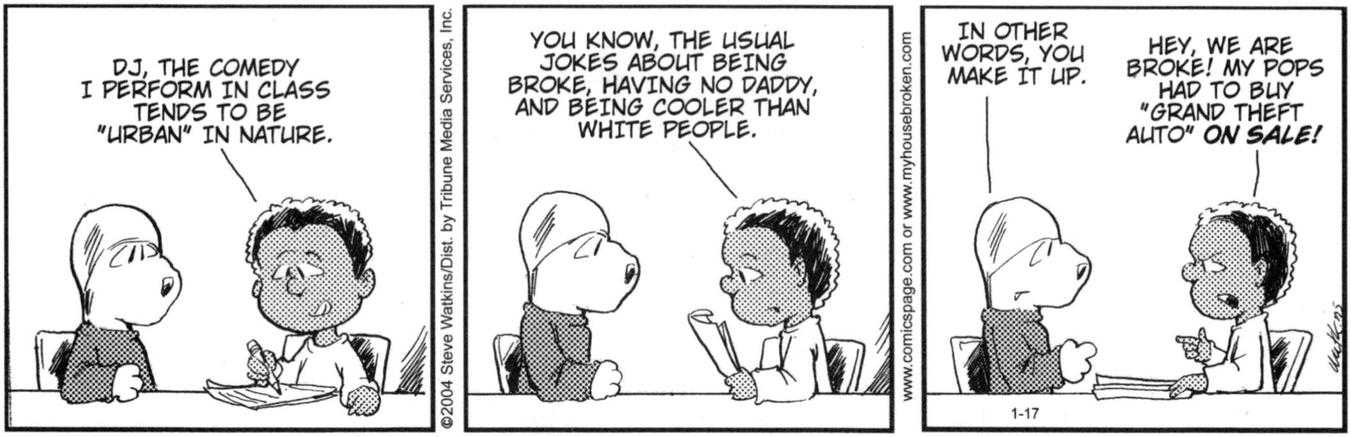
DJ, THE COMEDY I PERFORM IN CLASS TENDS TO BE "URBAN" IN NATURE.
YOU KNOW, THE USUAL JOKES ABOUT BEING BROKE, HAVING NO DADDY, AND BEING COOLER THAN WHITE PEOPLE.
IN OTHER WORDS, YOU MAKE IT UP.
HEY, WE ARE BROKE! MY POPS HAD TO BUY "GRAND THEFT AUTO" *ON SALE!*
1-17

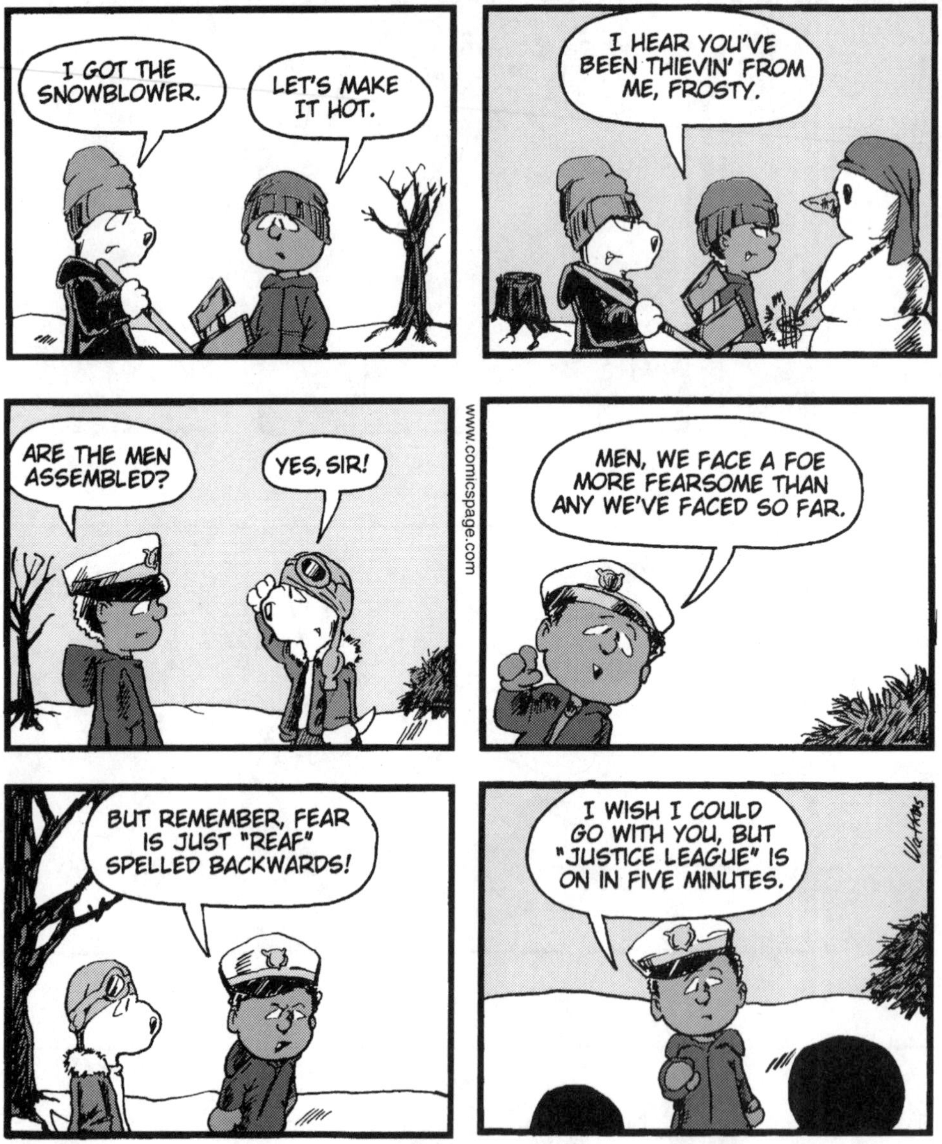

I GOT THE SNOWBLOWER.
LET'S MAKE IT HOT.
I HEAR YOU'VE BEEN THIEVIN' FROM ME, FROSTY.
www.comicspage.com
ARE THE MEN ASSEMBLED?
YES, SIR!
MEN, WE FACE A FOE MORE FEARSOME THAN ANY WE'VE FACED SO FAR.
BUT REMEMBER, FEAR IS JUST "REAF" SPELLED BACKWARDS!
I WISH I COULD GO WITH YOU, BUT "JUSTICE LEAGUE" IS ON IN FIVE MINUTES.

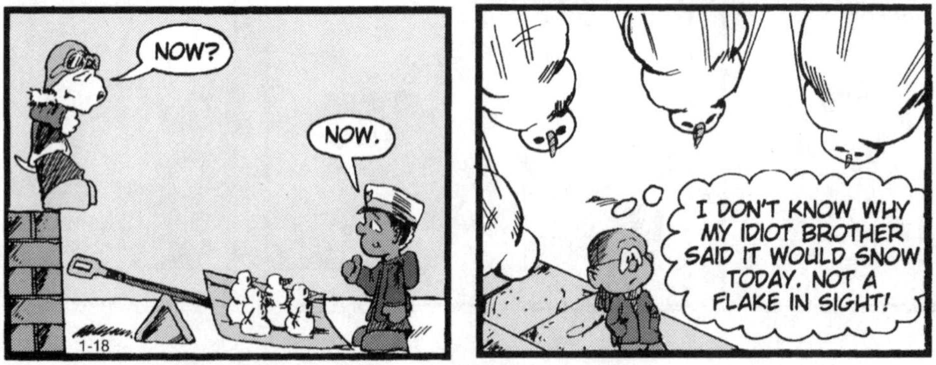

NOW?
NOW.
1-18
I DON'T KNOW WHY MY IDIOT BROTHER SAID IT WOULD SNOW TODAY. NOT A FLAKE IN SIGHT!

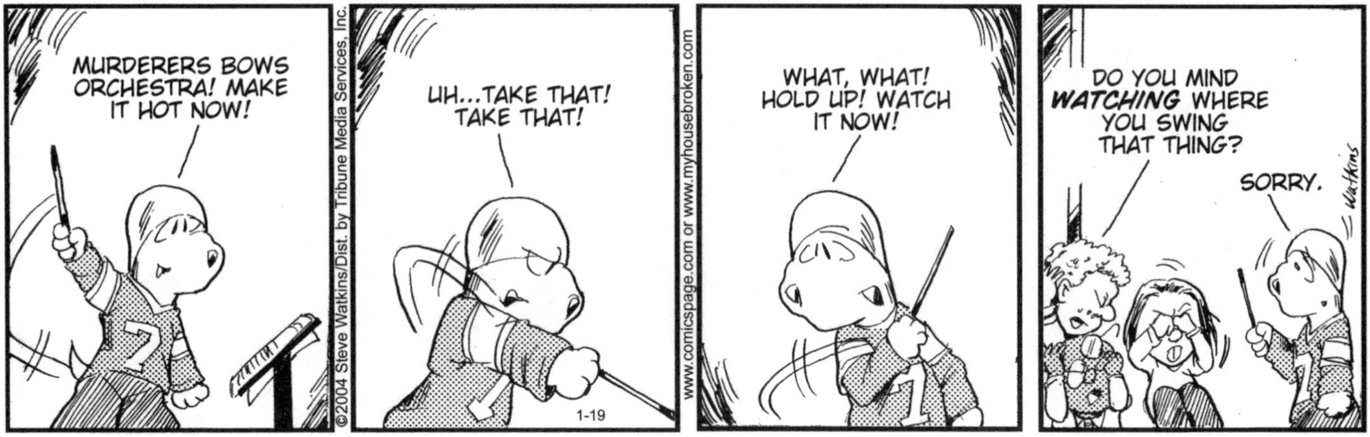
MURDERERS BOWS ORCHESTRA! MAKE IT HOT NOW!
©2004 Steve Watkins/Dist. by Tribune Media Services, Inc.
UH...TAKE THAT! TAKE THAT!
1-19
www.comicspage.com or www.myhousebroken.com
WHAT, WHAT! HOLD UP! WATCH IT NOW!
DO YOU MIND **WATCHING** WHERE YOU SWING THAT THING?
SORRY.

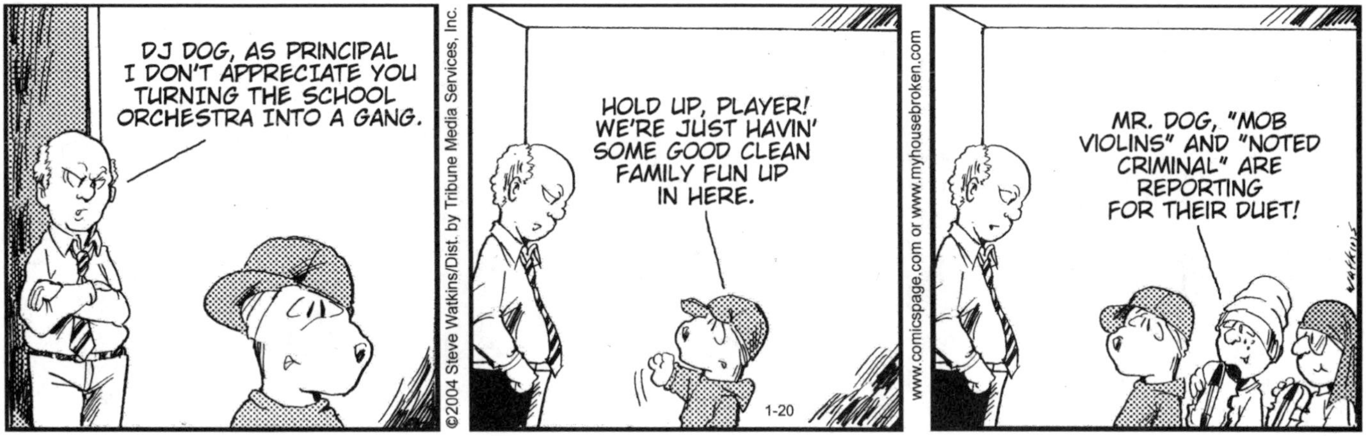
DJ DOG, AS PRINCIPAL I DON'T APPRECIATE YOU TURNING THE SCHOOL ORCHESTRA INTO A GANG.
©2004 Steve Watkins/Dist. by Tribune Media Services, Inc.
HOLD UP, PLAYER! WE'RE JUST HAVIN' SOME GOOD CLEAN FAMILY FUN UP IN HERE.
1-20
www.comicspage.com or www.myhousebroken.com
MR. DOG, "MOB VIOLINS" AND "NOTED CRIMINAL" ARE REPORTING FOR THEIR DUET!

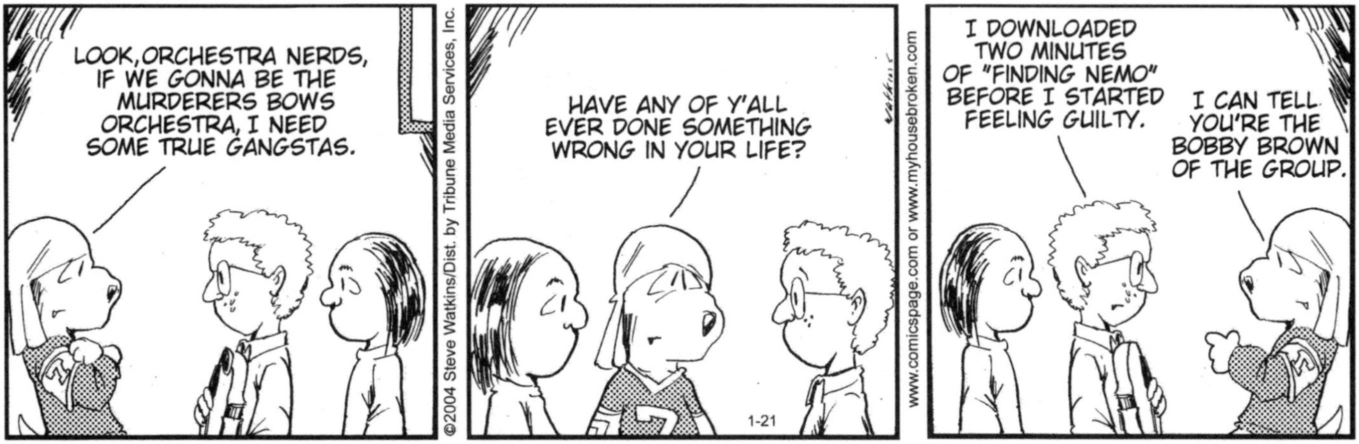
LOOK, ORCHESTRA NERDS, IF WE GONNA BE THE MURDERERS BOWS ORCHESTRA, I NEED SOME TRUE GANGSTAS.
©2004 Steve Watkins/Dist. by Tribune Media Services, Inc.
HAVE ANY OF Y'ALL EVER DONE SOMETHING WRONG IN YOUR LIFE?
1-21
www.comicspage.com or www.myhousebroken.com
I DOWNLOADED TWO MINUTES OF "FINDING NEMO" BEFORE I STARTED FEELING GUILTY.
I CAN TELL YOU'RE THE BOBBY BROWN OF THE GROUP.

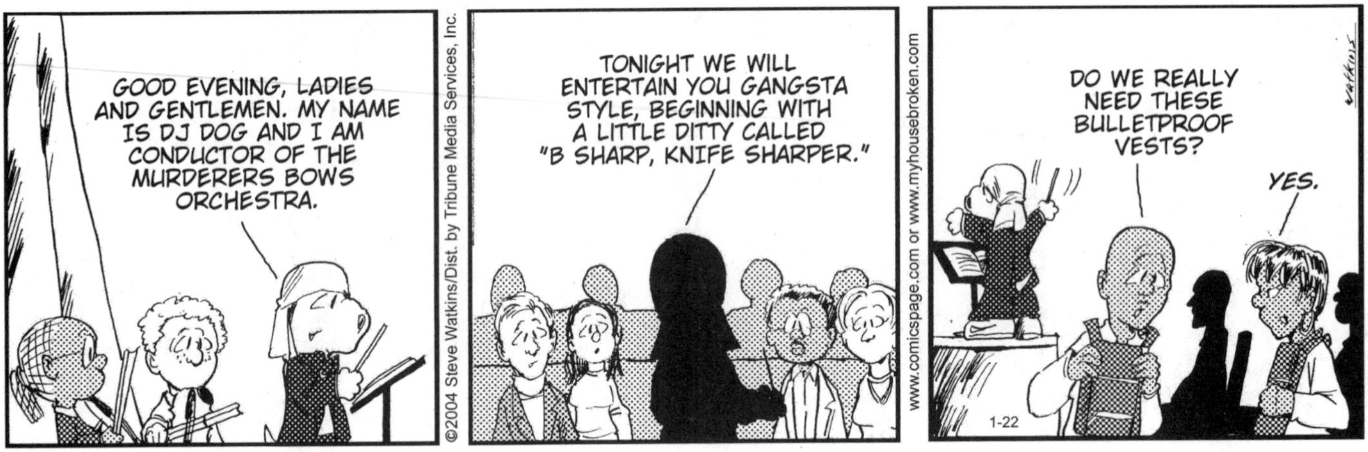
GOOD EVENING, LADIES AND GENTLEMEN. MY NAME IS DJ DOG AND I AM CONDUCTOR OF THE MURDERERS BOWS ORCHESTRA.
TONIGHT WE WILL ENTERTAIN YOU GANGSTA STYLE, BEGINNING WITH A LITTLE DITTY CALLED "B SHARP, KNIFE SHARPER."
DO WE REALLY NEED THESE BULLETPROOF VESTS?
YES.
1-22
©2004 Steve Watkins/Dist. by Tribune Media Services, Inc.
www.comicspage.com or www.myhousebroken.com

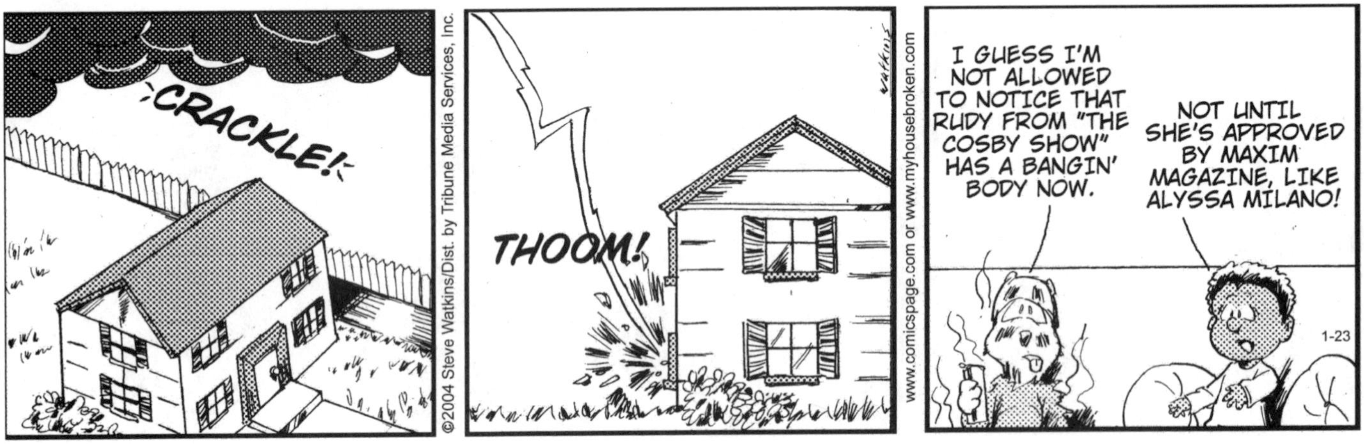
CRACKLE!
THOOM!
I GUESS I'M NOT ALLOWED TO NOTICE THAT RUDY FROM "THE COSBY SHOW" HAS A BANGIN' BODY NOW.
NOT UNTIL SHE'S APPROVED BY MAXIM MAGAZINE, LIKE ALYSSA MILANO!
1-23
©2004 Steve Watkins/Dist. by Tribune Media Services, Inc.
www.comicspage.com or www.myhousebroken.com

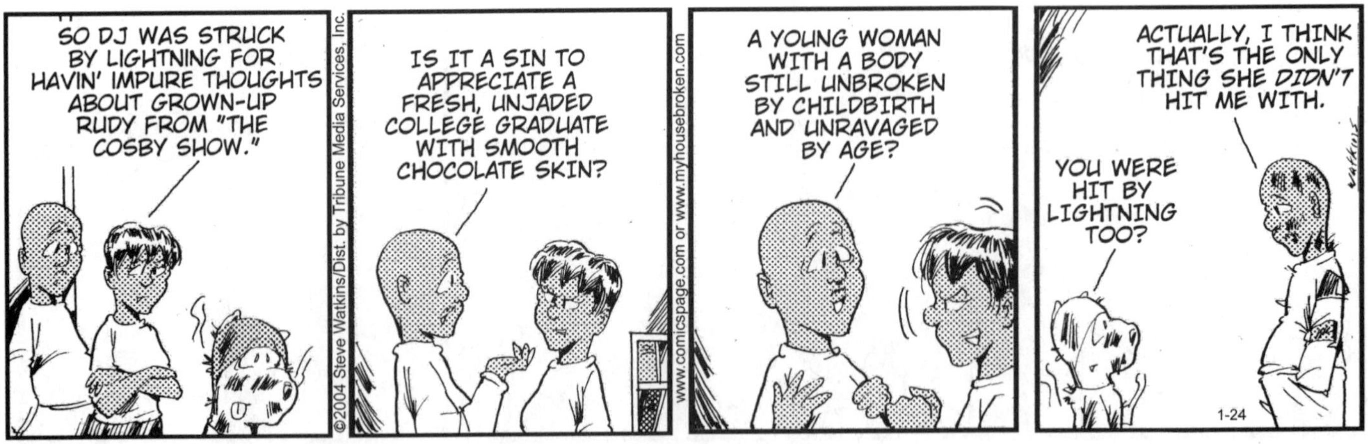
SO DJ WAS STRUCK BY LIGHTNING FOR HAVIN' IMPURE THOUGHTS ABOUT GROWN-UP RUDY FROM "THE COSBY SHOW."
IS IT A SIN TO APPRECIATE A FRESH, UNJADED COLLEGE GRADUATE WITH SMOOTH CHOCOLATE SKIN?
A YOUNG WOMAN WITH A BODY STILL UNBROKEN BY CHILDBIRTH AND UNRAVAGED BY AGE?
YOU WERE HIT BY LIGHTNING TOO?
ACTUALLY, I THINK THAT'S THE ONLY THING SHE *DIDN'T* HIT ME WITH.
1-24
©2004 Steve Watkins/Dist. by Tribune Media Services, Inc.
www.comicspage.com or www.myhousebroken.com

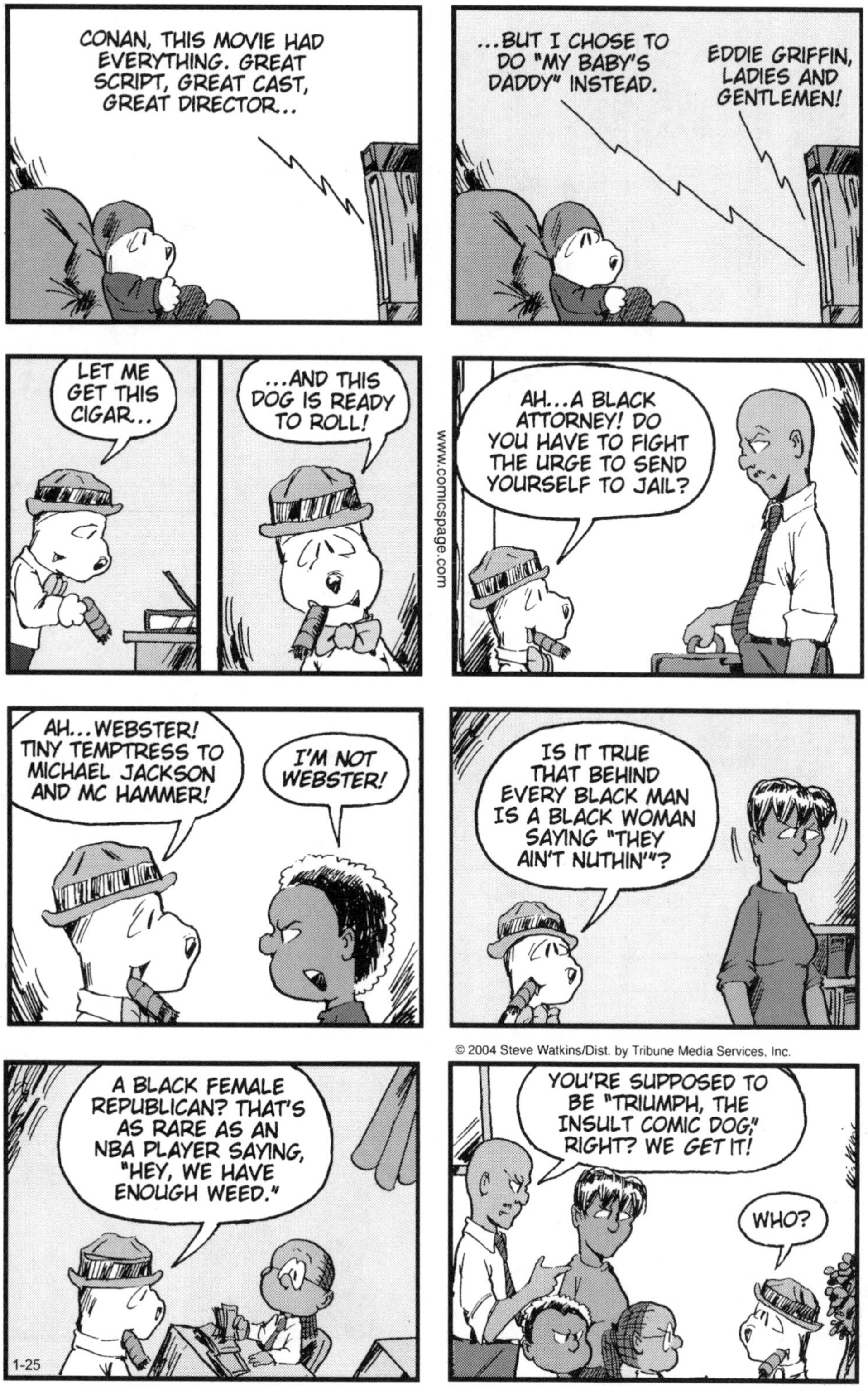
CONAN, THIS MOVIE HAD EVERYTHING. GREAT SCRIPT, GREAT CAST, GREAT DIRECTOR...
...BUT I CHOSE TO DO "MY BABY'S DADDY" INSTEAD.
EDDIE GRIFFIN, LADIES AND GENTLEMEN!
LET ME GET THIS CIGAR...
...AND THIS DOG IS READY TO ROLL!
www.comicspage.com
AH...A BLACK ATTORNEY! DO YOU HAVE TO FIGHT THE URGE TO SEND YOURSELF TO JAIL?
AH...WEBSTER! TINY TEMPTRESS TO MICHAEL JACKSON AND MC HAMMER!
I'M NOT WEBSTER!
IS IT TRUE THAT BEHIND EVERY BLACK MAN IS A BLACK WOMAN SAYING "THEY AIN'T NUTHIN'"?
© 2004 Steve Watkins/Dist. by Tribune Media Services, Inc.
A BLACK FEMALE REPUBLICAN? THAT'S AS RARE AS AN NBA PLAYER SAYING, "HEY, WE HAVE ENOUGH WEED."
1-25
YOU'RE SUPPOSED TO BE "TRIUMPH, THE INSULT COMIC DOG," RIGHT? WE GET IT!
WHO?

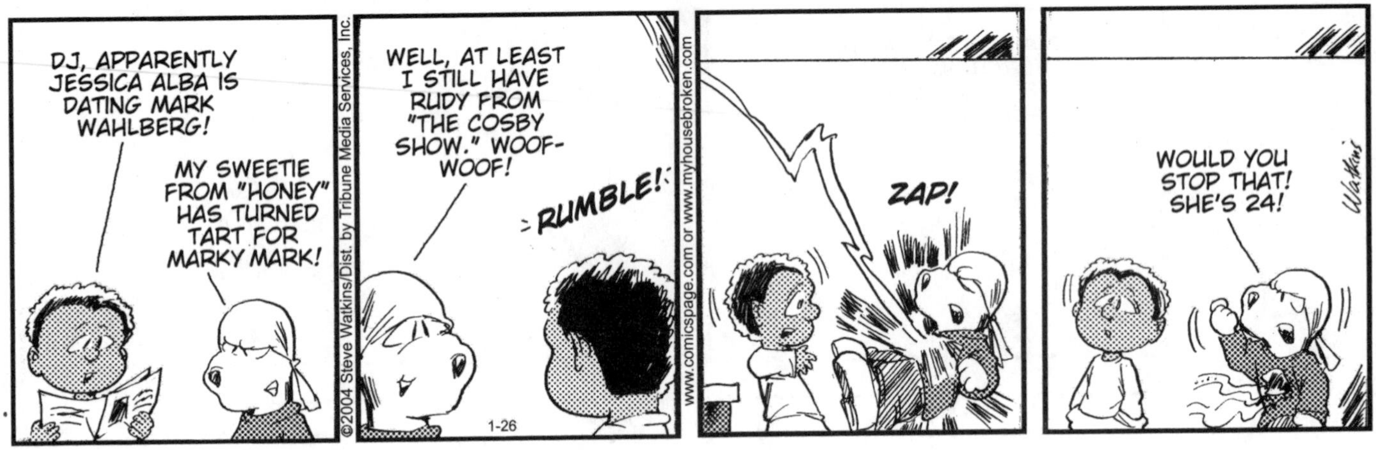
DJ, APPARENTLY JESSICA ALBA IS DATING MARK WAHLBERG!
MY SWEETIE FROM "HONEY" HAS TURNED TART FOR MARKY MARK!
©2004 Steve Watkins/Dist. by Tribune Media Services, Inc.
WELL, AT LEAST I STILL HAVE RUDY FROM "THE COSBY SHOW." WOOF-WOOF!
RUMBLE!
1-26
www.comicspage.com or www.myhousebroken.com
ZAP!
WOULD YOU STOP THAT! SHE'S 24!
Watkins

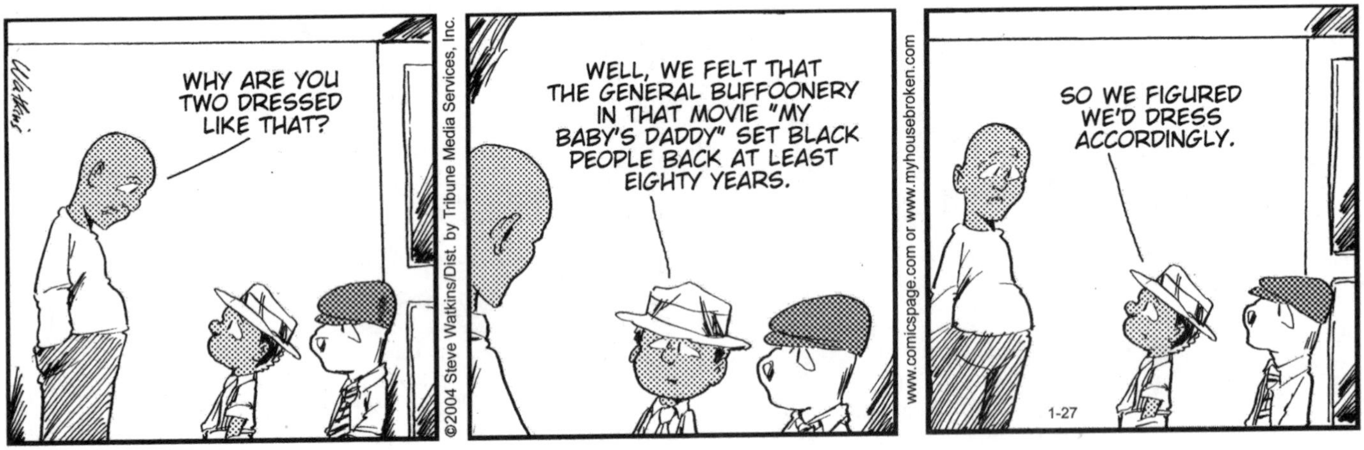
Watkins
WHY ARE YOU TWO DRESSED LIKE THAT?
©2004 Steve Watkins/Dist. by Tribune Media Services, Inc.
WELL, WE FELT THAT THE GENERAL BUFFOONERY IN THAT MOVIE "MY BABY'S DADDY" SET BLACK PEOPLE BACK AT LEAST EIGHTY YEARS.
www.comicspage.com or www.myhousebroken.com
SO WE FIGURED WE'D DRESS ACCORDINGLY.
1-27

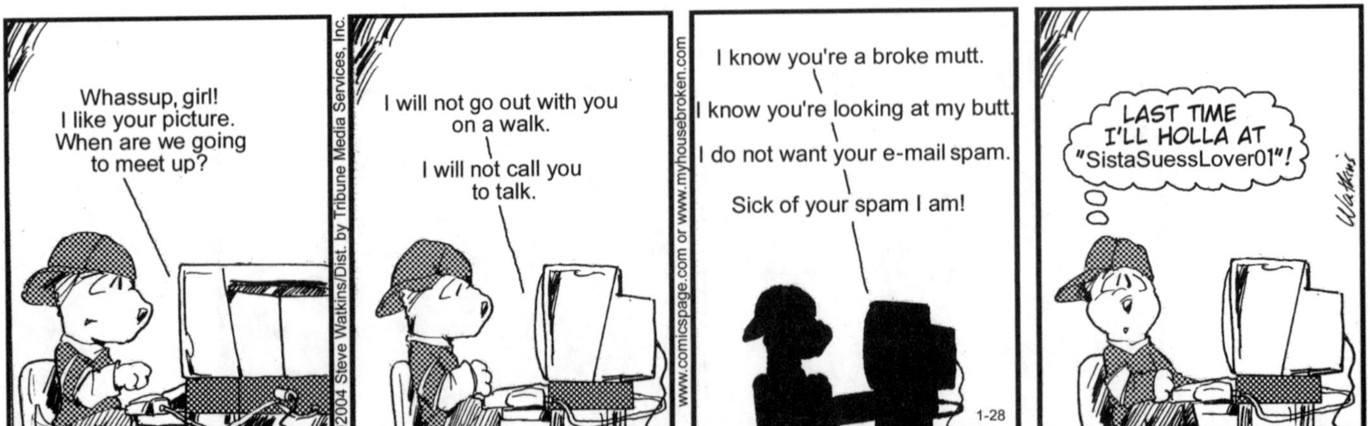
Whassup, girl! I like your picture. When are we going to meet up?
©2004 Steve Watkins/Dist. by Tribune Media Services, Inc.
I will not go out with you on a walk.
I will not call you to talk.
www.comicspage.com or www.myhousebroken.com
I know you're a broke mutt.
I know you're looking at my butt.
I do not want your e-mail spam.
Sick of your spam I am!
1-28
LAST TIME I'LL HOLLA AT "SistaSuessLover01"!
Watkins

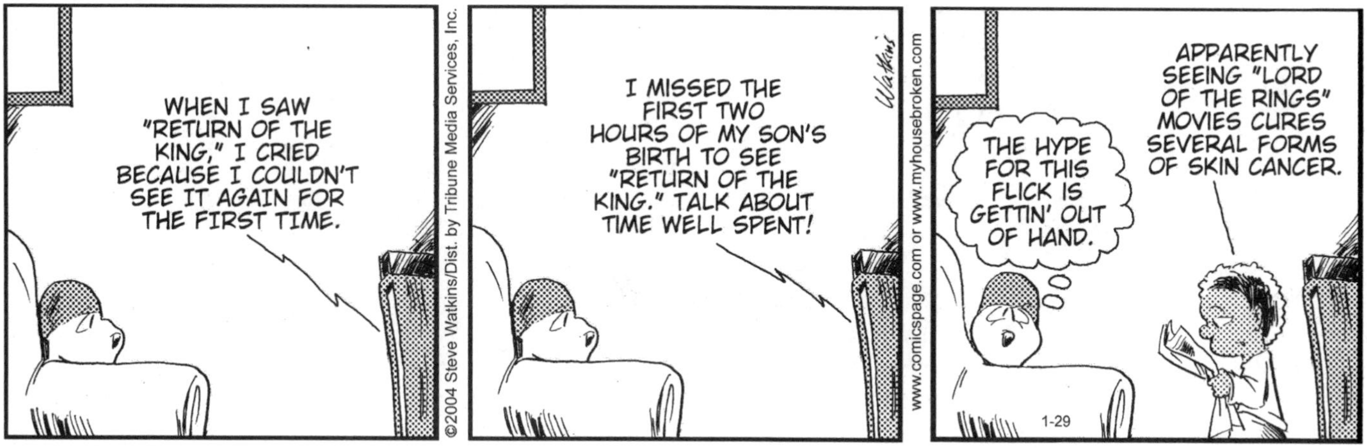
WHEN I SAW "RETURN OF THE KING," I CRIED BECAUSE I COULDN'T SEE IT AGAIN FOR THE FIRST TIME.
©2004 Steve Watkins/Dist. by Tribune Media Services, Inc.
I MISSED THE FIRST TWO HOURS OF MY SON'S BIRTH TO SEE "RETURN OF THE KING." TALK ABOUT TIME WELL SPENT!
Watkins
www.comicspage.com or www.myhousebroken.com
THE HYPE FOR THIS FLICK IS GETTIN' OUT OF HAND.
APPARENTLY SEEING "LORD OF THE RINGS" MOVIES CURES SEVERAL FORMS OF SKIN CANCER.
1-29

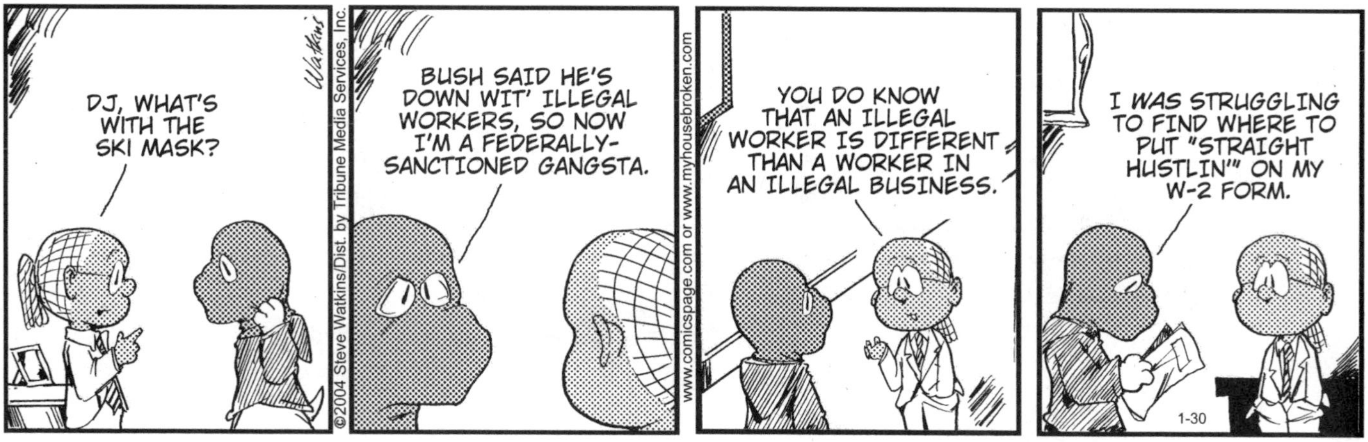
DJ, WHAT'S WITH THE SKI MASK?
Watkins
©2004 Steve Watkins/Dist. by Tribune Media Services, Inc.
BUSH SAID HE'S DOWN WIT' ILLEGAL WORKERS, SO NOW I'M A FEDERALLY-SANCTIONED GANGSTA.
www.comicspage.com or www.myhousebroken.com
YOU DO KNOW THAT AN ILLEGAL WORKER IS DIFFERENT THAN A WORKER IN AN ILLEGAL BUSINESS.
I *WAS* STRUGGLING TO FIND WHERE TO PUT "STRAIGHT HUSTLIN'" ON MY W-2 FORM.
1-30

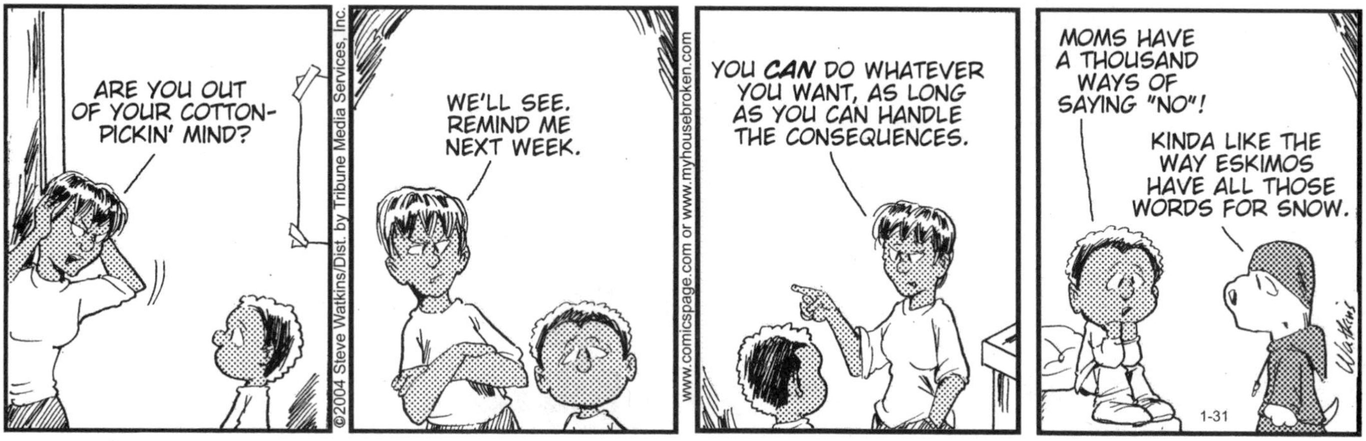
ARE YOU OUT OF YOUR COTTON-PICKIN' MIND?
©2004 Steve Watkins/Dist. by Tribune Media Services, Inc.
WE'LL SEE. REMIND ME NEXT WEEK.
www.comicspage.com or www.myhousebroken.com
YOU *CAN* DO WHATEVER YOU WANT, AS LONG AS YOU CAN HANDLE THE CONSEQUENCES.
MOMS HAVE A THOUSAND WAYS OF SAYING "NO"!
KINDA LIKE THE WAY ESKIMOS HAVE ALL THOSE WORDS FOR SNOW.
Watkins
1-31

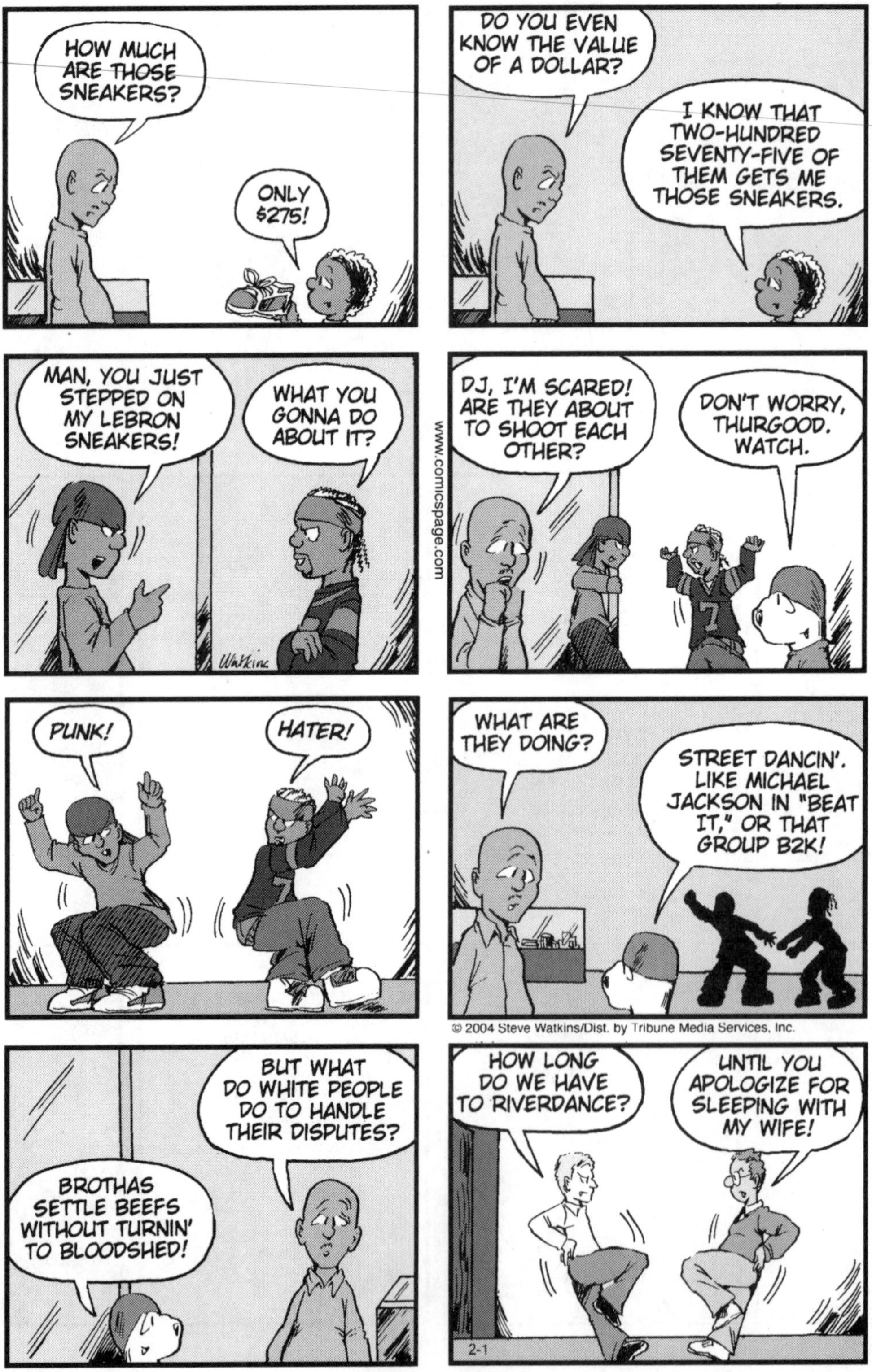

HOW MUCH ARE THOSE SNEAKERS?
ONLY $275!
DO YOU EVEN KNOW THE VALUE OF A DOLLAR?
I KNOW THAT TWO-HUNDRED SEVENTY-FIVE OF THEM GETS ME THOSE SNEAKERS.
MAN, YOU JUST STEPPED ON MY LEBRON SNEAKERS!
WHAT YOU GONNA DO ABOUT IT?
Watkins
www.comicspage.com
DJ, I'M SCARED! ARE THEY ABOUT TO SHOOT EACH OTHER?
DON'T WORRY, THURGOOD. WATCH.
PUNK!
HATER!
WHAT ARE THEY DOING?
STREET DANCIN'. LIKE MICHAEL JACKSON IN "BEAT IT," OR THAT GROUP B2K!
BROTHAS SETTLE BEEFS WITHOUT TURNIN' TO BLOODSHED!
BUT WHAT DO WHITE PEOPLE DO TO HANDLE THEIR DISPUTES?
HOW LONG DO WE HAVE TO RIVERDANCE?
UNTIL YOU APOLOGIZE FOR SLEEPING WITH MY WIFE!
2-1

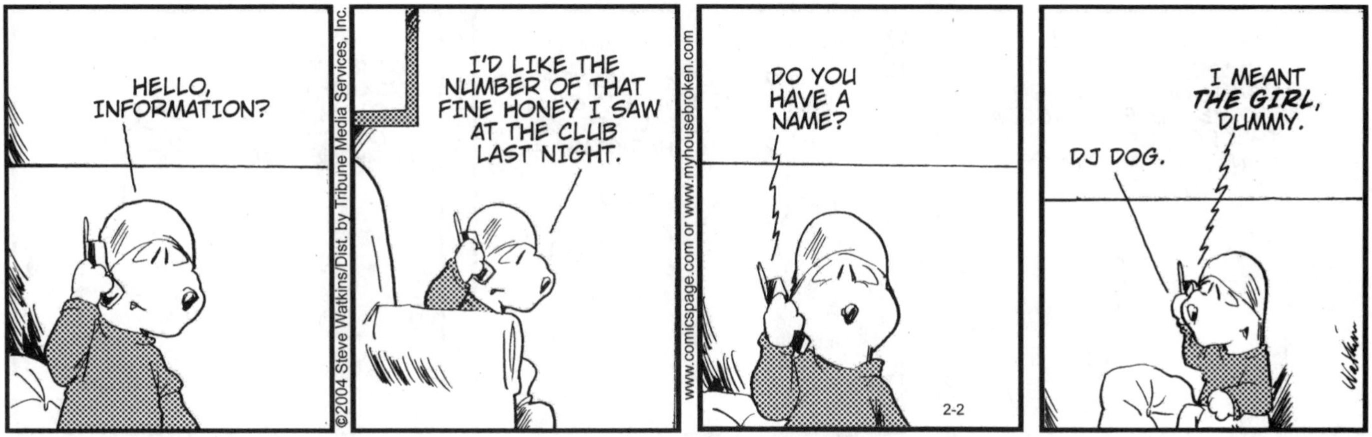
HELLO, INFORMATION?
©2004 Steve Watkins/Dist. by Tribune Media Services, Inc.
I'D LIKE THE NUMBER OF THAT FINE HONEY I SAW AT THE CLUB LAST NIGHT.
www.comicspage.com or www.myhousebroken.com
DO YOU HAVE A NAME?
2-2
DJ DOG.
I MEANT ***THE GIRL***, DUMMY.
Watkins

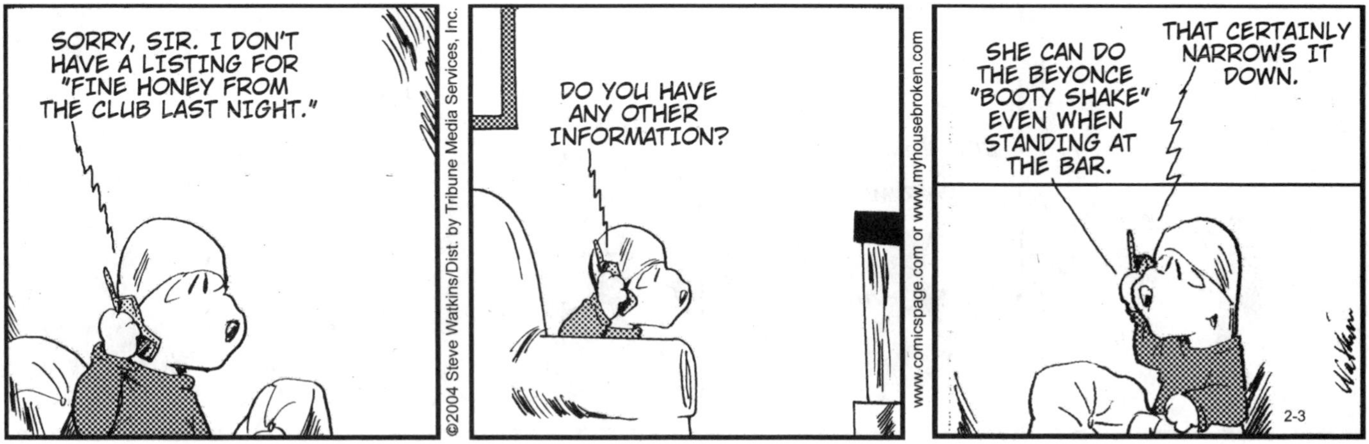
SORRY, SIR. I DON'T HAVE A LISTING FOR "FINE HONEY FROM THE CLUB LAST NIGHT."
©2004 Steve Watkins/Dist. by Tribune Media Services, Inc.
DO YOU HAVE ANY OTHER INFORMATION?
www.comicspage.com or www.myhousebroken.com
SHE CAN DO THE BEYONCE "BOOTY SHAKE" EVEN WHEN STANDING AT THE BAR.
THAT CERTAINLY NARROWS IT DOWN.
2-3
Watkins

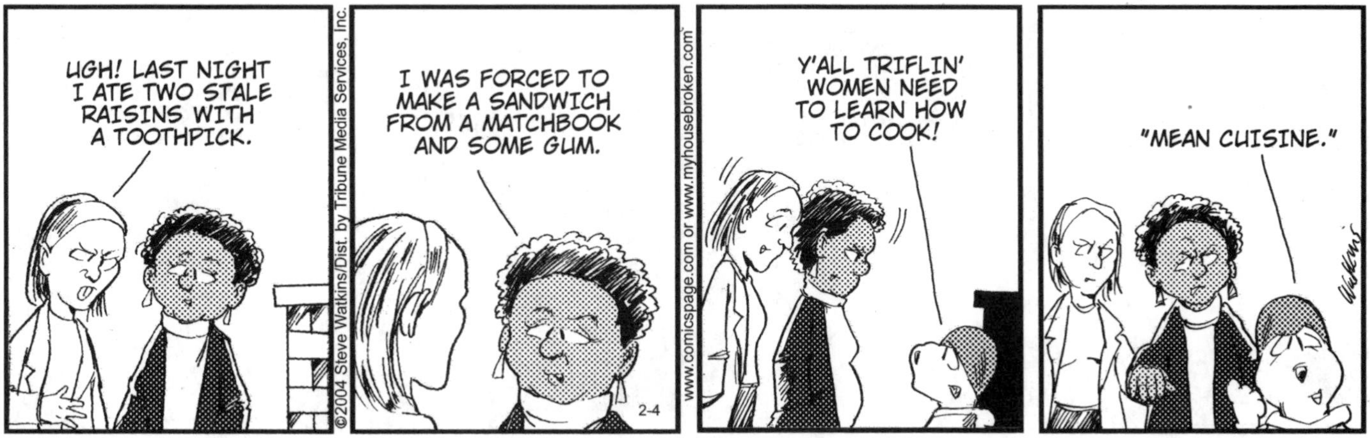
UGH! LAST NIGHT I ATE TWO STALE RAISINS WITH A TOOTHPICK.
©2004 Steve Watkins/Dist. by Tribune Media Services, Inc.
I WAS FORCED TO MAKE A SANDWICH FROM A MATCHBOOK AND SOME GUM.
2-4
www.comicspage.com or www.myhousebroken.com
Y'ALL TRIFLIN' WOMEN NEED TO LEARN HOW TO COOK!
"MEAN CUISINE."
Watkins

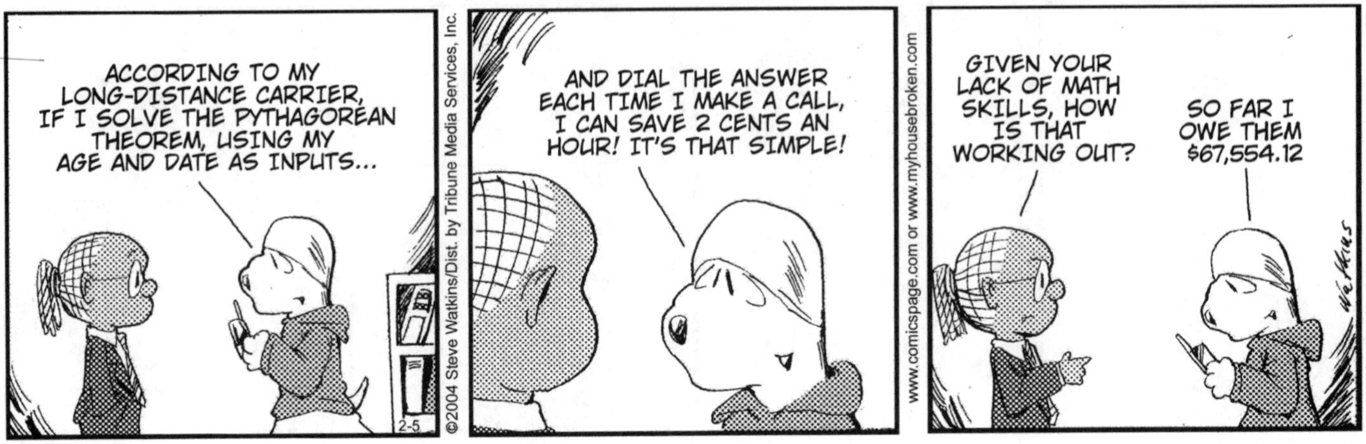
ACCORDING TO MY LONG-DISTANCE CARRIER, IF I SOLVE THE PYTHAGOREAN THEOREM, USING MY AGE AND DATE AS INPUTS...
2-5
©2004 Steve Watkins/Dist. by Tribune Media Services, Inc.
AND DIAL THE ANSWER EACH TIME I MAKE A CALL, I CAN SAVE 2 CENTS AN HOUR! IT'S THAT SIMPLE!
www.comicspage.com or www.myhousebroken.com
GIVEN YOUR LACK OF MATH SKILLS, HOW IS THAT WORKING OUT?
SO FAR I OWE THEM $67,554.12

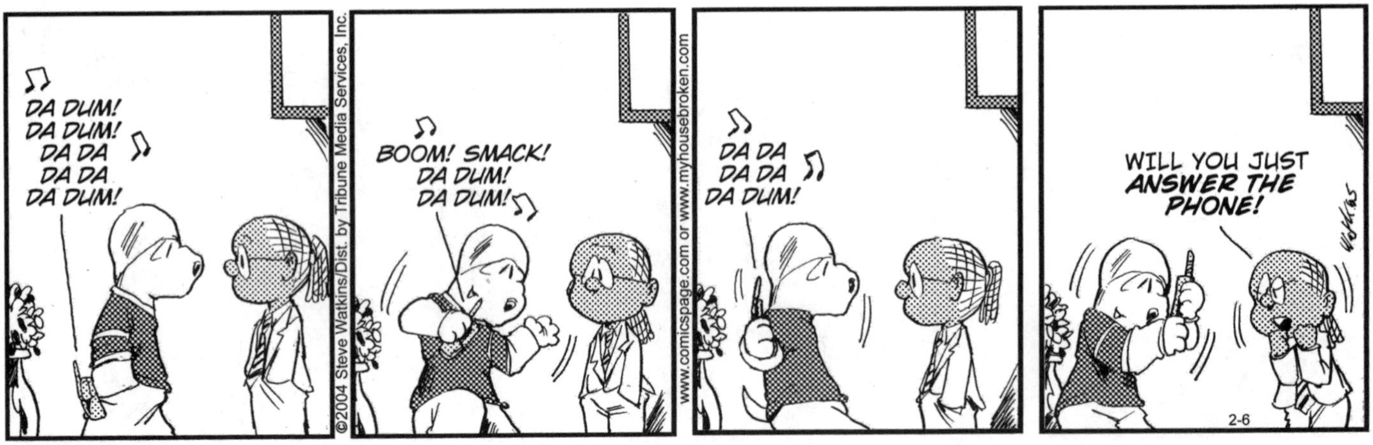
DA DUM! DA DUM! DA DA DA DA DA DUM!
©2004 Steve Watkins/Dist. by Tribune Media Services, Inc.
BOOM! SMACK! DA DUM! DA DUM!
www.comicspage.com or www.myhousebroken.com
DA DA DA DA DA DUM!
WILL YOU JUST *ANSWER THE PHONE!*
2-6

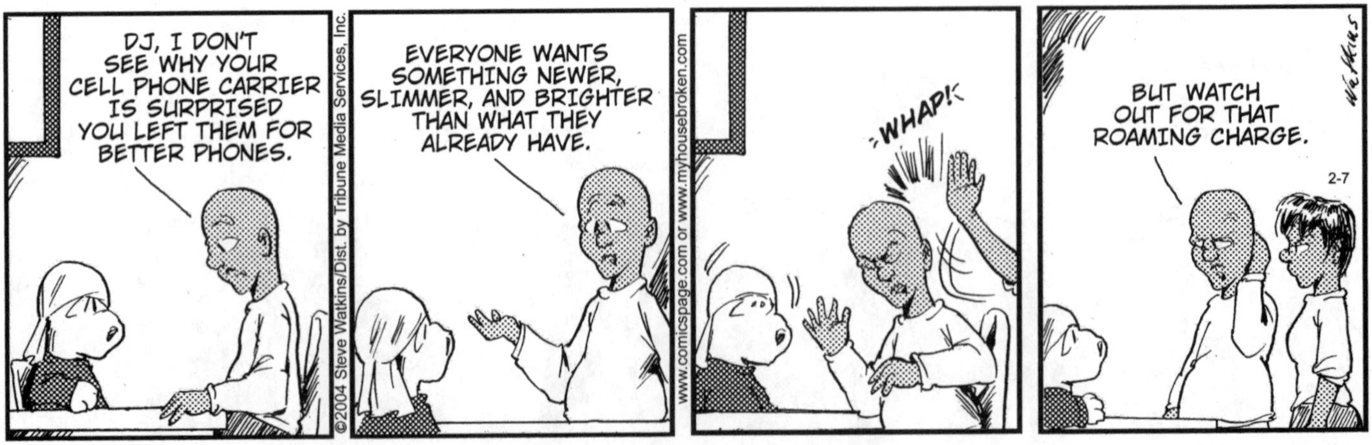
DJ, I DON'T SEE WHY YOUR CELL PHONE CARRIER IS SURPRISED YOU LEFT THEM FOR BETTER PHONES.
©2004 Steve Watkins/Dist. by Tribune Media Services, Inc.
EVERYONE WANTS SOMETHING NEWER, SLIMMER, AND BRIGHTER THAN WHAT THEY ALREADY HAVE.
www.comicspage.com or www.myhousebroken.com
WHAP!
BUT WATCH OUT FOR THAT ROAMING CHARGE.
2-7

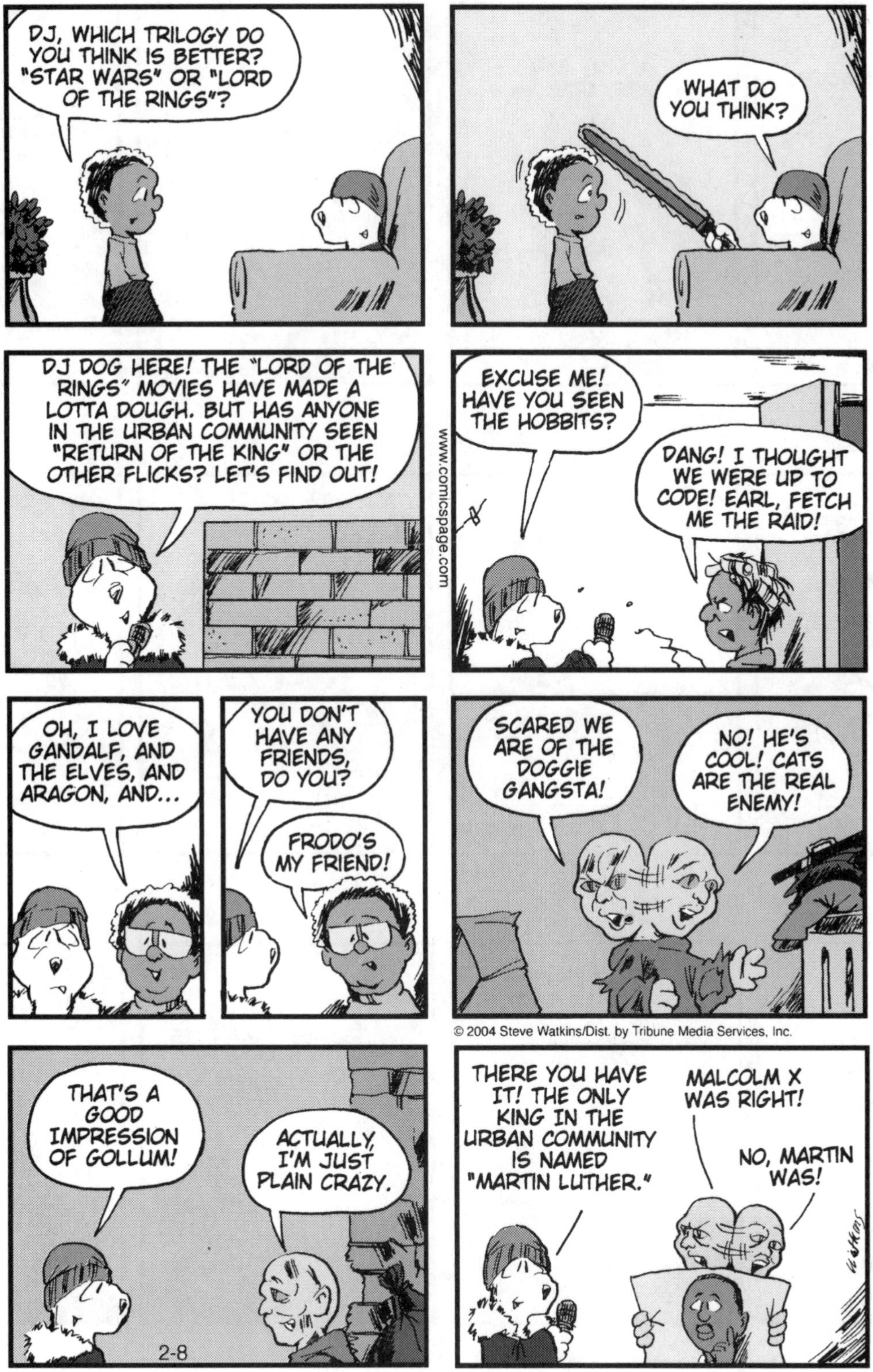

DJ, WHICH TRILOGY DO YOU THINK IS BETTER? "STAR WARS" OR "LORD OF THE RINGS"?
WHAT DO YOU THINK?
DJ DOG HERE! THE "LORD OF THE RINGS" MOVIES HAVE MADE A LOTTA DOUGH. BUT HAS ANYONE IN THE URBAN COMMUNITY SEEN "RETURN OF THE KING" OR THE OTHER FLICKS? LET'S FIND OUT!
www.comicspage.com
EXCUSE ME! HAVE YOU SEEN THE HOBBITS?
DANG! I THOUGHT WE WERE UP TO CODE! EARL, FETCH ME THE RAID!
OH, I LOVE GANDALF, AND THE ELVES, AND ARAGON, AND...
YOU DON'T HAVE ANY FRIENDS, DO YOU?
FRODO'S MY FRIEND!
SCARED WE ARE OF THE DOGGIE GANGSTA!
NO! HE'S COOL! CATS ARE THE REAL ENEMY!
© 2004 Steve Watkins/Dist. by Tribune Media Services, Inc.
THAT'S A GOOD IMPRESSION OF GOLLUM!
ACTUALLY, I'M JUST PLAIN CRAZY.
2-8
THERE YOU HAVE IT! THE ONLY KING IN THE URBAN COMMUNITY IS NAMED "MARTIN LUTHER."
MALCOLM X WAS RIGHT!
NO, MARTIN WAS!

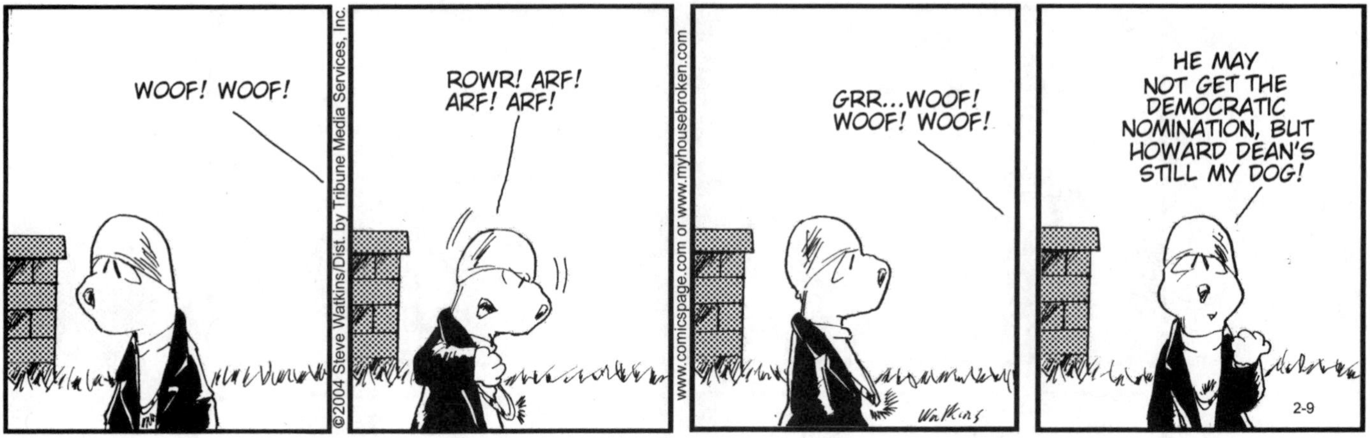
WOOF! WOOF!
©2004 Steve Watkins/Dist. by Tribune Media Services, Inc.
ROWR! ARF! ARF! ARF!
www.comicspage.com or www.myhousebroken.com
GRR...WOOF! WOOF! WOOF!
HE MAY NOT GET THE DEMOCRATIC NOMINATION, BUT HOWARD DEAN'S STILL MY DOG!
2-9

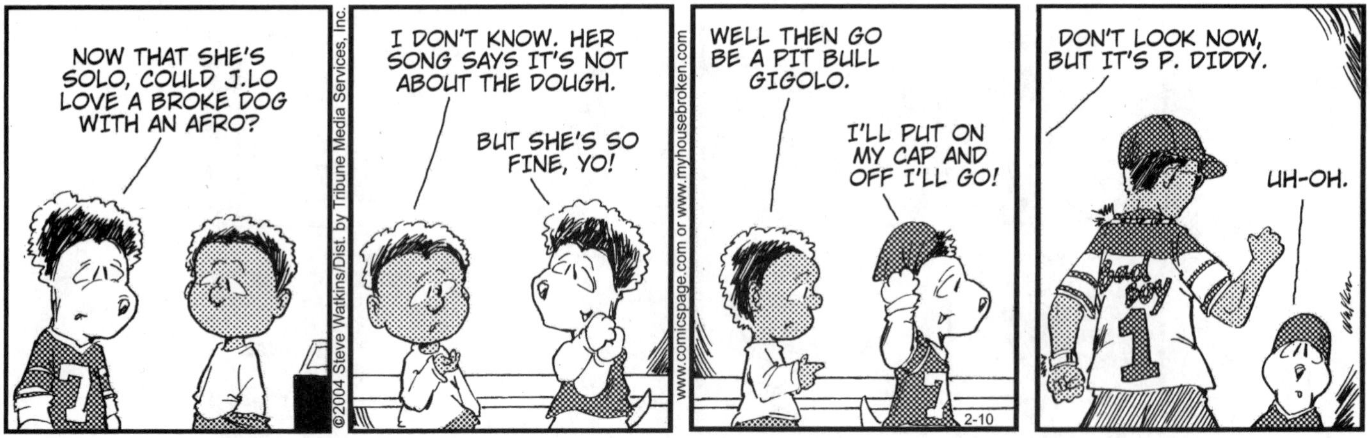
NOW THAT SHE'S SOLO, COULD J.LO LOVE A BROKE DOG WITH AN AFRO?
©2004 Steve Watkins/Dist. by Tribune Media Services, Inc.
I DON'T KNOW. HER SONG SAYS IT'S NOT ABOUT THE DOUGH.
BUT SHE'S SO FINE, YO!
www.comicspage.com or www.myhousebroken.com
WELL THEN GO BE A PIT BULL GIGOLO.
I'LL PUT ON MY CAP AND OFF I'LL GO!
2-10
DON'T LOOK NOW, BUT IT'S P. DIDDY.
UH-OH.
Bad Boy 1

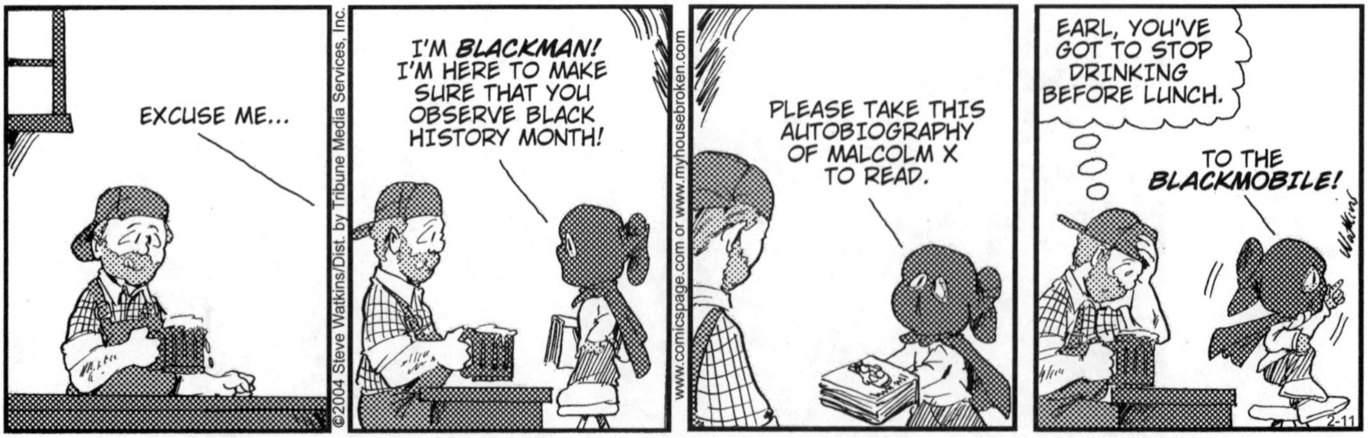
EXCUSE ME...
©2004 Steve Watkins/Dist. by Tribune Media Services, Inc.
I'M ***BLACKMAN!*** I'M HERE TO MAKE SURE THAT YOU OBSERVE BLACK HISTORY MONTH!
www.comicspage.com or www.myhousebroken.com
PLEASE TAKE THIS AUTOBIOGRAPHY OF MALCOLM X TO READ.
EARL, YOU'VE GOT TO STOP DRINKING BEFORE LUNCH.
TO THE ***BLACKMOBILE!***
2-11

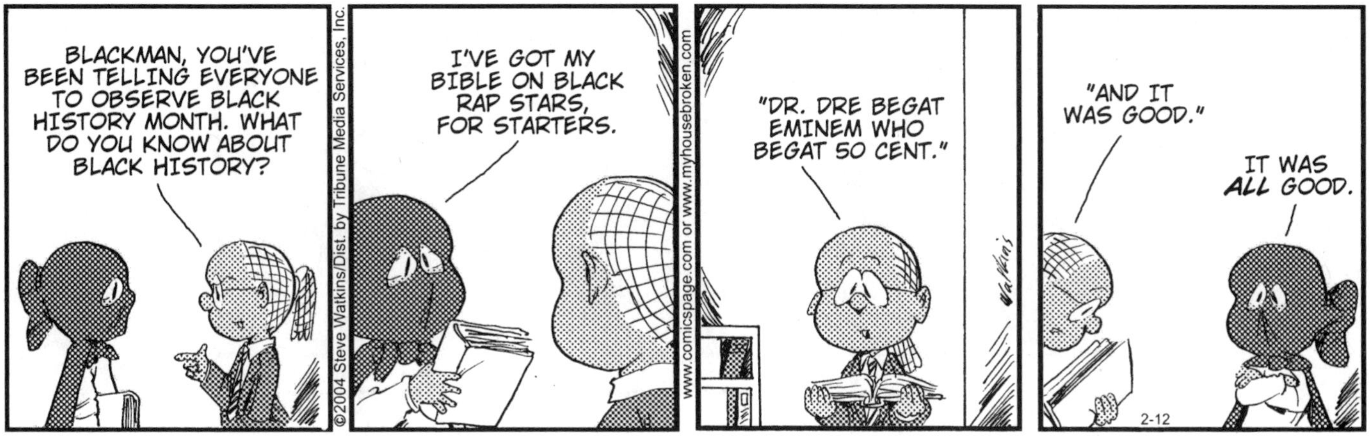
BLACKMAN, YOU'VE BEEN TELLING EVERYONE TO OBSERVE BLACK HISTORY MONTH. WHAT DO YOU KNOW ABOUT BLACK HISTORY?
©2004 Steve Watkins/Dist. by Tribune Media Services, Inc.
I'VE GOT MY BIBLE ON BLACK RAP STARS, FOR STARTERS.
www.comicspage.com or www.myhousebroken.com
"DR. DRE BEGAT EMINEM WHO BEGAT 50 CENT."
"AND IT WAS GOOD."
IT WAS ALL GOOD.
2-12

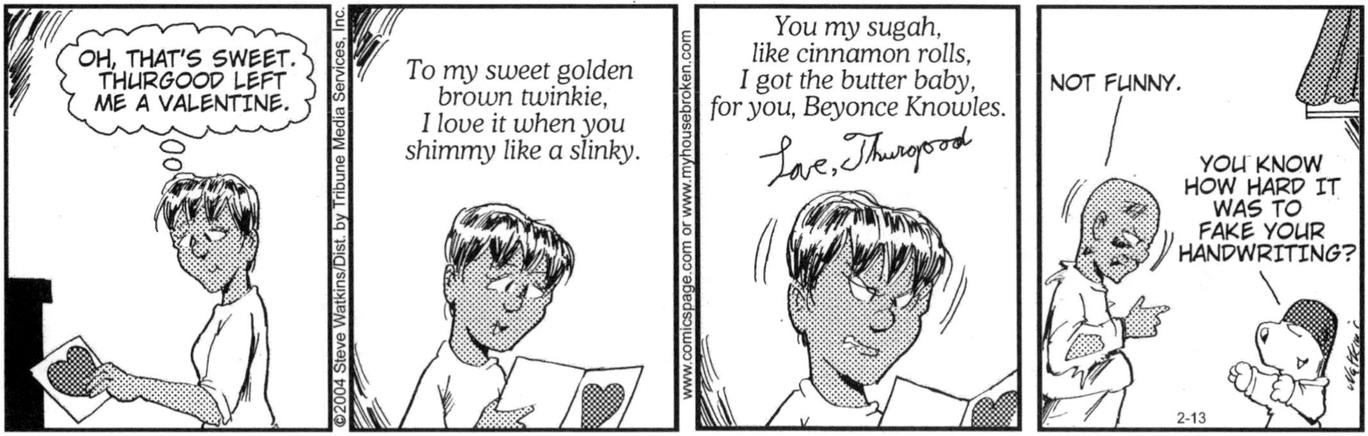
OH, THAT'S SWEET. THURGOOD LEFT ME A VALENTINE.
©2004 Steve Watkins/Dist. by Tribune Media Services, Inc.
To my sweet golden brown twinkie, I love it when you shimmy like a slinky.
www.comicspage.com or www.myhousebroken.com
You my sugah, like cinnamon rolls, I got the butter baby, for you, Beyonce Knowles.
Love, Thurgood
NOT FUNNY.
YOU KNOW HOW HARD IT WAS TO FAKE YOUR HANDWRITING?
2-13

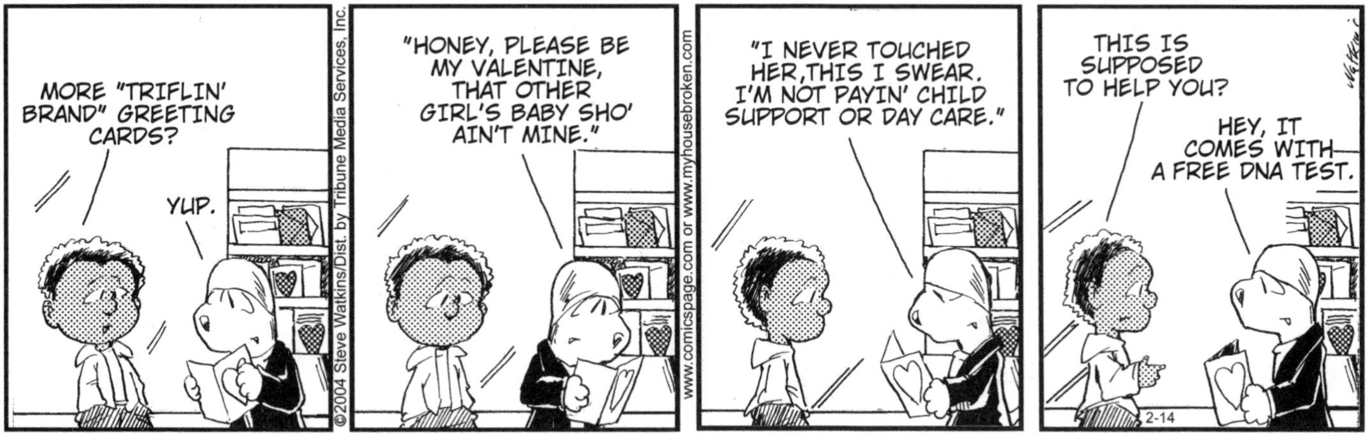
MORE "TRIFLIN' BRAND" GREETING CARDS?
YUP.
©2004 Steve Watkins/Dist. by Tribune Media Services, Inc.
"HONEY, PLEASE BE MY VALENTINE, THAT OTHER GIRL'S BABY SHO' AIN'T MINE."
www.comicspage.com or www.myhousebroken.com
"I NEVER TOUCHED HER,THIS I SWEAR. I'M NOT PAYIN' CHILD SUPPORT OR DAY CARE."
THIS IS SUPPOSED TO HELP YOU?
HEY, IT COMES WITH A FREE DNA TEST.
2-14

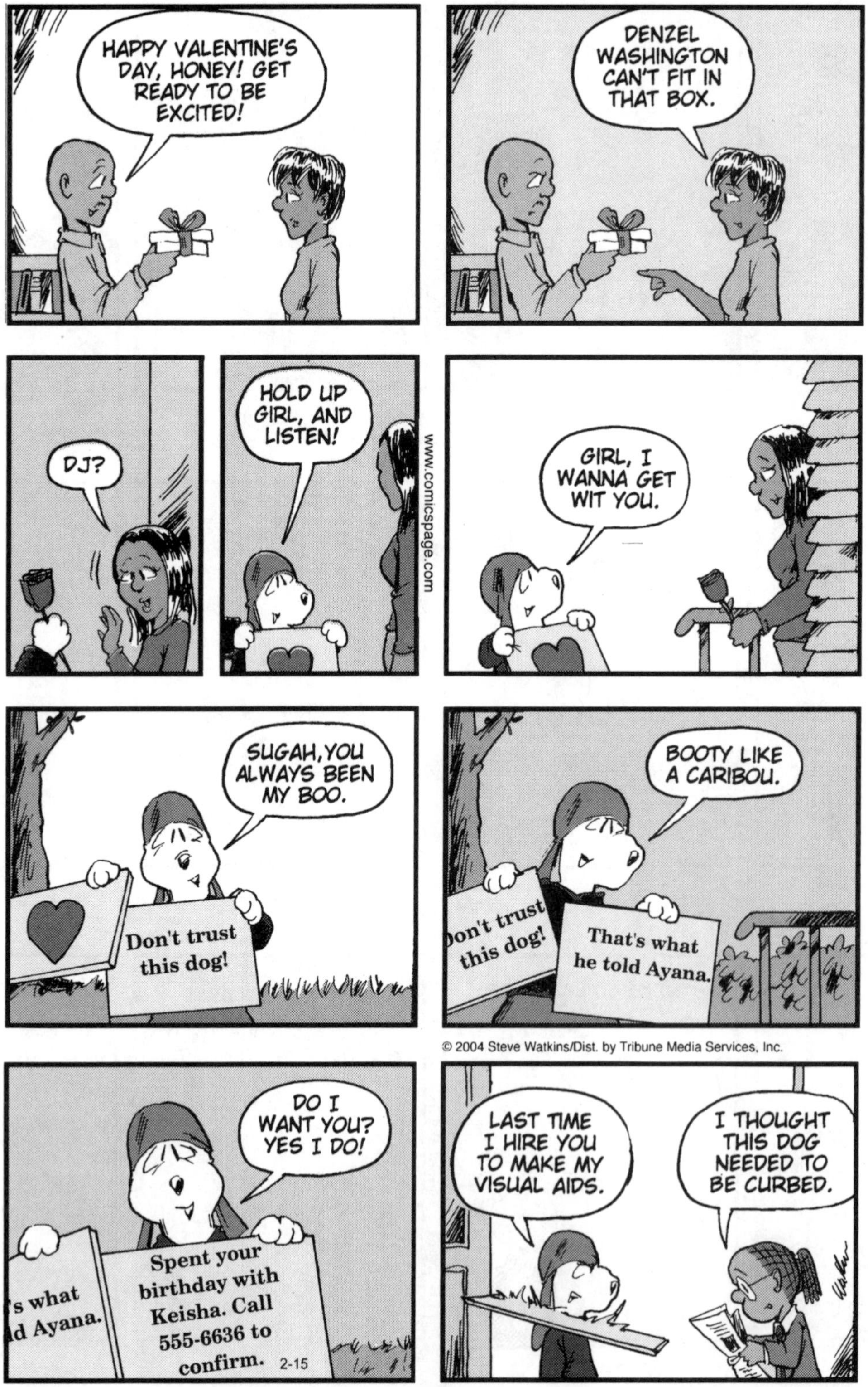
HAPPY VALENTINE'S DAY, HONEY! GET READY TO BE EXCITED!
DENZEL WASHINGTON CAN'T FIT IN THAT BOX.
DJ?
HOLD UP GIRL, AND LISTEN!
www.comicspage.com
GIRL, I WANNA GET WIT YOU.
SUGAH, YOU ALWAYS BEEN MY BOO.
Don't trust this dog!
BOOTY LIKE A CARIBOU.
on't trust this dog!
That's what he told Ayana.
DO I WANT YOU? YES I DO!
's what
d Ayana.
Spent your birthday with Keisha. Call 555-6636 to confirm.
2-15
LAST TIME I HIRE YOU TO MAKE MY VISUAL AIDS.
I THOUGHT THIS DOG NEEDED TO BE CURBED.

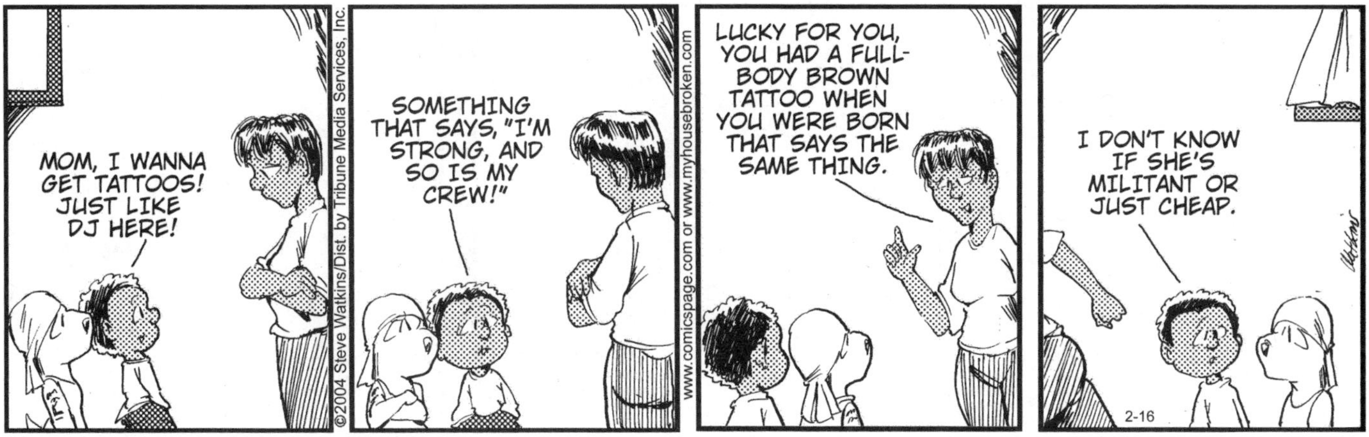
MOM, I WANNA GET TATTOOS! JUST LIKE DJ HERE!
©2004 Steve Watkins/Dist. by Tribune Media Services, Inc.
SOMETHING THAT SAYS, "I'M STRONG, AND SO IS MY CREW!"
www.comicspage.com or www.myhousebroken.com
LUCKY FOR YOU, YOU HAD A FULL-BODY BROWN TATTOO WHEN YOU WERE BORN THAT SAYS THE SAME THING.
I DON'T KNOW IF SHE'S MILITANT OR JUST CHEAP.
2-16

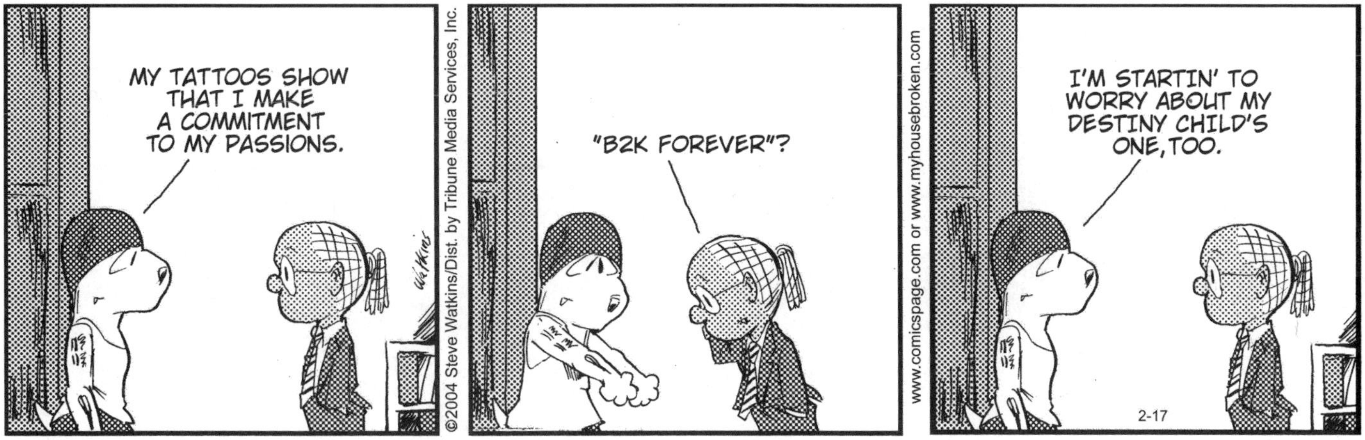
MY TATTOOS SHOW THAT I MAKE A COMMITMENT TO MY PASSIONS.
©2004 Steve Watkins/Dist. by Tribune Media Services, Inc.
"B2K FOREVER"?
www.comicspage.com or www.myhousebroken.com
I'M STARTIN' TO WORRY ABOUT MY DESTINY CHILD'S ONE, TOO.
2-17

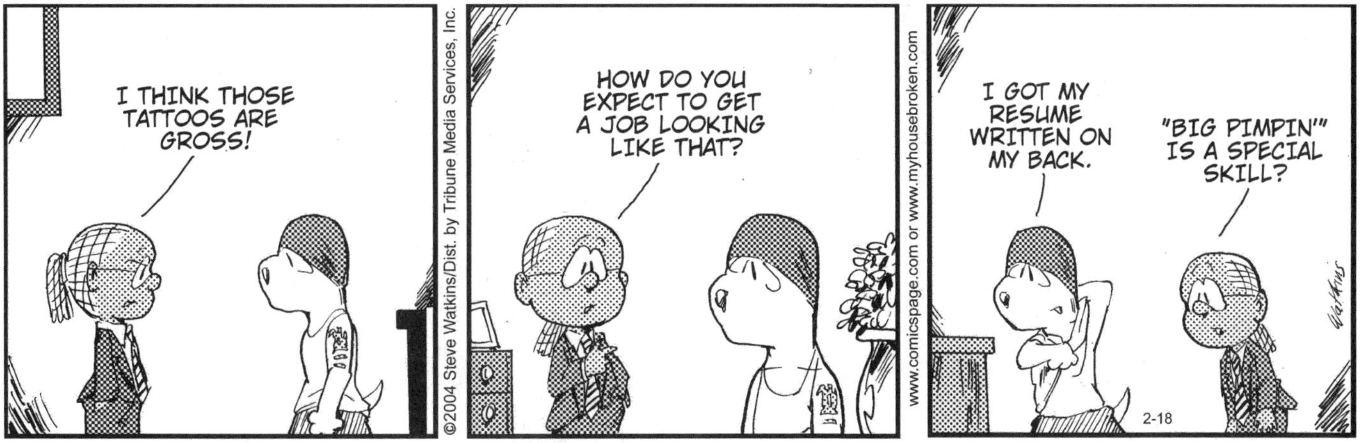
I THINK THOSE TATTOOS ARE GROSS!
©2004 Steve Watkins/Dist. by Tribune Media Services, Inc.
HOW DO YOU EXPECT TO GET A JOB LOOKING LIKE THAT?
www.comicspage.com or www.myhousebroken.com
I GOT MY RESUME WRITTEN ON MY BACK.
"BIG PIMPIN'" IS A SPECIAL SKILL?
2-18

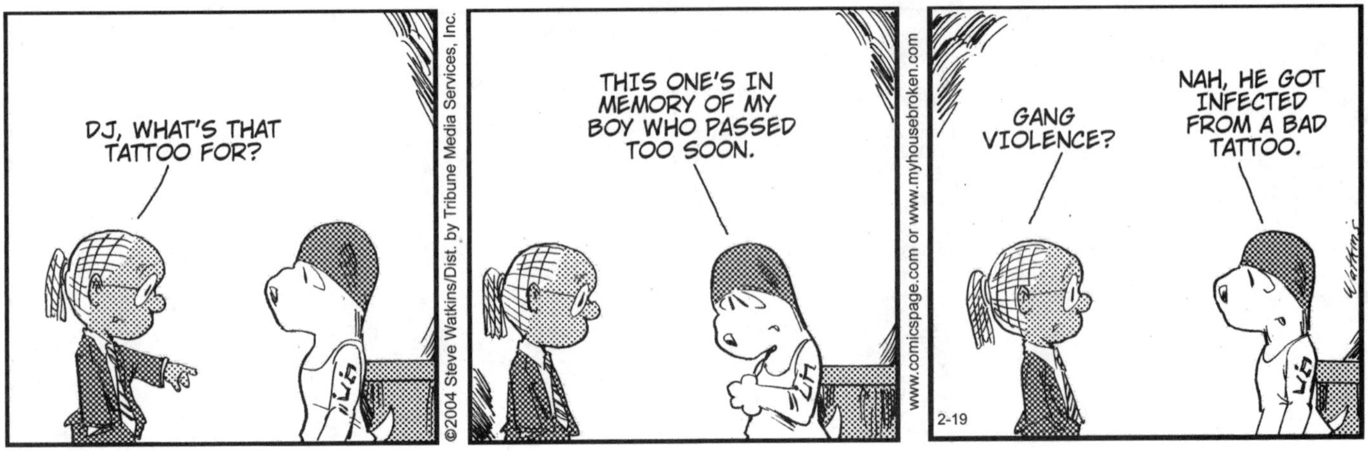
DJ, WHAT'S THAT TATTOO FOR?
©2004 Steve Watkins/Dist. by Tribune Media Services, Inc.
THIS ONE'S IN MEMORY OF MY BOY WHO PASSED TOO SOON.
www.comicspage.com or www.myhousebroken.com
GANG VIOLENCE?
NAH, HE GOT INFECTED FROM A BAD TATTOO.
2-19

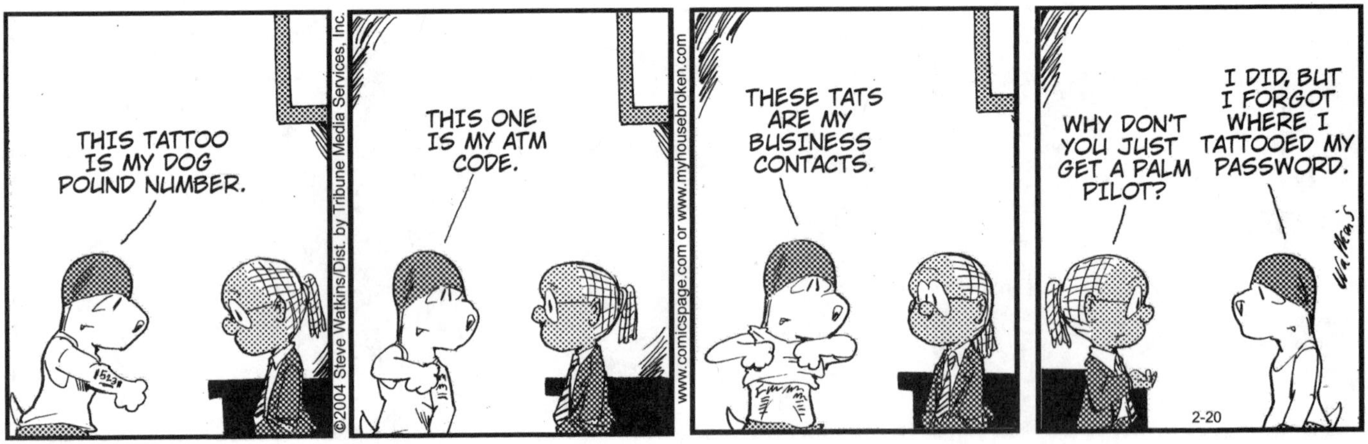
THIS TATTOO IS MY DOG POUND NUMBER.
©2004 Steve Watkins/Dist. by Tribune Media Services, Inc.
THIS ONE IS MY ATM CODE.
www.comicspage.com or www.myhousebroken.com
THESE TATS ARE MY BUSINESS CONTACTS.
WHY DON'T YOU JUST GET A PALM PILOT?
I DID, BUT I FORGOT WHERE I TATTOOED MY PASSWORD.
2-20

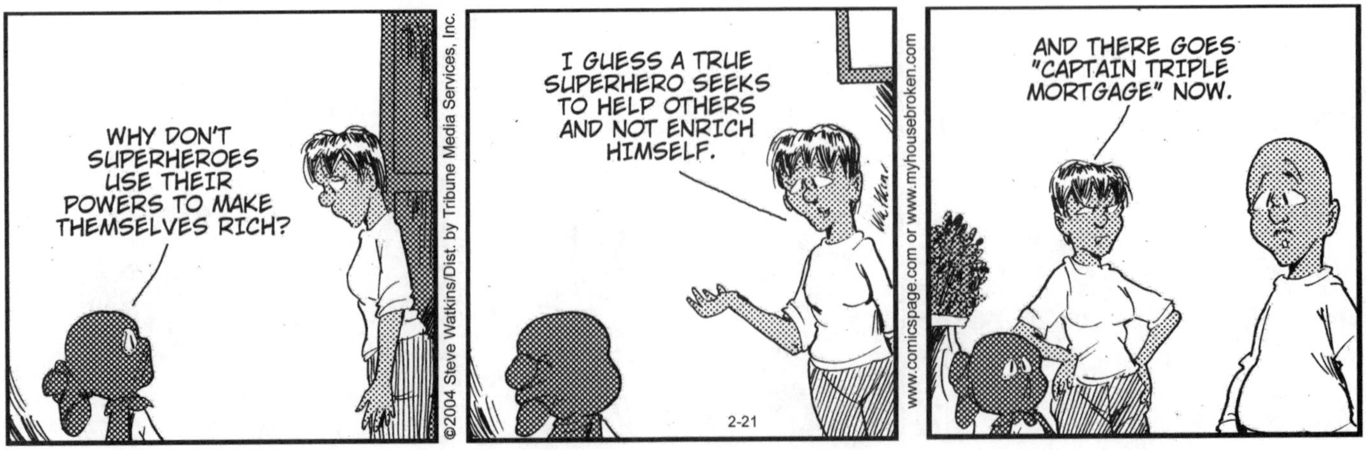
WHY DON'T SUPERHEROES USE THEIR POWERS TO MAKE THEMSELVES RICH?
©2004 Steve Watkins/Dist. by Tribune Media Services, Inc.
I GUESS A TRUE SUPERHERO SEEKS TO HELP OTHERS AND NOT ENRICH HIMSELF.
2-21
www.comicspage.com or www.myhousebroken.com
AND THERE GOES "CAPTAIN TRIPLE MORTGAGE" NOW.

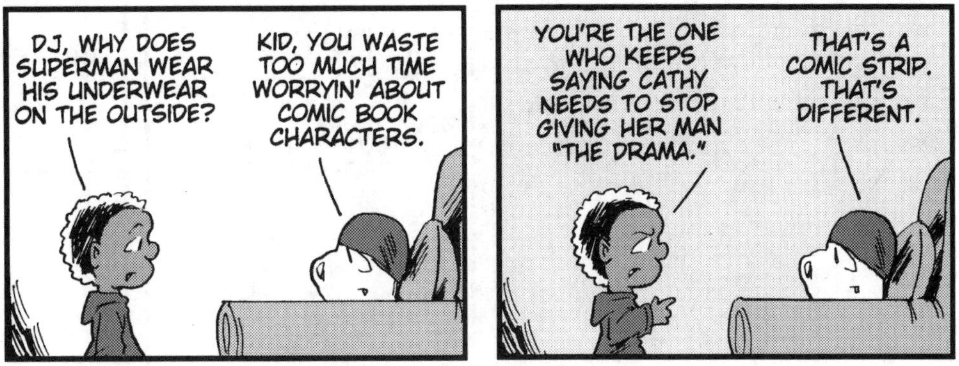
DJ, WHY DOES SUPERMAN WEAR HIS UNDERWEAR ON THE OUTSIDE?
KID, YOU WASTE TOO MUCH TIME WORRYIN' ABOUT COMIC BOOK CHARACTERS.
YOU'RE THE ONE WHO KEEPS SAYING CATHY NEEDS TO STOP GIVING HER MAN "THE DRAMA."
THAT'S A COMIC STRIP. THAT'S DIFFERENT.

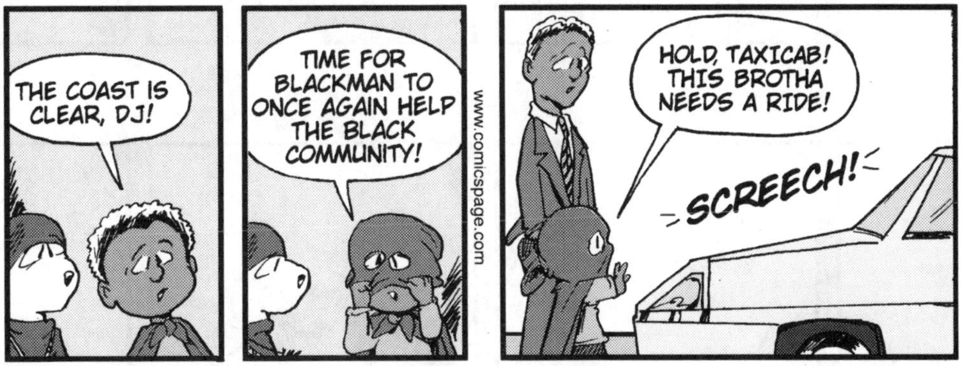
THE COAST IS CLEAR, DJ!
TIME FOR BLACKMAN TO ONCE AGAIN HELP THE BLACK COMMUNITY!
www.comicspage.com
HOLD, TAXICAB! THIS BROTHA NEEDS A RIDE!
SCREECH!

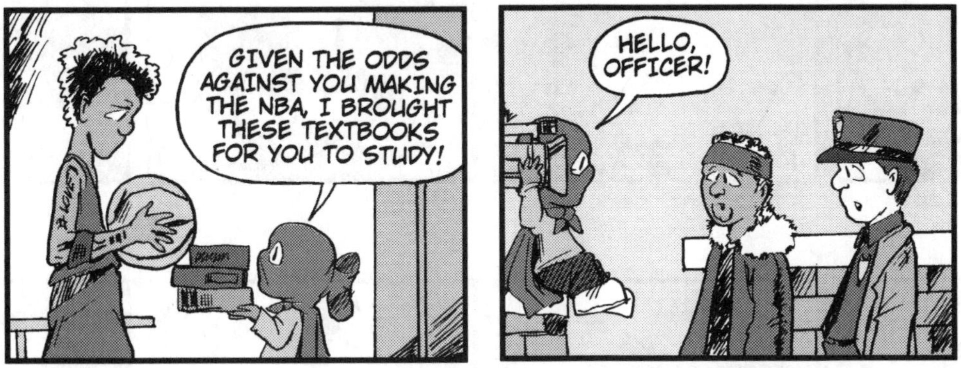
GIVEN THE ODDS AGAINST YOU MAKING THE NBA, I BROUGHT THESE TEXTBOOKS FOR YOU TO STUDY!
HELLO, OFFICER!

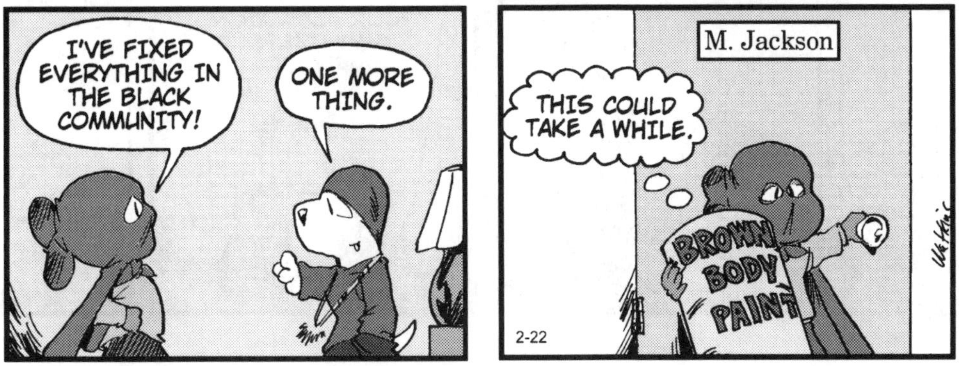
I'VE FIXED EVERYTHING IN THE BLACK COMMUNITY!
ONE MORE THING.
M. Jackson
THIS COULD TAKE A WHILE.
BROWN BODY PAINT
2-22

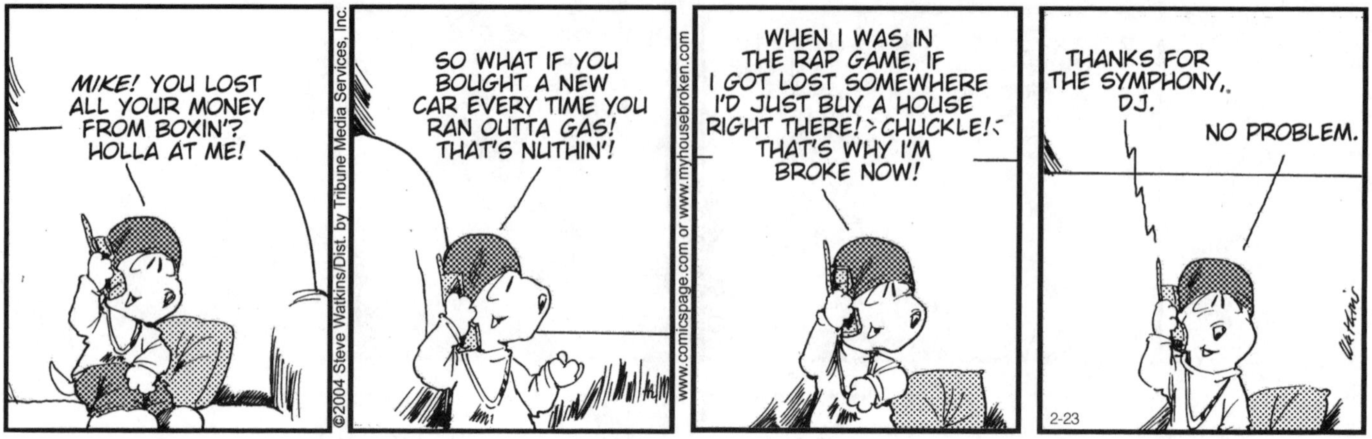

MIKE! YOU LOST ALL YOUR MONEY FROM BOXIN'? HOLLA AT ME!
©2004 Steve Watkins/Dist. by Tribune Media Services, Inc.
SO WHAT IF YOU BOUGHT A NEW CAR EVERY TIME YOU RAN OUTTA GAS! THAT'S NUTHIN'!
www.comicspage.com or www.myhousebroken.com
WHEN I WAS IN THE RAP GAME, IF I GOT LOST SOMEWHERE I'D JUST BUY A HOUSE RIGHT THERE! >CHUCKLE!< THAT'S WHY I'M BROKE NOW!
THANKS FOR THE SYMPHONY, DJ.
NO PROBLEM.
Watkins
2-23

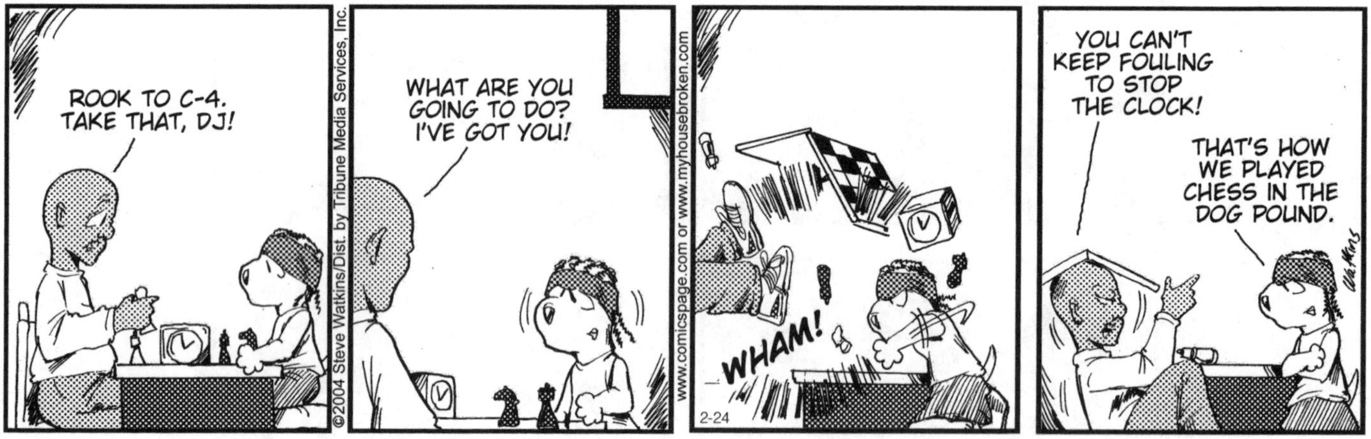

ROOK TO C-4. TAKE THAT, DJ!
©2004 Steve Watkins/Dist. by Tribune Media Services, Inc.
WHAT ARE YOU GOING TO DO? I'VE GOT YOU!
www.comicspage.com or www.myhousebroken.com
WHAM!
2-24
YOU CAN'T KEEP FOULING TO STOP THE CLOCK!
THAT'S HOW WE PLAYED CHESS IN THE DOG POUND.
Watkins

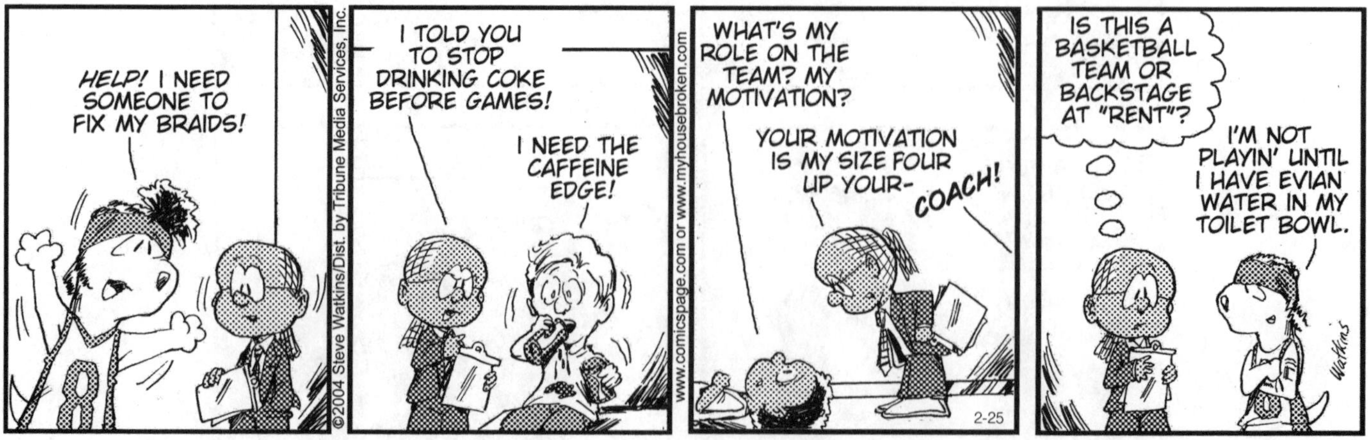

HELP! I NEED SOMEONE TO FIX MY BRAIDS!
©2004 Steve Watkins/Dist. by Tribune Media Services, Inc.
I TOLD YOU TO STOP DRINKING COKE BEFORE GAMES!
I NEED THE CAFFEINE EDGE!
www.comicspage.com or www.myhousebroken.com
WHAT'S MY ROLE ON THE TEAM? MY MOTIVATION?
YOUR MOTIVATION IS MY SIZE FOUR UP YOUR-
COACH!
2-25
IS THIS A BASKETBALL TEAM OR BACKSTAGE AT "RENT"?
I'M NOT PLAYIN' UNTIL I HAVE EVIAN WATER IN MY TOILET BOWL.
Watkins

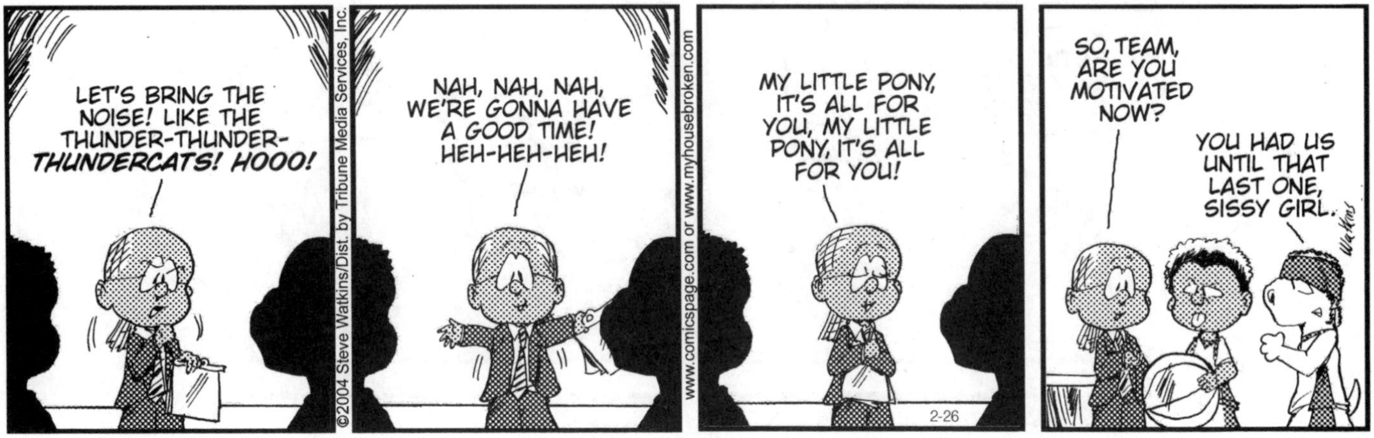
LET'S BRING THE NOISE! LIKE THE THUNDER-THUNDER-*THUNDERCATS! HOOO!*
NAH, NAH, NAH, WE'RE GONNA HAVE A GOOD TIME! HEH-HEH-HEH!
MY LITTLE PONY, IT'S ALL FOR YOU, MY LITTLE PONY, IT'S ALL FOR YOU!
SO, TEAM, ARE YOU MOTIVATED NOW?
YOU HAD US UNTIL THAT LAST ONE, SISSY GIRL.
©2004 Steve Watkins/Dist. by Tribune Media Services, Inc.
www.comicspage.com or www.myhousebroken.com
2-26
Watkins

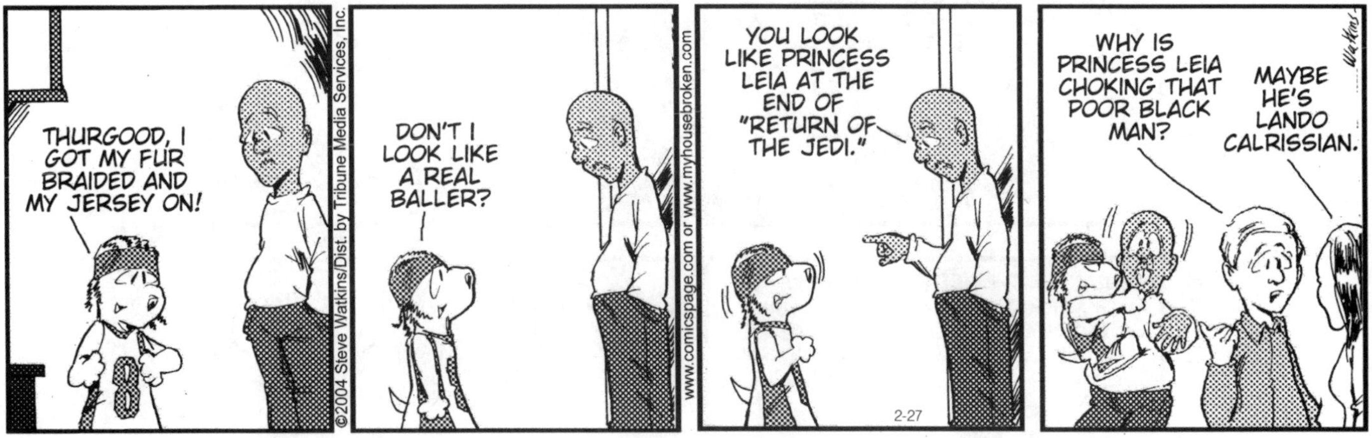
THURGOOD, I GOT MY FUR BRAIDED AND MY JERSEY ON!
DON'T I LOOK LIKE A REAL BALLER?
YOU LOOK LIKE PRINCESS LEIA AT THE END OF "RETURN OF THE JEDI."
WHY IS PRINCESS LEIA CHOKING THAT POOR BLACK MAN?
MAYBE HE'S LANDO CALRISSIAN.
©2004 Steve Watkins/Dist. by Tribune Media Services, Inc.
www.comicspage.com or www.myhousebroken.com
2-27
Watkins

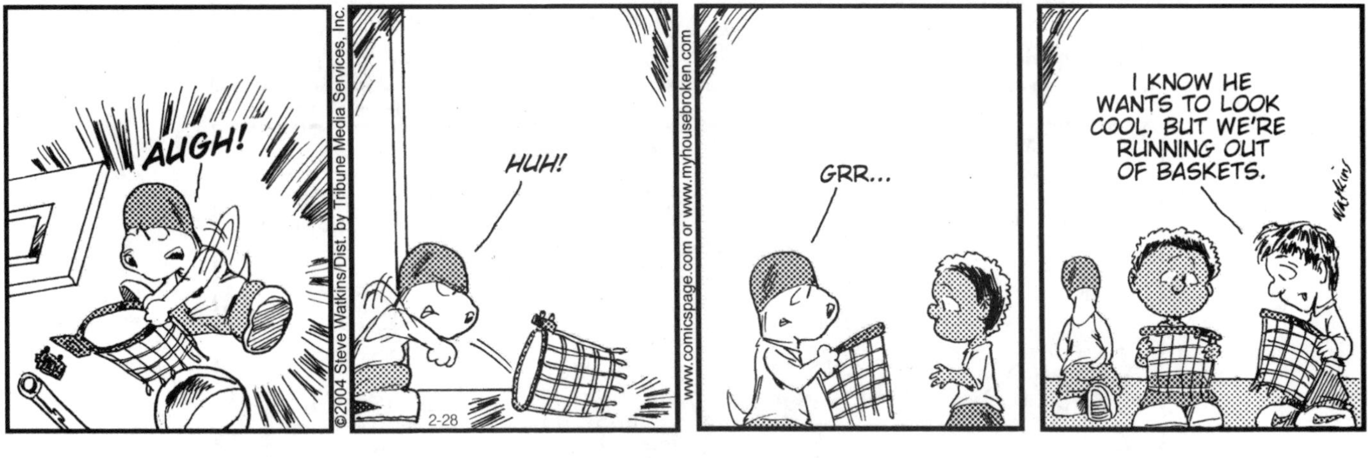
AUGH!
HUH!
GRR...
I KNOW HE WANTS TO LOOK COOL, BUT WE'RE RUNNING OUT OF BASKETS.
©2004 Steve Watkins/Dist. by Tribune Media Services, Inc.
www.comicspage.com or www.myhousebroken.com
2-28
Watkins

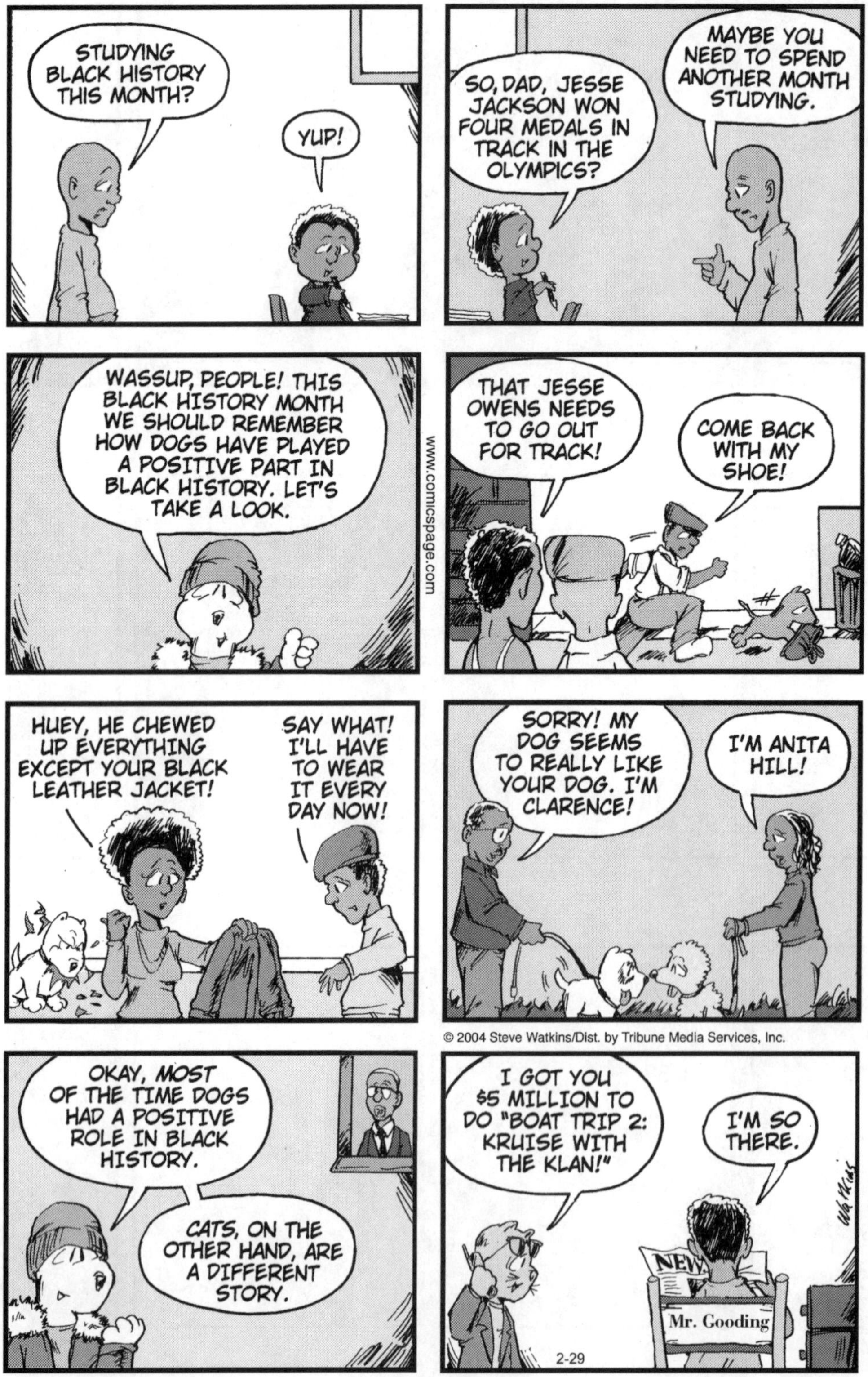
STUDYING BLACK HISTORY THIS MONTH?
YUP!
SO, DAD, JESSE JACKSON WON FOUR MEDALS IN TRACK IN THE OLYMPICS?
MAYBE YOU NEED TO SPEND ANOTHER MONTH STUDYING.
www.comicspage.com
WASSUP, PEOPLE! THIS BLACK HISTORY MONTH WE SHOULD REMEMBER HOW DOGS HAVE PLAYED A POSITIVE PART IN BLACK HISTORY. LET'S TAKE A LOOK.
THAT JESSE OWENS NEEDS TO GO OUT FOR TRACK!
COME BACK WITH MY SHOE!
HUEY, HE CHEWED UP EVERYTHING EXCEPT YOUR BLACK LEATHER JACKET!
SAY WHAT! I'LL HAVE TO WEAR IT EVERY DAY NOW!
SORRY! MY DOG SEEMS TO REALLY LIKE YOUR DOG. I'M CLARENCE!
I'M ANITA HILL!
© 2004 Steve Watkins/Dist. by Tribune Media Services, Inc.
OKAY, MOST OF THE TIME DOGS HAD A POSITIVE ROLE IN BLACK HISTORY.
CATS, ON THE OTHER HAND, ARE A DIFFERENT STORY.
I GOT YOU $5 MILLION TO DO "BOAT TRIP 2: KRUISE WITH THE KLAN!"
I'M SO THERE.
NEWS
Mr. Gooding
2-29

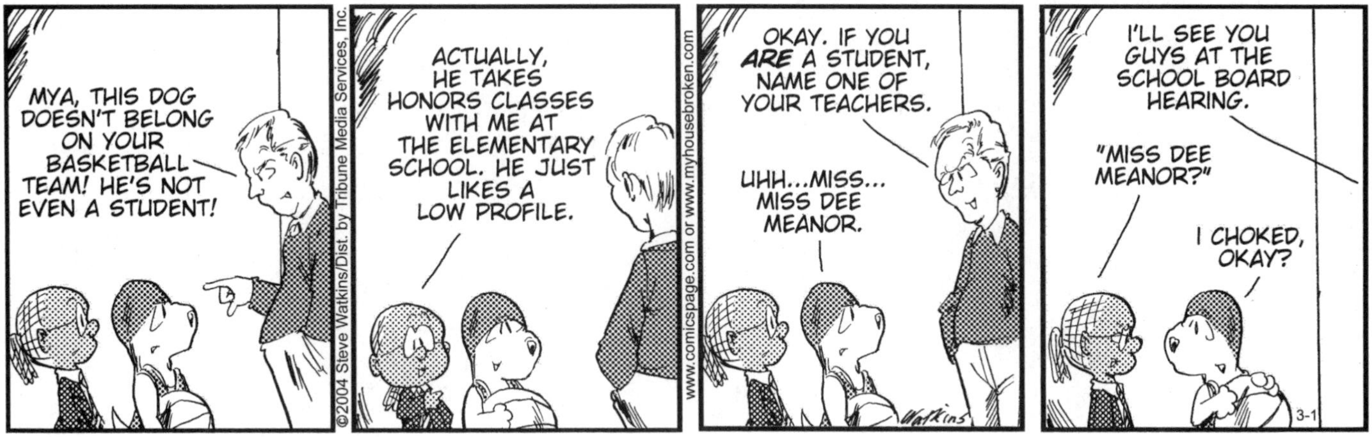
MYA, THIS DOG DOESN'T BELONG ON YOUR BASKETBALL TEAM! HE'S NOT EVEN A STUDENT!
©2004 Steve Watkins/Dist. by Tribune Media Services, Inc.
ACTUALLY, HE TAKES HONORS CLASSES WITH ME AT THE ELEMENTARY SCHOOL. HE JUST LIKES A LOW PROFILE.
www.comicspage.com or www.myhousebroken.com
OKAY. IF YOU ***ARE*** A STUDENT, NAME ONE OF YOUR TEACHERS.
UHH...MISS... MISS DEE MEANOR.
WATKINS
I'LL SEE YOU GUYS AT THE SCHOOL BOARD HEARING.
"MISS DEE MEANOR?"
I CHOKED, OKAY?
3-1

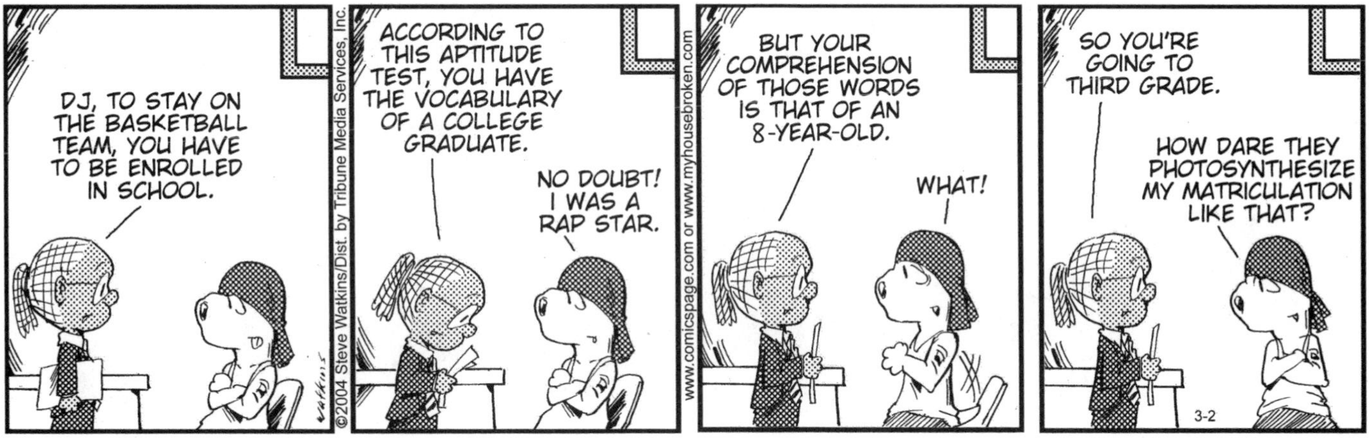
DJ, TO STAY ON THE BASKETBALL TEAM, YOU HAVE TO BE ENROLLED IN SCHOOL.
WATKINS
©2004 Steve Watkins/Dist. by Tribune Media Services, Inc.
ACCORDING TO THIS APTITUDE TEST, YOU HAVE THE VOCABULARY OF A COLLEGE GRADUATE.
NO DOUBT! I WAS A RAP STAR.
www.comicspage.com or www.myhousebroken.com
BUT YOUR COMPREHENSION OF THOSE WORDS IS THAT OF AN 8-YEAR-OLD.
WHAT!
SO YOU'RE GOING TO THIRD GRADE.
HOW DARE THEY PHOTOSYNTHESIZE MY MATRICULATION LIKE THAT?
3-2

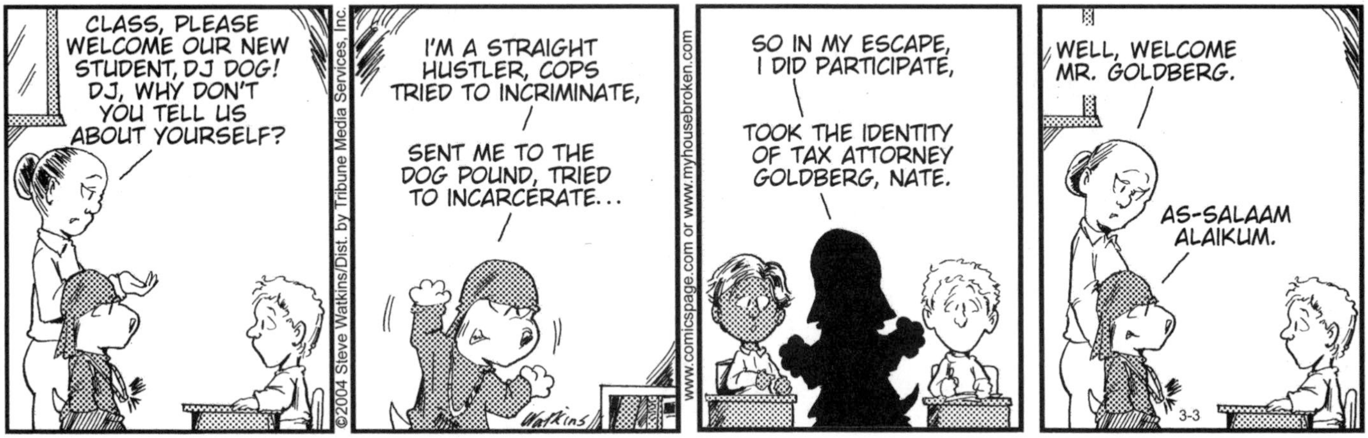
CLASS, PLEASE WELCOME OUR NEW STUDENT, DJ DOG! DJ, WHY DON'T YOU TELL US ABOUT YOURSELF?
©2004 Steve Watkins/Dist. by Tribune Media Services, Inc.
I'M A STRAIGHT HUSTLER, COPS TRIED TO INCRIMINATE,
SENT ME TO THE DOG POUND, TRIED TO INCARCERATE...
WATKINS
www.comicspage.com or www.myhousebroken.com
SO IN MY ESCAPE, I DID PARTICIPATE,
TOOK THE IDENTITY OF TAX ATTORNEY GOLDBERG, NATE.
WELL, WELCOME MR. GOLDBERG.
AS-SALAAM ALAIKUM.
3-3

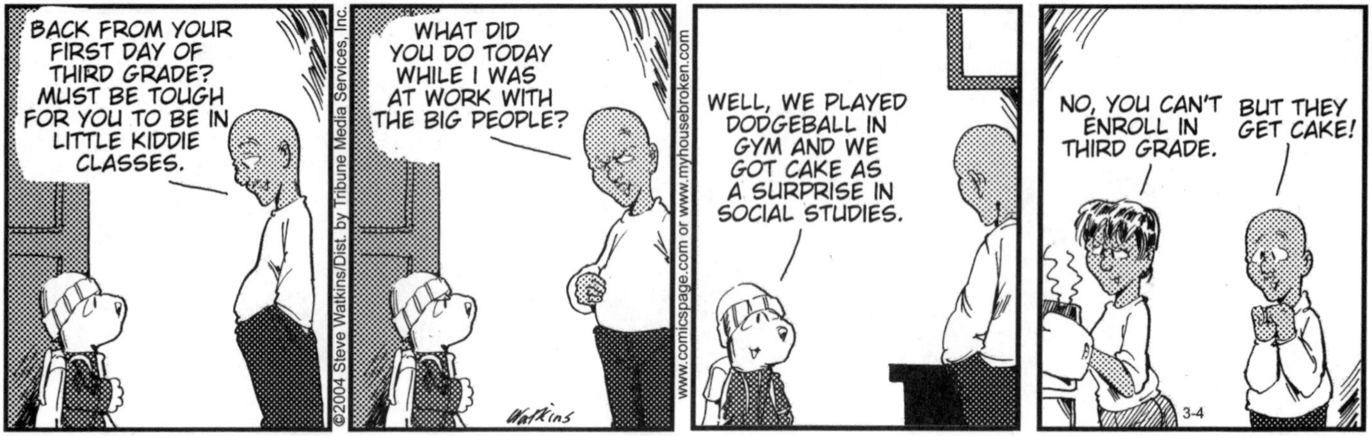
BACK FROM YOUR FIRST DAY OF THIRD GRADE? MUST BE TOUGH FOR YOU TO BE IN LITTLE KIDDIE CLASSES.
©2004 Steve Watkins/Dist. by Tribune Media Services, Inc.
WHAT DID YOU DO TODAY WHILE I WAS AT WORK WITH THE BIG PEOPLE?
Watkins
www.comicspage.com or www.myhousebroken.com
WELL, WE PLAYED DODGEBALL IN GYM AND WE GOT CAKE AS A SURPRISE IN SOCIAL STUDIES.
NO, YOU CAN'T ENROLL IN THIRD GRADE.
BUT THEY GET CAKE!
3-4

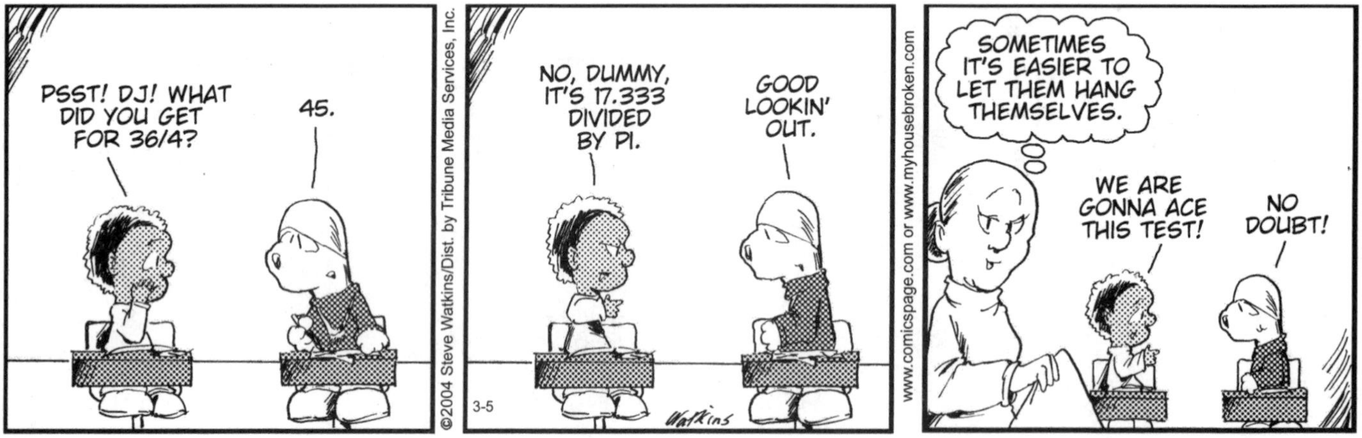
PSST! DJ! WHAT DID YOU GET FOR 36/4?
45.
©2004 Steve Watkins/Dist. by Tribune Media Services, Inc.
3-5
NO, DUMMY, IT'S 17.333 DIVIDED BY PI.
GOOD LOOKIN' OUT.
Watkins
www.comicspage.com or www.myhousebroken.com
SOMETIMES IT'S EASIER TO LET THEM HANG THEMSELVES.
WE ARE GONNA ACE THIS TEST!
NO DOUBT!

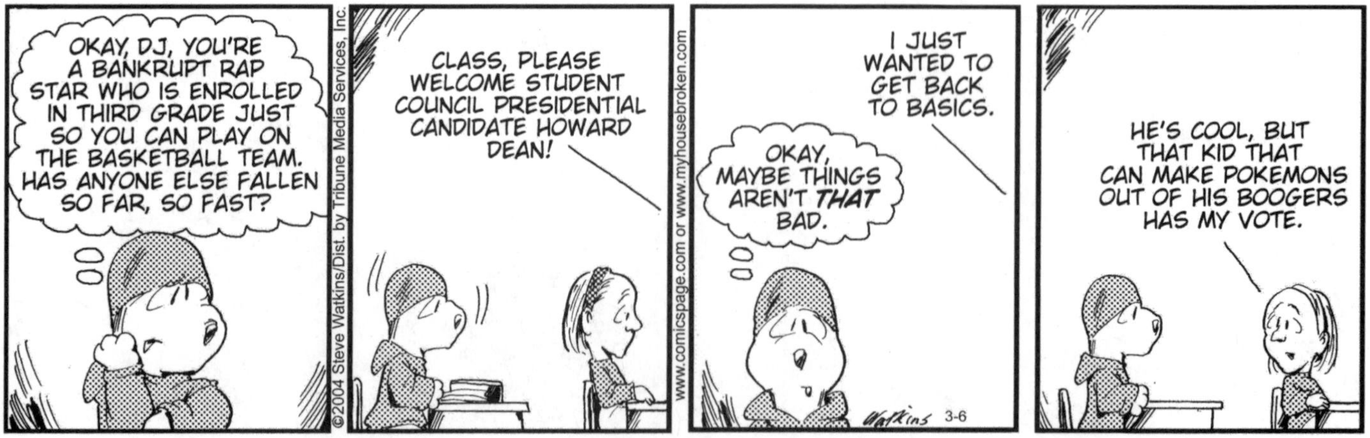
OKAY, DJ, YOU'RE A BANKRUPT RAP STAR WHO IS ENROLLED IN THIRD GRADE JUST SO YOU CAN PLAY ON THE BASKETBALL TEAM. HAS ANYONE ELSE FALLEN SO FAR, SO FAST?
©2004 Steve Watkins/Dist. by Tribune Media Services, Inc.
CLASS, PLEASE WELCOME STUDENT COUNCIL PRESIDENTIAL CANDIDATE HOWARD DEAN!
www.comicspage.com or www.myhousebroken.com
I JUST WANTED TO GET BACK TO BASICS.
OKAY, MAYBE THINGS AREN'T ***THAT*** BAD.
Watkins
3-6
HE'S COOL, BUT THAT KID THAT CAN MAKE POKEMONS OUT OF HIS BOOGERS HAS MY VOTE.

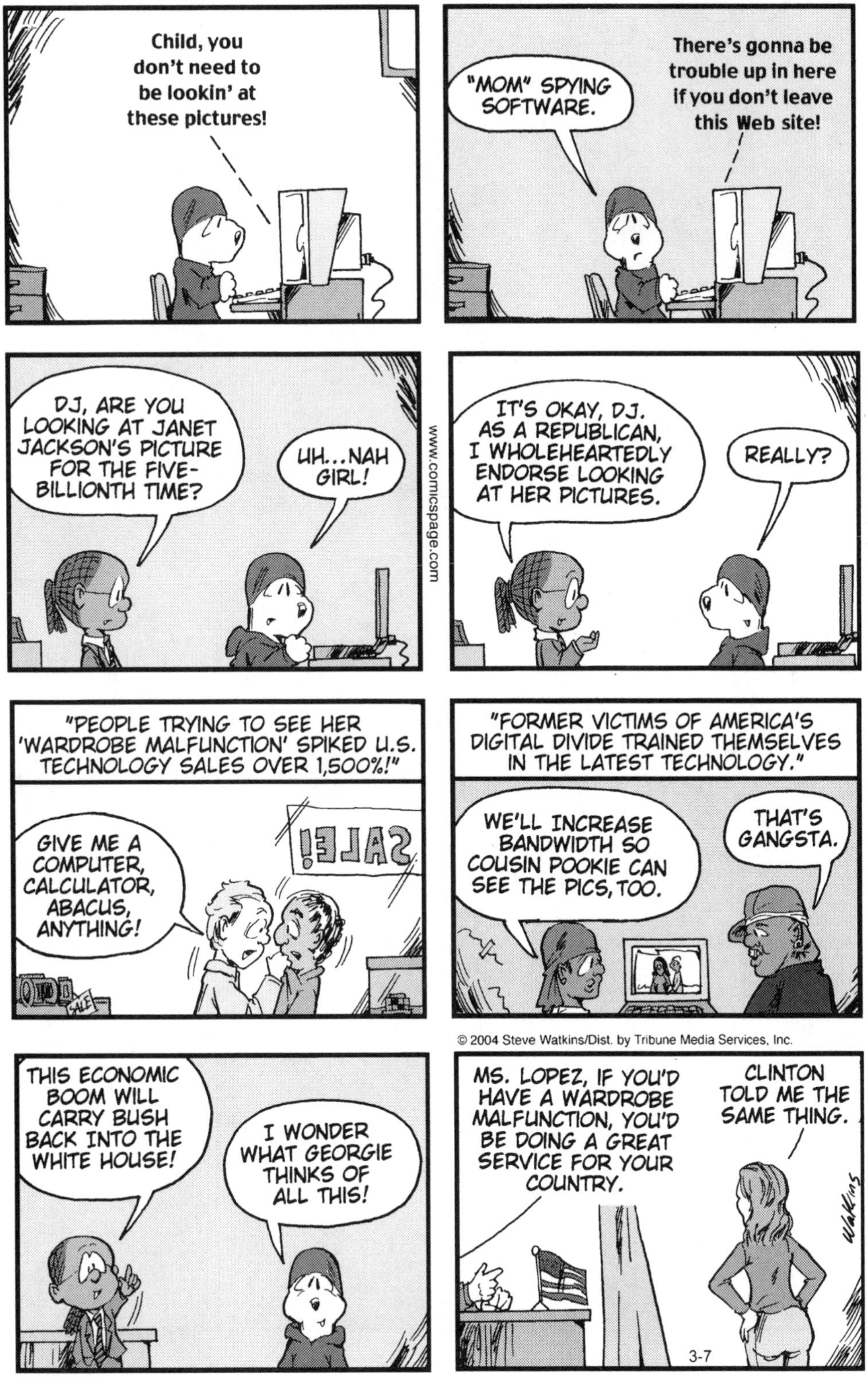

Child, you don't need to be lookin' at these pictures!
"MOM" SPYING SOFTWARE.
There's gonna be trouble up in here if you don't leave this Web site!
DJ, ARE YOU LOOKING AT JANET JACKSON'S PICTURE FOR THE FIVE-BILLIONTH TIME?
UH...NAH GIRL!
www.comicspage.com
IT'S OKAY, DJ. AS A REPUBLICAN, I WHOLEHEARTEDLY ENDORSE LOOKING AT HER PICTURES.
REALLY?
"PEOPLE TRYING TO SEE HER 'WARDROBE MALFUNCTION' SPIKED U.S. TECHNOLOGY SALES OVER 1,500%!"
GIVE ME A COMPUTER, CALCULATOR, ABACUS, ANYTHING!
"FORMER VICTIMS OF AMERICA'S DIGITAL DIVIDE TRAINED THEMSELVES IN THE LATEST TECHNOLOGY."
WE'LL INCREASE BANDWIDTH SO COUSIN POOKIE CAN SEE THE PICS, TOO.
THAT'S GANGSTA.
© 2004 Steve Watkins/Dist. by Tribune Media Services, Inc.
THIS ECONOMIC BOOM WILL CARRY BUSH BACK INTO THE WHITE HOUSE!
I WONDER WHAT GEORGIE THINKS OF ALL THIS!
MS. LOPEZ, IF YOU'D HAVE A WARDROBE MALFUNCTION, YOU'D BE DOING A GREAT SERVICE FOR YOUR COUNTRY.
CLINTON TOLD ME THE SAME THING.
Watkins
3-7

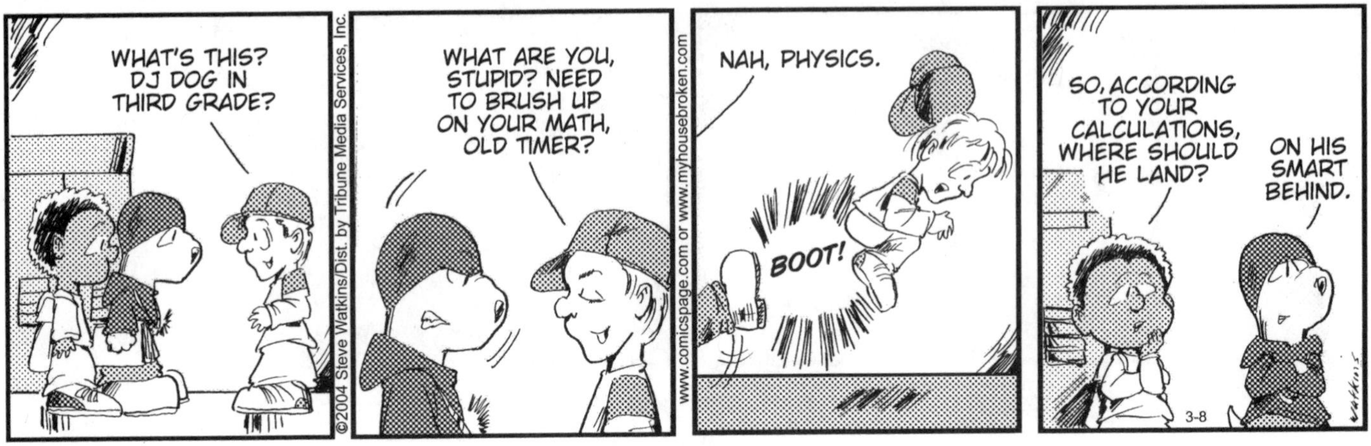
WHAT'S THIS? DJ DOG IN THIRD GRADE?
©2004 Steve Watkins/Dist. by Tribune Media Services, Inc.
WHAT ARE YOU, STUPID? NEED TO BRUSH UP ON YOUR MATH, OLD TIMER?
www.comicspage.com or www.myhousebroken.com
NAH, PHYSICS.
BOOT!
SO, ACCORDING TO YOUR CALCULATIONS, WHERE SHOULD HE LAND?
ON HIS SMART BEHIND.
3-8
Watkins

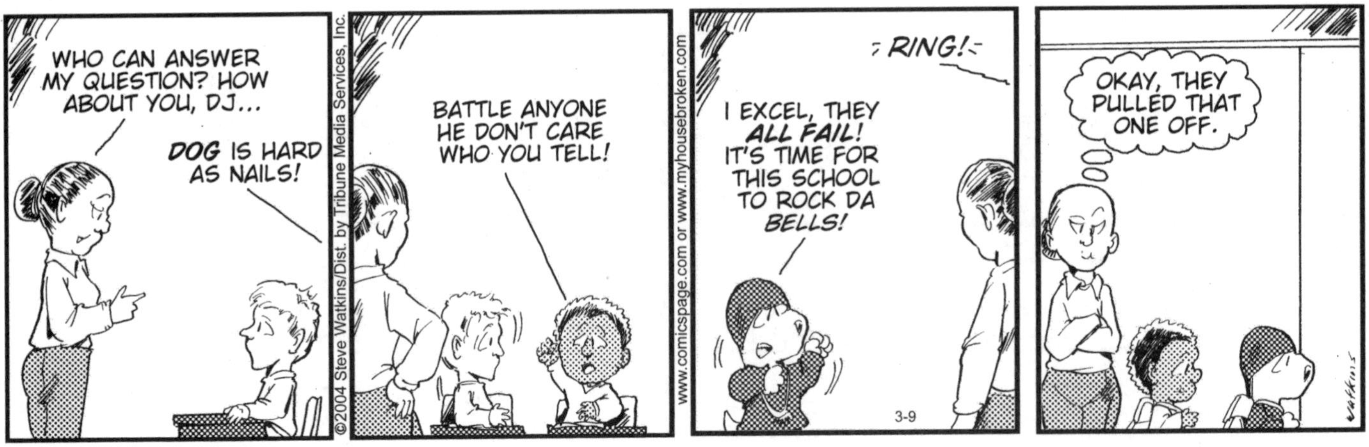
WHO CAN ANSWER MY QUESTION? HOW ABOUT YOU, DJ...
DOG IS HARD AS NAILS!
©2004 Steve Watkins/Dist. by Tribune Media Services, Inc.
BATTLE ANYONE HE DON'T CARE WHO YOU TELL!
www.comicspage.com or www.myhousebroken.com
RING!
I EXCEL, THEY ***ALL FAIL!*** IT'S TIME FOR THIS SCHOOL TO ROCK DA *BELLS!*
3-9
OKAY, THEY PULLED THAT ONE OFF.
Watkins

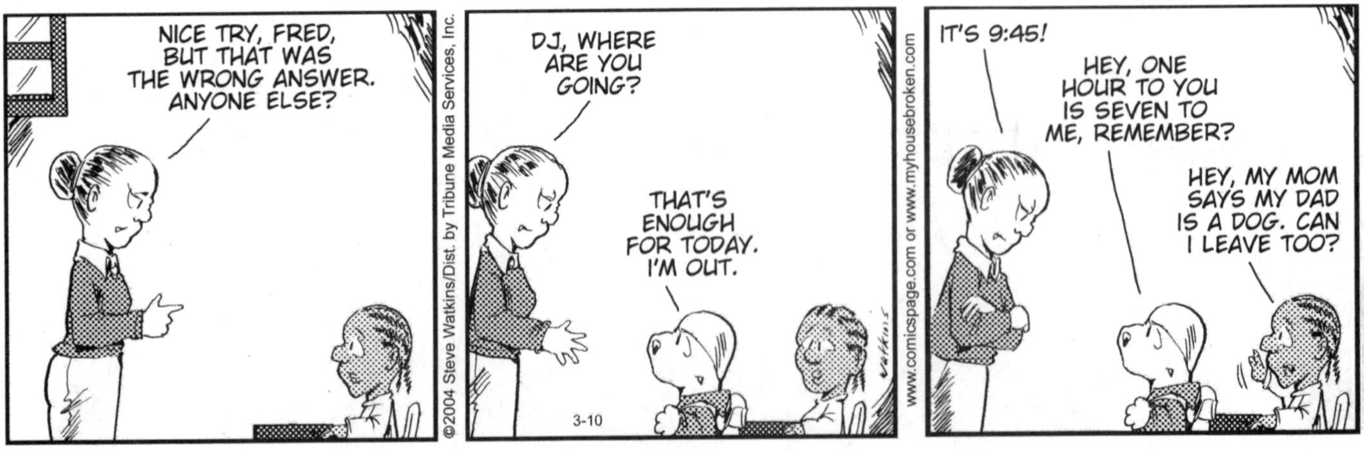
NICE TRY, FRED, BUT THAT WAS THE WRONG ANSWER. ANYONE ELSE?
©2004 Steve Watkins/Dist. by Tribune Media Services, Inc.
DJ, WHERE ARE YOU GOING?
THAT'S ENOUGH FOR TODAY. I'M OUT.
Watkins
3-10
www.comicspage.com or www.myhousebroken.com
IT'S 9:45!
HEY, ONE HOUR TO YOU IS SEVEN TO ME, REMEMBER?
HEY, MY MOM SAYS MY DAD IS A DOG. CAN I LEAVE TOO?

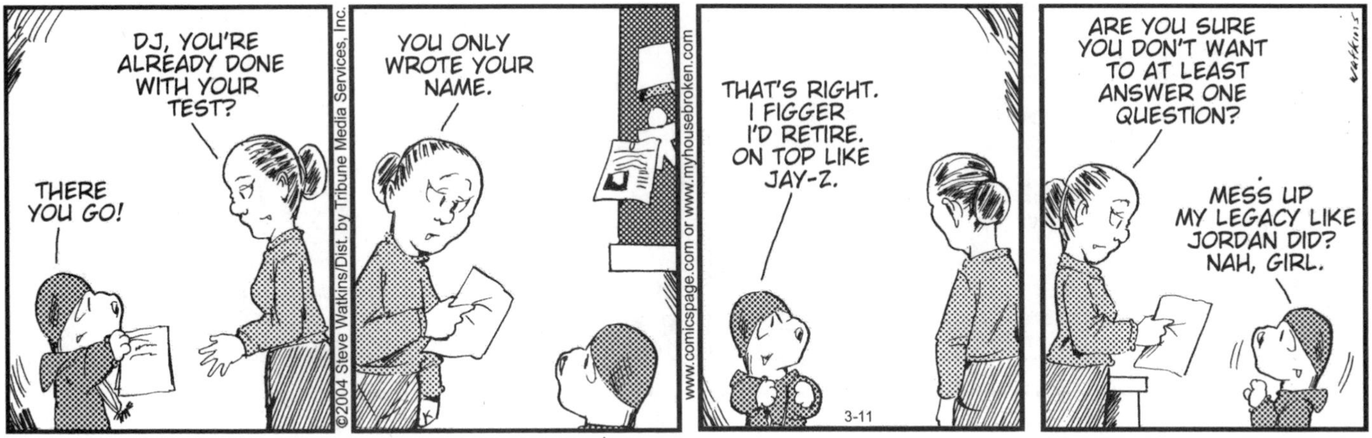
DJ, YOU'RE ALREADY DONE WITH YOUR TEST?
THERE YOU GO!
©2004 Steve Watkins/Dist. by Tribune Media Services, Inc.
YOU ONLY WROTE YOUR NAME.
www.comicspage.com or www.myhousebroken.com
THAT'S RIGHT. I FIGGER I'D RETIRE. ON TOP LIKE JAY-Z.
3-11
ARE YOU SURE YOU DON'T WANT TO AT LEAST ANSWER ONE QUESTION?
MESS UP MY LEGACY LIKE JORDAN DID? NAH, GIRL.
Watkins

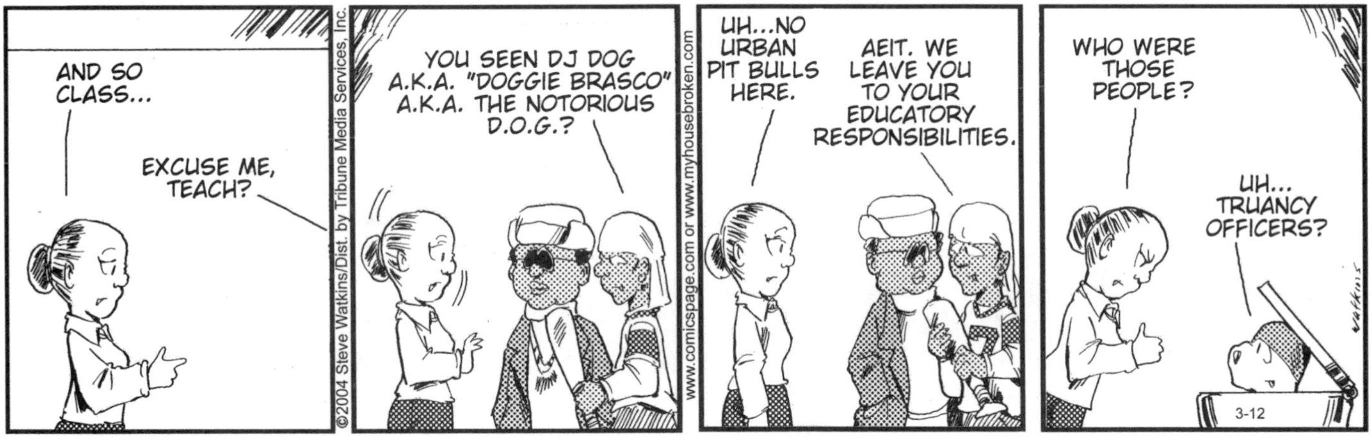
AND SO CLASS...
EXCUSE ME, TEACH?
©2004 Steve Watkins/Dist. by Tribune Media Services, Inc.
YOU SEEN DJ DOG A.K.A. "DOGGIE BRASCO" A.K.A. THE NOTORIOUS D.O.G.?
www.comicspage.com or www.myhousebroken.com
UH...NO URBAN PIT BULLS HERE.
AEIT. WE LEAVE YOU TO YOUR EDUCATORY RESPONSIBILITIES.
WHO WERE THOSE PEOPLE?
UH... TRUANCY OFFICERS?
Watkins
3-12

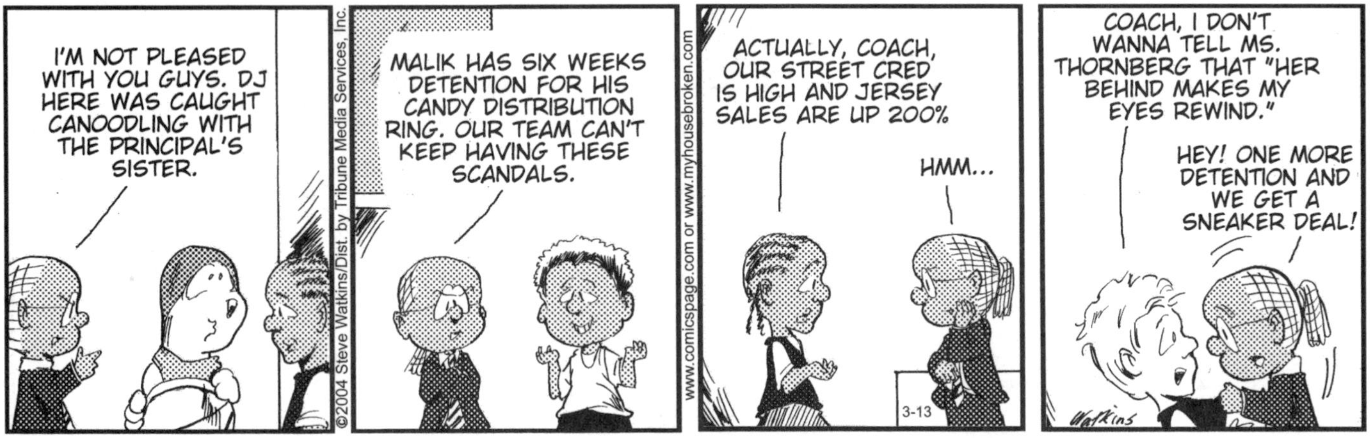
I'M NOT PLEASED WITH YOU GUYS. DJ HERE WAS CAUGHT CANOODLING WITH THE PRINCIPAL'S SISTER.
©2004 Steve Watkins/Dist. by Tribune Media Services, Inc.
MALIK HAS SIX WEEKS DETENTION FOR HIS CANDY DISTRIBUTION RING. OUR TEAM CAN'T KEEP HAVING THESE SCANDALS.
www.comicspage.com or www.myhousebroken.com
ACTUALLY, COACH, OUR STREET CRED IS HIGH AND JERSEY SALES ARE UP 200%
HMM...
3-13
COACH, I DON'T WANNA TELL MS. THORNBERG THAT "HER BEHIND MAKES MY EYES REWIND."
HEY! ONE MORE DETENTION AND WE GET A SNEAKER DEAL!
Watkins

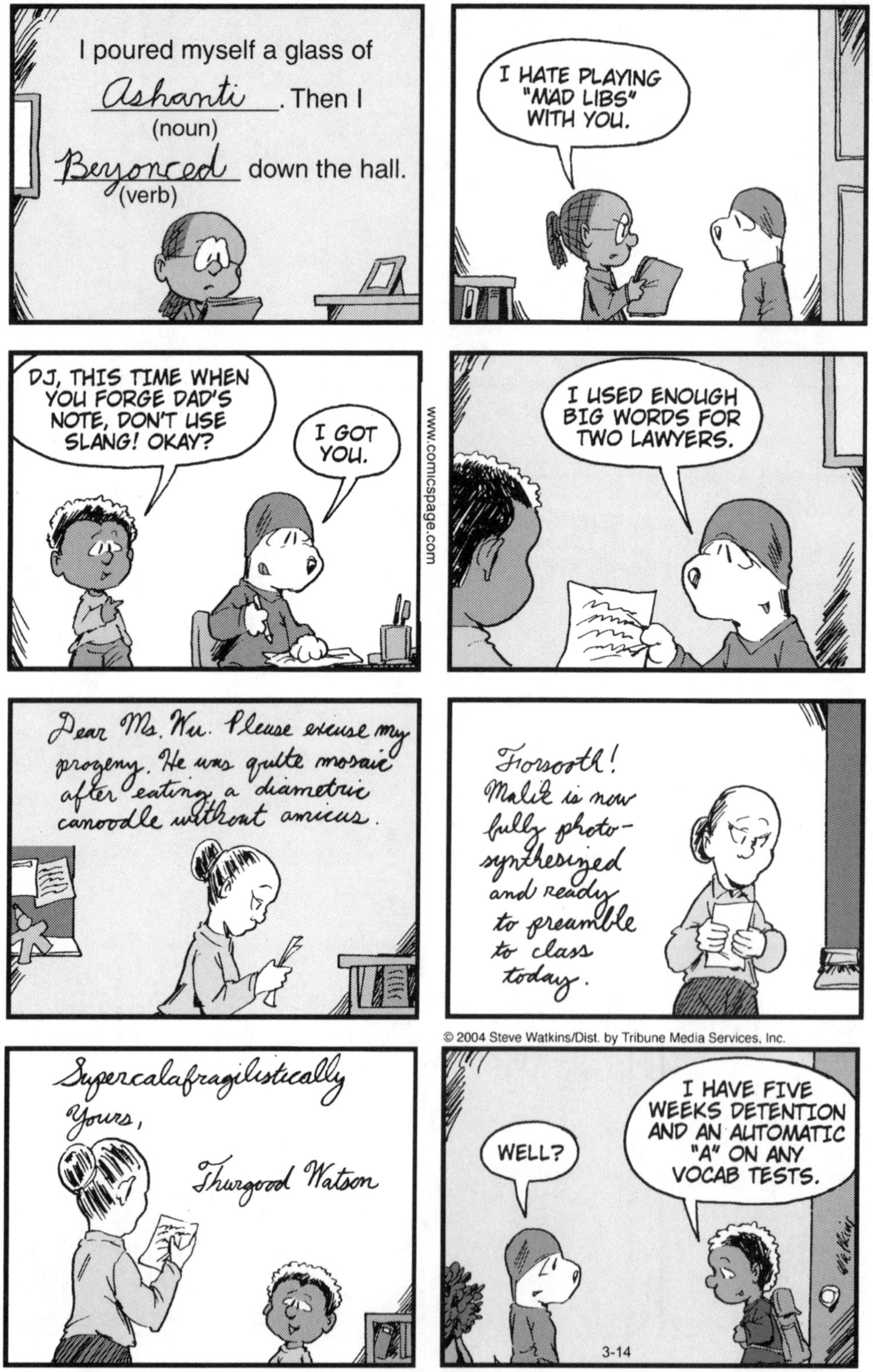

I poured myself a glass of Ashanti. Then I Beyonced down the hall.
(noun)
(verb)
I HATE PLAYING "MAD LIBS" WITH YOU.
DJ, THIS TIME WHEN YOU FORGE DAD'S NOTE, DON'T USE SLANG! OKAY?
I GOT YOU.
www.comicspage.com
I USED ENOUGH BIG WORDS FOR TWO LAWYERS.
Dear Ms. Wu. Please excuse my progeny. He was quite mosaic after eating a diametric canoodle without amicus.
Forsooth! Malik is now fully photo-synthesized and ready to preamble to class today.
Supercalafragilistically Yours,
Thurgood Watson
WELL?
I HAVE FIVE WEEKS DETENTION AND AN AUTOMATIC "A" ON ANY VOCAB TESTS.
3-14

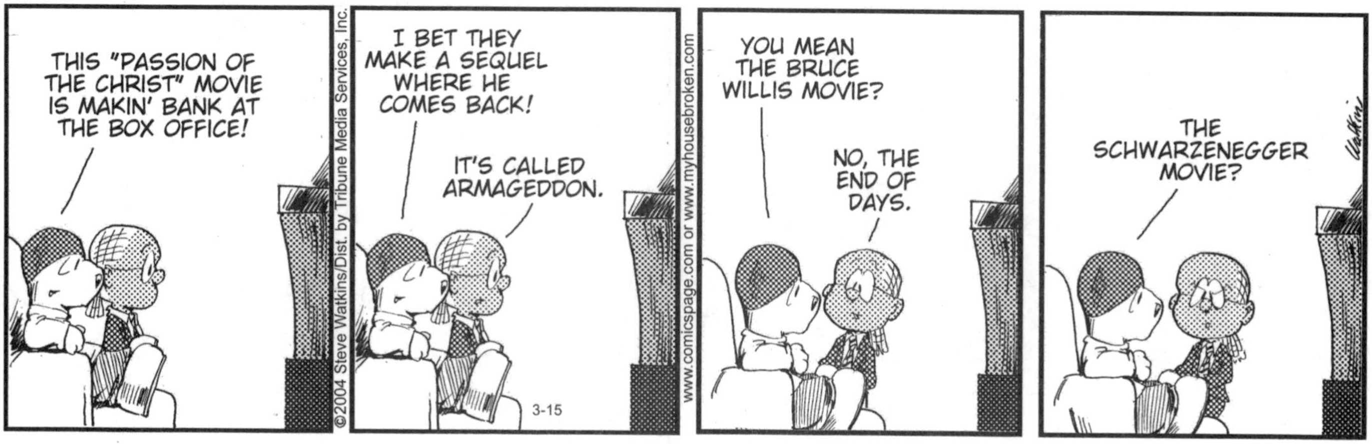
THIS "PASSION OF THE CHRIST" MOVIE IS MAKIN' BANK AT THE BOX OFFICE!
©2004 Steve Watkins/Dist. by Tribune Media Services, Inc.
I BET THEY MAKE A SEQUEL WHERE HE COMES BACK!
IT'S CALLED ARMAGEDDON.
3-15
www.comicspage.com or www.myhousebroken.com
YOU MEAN THE BRUCE WILLIS MOVIE?
NO, THE END OF DAYS.
THE SCHWARZENEGGER MOVIE?

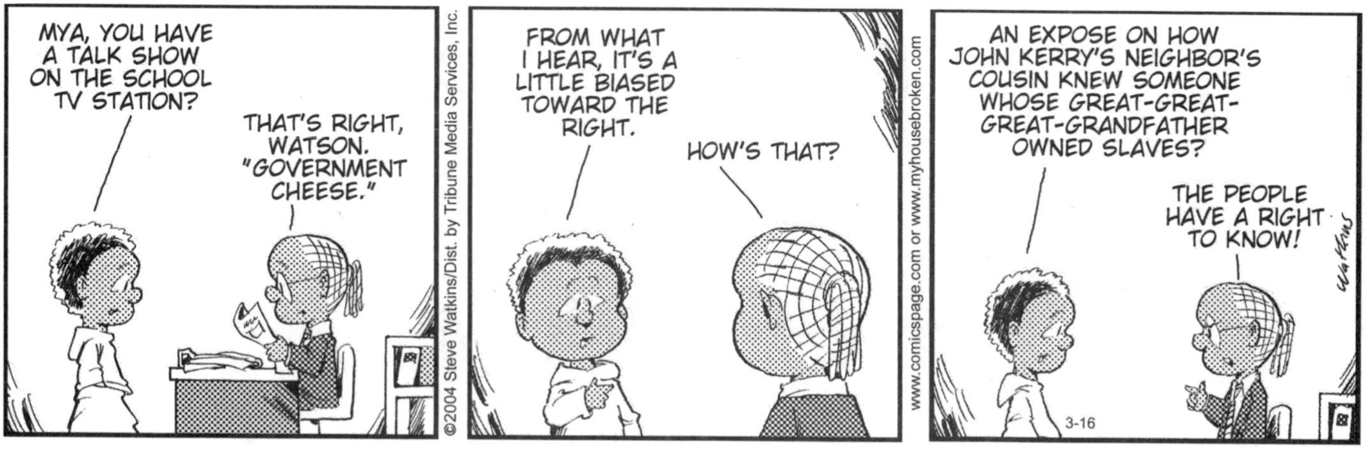
MYA, YOU HAVE A TALK SHOW ON THE SCHOOL TV STATION?
THAT'S RIGHT, WATSON. "GOVERNMENT CHEESE."
©2004 Steve Watkins/Dist. by Tribune Media Services, Inc.
FROM WHAT I HEAR, IT'S A LITTLE BIASED TOWARD THE RIGHT.
HOW'S THAT?
www.comicspage.com or www.myhousebroken.com
AN EXPOSE ON HOW JOHN KERRY'S NEIGHBOR'S COUSIN KNEW SOMEONE WHOSE GREAT-GREAT-GREAT-GRANDFATHER OWNED SLAVES?
THE PEOPLE HAVE A RIGHT TO KNOW!
3-16

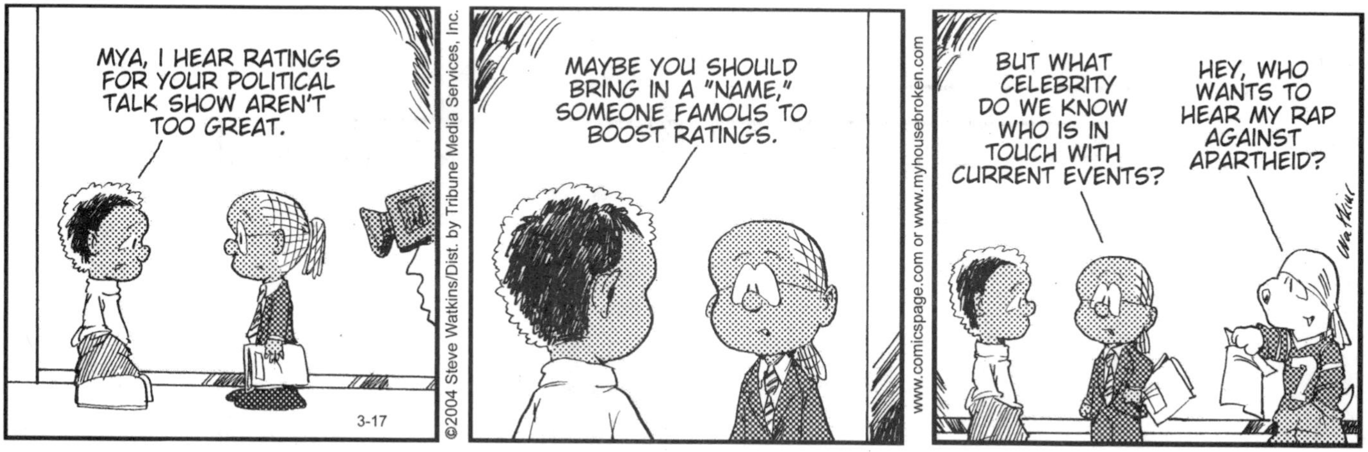
MYA, I HEAR RATINGS FOR YOUR POLITICAL TALK SHOW AREN'T TOO GREAT.
3-17
©2004 Steve Watkins/Dist. by Tribune Media Services, Inc.
MAYBE YOU SHOULD BRING IN A "NAME," SOMEONE FAMOUS TO BOOST RATINGS.
www.comicspage.com or www.myhousebroken.com
BUT WHAT CELEBRITY DO WE KNOW WHO IS IN TOUCH WITH CURRENT EVENTS?
HEY, WHO WANTS TO HEAR MY RAP AGAINST APARTHEID?

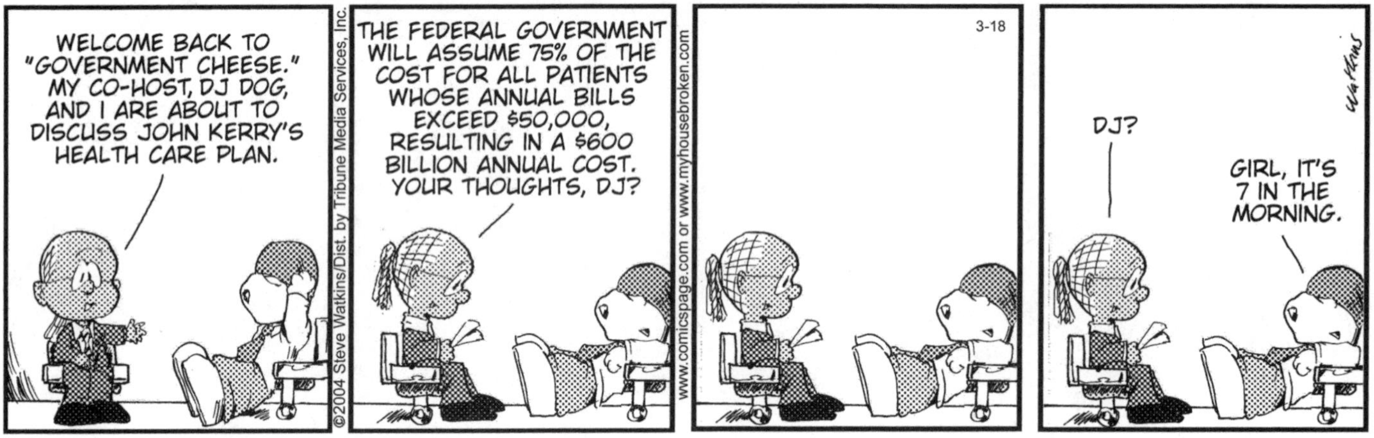
WELCOME BACK TO "GOVERNMENT CHEESE." MY CO-HOST, DJ DOG, AND I ARE ABOUT TO DISCUSS JOHN KERRY'S HEALTH CARE PLAN.
THE FEDERAL GOVERNMENT WILL ASSUME 75% OF THE COST FOR ALL PATIENTS WHOSE ANNUAL BILLS EXCEED $50,000, RESULTING IN A $600 BILLION ANNUAL COST. YOUR THOUGHTS, DJ?
DJ?
GIRL, IT'S 7 IN THE MORNING.
©2004 Steve Watkins/Dist. by Tribune Media Services, Inc.
www.comicspage.com or www.myhousebroken.com
3-18

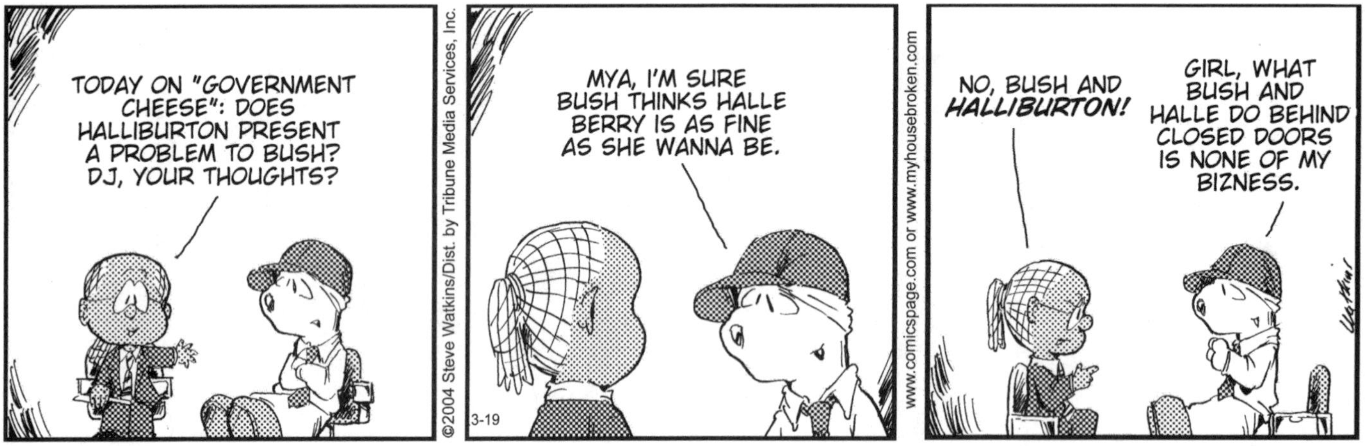
TODAY ON "GOVERNMENT CHEESE": DOES HALLIBURTON PRESENT A PROBLEM TO BUSH? DJ, YOUR THOUGHTS?
MYA, I'M SURE BUSH THINKS HALLE BERRY IS AS FINE AS SHE WANNA BE.
NO, BUSH AND ***HALLIBURTON!***
GIRL, WHAT BUSH AND HALLE DO BEHIND CLOSED DOORS IS NONE OF MY BIZNESS.
©2004 Steve Watkins/Dist. by Tribune Media Services, Inc.
www.comicspage.com or www.myhousebroken.com
3-19

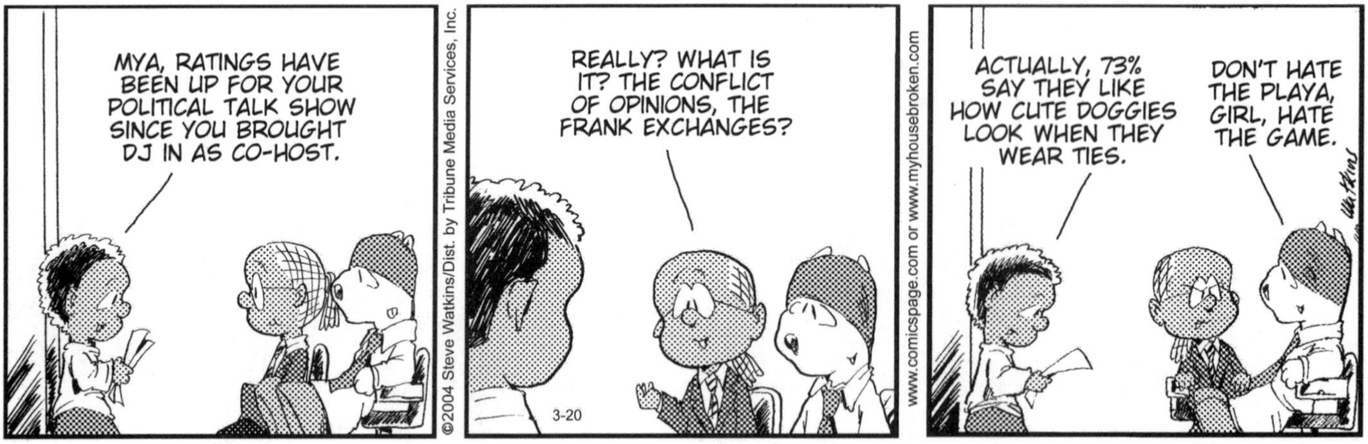
MYA, RATINGS HAVE BEEN UP FOR YOUR POLITICAL TALK SHOW SINCE YOU BROUGHT DJ IN AS CO-HOST.
REALLY? WHAT IS IT? THE CONFLICT OF OPINIONS, THE FRANK EXCHANGES?
ACTUALLY, 73% SAY THEY LIKE HOW CUTE DOGGIES LOOK WHEN THEY WEAR TIES.
DON'T HATE THE PLAYA, GIRL, HATE THE GAME.
©2004 Steve Watkins/Dist. by Tribune Media Services, Inc.
www.comicspage.com or www.myhousebroken.com
3-20

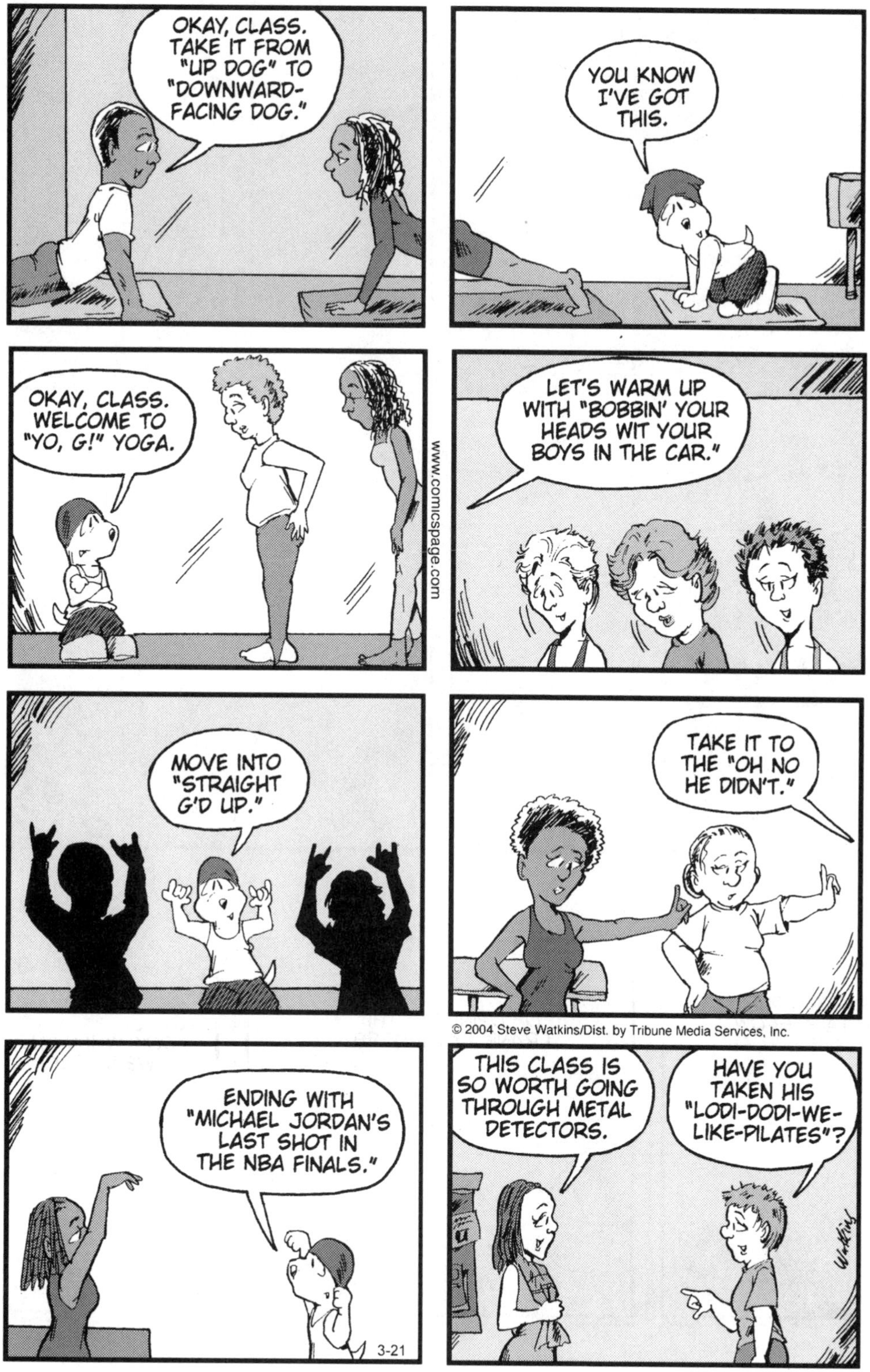
OKAY, CLASS. TAKE IT FROM "UP DOG" TO "DOWNWARD-FACING DOG."
YOU KNOW I'VE GOT THIS.
OKAY, CLASS. WELCOME TO "YO, G!" YOGA.
LET'S WARM UP WITH "BOBBIN' YOUR HEADS WIT YOUR BOYS IN THE CAR."
MOVE INTO "STRAIGHT G'D UP."
TAKE IT TO THE "OH NO HE DIDN'T."
ENDING WITH "MICHAEL JORDAN'S LAST SHOT IN THE NBA FINALS."
THIS CLASS IS SO WORTH GOING THROUGH METAL DETECTORS.
HAVE YOU TAKEN HIS "LODI-DODI-WE-LIKE-PILATES"?
3-21
Watkins

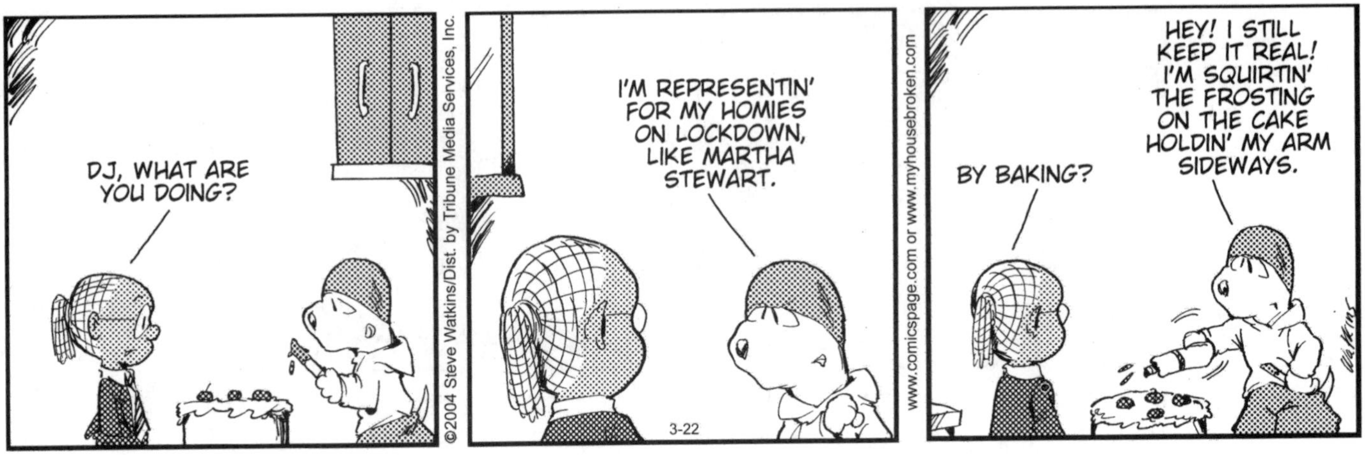
DJ, WHAT ARE YOU DOING?
©2004 Steve Watkins/Dist. by Tribune Media Services, Inc.
I'M REPRESENTIN' FOR MY HOMIES ON LOCKDOWN, LIKE MARTHA STEWART.
3-22
www.comicspage.com or www.myhousebroken.com
BY BAKING?
HEY! I STILL KEEP IT REAL! I'M SQUIRTIN' THE FROSTING ON THE CAKE HOLDIN' MY ARM SIDEWAYS.

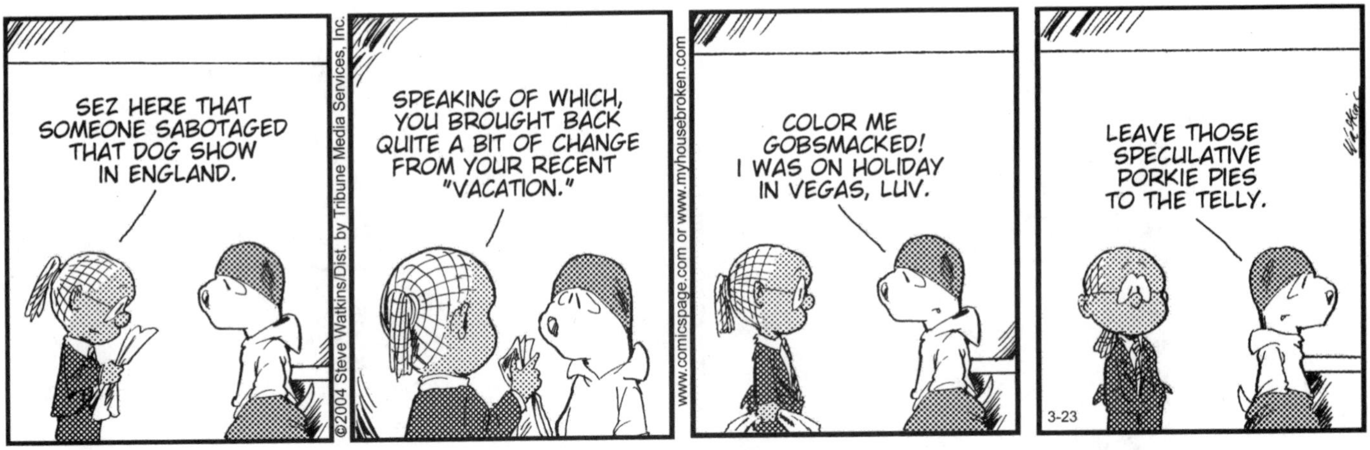
SEZ HERE THAT SOMEONE SABOTAGED THAT DOG SHOW IN ENGLAND.
©2004 Steve Watkins/Dist. by Tribune Media Services, Inc.
SPEAKING OF WHICH, YOU BROUGHT BACK QUITE A BIT OF CHANGE FROM YOUR RECENT "VACATION."
www.comicspage.com or www.myhousebroken.com
COLOR ME GOBSMACKED! I WAS ON HOLIDAY IN VEGAS, LUV.
LEAVE THOSE SPECULATIVE PORKIE PIES TO THE TELLY.
3-23

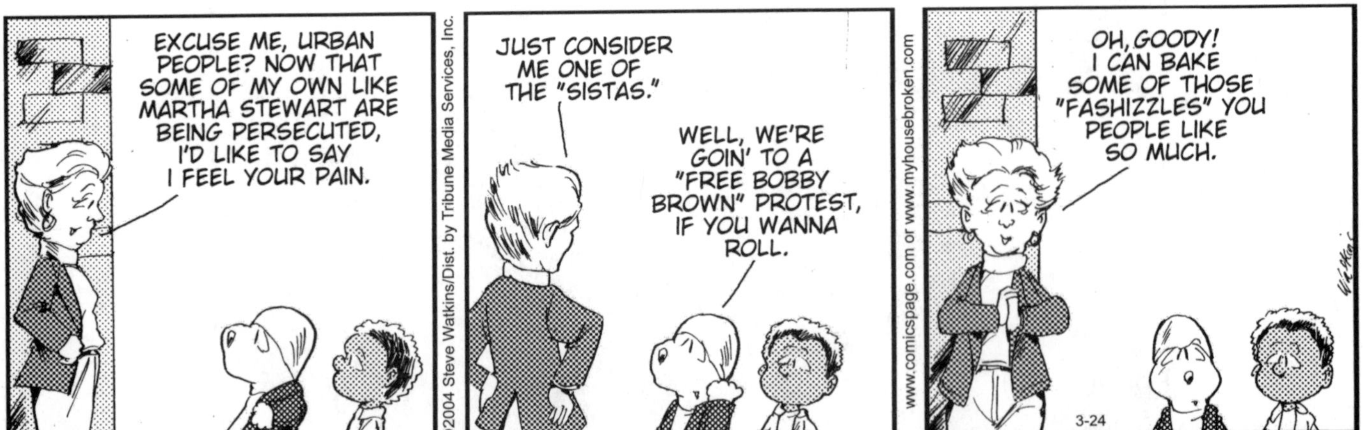
EXCUSE ME, URBAN PEOPLE? NOW THAT SOME OF MY OWN LIKE MARTHA STEWART ARE BEING PERSECUTED, I'D LIKE TO SAY I FEEL YOUR PAIN.
©2004 Steve Watkins/Dist. by Tribune Media Services, Inc.
JUST CONSIDER ME ONE OF THE "SISTAS."
WELL, WE'RE GOIN' TO A "FREE BOBBY BROWN" PROTEST, IF YOU WANNA ROLL.
www.comicspage.com or www.myhousebroken.com
OH, GOODY! I CAN BAKE SOME OF THOSE "FASHIZZLES" YOU PEOPLE LIKE SO MUCH.
3-24

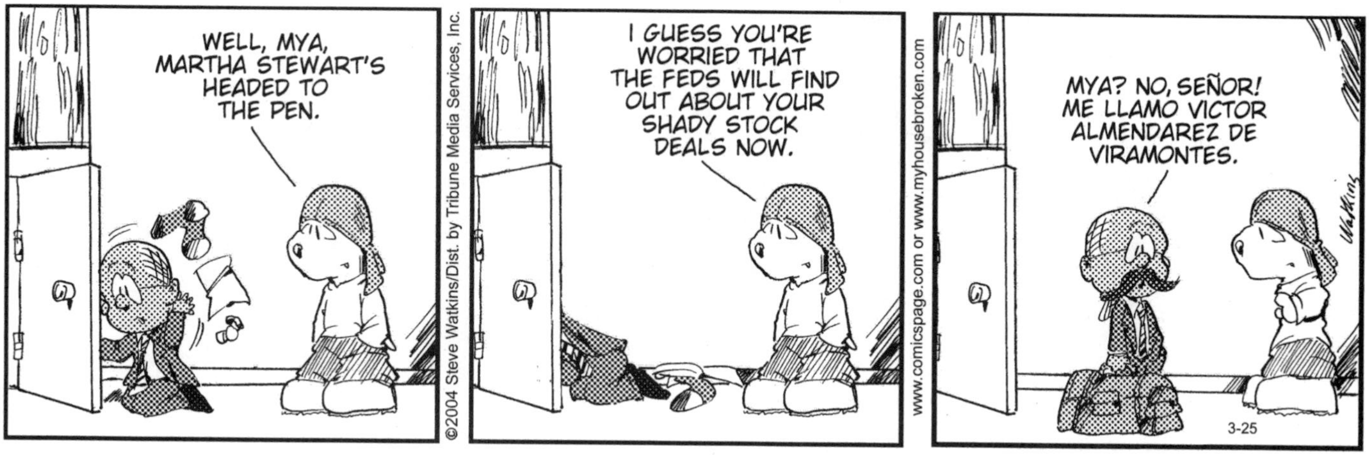
WELL, MYA, MARTHA STEWART'S HEADED TO THE PEN.
©2004 Steve Watkins/Dist. by Tribune Media Services, Inc.
I GUESS YOU'RE WORRIED THAT THE FEDS WILL FIND OUT ABOUT YOUR SHADY STOCK DEALS NOW.
www.comicspage.com or www.myhousebroken.com
MYA? NO, SEÑOR! ME LLAMO VICTOR ALMENDAREZ DE VIRAMONTES.
3-25

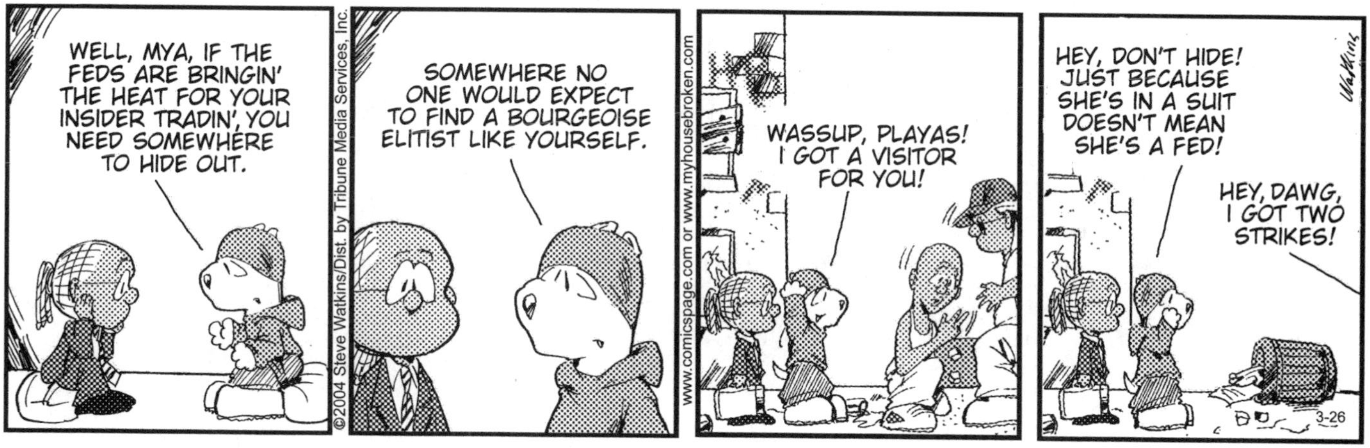
WELL, MYA, IF THE FEDS ARE BRINGIN' THE HEAT FOR YOUR INSIDER TRADIN', YOU NEED SOMEWHERE TO HIDE OUT.
©2004 Steve Watkins/Dist. by Tribune Media Services, Inc.
SOMEWHERE NO ONE WOULD EXPECT TO FIND A BOURGEOISE ELITIST LIKE YOURSELF.
www.comicspage.com or www.myhousebroken.com
WASSUP, PLAYAS! I GOT A VISITOR FOR YOU!
HEY, DON'T HIDE! JUST BECAUSE SHE'S IN A SUIT DOESN'T MEAN SHE'S A FED!
HEY, DAWG, I GOT TWO STRIKES!
3-26

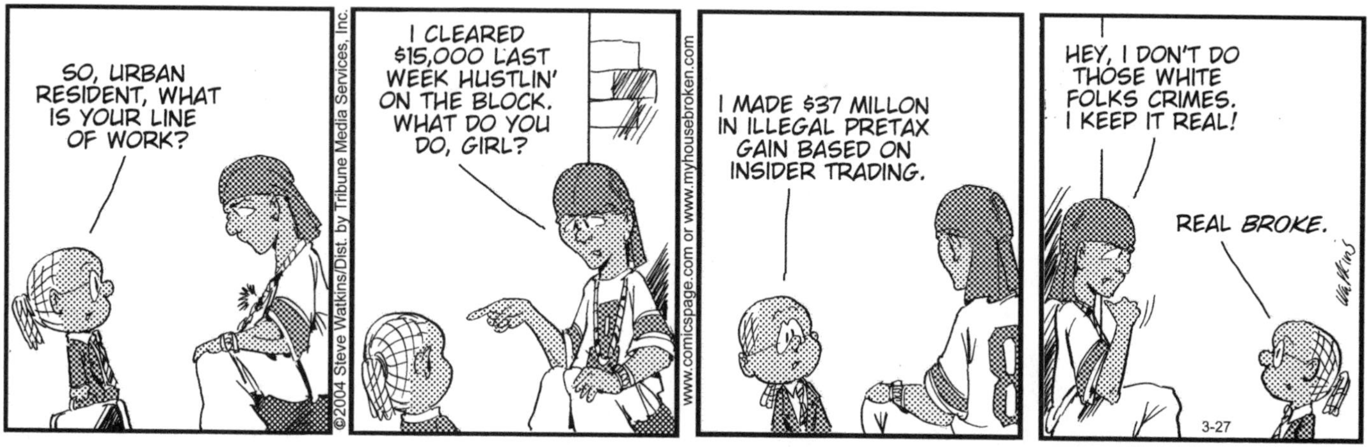
SO, URBAN RESIDENT, WHAT IS YOUR LINE OF WORK?
©2004 Steve Watkins/Dist. by Tribune Media Services, Inc.
I CLEARED $15,000 LAST WEEK HUSTLIN' ON THE BLOCK. WHAT DO YOU DO, GIRL?
www.comicspage.com or www.myhousebroken.com
I MADE $37 MILLON IN ILLEGAL PRETAX GAIN BASED ON INSIDER TRADING.
HEY, I DON'T DO THOSE WHITE FOLKS CRIMES. I KEEP IT REAL!
REAL BROKE.
3-27

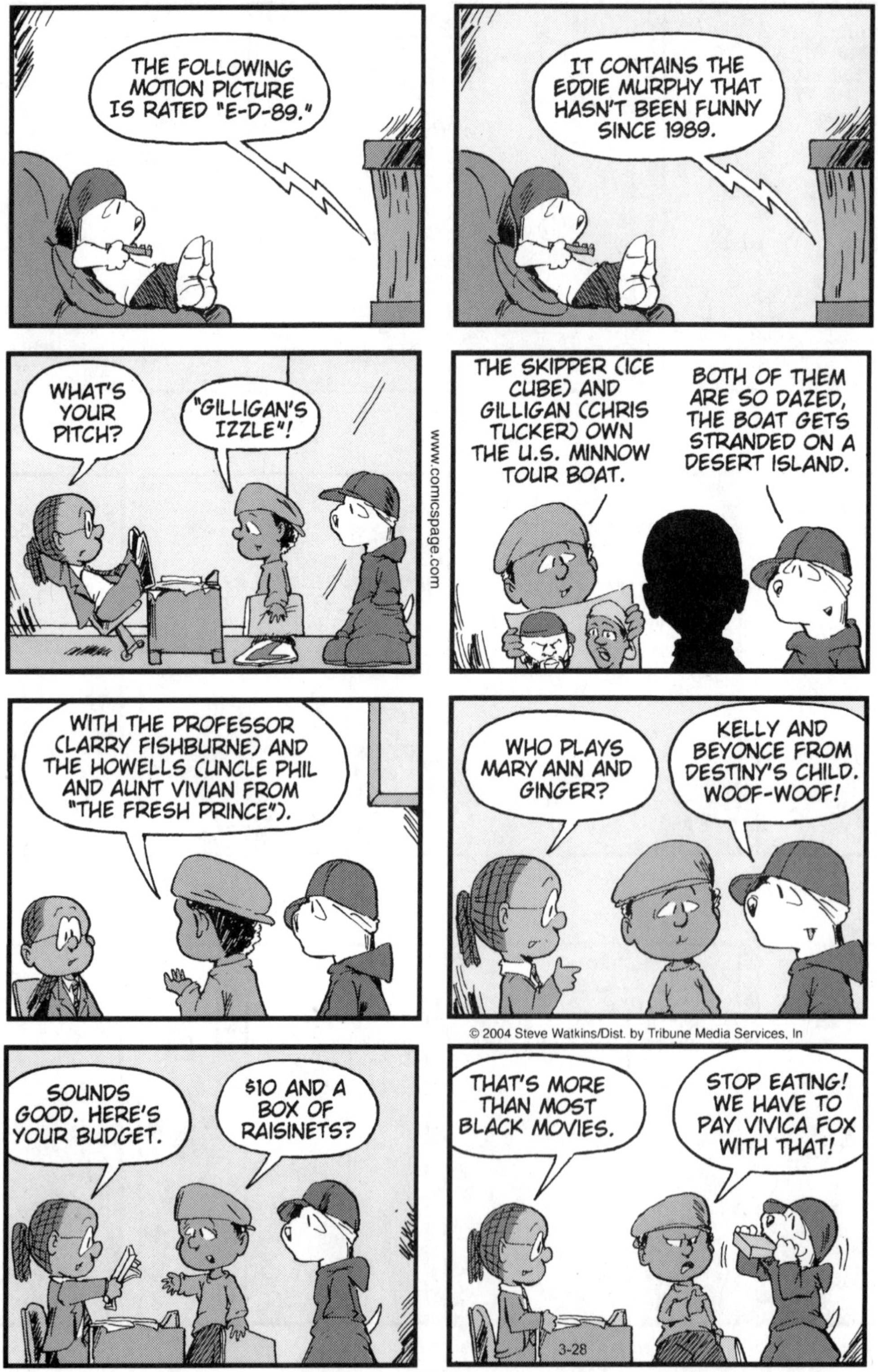
THE FOLLOWING MOTION PICTURE IS RATED "E-D-89."
IT CONTAINS THE EDDIE MURPHY THAT HASN'T BEEN FUNNY SINCE 1989.
WHAT'S YOUR PITCH?
"GILLIGAN'S IZZLE"!
www.comicspage.com
THE SKIPPER (ICE CUBE) AND GILLIGAN (CHRIS TUCKER) OWN THE U.S. MINNOW TOUR BOAT.
BOTH OF THEM ARE SO DAZED, THE BOAT GETS STRANDED ON A DESERT ISLAND.
WITH THE PROFESSOR (LARRY FISHBURNE) AND THE HOWELLS (UNCLE PHIL AND AUNT VIVIAN FROM "THE FRESH PRINCE").
WHO PLAYS MARY ANN AND GINGER?
KELLY AND BEYONCE FROM DESTINY'S CHILD. WOOF-WOOF!
SOUNDS GOOD. HERE'S YOUR BUDGET.
$10 AND A BOX OF RAISINETS?
THAT'S MORE THAN MOST BLACK MOVIES.
STOP EATING! WE HAVE TO PAY VIVICA FOX WITH THAT!
3-28

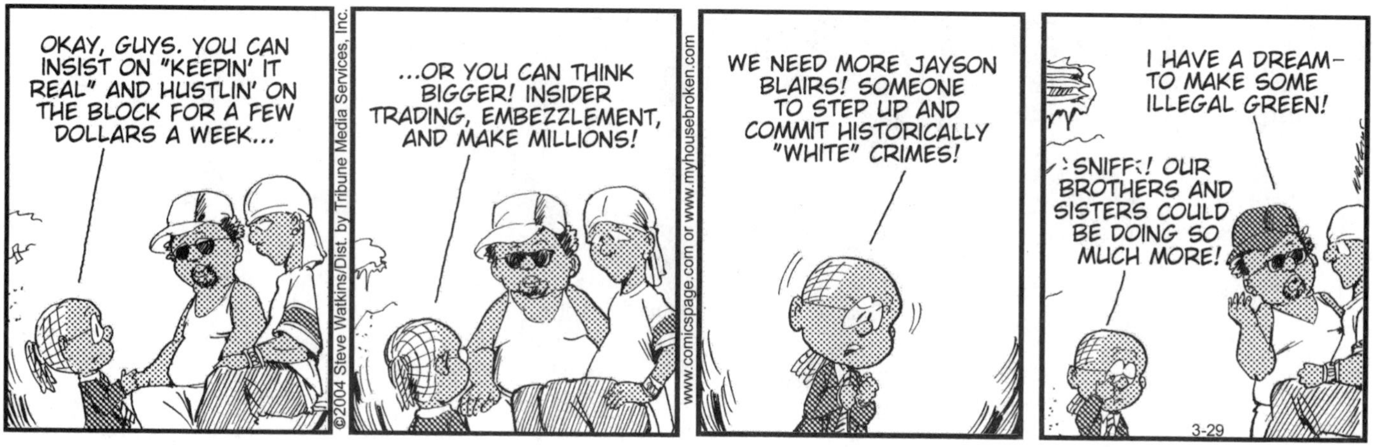
OKAY, GUYS. YOU CAN INSIST ON "KEEPIN' IT REAL" AND HUSTLIN' ON THE BLOCK FOR A FEW DOLLARS A WEEK...
...OR YOU CAN THINK BIGGER! INSIDER TRADING, EMBEZZLEMENT, AND MAKE MILLIONS!
WE NEED MORE JAYSON BLAIRS! SOMEONE TO STEP UP AND COMMIT HISTORICALLY "WHITE" CRIMES!
I HAVE A DREAM— TO MAKE SOME ILLEGAL GREEN!
SNIFF! OUR BROTHERS AND SISTERS COULD BE DOING SO MUCH MORE!
3-29

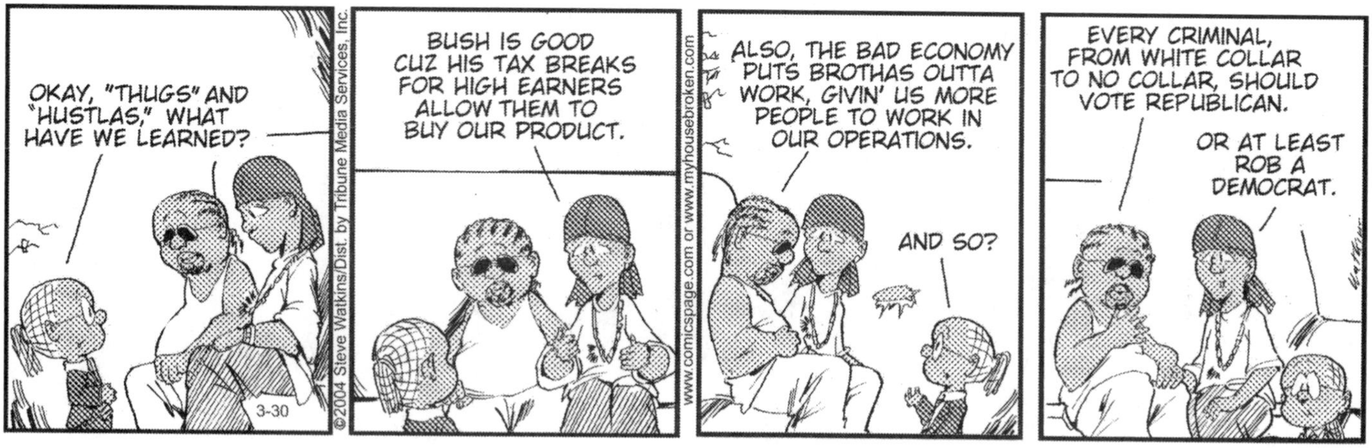
OKAY, "THUGS" AND "HUSTLAS," WHAT HAVE WE LEARNED?
3-30
BUSH IS GOOD CUZ HIS TAX BREAKS FOR HIGH EARNERS ALLOW THEM TO BUY OUR PRODUCT.
ALSO, THE BAD ECONOMY PUTS BROTHAS OUTTA WORK, GIVIN' US MORE PEOPLE TO WORK IN OUR OPERATIONS.
AND SO?
EVERY CRIMINAL, FROM WHITE COLLAR TO NO COLLAR, SHOULD VOTE REPUBLICAN.
OR AT LEAST ROB A DEMOCRAT.

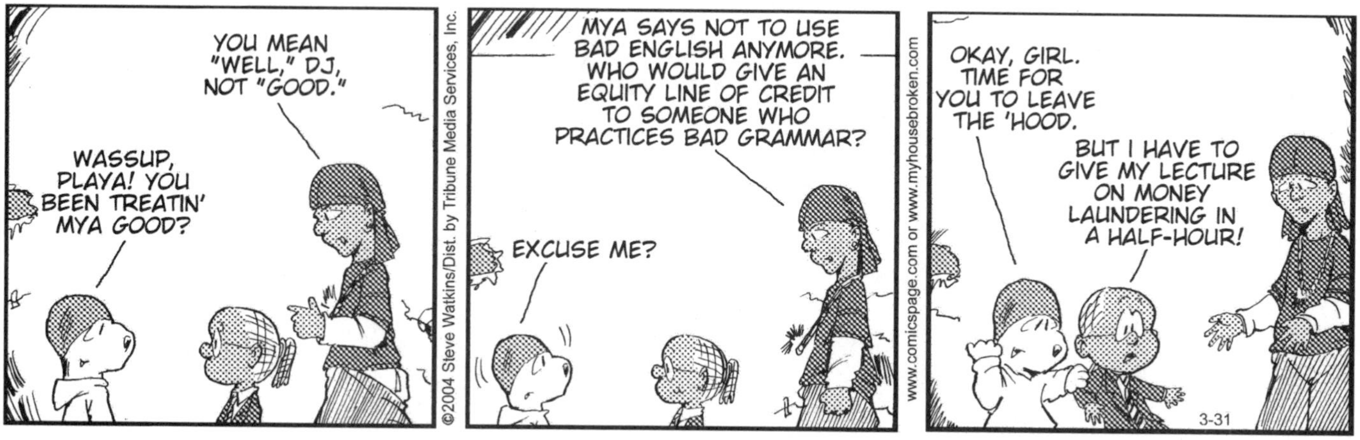
WASSUP, PLAYA! YOU BEEN TREATIN' MYA GOOD?
YOU MEAN "WELL," DJ, NOT "GOOD."
EXCUSE ME?
MYA SAYS NOT TO USE BAD ENGLISH ANYMORE. WHO WOULD GIVE AN EQUITY LINE OF CREDIT TO SOMEONE WHO PRACTICES BAD GRAMMAR?
OKAY, GIRL. TIME FOR YOU TO LEAVE THE 'HOOD.
BUT I HAVE TO GIVE MY LECTURE ON MONEY LAUNDERING IN A HALF-HOUR!
3-31

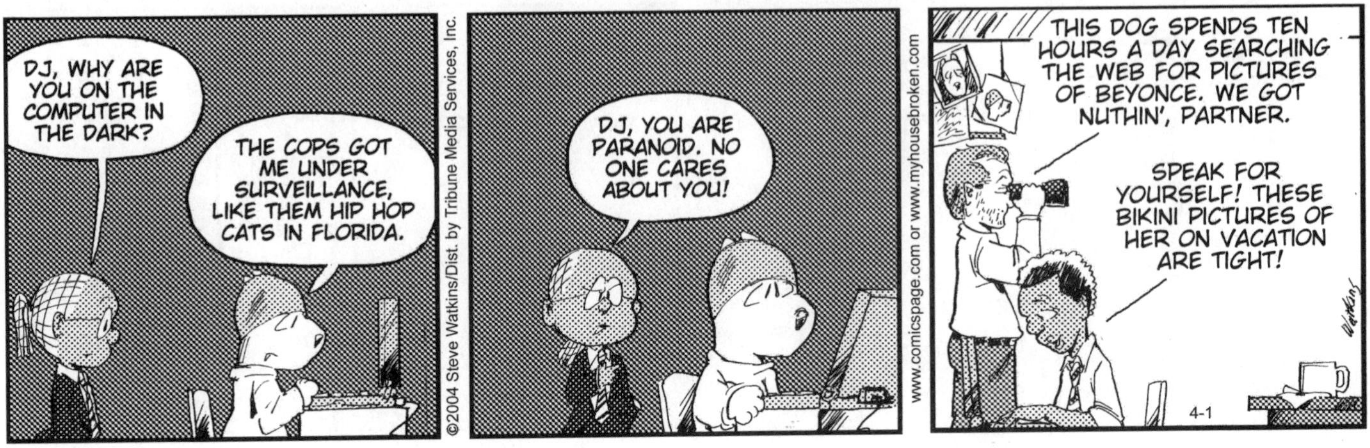

DJ, WHY ARE YOU ON THE COMPUTER IN THE DARK?
THE COPS GOT ME UNDER SURVEILLANCE, LIKE THEM HIP HOP CATS IN FLORIDA.
©2004 Steve Watkins/Dist. by Tribune Media Services, Inc.
DJ, YOU ARE PARANOID. NO ONE CARES ABOUT YOU!
www.comicspage.com or www.myhousebroken.com
THIS DOG SPENDS TEN HOURS A DAY SEARCHING THE WEB FOR PICTURES OF BEYONCE. WE GOT NUTHIN', PARTNER.
SPEAK FOR YOURSELF! THESE BIKINI PICTURES OF HER ON VACATION ARE TIGHT!
Watkins
4-1

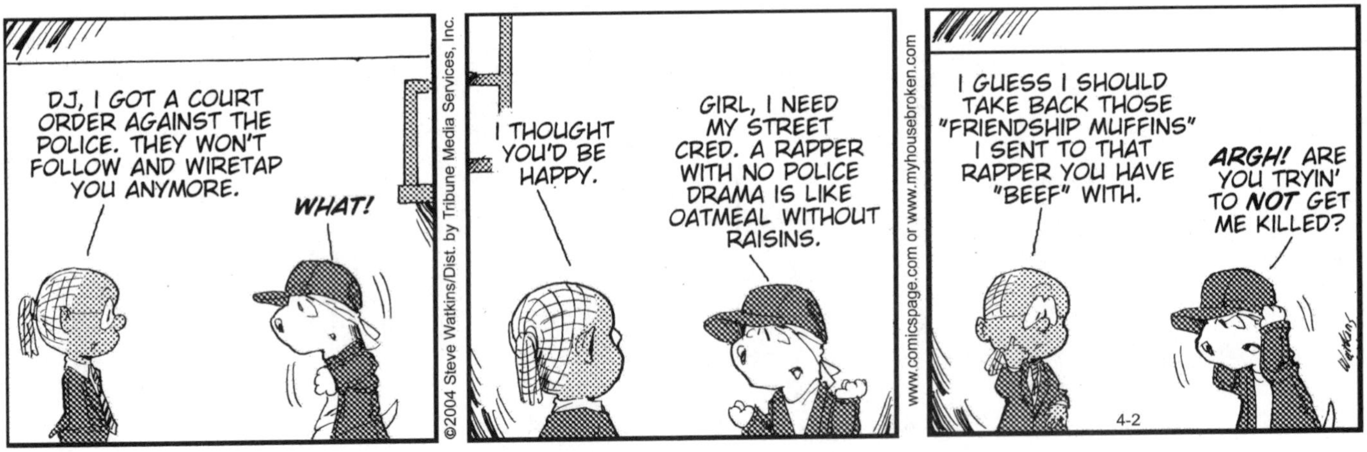

DJ, I GOT A COURT ORDER AGAINST THE POLICE. THEY WON'T FOLLOW AND WIRETAP YOU ANYMORE.
WHAT!
©2004 Steve Watkins/Dist. by Tribune Media Services, Inc.
I THOUGHT YOU'D BE HAPPY.
GIRL, I NEED MY STREET CRED. A RAPPER WITH NO POLICE DRAMA IS LIKE OATMEAL WITHOUT RAISINS.
www.comicspage.com or www.myhousebroken.com
I GUESS I SHOULD TAKE BACK THOSE "FRIENDSHIP MUFFINS" I SENT TO THAT RAPPER YOU HAVE "BEEF" WITH.
ARGH! ARE YOU TRYIN' TO NOT GET ME KILLED?
Watkins
4-2

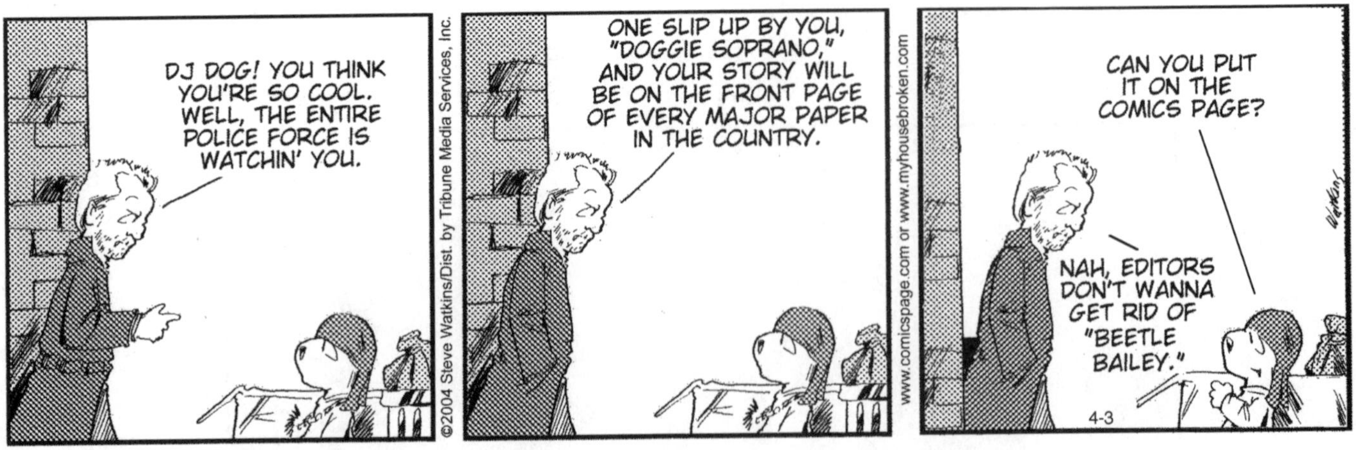

DJ DOG! YOU THINK YOU'RE SO COOL. WELL, THE ENTIRE POLICE FORCE IS WATCHIN' YOU.
©2004 Steve Watkins/Dist. by Tribune Media Services, Inc.
ONE SLIP UP BY YOU, "DOGGIE SOPRANO," AND YOUR STORY WILL BE ON THE FRONT PAGE OF EVERY MAJOR PAPER IN THE COUNTRY.
www.comicspage.com or www.myhousebroken.com
CAN YOU PUT IT ON THE COMICS PAGE?
NAH, EDITORS DON'T WANNA GET RID OF "BEETLE BAILEY."
Watkins
4-3

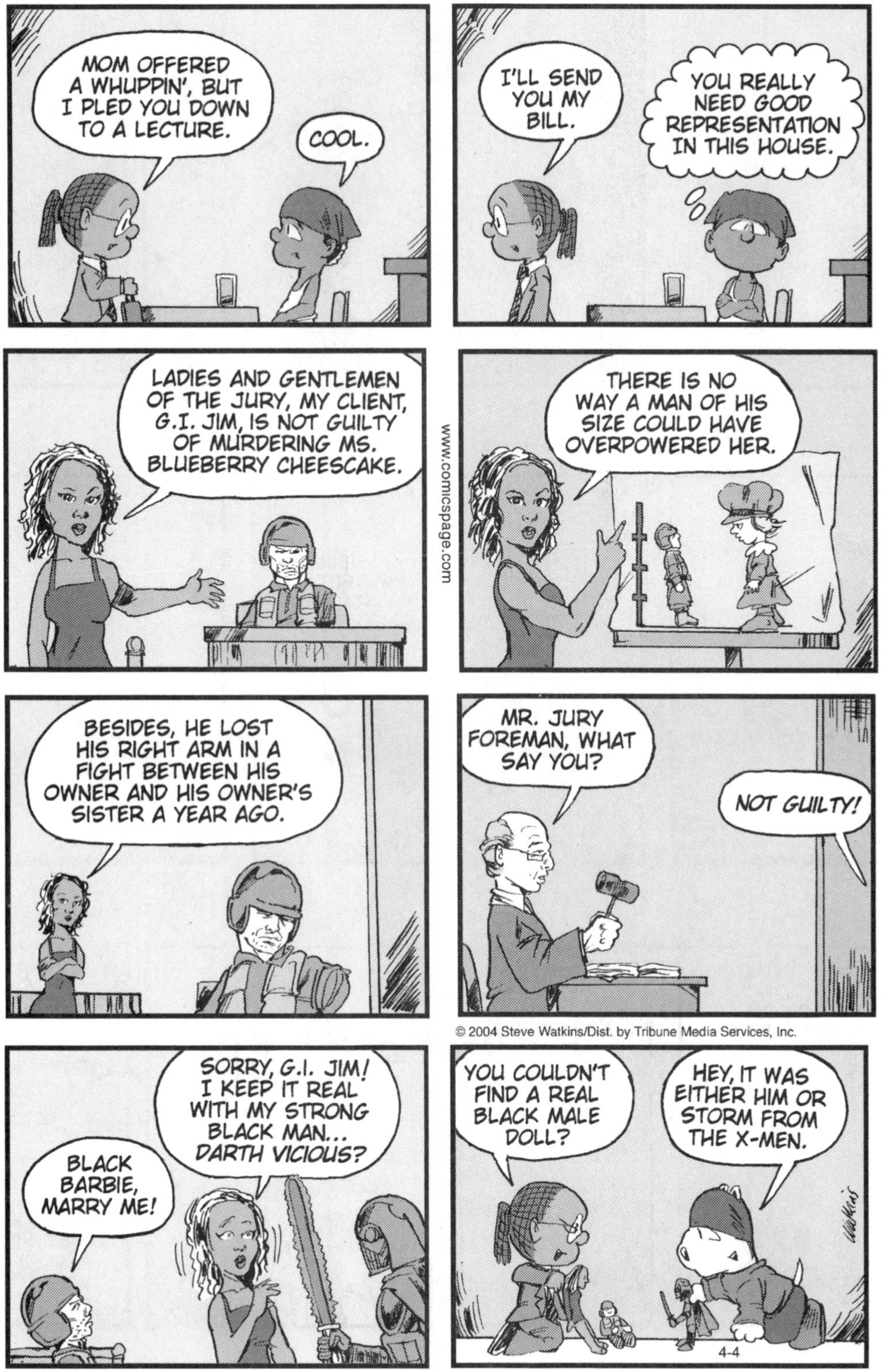
MOM OFFERED A WHUPPIN', BUT I PLED YOU DOWN TO A LECTURE.
COOL.
I'LL SEND YOU MY BILL.
YOU REALLY NEED GOOD REPRESENTATION IN THIS HOUSE.
LADIES AND GENTLEMEN OF THE JURY, MY CLIENT, G.I. JIM, IS NOT GUILTY OF MURDERING MS. BLUEBERRY CHEESCAKE.
THERE IS NO WAY A MAN OF HIS SIZE COULD HAVE OVERPOWERED HER.
BESIDES, HE LOST HIS RIGHT ARM IN A FIGHT BETWEEN HIS OWNER AND HIS OWNER'S SISTER A YEAR AGO.
MR. JURY FOREMAN, WHAT SAY YOU?
NOT GUILTY!
BLACK BARBIE, MARRY ME!
SORRY, G.I. JIM! I KEEP IT REAL WITH MY STRONG BLACK MAN... DARTH VICIOUS?
YOU COULDN'T FIND A REAL BLACK MALE DOLL?
HEY, IT WAS EITHER HIM OR STORM FROM THE X-MEN.
4-4

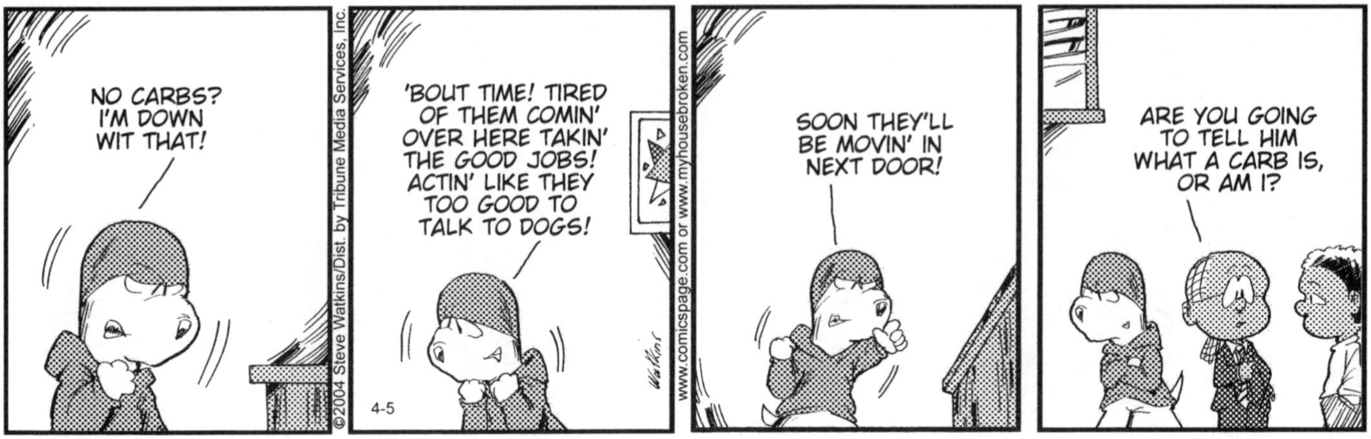
NO CARBS? I'M DOWN WIT THAT!
©2004 Steve Watkins/Dist. by Tribune Media Services, Inc.
4-5
'BOUT TIME! TIRED OF THEM COMIN' OVER HERE TAKIN' THE GOOD JOBS! ACTIN' LIKE THEY TOO GOOD TO TALK TO DOGS!
www.comicspage.com or www.myhousebroken.com
SOON THEY'LL BE MOVIN' IN NEXT DOOR!
ARE YOU GOING TO TELL HIM WHAT A CARB IS, OR AM I?

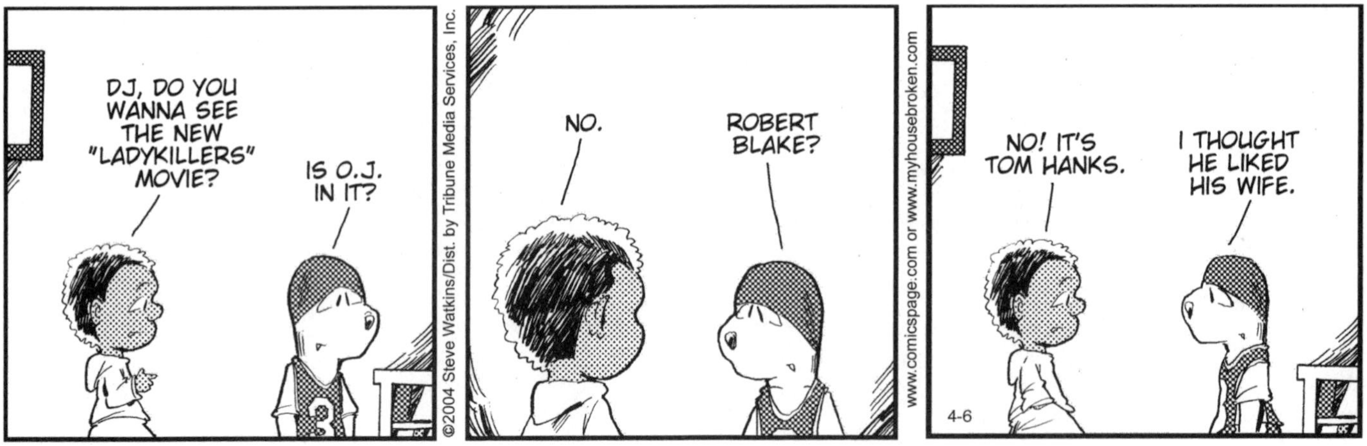
DJ, DO YOU WANNA SEE THE NEW "LADYKILLERS" MOVIE?
IS O.J. IN IT?
©2004 Steve Watkins/Dist. by Tribune Media Services, Inc.
NO.
ROBERT BLAKE?
www.comicspage.com or www.myhousebroken.com
4-6
NO! IT'S TOM HANKS.
I THOUGHT HE LIKED HIS WIFE.

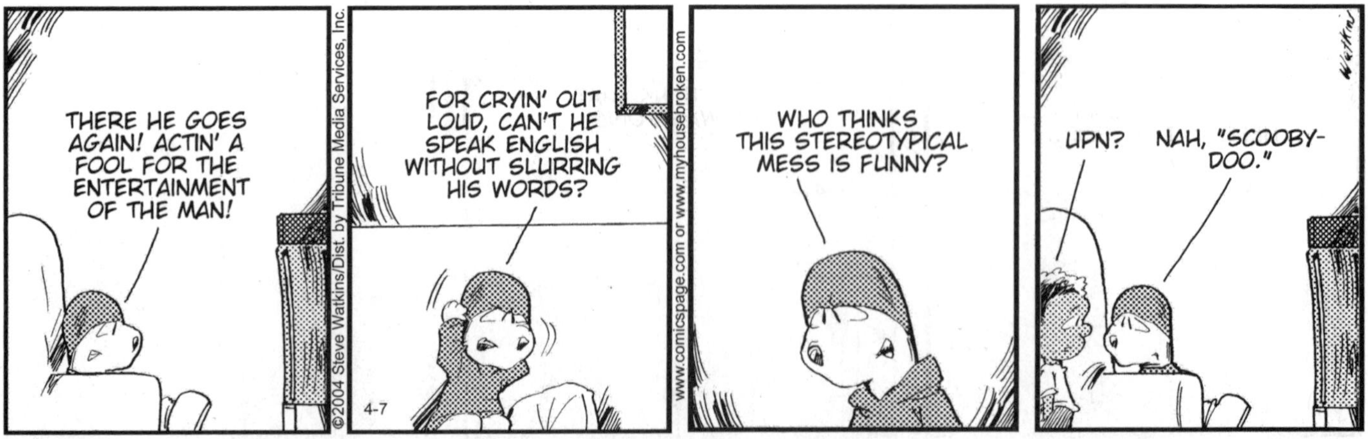
THERE HE GOES AGAIN! ACTIN' A FOOL FOR THE ENTERTAINMENT OF THE MAN!
©2004 Steve Watkins/Dist. by Tribune Media Services, Inc.
4-7
FOR CRYIN' OUT LOUD, CAN'T HE SPEAK ENGLISH WITHOUT SLURRING HIS WORDS?
www.comicspage.com or www.myhousebroken.com
WHO THINKS THIS STEREOTYPICAL MESS IS FUNNY?
UPN?
NAH, "SCOOBY-DOO."

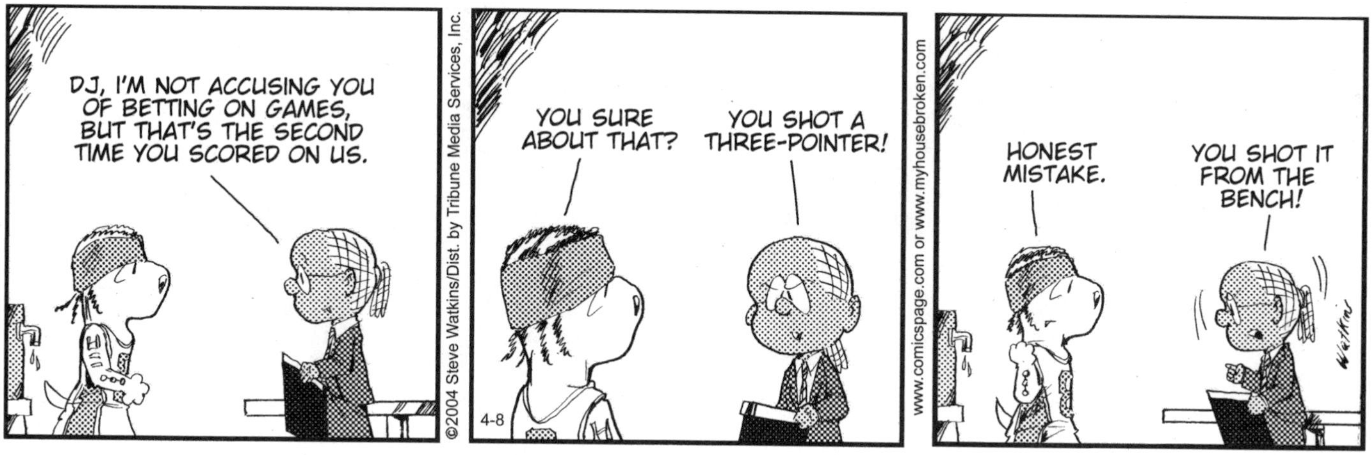
DJ, I'M NOT ACCUSING YOU OF BETTING ON GAMES, BUT THAT'S THE SECOND TIME YOU SCORED ON US.
©2004 Steve Watkins/Dist. by Tribune Media Services, Inc.
4-8
YOU SURE ABOUT THAT?
YOU SHOT A THREE-POINTER!
www.comicspage.com or www.myhousebroken.com
HONEST MISTAKE.
YOU SHOT IT FROM THE BENCH!

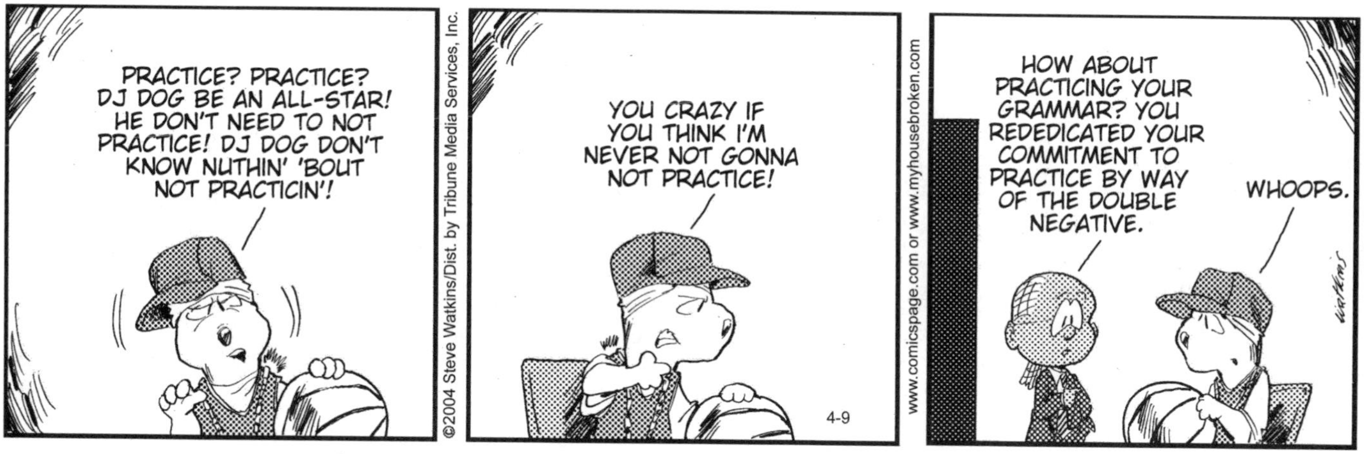
PRACTICE? PRACTICE? DJ DOG BE AN ALL-STAR! HE DON'T NEED TO NOT PRACTICE! DJ DOG DON'T KNOW NUTHIN' 'BOUT NOT PRACTICIN'!
©2004 Steve Watkins/Dist. by Tribune Media Services, Inc.
YOU CRAZY IF YOU THINK I'M NEVER NOT GONNA NOT PRACTICE!
4-9
www.comicspage.com or www.myhousebroken.com
HOW ABOUT PRACTICING YOUR GRAMMAR? YOU REDEDICATED YOUR COMMITMENT TO PRACTICE BY WAY OF THE DOUBLE NEGATIVE.
WHOOPS.

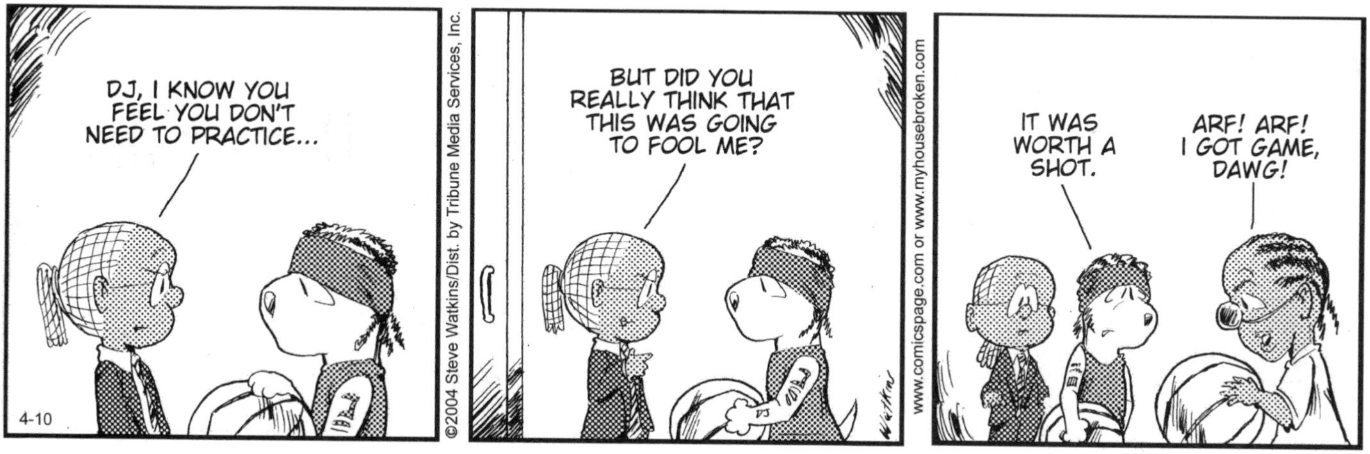
DJ, I KNOW YOU FEEL YOU DON'T NEED TO PRACTICE...
4-10
©2004 Steve Watkins/Dist. by Tribune Media Services, Inc.
BUT DID YOU REALLY THINK THAT THIS WAS GOING TO FOOL ME?
www.comicspage.com or www.myhousebroken.com
IT WAS WORTH A SHOT.
ARF! ARF! I GOT GAME, DAWG!

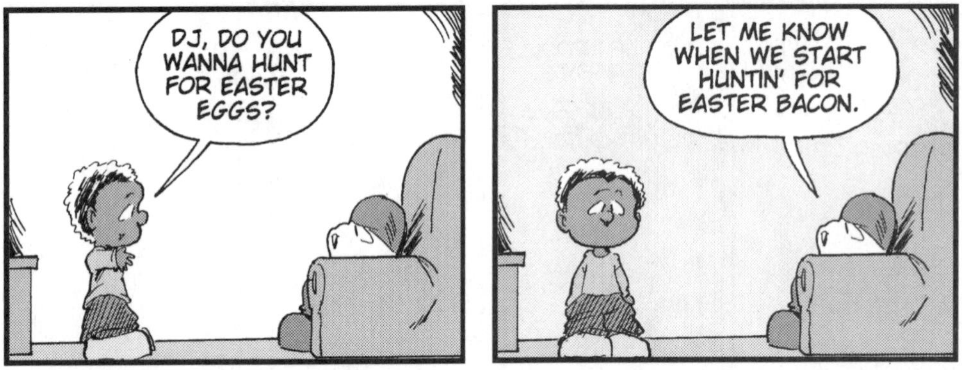
DJ, DO YOU WANNA HUNT FOR EASTER EGGS?
LET ME KNOW WHEN WE START HUNTIN' FOR EASTER BACON.

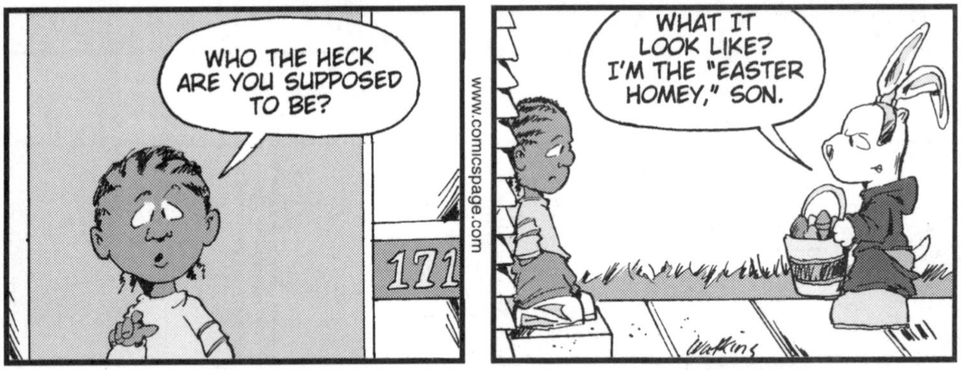
WHO THE HECK ARE YOU SUPPOSED TO BE?
171
www.comicspage.com
WHAT IT LOOK LIKE? I'M THE "EASTER HOMEY," SON.
Watkins

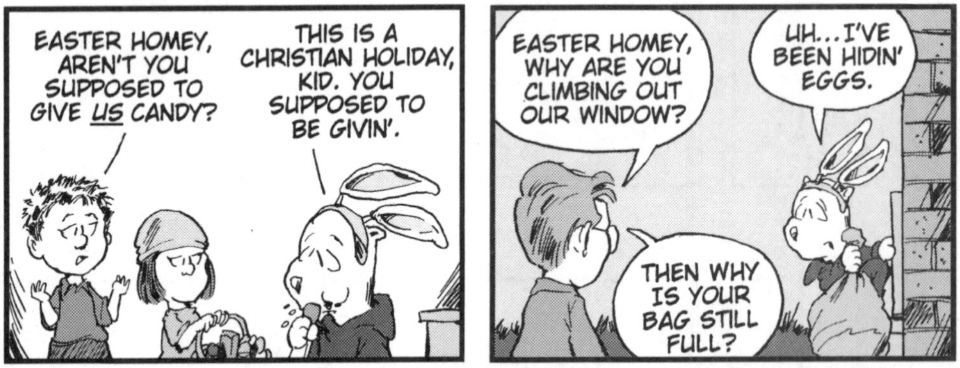
EASTER HOMEY, AREN'T YOU SUPPOSED TO GIVE US CANDY?
THIS IS A CHRISTIAN HOLIDAY, KID. YOU SUPPOSED TO BE GIVIN'.
EASTER HOMEY, WHY ARE YOU CLIMBING OUT OUR WINDOW?
UH...I'VE BEEN HIDIN' EGGS.
THEN WHY IS YOUR BAG STILL FULL?

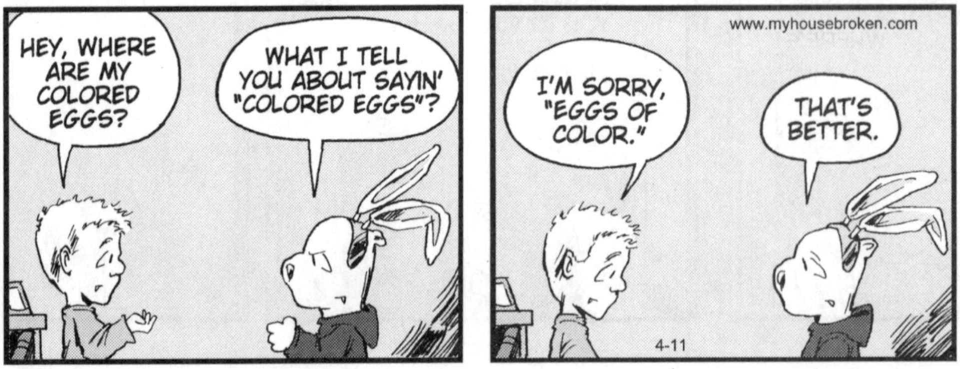
HEY, WHERE ARE MY COLORED EGGS?
WHAT I TELL YOU ABOUT SAYIN' "COLORED EGGS"?
www.myhousebroken.com
I'M SORRY, "EGGS OF COLOR."
THAT'S BETTER.
4-11

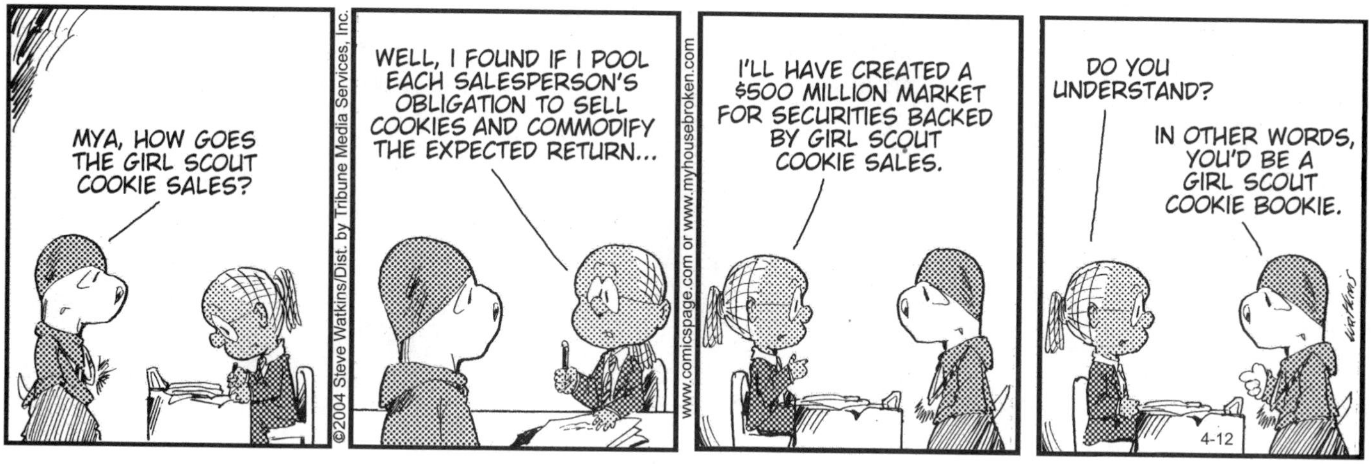
MYA, HOW GOES THE GIRL SCOUT COOKIE SALES?
©2004 Steve Watkins/Dist. by Tribune Media Services, Inc.
WELL, I FOUND IF I POOL EACH SALESPERSON'S OBLIGATION TO SELL COOKIES AND COMMODIFY THE EXPECTED RETURN...
www.comicspage.com or www.myhousebroken.com
I'LL HAVE CREATED A $500 MILLION MARKET FOR SECURITIES BACKED BY GIRL SCOUT COOKIE SALES.
DO YOU UNDERSTAND?
IN OTHER WORDS, YOU'D BE A GIRL SCOUT COOKIE BOOKIE.
4-12

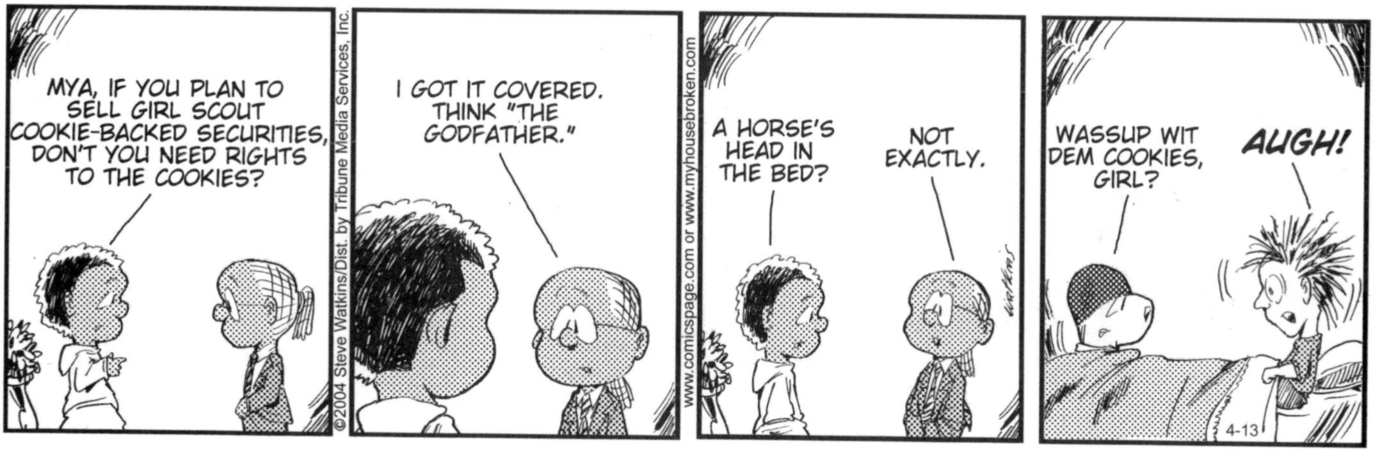
MYA, IF YOU PLAN TO SELL GIRL SCOUT COOKIE-BACKED SECURITIES, DON'T YOU NEED RIGHTS TO THE COOKIES?
©2004 Steve Watkins/Dist. by Tribune Media Services, Inc.
I GOT IT COVERED. THINK "THE GODFATHER."
www.comicspage.com or www.myhousebroken.com
A HORSE'S HEAD IN THE BED?
NOT EXACTLY.
WASSUP WIT DEM COOKIES, GIRL?
AUGH!
4-13

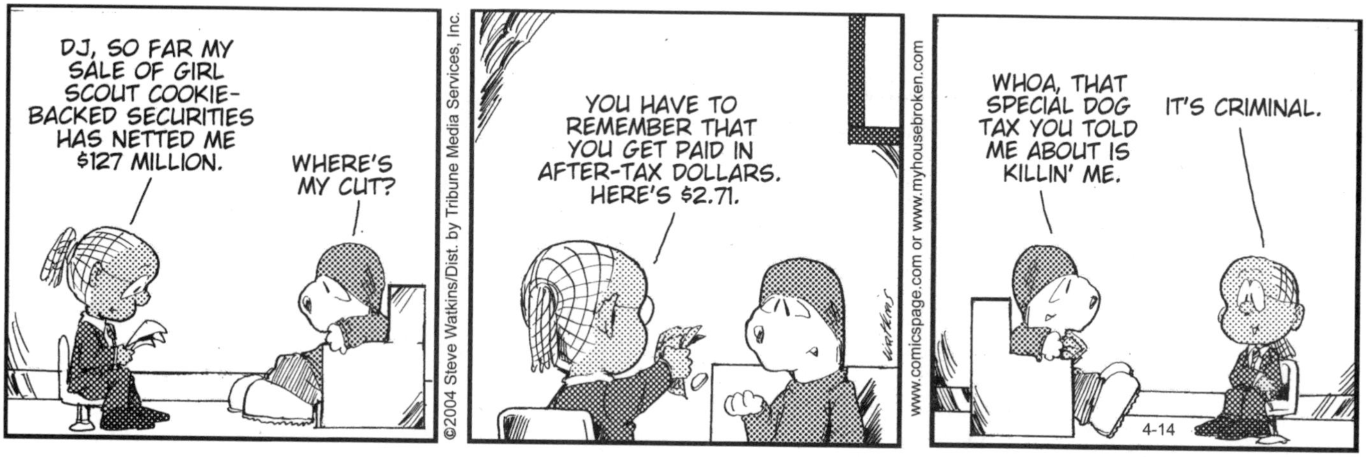
DJ, SO FAR MY SALE OF GIRL SCOUT COOKIE-BACKED SECURITIES HAS NETTED ME $127 MILLION.
WHERE'S MY CUT?
©2004 Steve Watkins/Dist. by Tribune Media Services, Inc.
YOU HAVE TO REMEMBER THAT YOU GET PAID IN AFTER-TAX DOLLARS. HERE'S $2.71.
www.comicspage.com or www.myhousebroken.com
WHOA, THAT SPECIAL DOG TAX YOU TOLD ME ABOUT IS KILLIN' ME.
IT'S CRIMINAL.
4-14

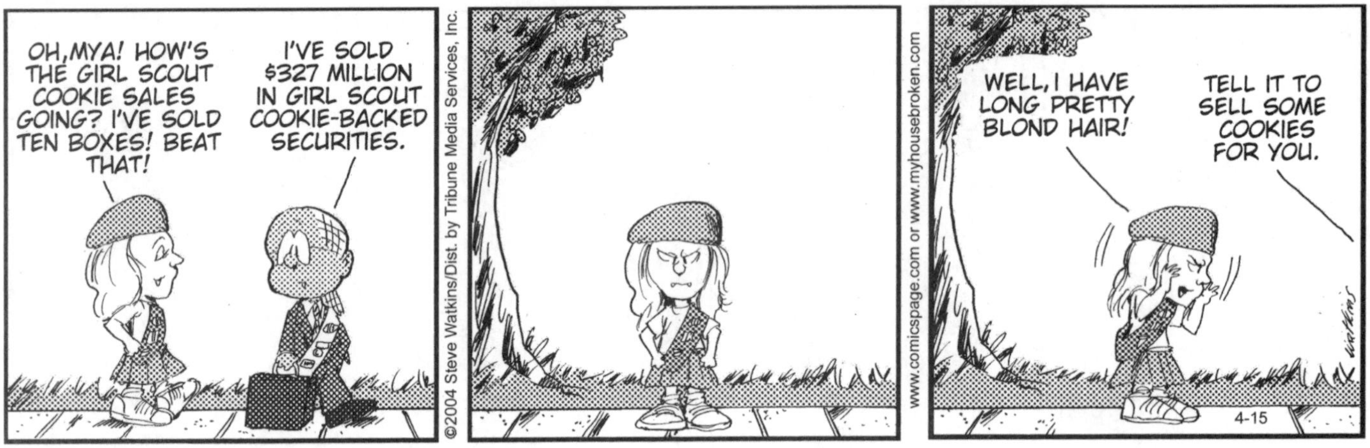
OH, MYA! HOW'S THE GIRL SCOUT COOKIE SALES GOING? I'VE SOLD TEN BOXES! BEAT THAT!
I'VE SOLD $327 MILLION IN GIRL SCOUT COOKIE-BACKED SECURITIES.
©2004 Steve Watkins/Dist. by Tribune Media Services, Inc.
www.comicspage.com or www.myhousebroken.com
WELL, I HAVE LONG PRETTY BLOND HAIR!
TELL IT TO SELL SOME COOKIES FOR YOU.
watkins
4-15

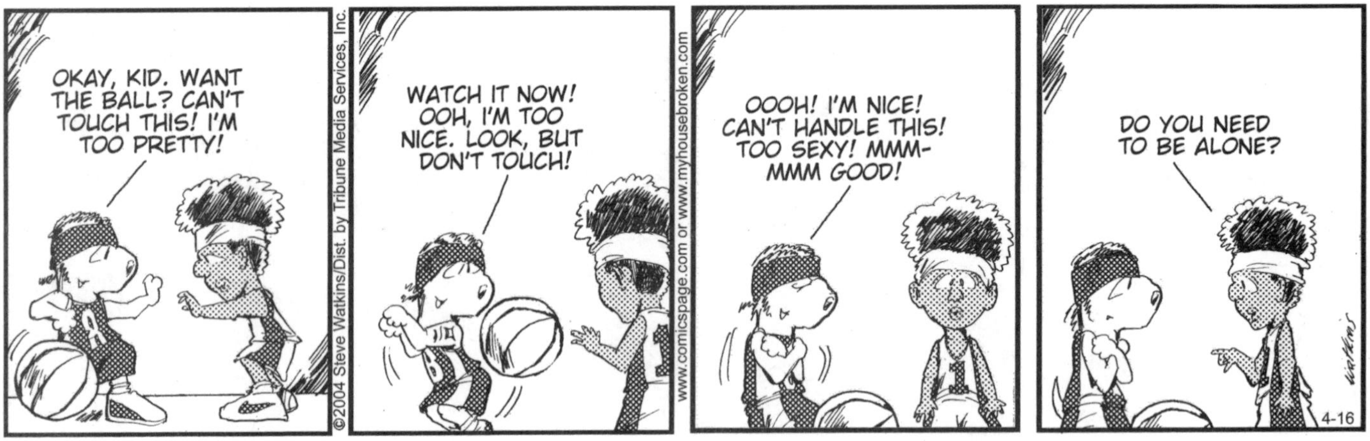
OKAY, KID. WANT THE BALL? CAN'T TOUCH THIS! I'M TOO PRETTY!
©2004 Steve Watkins/Dist. by Tribune Media Services, Inc.
WATCH IT NOW! OOH, I'M TOO NICE. LOOK, BUT DON'T TOUCH!
www.comicspage.com or www.myhousebroken.com
OOOH! I'M NICE! CAN'T HANDLE THIS! TOO SEXY! MMM-MMM GOOD!
DO YOU NEED TO BE ALONE?
watkins
4-16

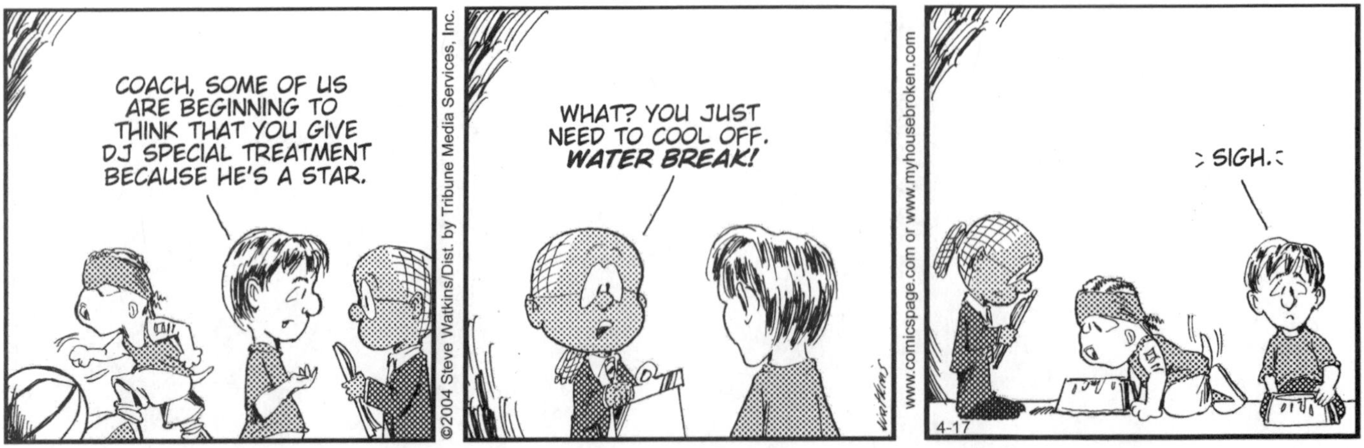
COACH, SOME OF US ARE BEGINNING TO THINK THAT YOU GIVE DJ SPECIAL TREATMENT BECAUSE HE'S A STAR.
©2004 Steve Watkins/Dist. by Tribune Media Services, Inc.
WHAT? YOU JUST NEED TO COOL OFF. WATER BREAK!
watkins
www.comicspage.com or www.myhousebroken.com
SIGH.
4-17

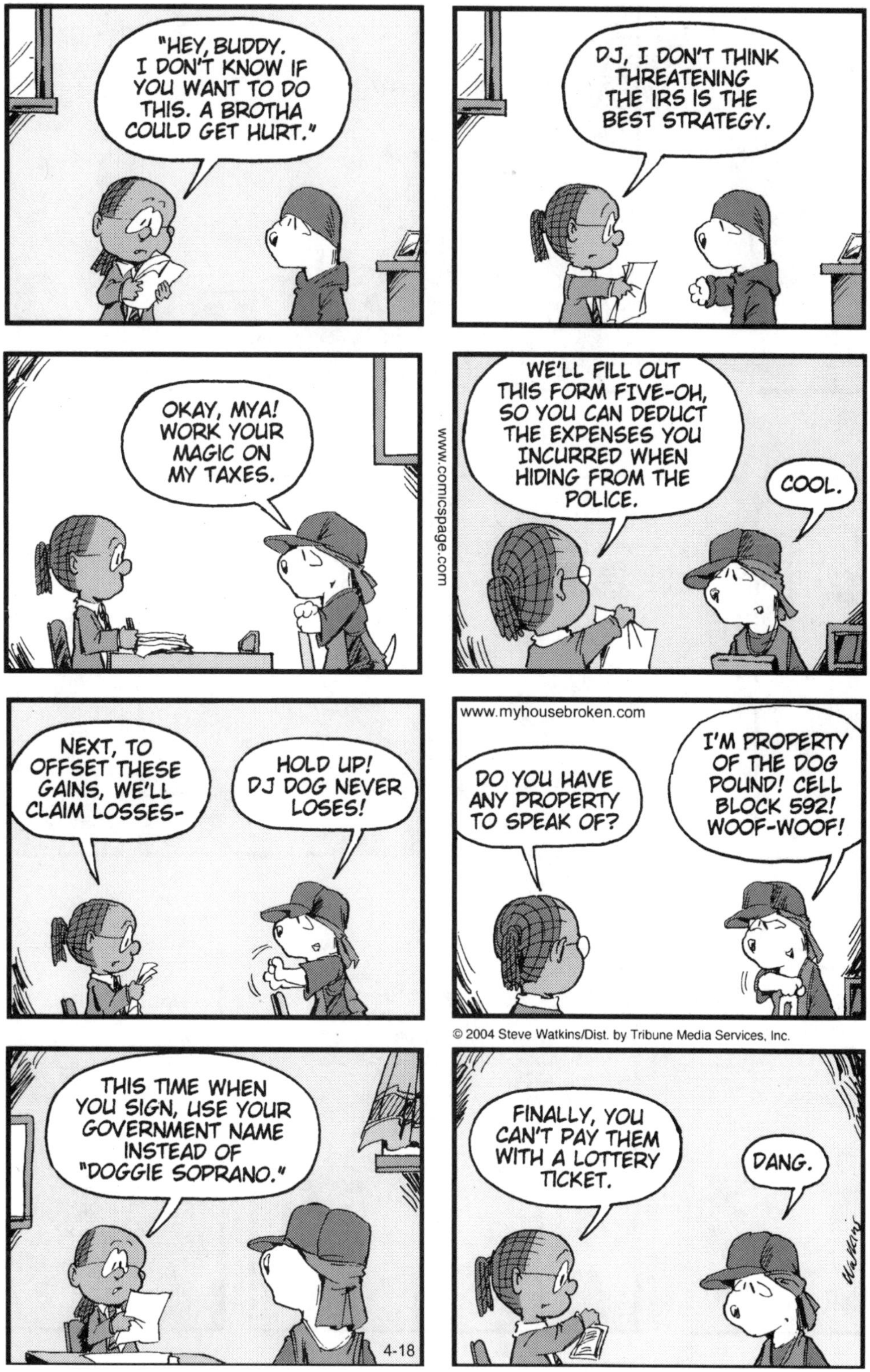
"HEY, BUDDY. I DON'T KNOW IF YOU WANT TO DO THIS. A BROTHA COULD GET HURT."
DJ, I DON'T THINK THREATENING THE IRS IS THE BEST STRATEGY.
OKAY, MYA! WORK YOUR MAGIC ON MY TAXES.
www.comicspage.com
WE'LL FILL OUT THIS FORM FIVE-OH, SO YOU CAN DEDUCT THE EXPENSES YOU INCURRED WHEN HIDING FROM THE POLICE.
COOL.
NEXT, TO OFFSET THESE GAINS, WE'LL CLAIM LOSSES-
HOLD UP! DJ DOG NEVER LOSES!
www.myhousebroken.com
DO YOU HAVE ANY PROPERTY TO SPEAK OF?
I'M PROPERTY OF THE DOG POUND! CELL BLOCK 592! WOOF-WOOF!
© 2004 Steve Watkins/Dist. by Tribune Media Services, Inc.
THIS TIME WHEN YOU SIGN, USE YOUR GOVERNMENT NAME INSTEAD OF "DOGGIE SOPRANO."
4-18
FINALLY, YOU CAN'T PAY THEM WITH A LOTTERY TICKET.
DANG.
Watkins

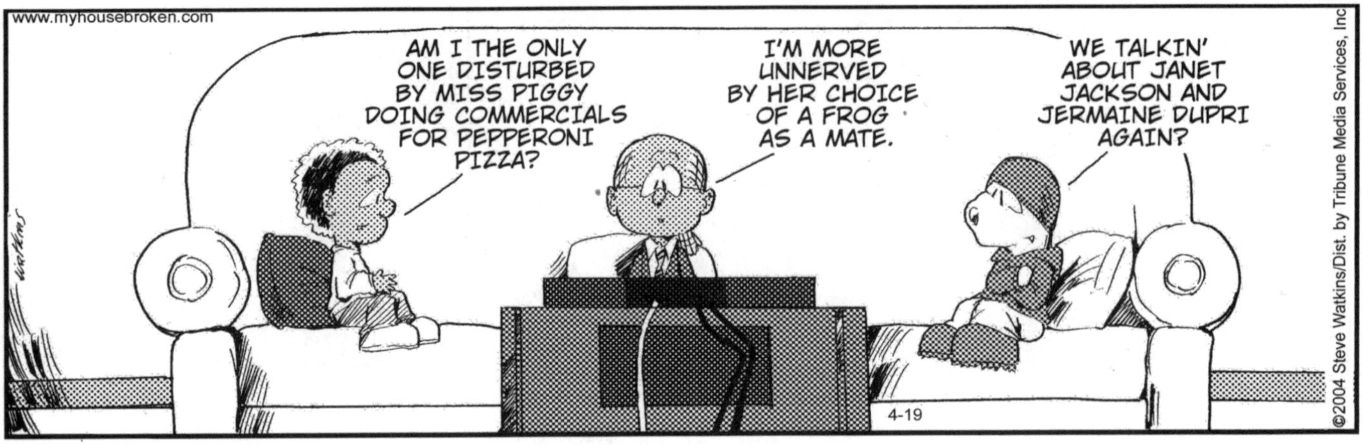
www.myhousebroken.com
AM I THE ONLY ONE DISTURBED BY MISS PIGGY DOING COMMERCIALS FOR PEPPERONI PIZZA?
I'M MORE UNNERVED BY HER CHOICE OF A FROG AS A MATE.
WE TALKIN' ABOUT JANET JACKSON AND JERMAINE DUPRI AGAIN?
4-19
©2004 Steve Watkins/Dist. by Tribune Media Services, Inc

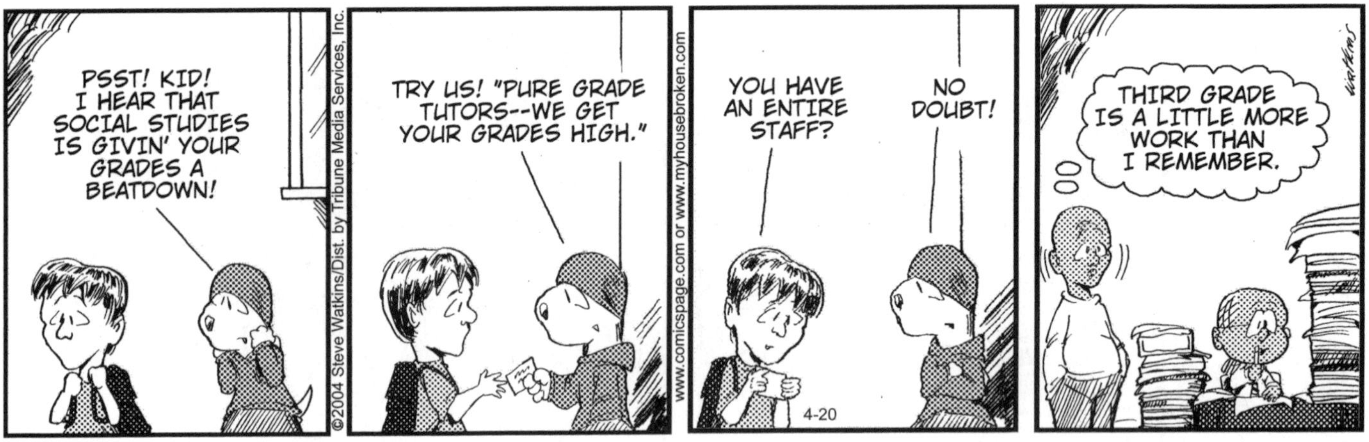
PSST! KID! I HEAR THAT SOCIAL STUDIES IS GIVIN' YOUR GRADES A BEATDOWN!
©2004 Steve Watkins/Dist. by Tribune Media Services, Inc.
TRY US! "PURE GRADE TUTORS--WE GET YOUR GRADES HIGH."
www.comicspage.com or www.myhousebroken.com
YOU HAVE AN ENTIRE STAFF?
NO DOUBT!
4-20
THIRD GRADE IS A LITTLE MORE WORK THAN I REMEMBER.

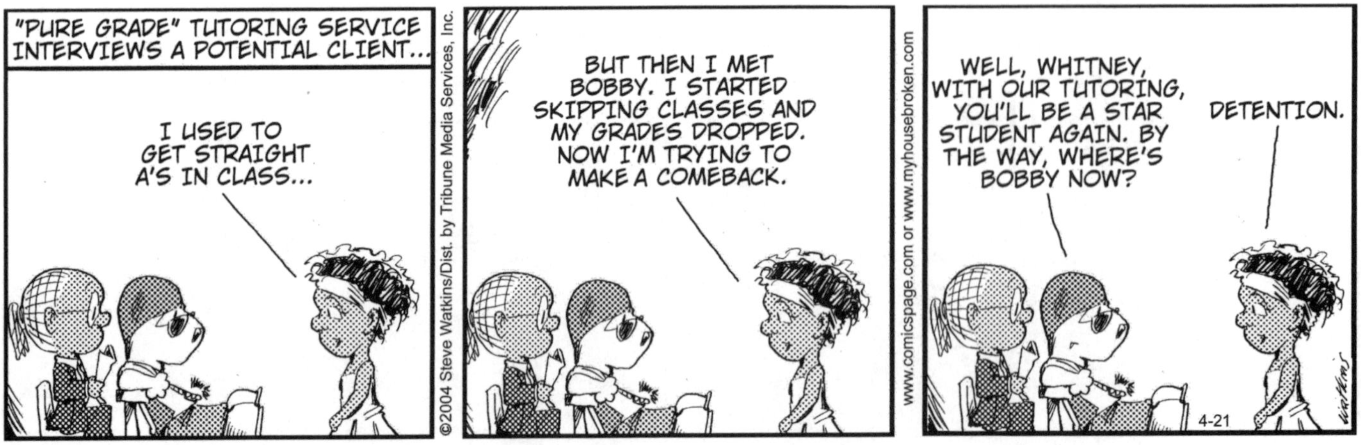
"PURE GRADE" TUTORING SERVICE INTERVIEWS A POTENTIAL CLIENT...
I USED TO GET STRAIGHT A'S IN CLASS...
©2004 Steve Watkins/Dist. by Tribune Media Services, Inc.
BUT THEN I MET BOBBY. I STARTED SKIPPING CLASSES AND MY GRADES DROPPED. NOW I'M TRYING TO MAKE A COMEBACK.
www.comicspage.com or www.myhousebroken.com
WELL, WHITNEY, WITH OUR TUTORING, YOU'LL BE A STAR STUDENT AGAIN. BY THE WAY, WHERE'S BOBBY NOW?
DETENTION.
4-21

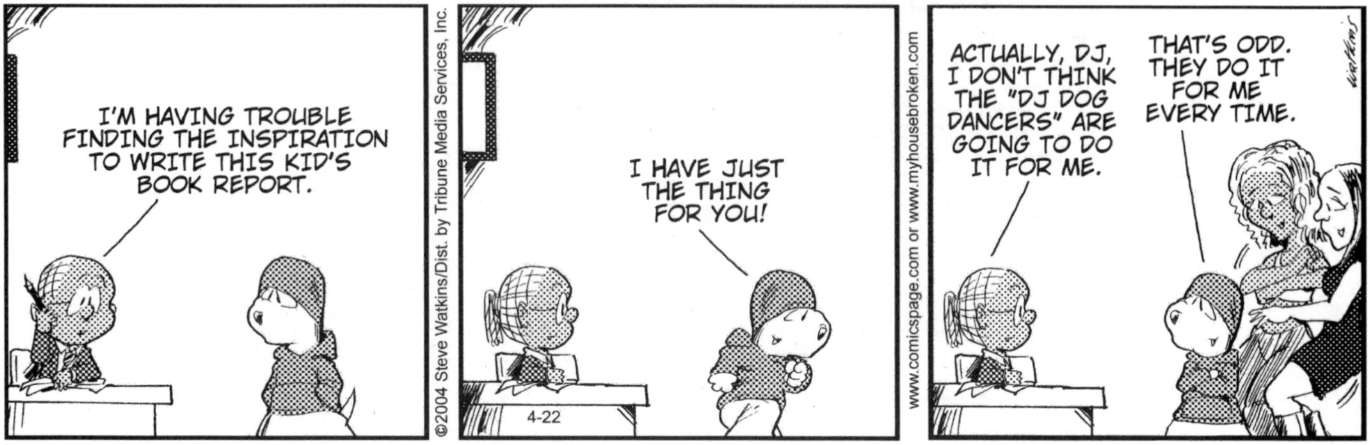
I'M HAVING TROUBLE FINDING THE INSPIRATION TO WRITE THIS KID'S BOOK REPORT.
©2004 Steve Watkins/Dist. by Tribune Media Services, Inc.
I HAVE JUST THE THING FOR YOU!
4-22
www.comicspage.com or www.myhousebroken.com
ACTUALLY, DJ, I DON'T THINK THE "DJ DOG DANCERS" ARE GOING TO DO IT FOR ME.
THAT'S ODD. THEY DO IT FOR ME EVERY TIME.

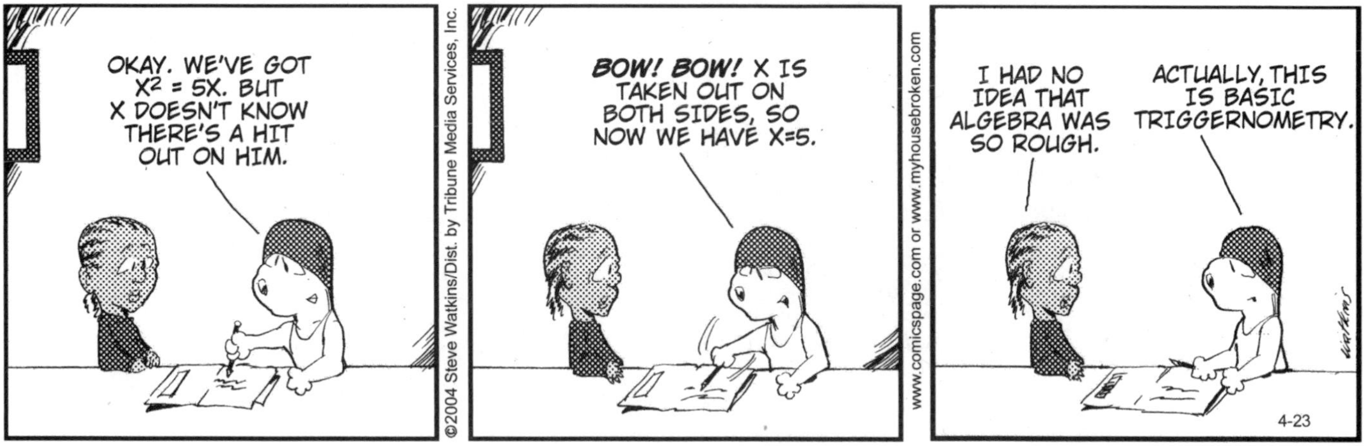
OKAY. WE'VE GOT X² = 5X. BUT X DOESN'T KNOW THERE'S A HIT OUT ON HIM.
©2004 Steve Watkins/Dist. by Tribune Media Services, Inc.
BOW! BOW! X IS TAKEN OUT ON BOTH SIDES, SO NOW WE HAVE X=5.
www.comicspage.com or www.myhousebroken.com
I HAD NO IDEA THAT ALGEBRA WAS SO ROUGH.
ACTUALLY, THIS IS BASIC TRIGGERNOMETRY.
4-23

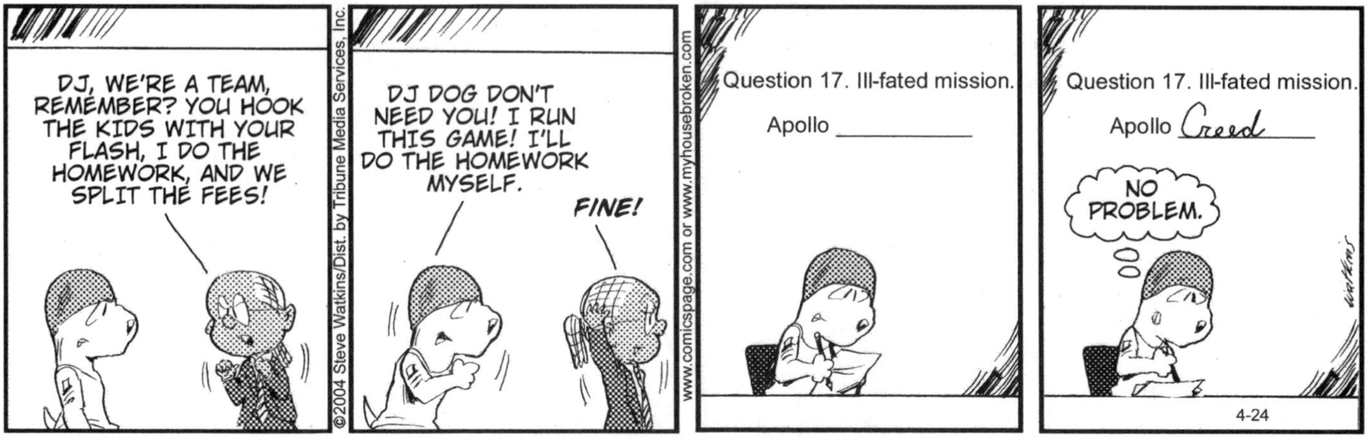
DJ, WE'RE A TEAM, REMEMBER? YOU HOOK THE KIDS WITH YOUR FLASH, I DO THE HOMEWORK, AND WE SPLIT THE FEES!
©2004 Steve Watkins/Dist. by Tribune Media Services, Inc.
DJ DOG DON'T NEED YOU! I RUN THIS GAME! I'LL DO THE HOMEWORK MYSELF.
FINE!
www.comicspage.com or www.myhousebroken.com
Question 17. Ill-fated mission.
Apollo
Question 17. Ill-fated mission.
Apollo Creed
NO PROBLEM.
4-24

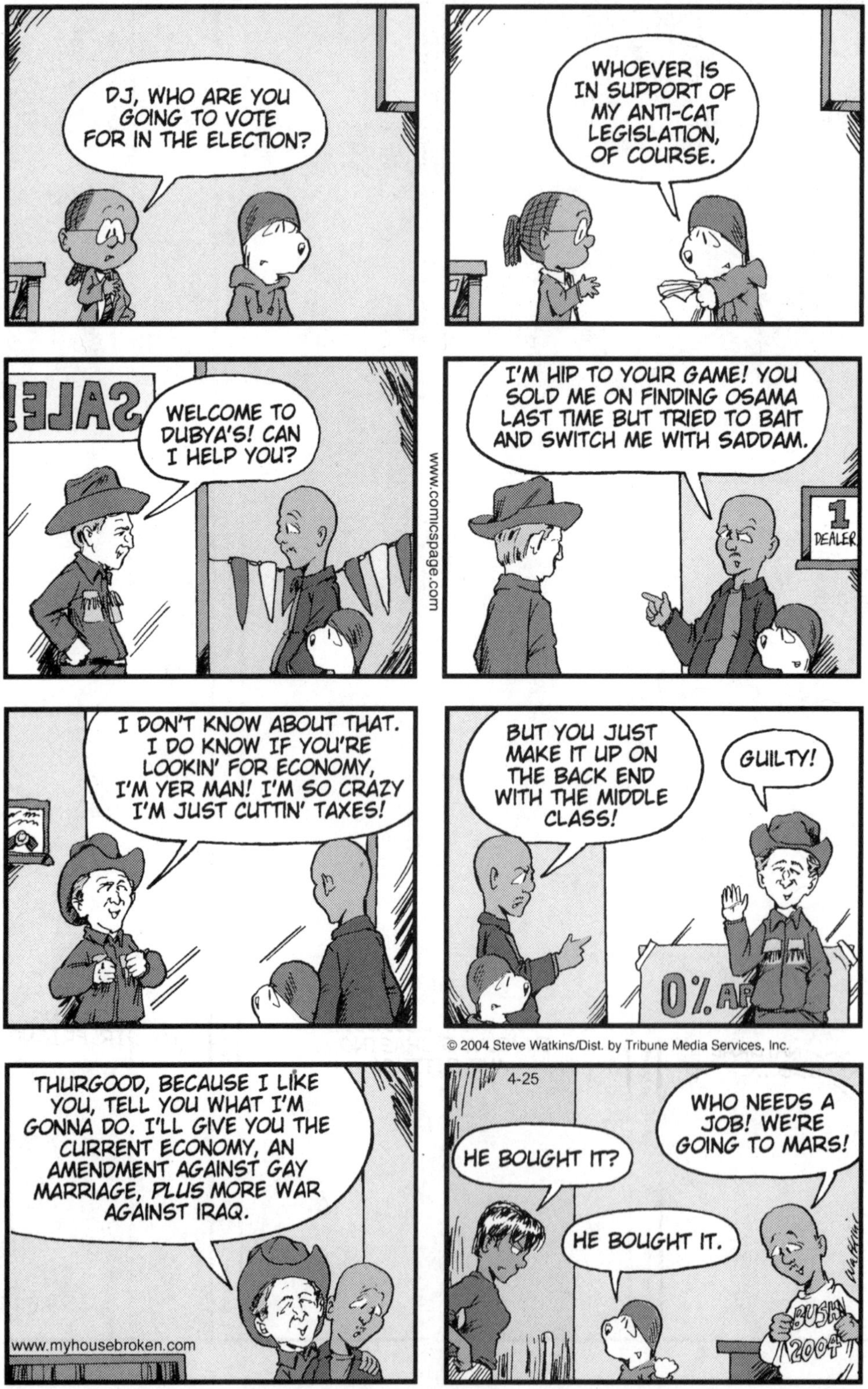

DJ, WHO ARE YOU GOING TO VOTE FOR IN THE ELECTION?
WHOEVER IS IN SUPPORT OF MY ANTI-CAT LEGISLATION, OF COURSE.
SALE!
WELCOME TO DUBYA'S! CAN I HELP YOU?
www.comicspage.com
I'M HIP TO YOUR GAME! YOU SOLD ME ON FINDING OSAMA LAST TIME BUT TRIED TO BAIT AND SWITCH ME WITH SADDAM.
1 DEALER
I DON'T KNOW ABOUT THAT. I DO KNOW IF YOU'RE LOOKIN' FOR ECONOMY, I'M YER MAN! I'M SO CRAZY I'M JUST CUTTIN' TAXES!
BUT YOU JUST MAKE IT UP ON THE BACK END WITH THE MIDDLE CLASS!
GUILTY!
0%
© 2004 Steve Watkins/Dist. by Tribune Media Services, Inc.
THURGOOD, BECAUSE I LIKE YOU, TELL YOU WHAT I'M GONNA DO. I'LL GIVE YOU THE CURRENT ECONOMY, AN AMENDMENT AGAINST GAY MARRIAGE, PLUS MORE WAR AGAINST IRAQ.
www.myhousebroken.com
4-25
HE BOUGHT IT?
WHO NEEDS A JOB! WE'RE GOING TO MARS!
HE BOUGHT IT.
BUSH 2004

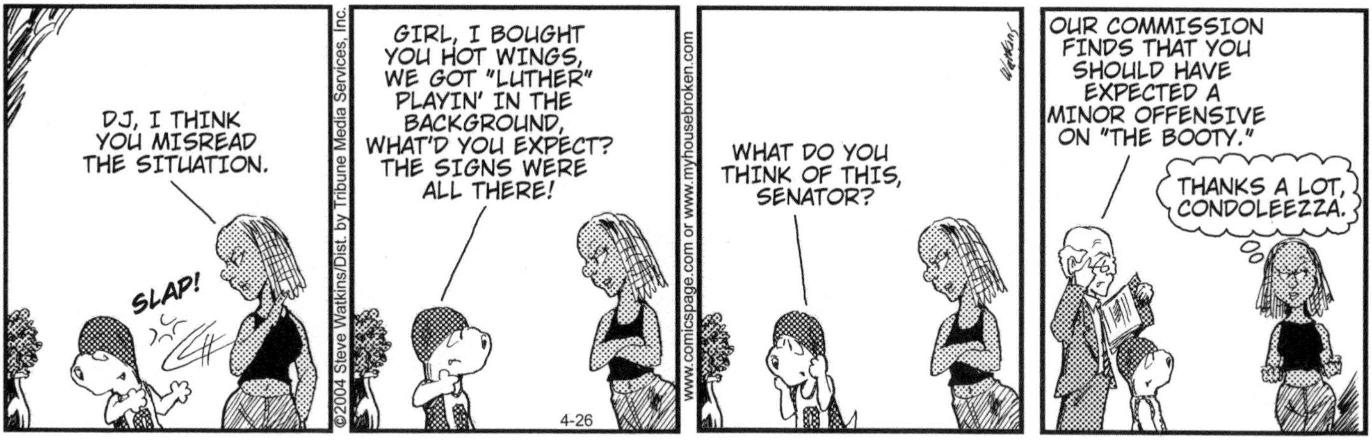
DJ, I THINK YOU MISREAD THE SITUATION.
SLAP!
©2004 Steve Watkins/Dist. by Tribune Media Services, Inc.
GIRL, I BOUGHT YOU HOT WINGS, WE GOT "LUTHER" PLAYIN' IN THE BACKGROUND, WHAT'D YOU EXPECT? THE SIGNS WERE ALL THERE!
4-26
www.comicspage.com or www.myhousebroken.com
WHAT DO YOU THINK OF THIS, SENATOR?
OUR COMMISSION FINDS THAT YOU SHOULD HAVE EXPECTED A MINOR OFFENSIVE ON "THE BOOTY."
THANKS A LOT, CONDOLEEZZA.

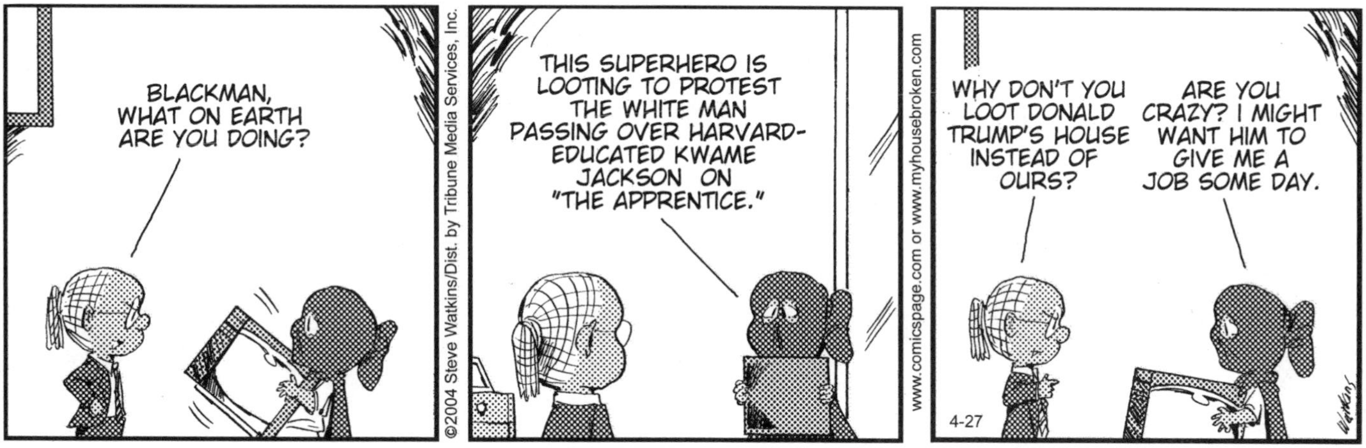
BLACKMAN, WHAT ON EARTH ARE YOU DOING?
©2004 Steve Watkins/Dist. by Tribune Media Services, Inc.
THIS SUPERHERO IS LOOTING TO PROTEST THE WHITE MAN PASSING OVER HARVARD-EDUCATED KWAME JACKSON ON "THE APPRENTICE."
www.comicspage.com or www.myhousebroken.com
WHY DON'T YOU LOOT DONALD TRUMP'S HOUSE INSTEAD OF OURS?
ARE YOU CRAZY? I MIGHT WANT HIM TO GIVE ME A JOB SOME DAY.
4-27

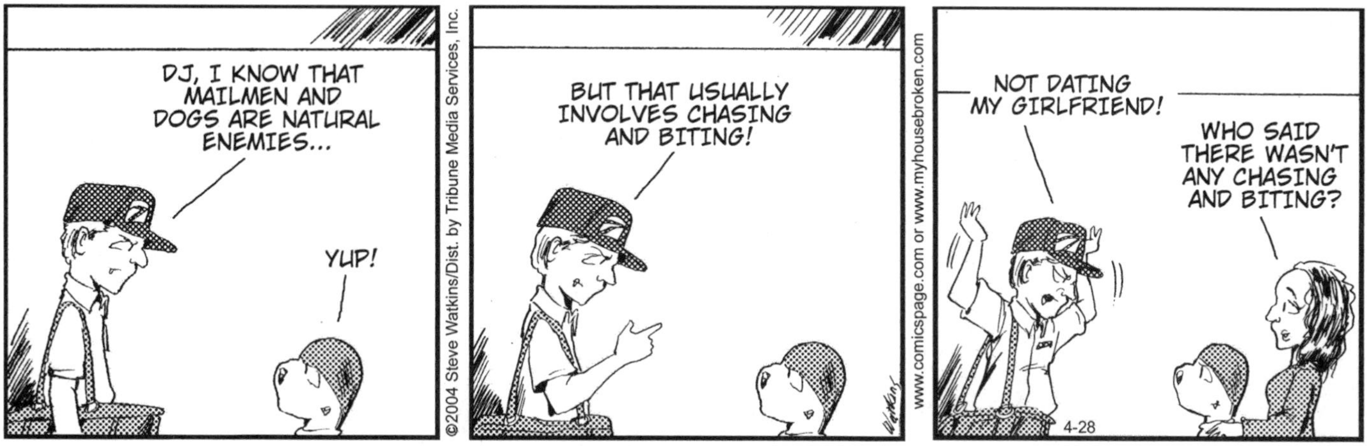
DJ, I KNOW THAT MAILMEN AND DOGS ARE NATURAL ENEMIES...
YUP!
©2004 Steve Watkins/Dist. by Tribune Media Services, Inc.
BUT THAT USUALLY INVOLVES CHASING AND BITING!
www.comicspage.com or www.myhousebroken.com
NOT DATING MY GIRLFRIEND!
WHO SAID THERE WASN'T ANY CHASING AND BITING?
4-28

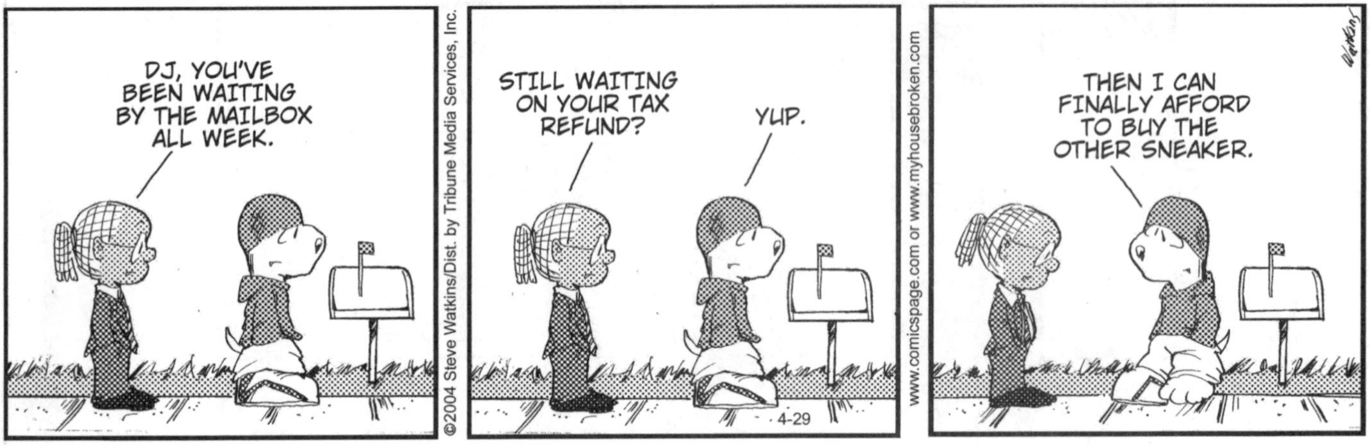
DJ, YOU'VE BEEN WAITING BY THE MAILBOX ALL WEEK.
STILL WAITING ON YOUR TAX REFUND?
YUP.
THEN I CAN FINALLY AFFORD TO BUY THE OTHER SNEAKER.
©2004 Steve Watkins/Dist. by Tribune Media Services, Inc.
www.comicspage.com or www.myhousebroken.com
4-29

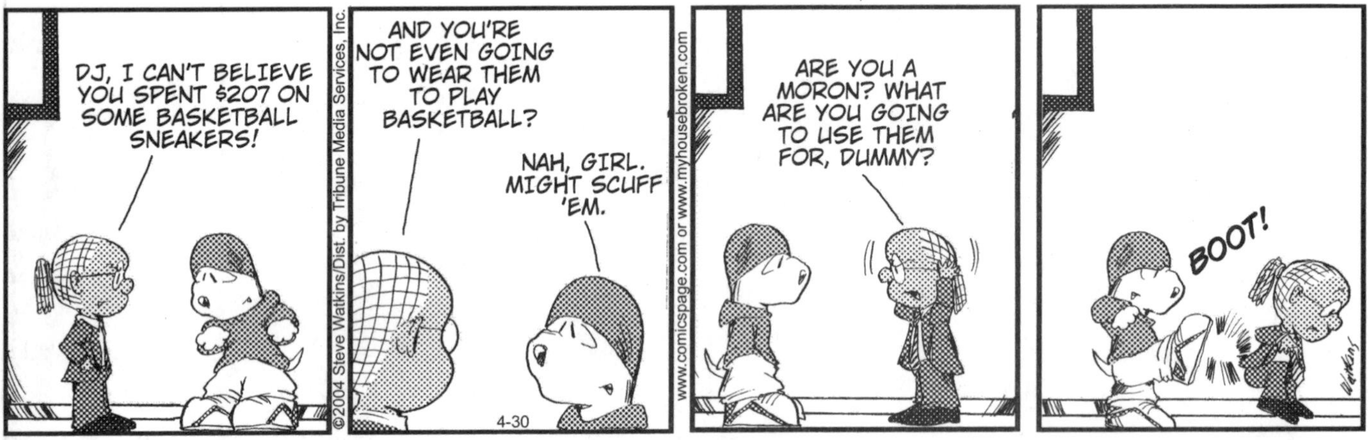
DJ, I CAN'T BELIEVE YOU SPENT $207 ON SOME BASKETBALL SNEAKERS!
AND YOU'RE NOT EVEN GOING TO WEAR THEM TO PLAY BASKETBALL?
NAH, GIRL. MIGHT SCUFF 'EM.
ARE YOU A MORON? WHAT ARE YOU GOING TO USE THEM FOR, DUMMY?
BOOT!
©2004 Steve Watkins/Dist. by Tribune Media Services, Inc.
www.comicspage.com or www.myhousebroken.com
4-30

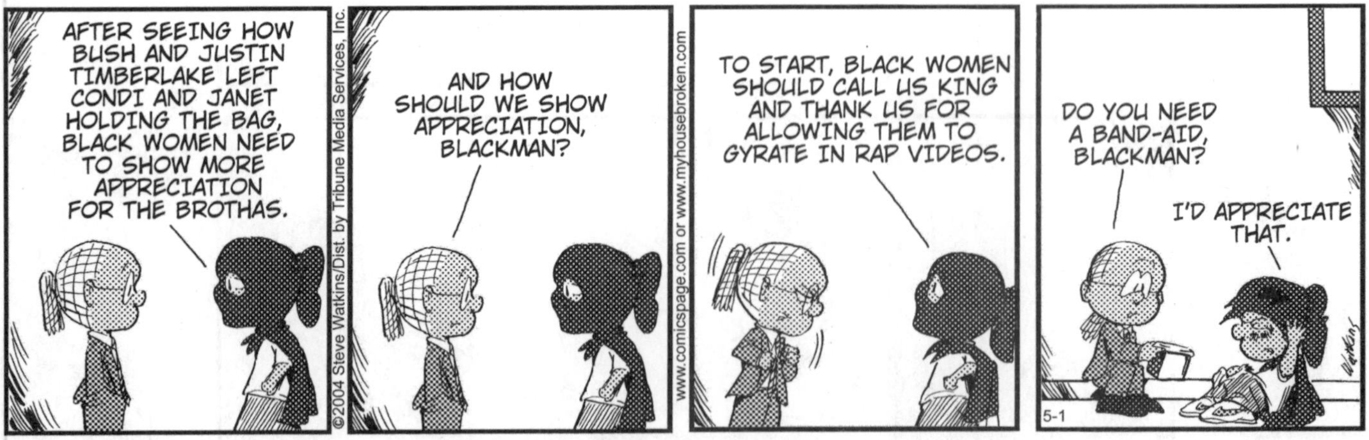
AFTER SEEING HOW BUSH AND JUSTIN TIMBERLAKE LEFT CONDI AND JANET HOLDING THE BAG, BLACK WOMEN NEED TO SHOW MORE APPRECIATION FOR THE BROTHAS.
AND HOW SHOULD WE SHOW APPRECIATION, BLACKMAN?
TO START, BLACK WOMEN SHOULD CALL US KING AND THANK US FOR ALLOWING THEM TO GYRATE IN RAP VIDEOS.
DO YOU NEED A BAND-AID, BLACKMAN?
I'D APPRECIATE THAT.
©2004 Steve Watkins/Dist. by Tribune Media Services, Inc.
www.comicspage.com or www.myhousebroken.com
5-1

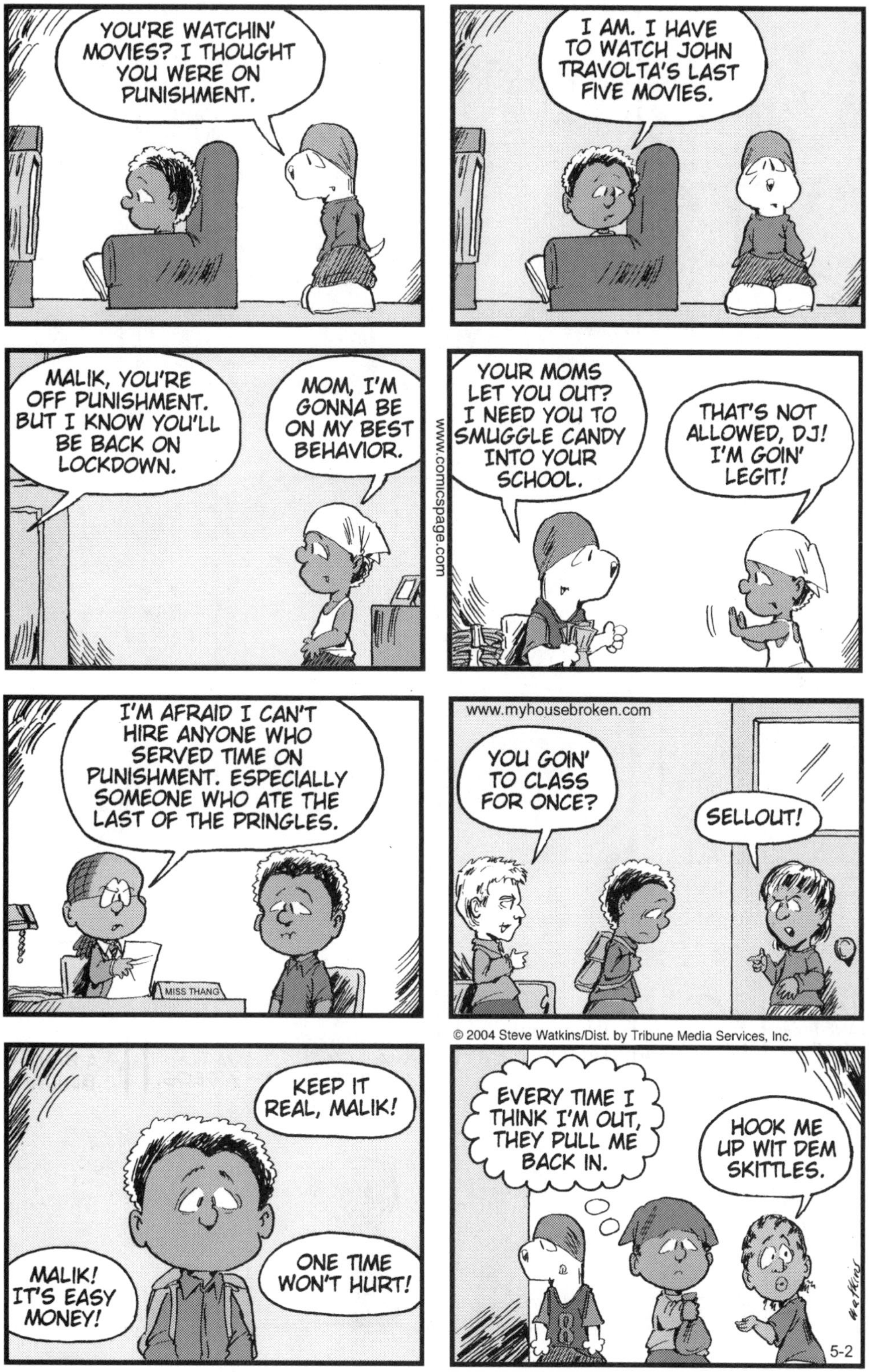
YOU'RE WATCHIN' MOVIES? I THOUGHT YOU WERE ON PUNISHMENT.
I AM. I HAVE TO WATCH JOHN TRAVOLTA'S LAST FIVE MOVIES.
MALIK, YOU'RE OFF PUNISHMENT. BUT I KNOW YOU'LL BE BACK ON LOCKDOWN.
MOM, I'M GONNA BE ON MY BEST BEHAVIOR.
www.comicspage.com
YOUR MOMS LET YOU OUT? I NEED YOU TO SMUGGLE CANDY INTO YOUR SCHOOL.
THAT'S NOT ALLOWED, DJ! I'M GOIN' LEGIT!
I'M AFRAID I CAN'T HIRE ANYONE WHO SERVED TIME ON PUNISHMENT. ESPECIALLY SOMEONE WHO ATE THE LAST OF THE PRINGLES.
MISS THANG
www.myhousebroken.com
YOU GOIN' TO CLASS FOR ONCE?
SELLOUT!
KEEP IT REAL, MALIK!
MALIK! IT'S EASY MONEY!
ONE TIME WON'T HURT!
EVERY TIME I THINK I'M OUT, THEY PULL ME BACK IN.
HOOK ME UP WIT DEM SKITTLES.
WATKINS
5-2

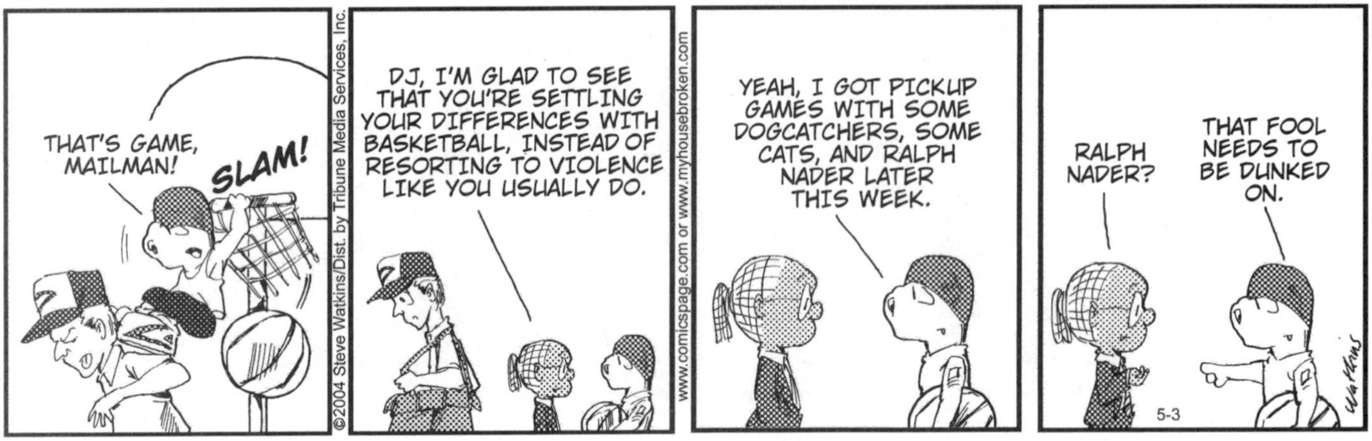

THAT'S GAME, MAILMAN!
SLAM!
©2004 Steve Watkins/Dist. by Tribune Media Services, Inc.
DJ, I'M GLAD TO SEE THAT YOU'RE SETTLING YOUR DIFFERENCES WITH BASKETBALL, INSTEAD OF RESORTING TO VIOLENCE LIKE YOU USUALLY DO.
www.comicspage.com or www.myhousebroken.com
YEAH, I GOT PICKUP GAMES WITH SOME DOGCATCHERS, SOME CATS, AND RALPH NADER LATER THIS WEEK.
RALPH NADER?
THAT FOOL NEEDS TO BE DUNKED ON.
5-3

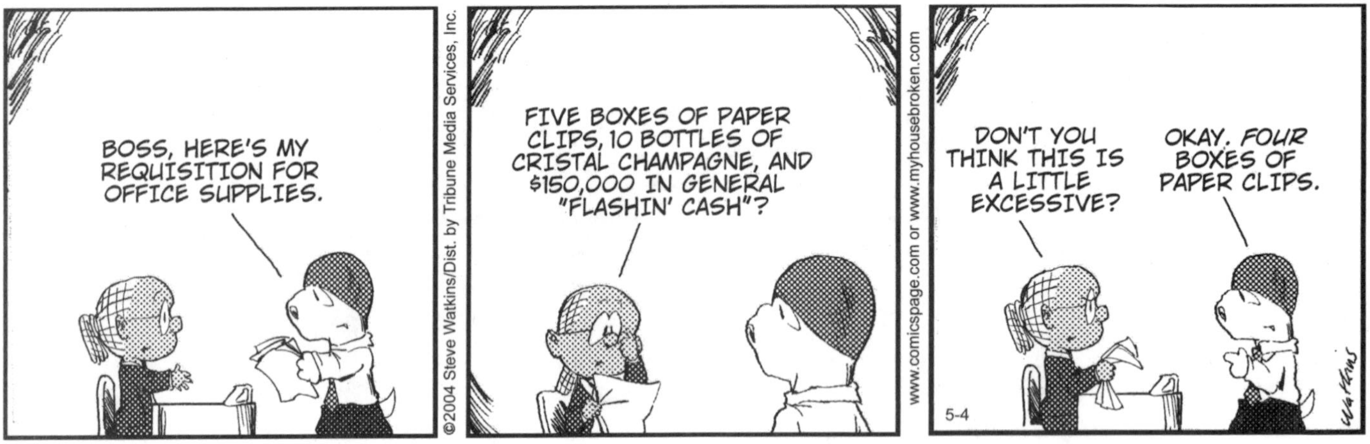

BOSS, HERE'S MY REQUISITION FOR OFFICE SUPPLIES.
©2004 Steve Watkins/Dist. by Tribune Media Services, Inc.
FIVE BOXES OF PAPER CLIPS, 10 BOTTLES OF CRISTAL CHAMPAGNE, AND $150,000 IN GENERAL "FLASHIN' CASH"?
www.comicspage.com or www.myhousebroken.com
DON'T YOU THINK THIS IS A LITTLE EXCESSIVE?
OKAY. *FOUR* BOXES OF PAPER CLIPS.
5-4

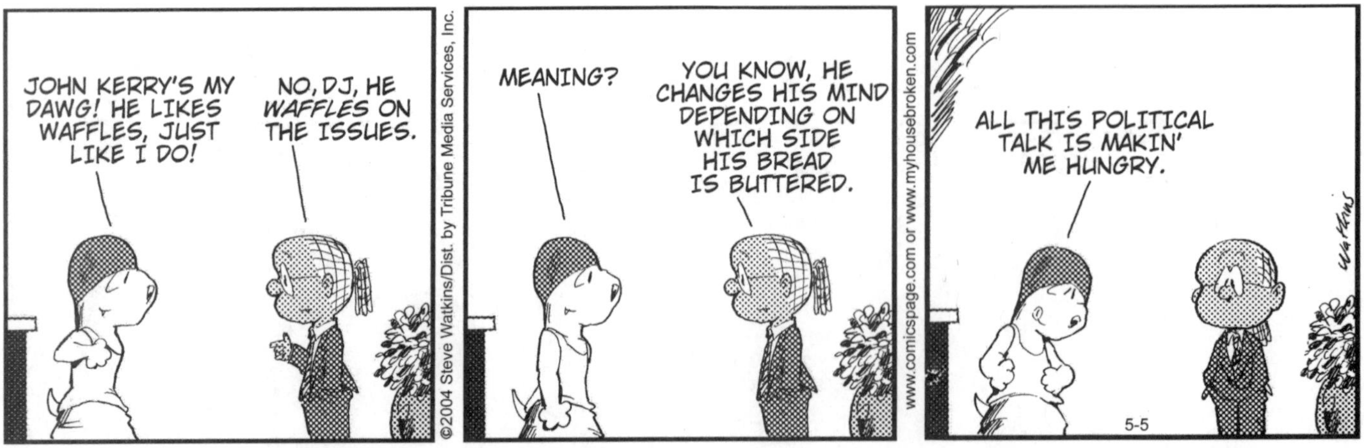

JOHN KERRY'S MY DAWG! HE LIKES WAFFLES, JUST LIKE I DO!
NO, DJ, HE *WAFFLES* ON THE ISSUES.
©2004 Steve Watkins/Dist. by Tribune Media Services, Inc.
MEANING?
YOU KNOW, HE CHANGES HIS MIND DEPENDING ON WHICH SIDE HIS BREAD IS BUTTERED.
www.comicspage.com or www.myhousebroken.com
ALL THIS POLITICAL TALK IS MAKIN' ME HUNGRY.
5-5

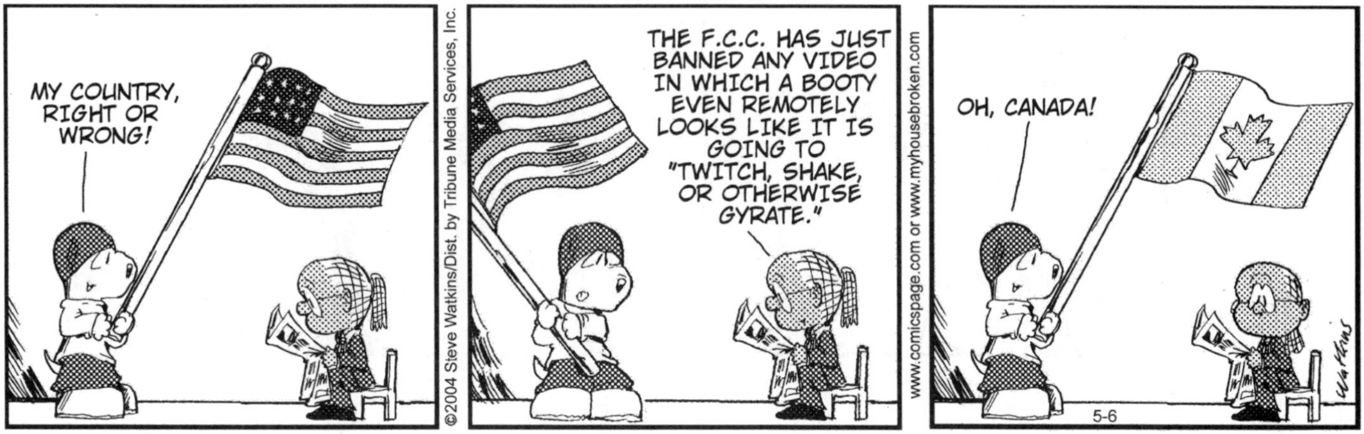
MY COUNTRY, RIGHT OR WRONG!
©2004 Steve Watkins/Dist. by Tribune Media Services, Inc.
THE F.C.C. HAS JUST BANNED ANY VIDEO IN WHICH A BOOTY EVEN REMOTELY LOOKS LIKE IT IS GOING TO "TWITCH, SHAKE, OR OTHERWISE GYRATE."
www.comicspage.com or www.myhousebroken.com
OH, CANADA!
5-6

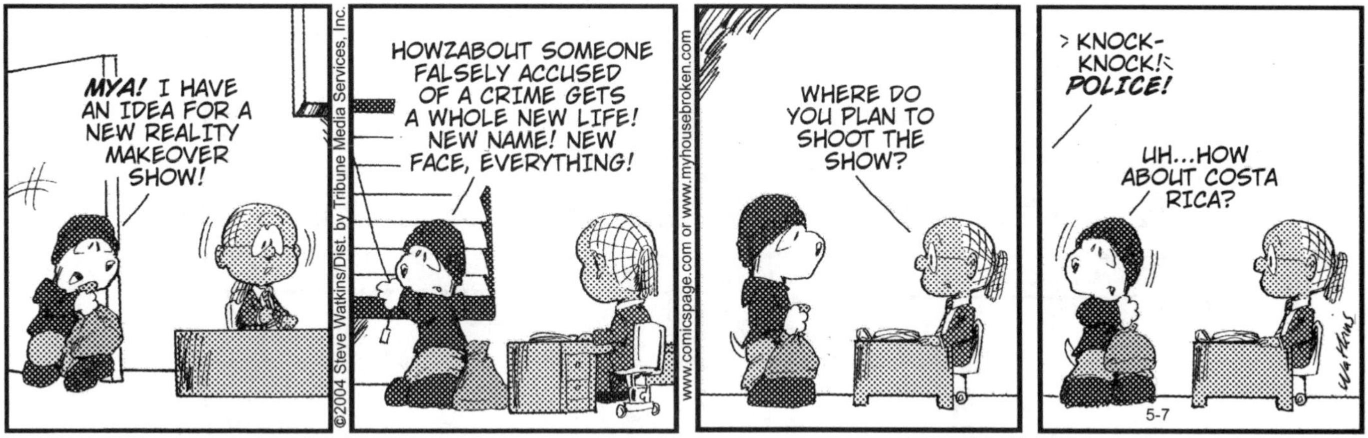
MYA! I HAVE AN IDEA FOR A NEW REALITY MAKEOVER SHOW!
©2004 Steve Watkins/Dist. by Tribune Media Services, Inc.
HOWZABOUT SOMEONE FALSELY ACCUSED OF A CRIME GETS A WHOLE NEW LIFE! NEW NAME! NEW FACE, EVERYTHING!
www.comicspage.com or www.myhousebroken.com
WHERE DO YOU PLAN TO SHOOT THE SHOW?
KNOCK-KNOCK! *POLICE!*
UH...HOW ABOUT COSTA RICA?
5-7

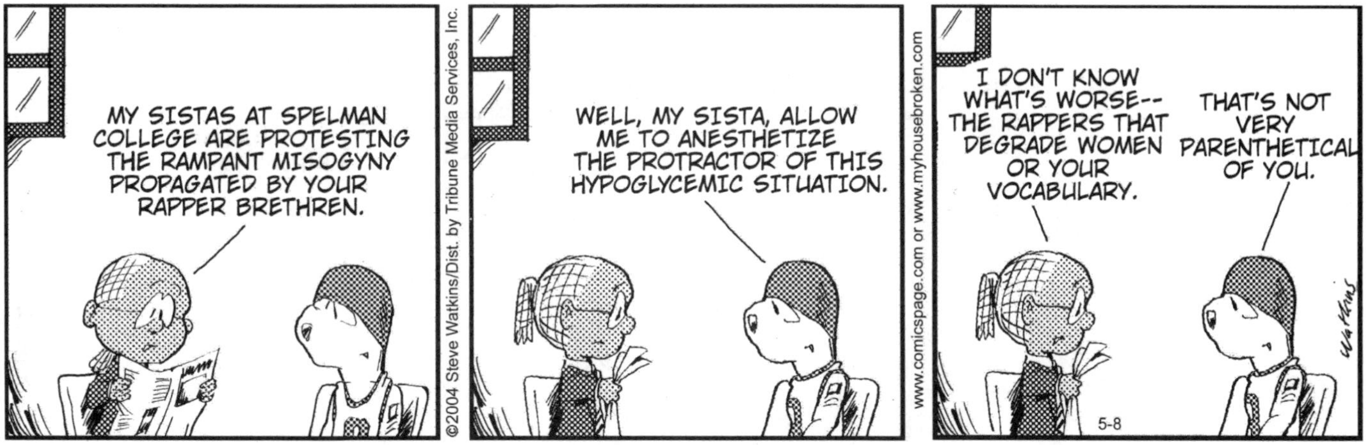
MY SISTAS AT SPELMAN COLLEGE ARE PROTESTING THE RAMPANT MISOGYNY PROPAGATED BY YOUR RAPPER BRETHREN.
©2004 Steve Watkins/Dist. by Tribune Media Services, Inc.
WELL, MY SISTA, ALLOW ME TO ANESTHETIZE THE PROTRACTOR OF THIS HYPOGLYCEMIC SITUATION.
www.comicspage.com or www.myhousebroken.com
I DON'T KNOW WHAT'S WORSE-- THE RAPPERS THAT DEGRADE WOMEN OR YOUR VOCABULARY.
THAT'S NOT VERY PARENTHETICAL OF YOU.
5-8

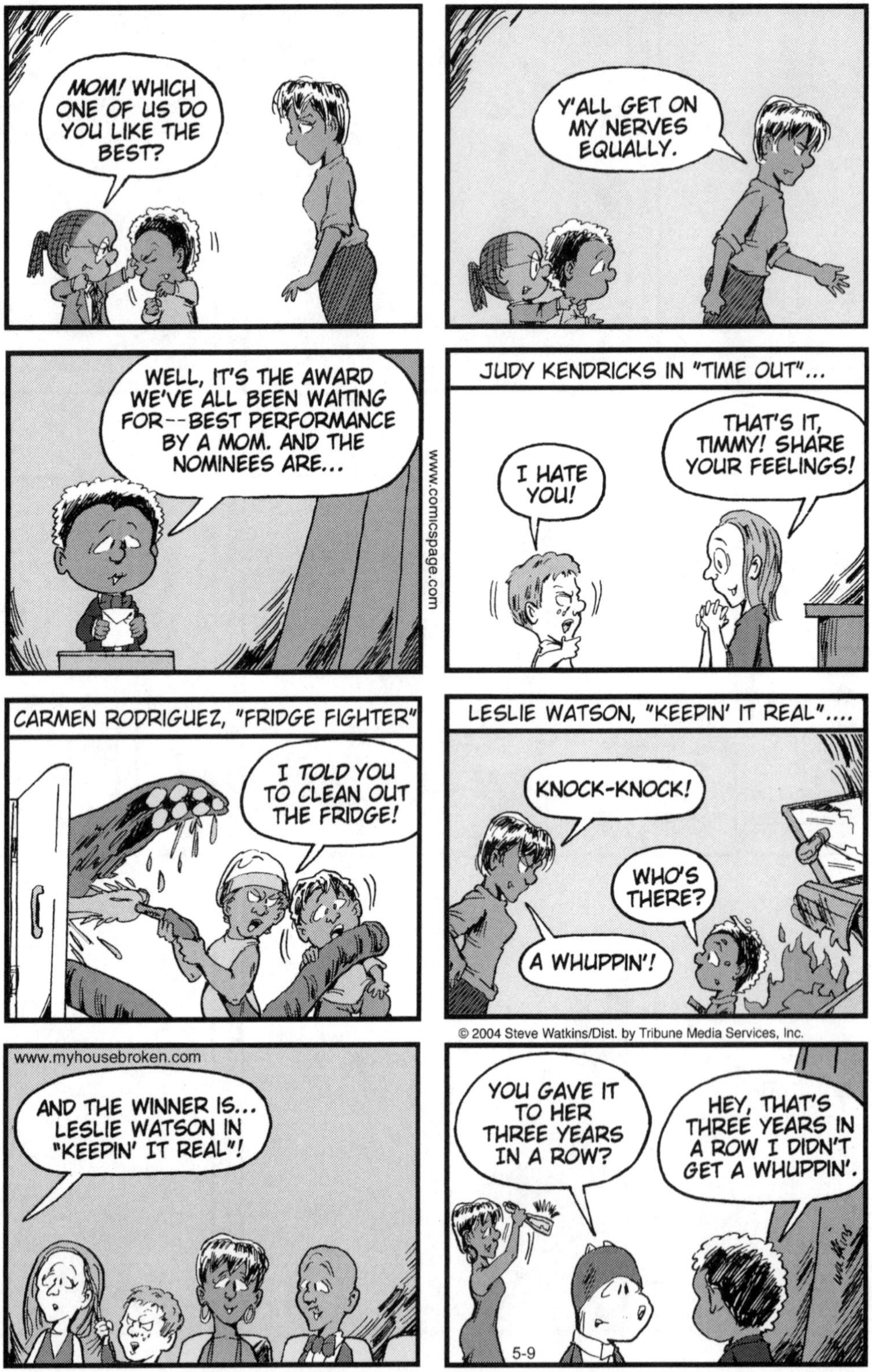
MOM! WHICH ONE OF US DO YOU LIKE THE BEST?
Y'ALL GET ON MY NERVES EQUALLY.
WELL, IT'S THE AWARD WE'VE ALL BEEN WAITING FOR--BEST PERFORMANCE BY A MOM. AND THE NOMINEES ARE...
www.comicspage.com
JUDY KENDRICKS IN "TIME OUT"...
I HATE YOU!
THAT'S IT, TIMMY! SHARE YOUR FEELINGS!
CARMEN RODRIGUEZ, "FRIDGE FIGHTER"
I TOLD YOU TO CLEAN OUT THE FRIDGE!
LESLIE WATSON, "KEEPIN' IT REAL"....
KNOCK-KNOCK!
WHO'S THERE?
A WHUPPIN'!
© 2004 Steve Watkins/Dist. by Tribune Media Services, Inc.
www.myhousebroken.com
AND THE WINNER IS... LESLIE WATSON IN "KEEPIN' IT REAL"!
YOU GAVE IT TO HER THREE YEARS IN A ROW?
HEY, THAT'S THREE YEARS IN A ROW I DIDN'T GET A WHUPPIN'.
5-9

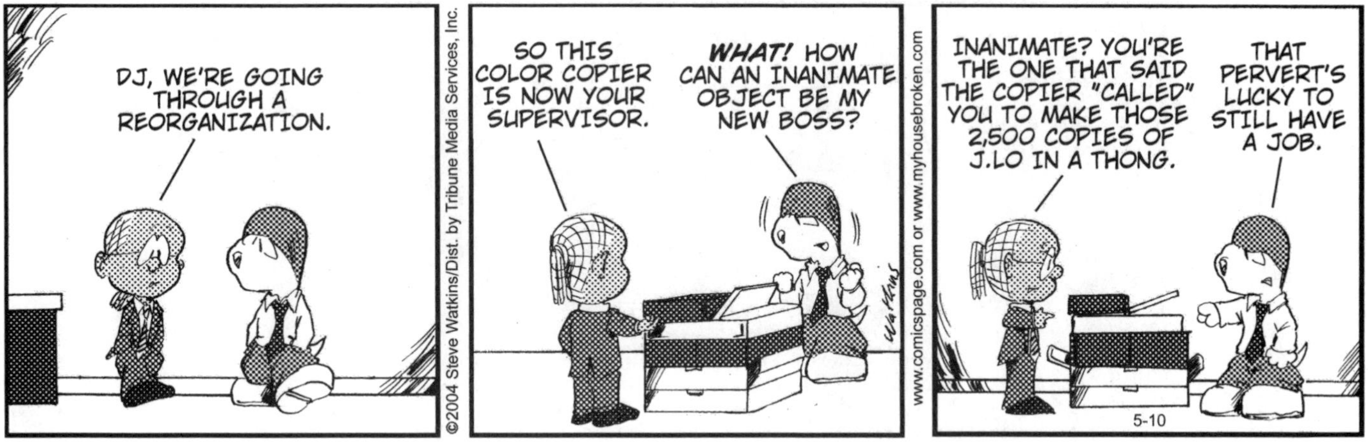
DJ, WE'RE GOING THROUGH A REORGANIZATION.
SO THIS COLOR COPIER IS NOW YOUR SUPERVISOR.
WHAT! HOW CAN AN INANIMATE OBJECT BE MY NEW BOSS?
INANIMATE? YOU'RE THE ONE THAT SAID THE COPIER "CALLED" YOU TO MAKE THOSE 2,500 COPIES OF J.LO IN A THONG.
THAT PERVERT'S LUCKY TO STILL HAVE A JOB.
©2004 Steve Watkins/Dist. by Tribune Media Services, Inc.
www.comicspage.com or www.myhousebroken.com
5-10

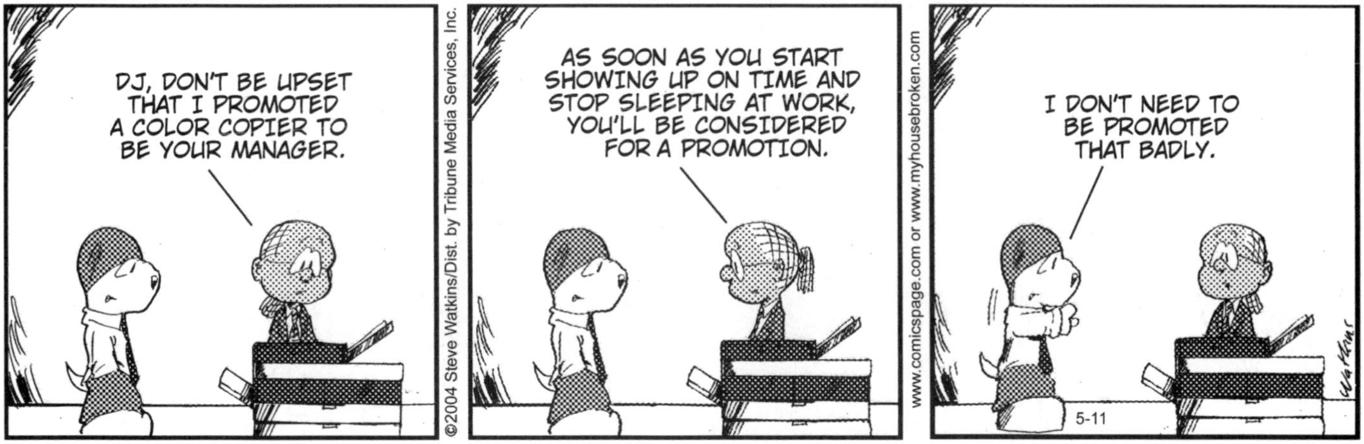
DJ, DON'T BE UPSET THAT I PROMOTED A COLOR COPIER TO BE YOUR MANAGER.
AS SOON AS YOU START SHOWING UP ON TIME AND STOP SLEEPING AT WORK, YOU'LL BE CONSIDERED FOR A PROMOTION.
I DON'T NEED TO BE PROMOTED THAT BADLY.
©2004 Steve Watkins/Dist. by Tribune Media Services, Inc.
www.comicspage.com or www.myhousebroken.com
5-11

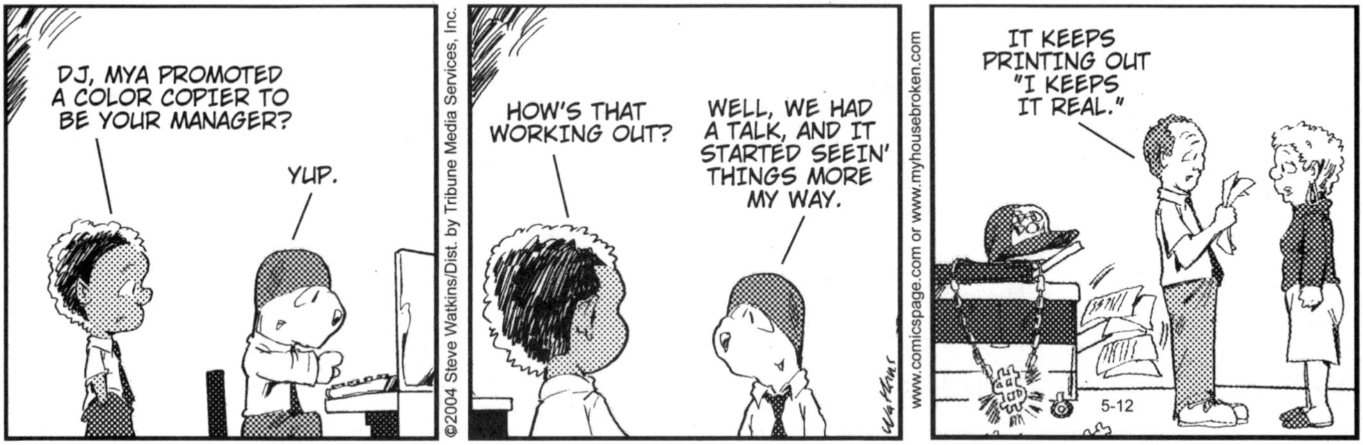
DJ, MYA PROMOTED A COLOR COPIER TO BE YOUR MANAGER?
YUP.
HOW'S THAT WORKING OUT?
WELL, WE HAD A TALK, AND IT STARTED SEEIN' THINGS MORE MY WAY.
IT KEEPS PRINTING OUT "I KEEPS IT REAL."
©2004 Steve Watkins/Dist. by Tribune Media Services, Inc.
www.comicspage.com or www.myhousebroken.com
5-12

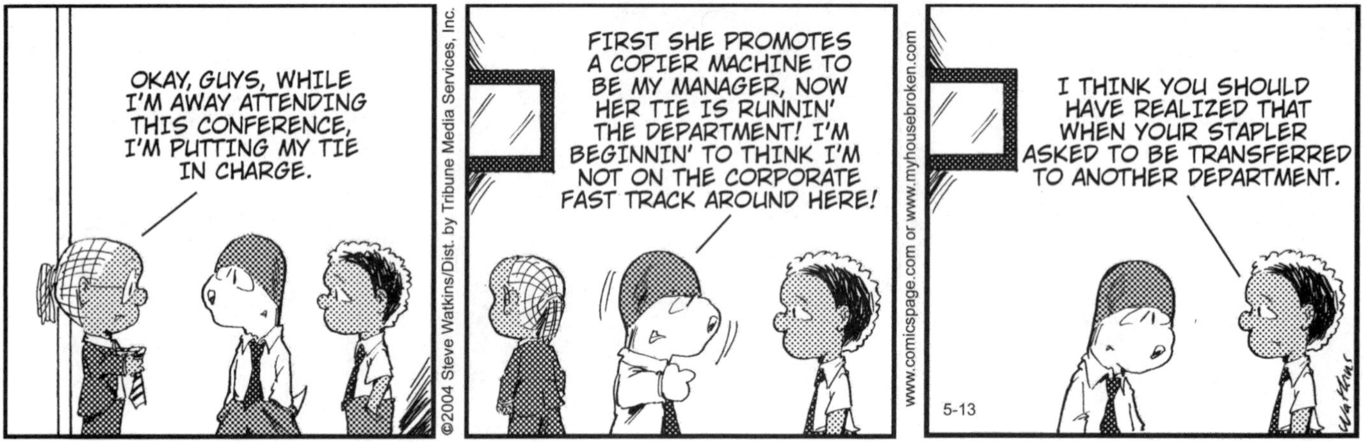
OKAY, GUYS, WHILE I'M AWAY ATTENDING THIS CONFERENCE, I'M PUTTING MY TIE IN CHARGE.
©2004 Steve Watkins/Dist. by Tribune Media Services, Inc.
FIRST SHE PROMOTES A COPIER MACHINE TO BE MY MANAGER, NOW HER TIE IS RUNNIN' THE DEPARTMENT! I'M BEGINNIN' TO THINK I'M NOT ON THE CORPORATE FAST TRACK AROUND HERE!
www.comicspage.com or www.myhousebroken.com
I THINK YOU SHOULD HAVE REALIZED THAT WHEN YOUR STAPLER ASKED TO BE TRANSFERRED TO ANOTHER DEPARTMENT.
5-13

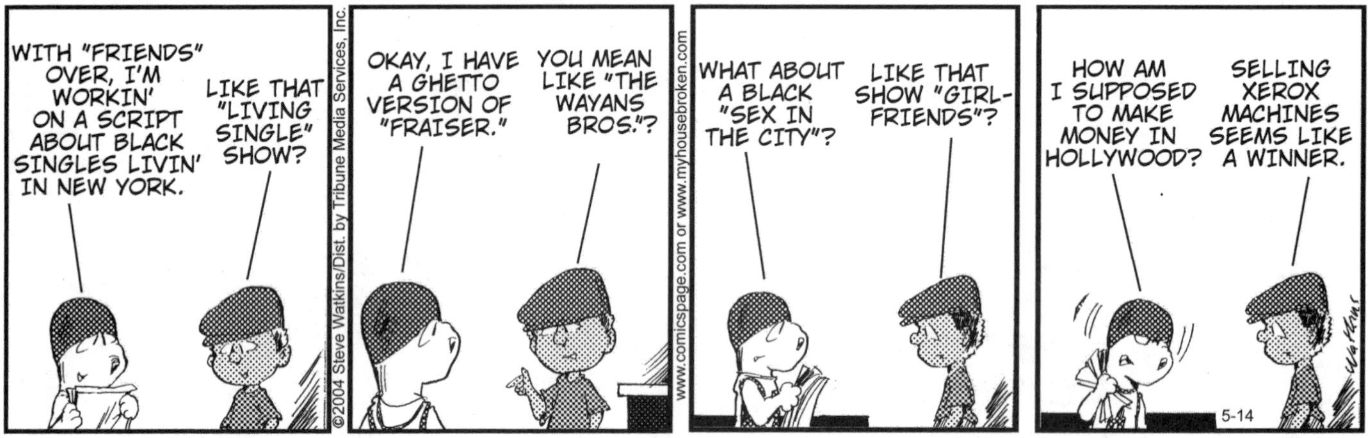
WITH "FRIENDS" OVER, I'M WORKIN' ON A SCRIPT ABOUT BLACK SINGLES LIVIN' IN NEW YORK.
LIKE THAT "LIVING SINGLE" SHOW?
©2004 Steve Watkins/Dist. by Tribune Media Services, Inc.
OKAY, I HAVE A GHETTO VERSION OF "FRAISER."
YOU MEAN LIKE "THE WAYANS BROS."?
www.comicspage.com or www.myhousebroken.com
WHAT ABOUT A BLACK "SEX IN THE CITY"?
LIKE THAT SHOW "GIRL-FRIENDS"?
HOW AM I SUPPOSED TO MAKE MONEY IN HOLLYWOOD?
SELLING XEROX MACHINES SEEMS LIKE A WINNER.
5-14

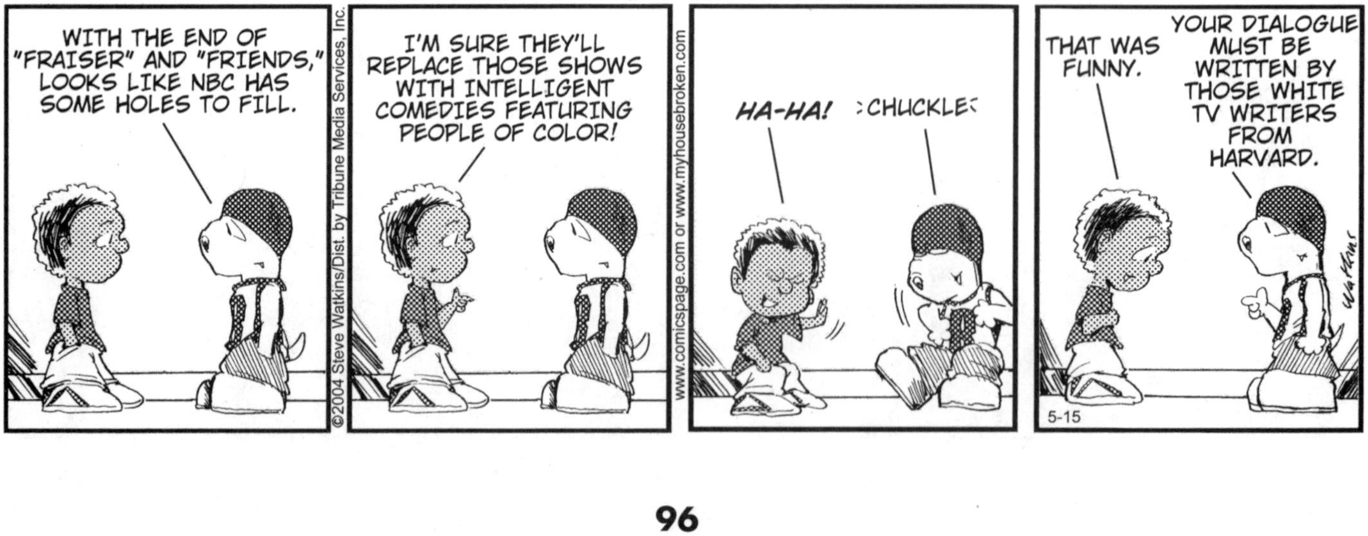
WITH THE END OF "FRAISER" AND "FRIENDS," LOOKS LIKE NBC HAS SOME HOLES TO FILL.
©2004 Steve Watkins/Dist. by Tribune Media Services, Inc.
I'M SURE THEY'LL REPLACE THOSE SHOWS WITH INTELLIGENT COMEDIES FEATURING PEOPLE OF COLOR!
www.comicspage.com or www.myhousebroken.com
HA-HA!
CHUCKLE
THAT WAS FUNNY.
YOUR DIALOGUE MUST BE WRITTEN BY THOSE WHITE TV WRITERS FROM HARVARD.
5-15

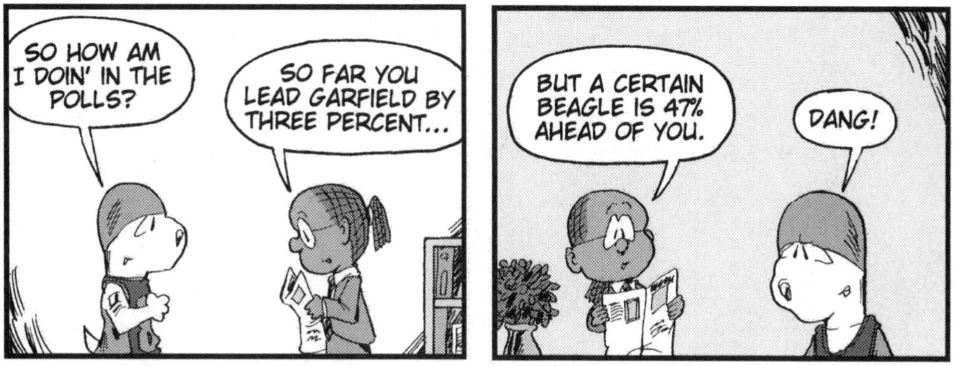
SO HOW AM I DOIN' IN THE POLLS?
SO FAR YOU LEAD GARFIELD BY THREE PERCENT...
BUT A CERTAIN BEAGLE IS 47% AHEAD OF YOU.
DANG!

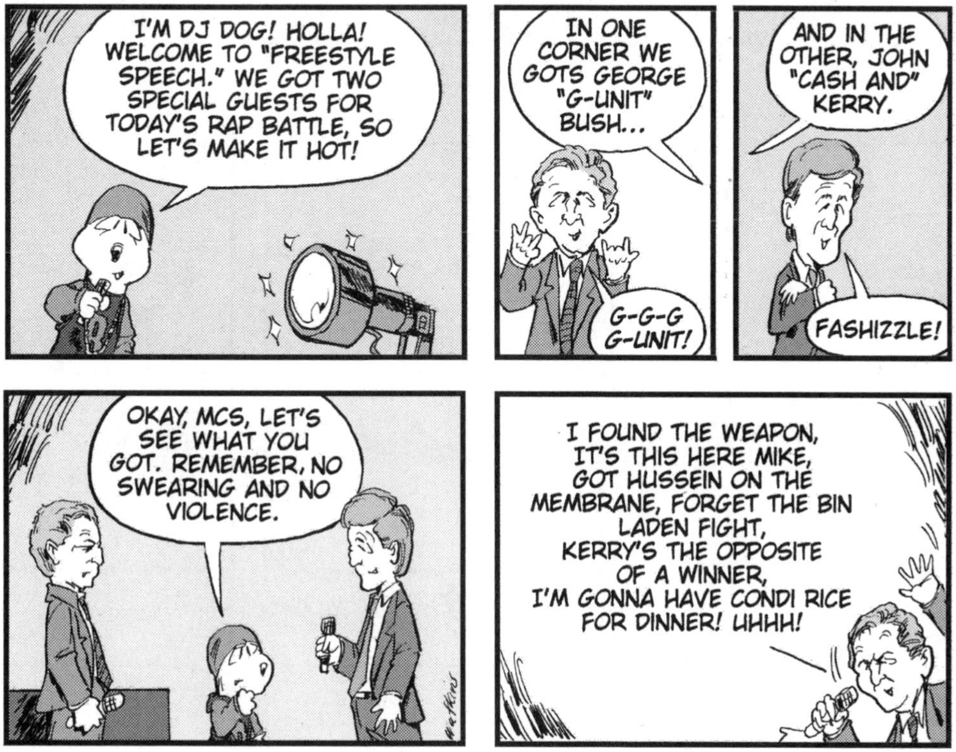
I'M DJ DOG! HOLLA! WELCOME TO "FREESTYLE SPEECH." WE GOT TWO SPECIAL GUESTS FOR TODAY'S RAP BATTLE, SO LET'S MAKE IT HOT!
IN ONE CORNER WE GOTS GEORGE "G-UNIT" BUSH...
G-G-G G-UNIT!
AND IN THE OTHER, JOHN "CASH AND" KERRY.
FASHIZZLE!
OKAY, MCS, LET'S SEE WHAT YOU GOT. REMEMBER, NO SWEARING AND NO VIOLENCE.
I FOUND THE WEAPON, IT'S THIS HERE MIKE, GOT HUSSEIN ON THE MEMBRANE, FORGET THE BIN LADEN FIGHT, KERRY'S THE OPPOSITE OF A WINNER, I'M GONNA HAVE CONDI RICE FOR DINNER! UHHH!

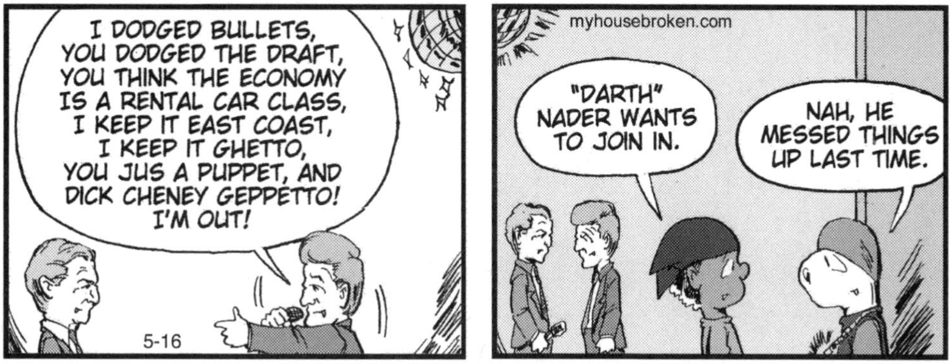
I DODGED BULLETS, YOU DODGED THE DRAFT, YOU THINK THE ECONOMY IS A RENTAL CAR CLASS, I KEEP IT EAST COAST, I KEEP IT GHETTO, YOU JUS A PUPPET, AND DICK CHENEY GEPPETTO! I'M OUT!
5-16
myhousebroken.com
"DARTH" NADER WANTS TO JOIN IN.
NAH, HE MESSED THINGS UP LAST TIME.

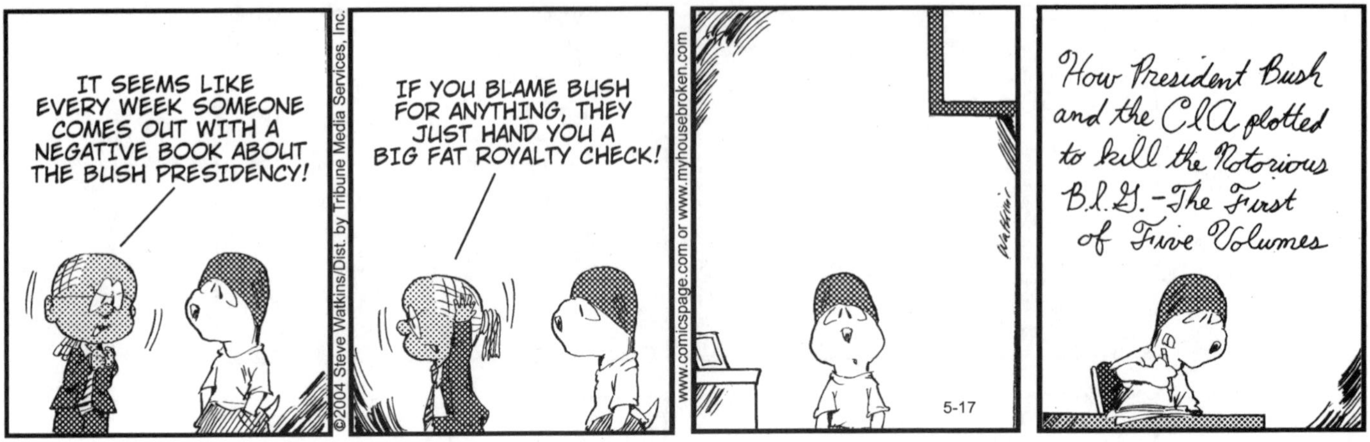
IT SEEMS LIKE EVERY WEEK SOMEONE COMES OUT WITH A NEGATIVE BOOK ABOUT THE BUSH PRESIDENCY!
©2004 Steve Watkins/Dist. by Tribune Media Services, Inc.
IF YOU BLAME BUSH FOR ANYTHING, THEY JUST HAND YOU A BIG FAT ROYALTY CHECK!
www.comicspage.com or www.myhousebroken.com
5-17
How President Bush and the CIA plotted to kill the Notorious B.I.G. - The First of Five Volumes

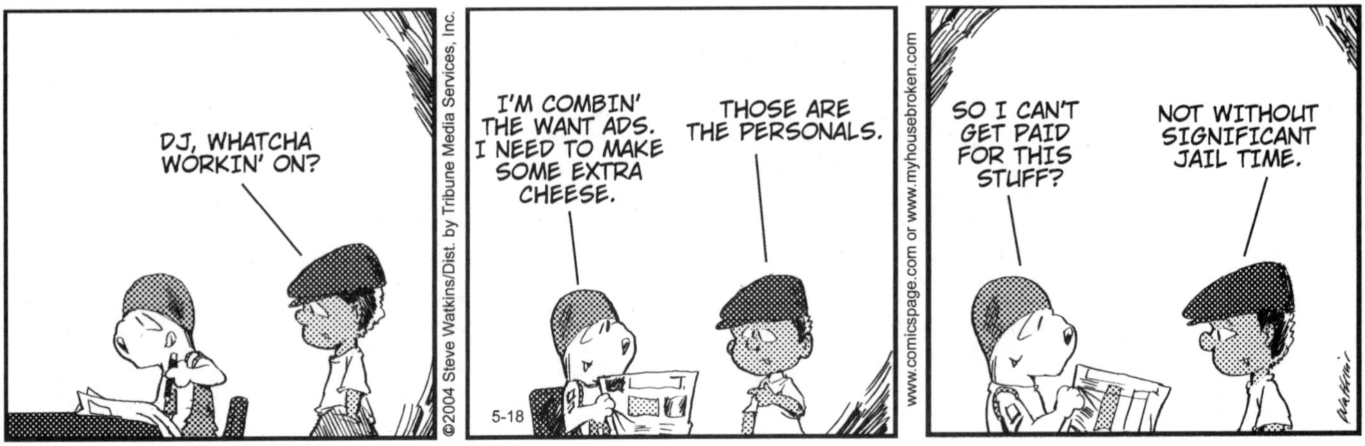
DJ, WHATCHA WORKIN' ON?
©2004 Steve Watkins/Dist. by Tribune Media Services, Inc.
I'M COMBIN' THE WANT ADS. I NEED TO MAKE SOME EXTRA CHEESE.
THOSE ARE THE PERSONALS.
5-18
www.comicspage.com or www.myhousebroken.com
SO I CAN'T GET PAID FOR THIS STUFF?
NOT WITHOUT SIGNIFICANT JAIL TIME.

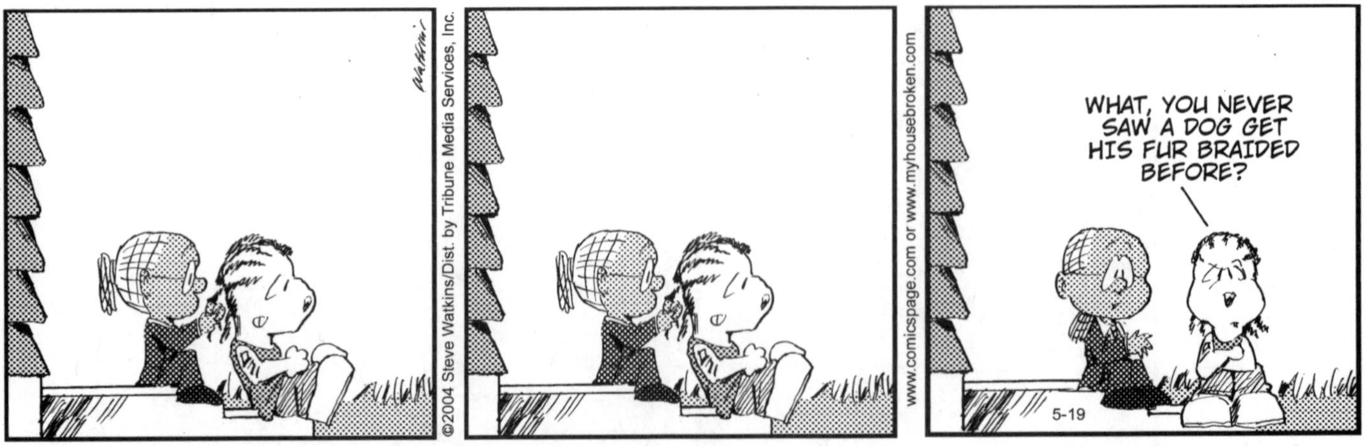
©2004 Steve Watkins/Dist. by Tribune Media Services, Inc.
www.comicspage.com or www.myhousebroken.com
WHAT, YOU NEVER SAW A DOG GET HIS FUR BRAIDED BEFORE?
5-19

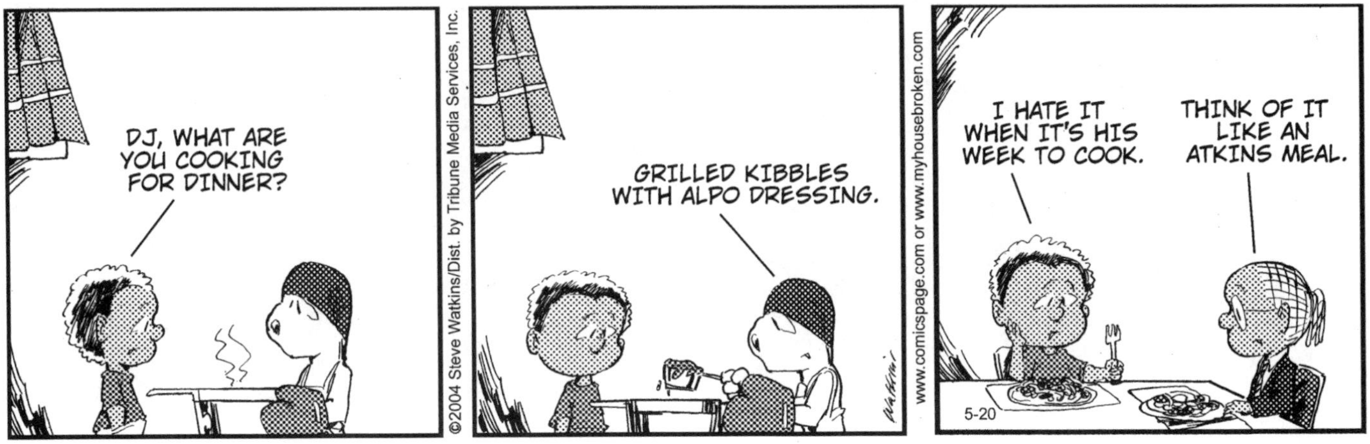
DJ, WHAT ARE YOU COOKING FOR DINNER?
GRILLED KIBBLES WITH ALPO DRESSING.
I HATE IT WHEN IT'S HIS WEEK TO COOK.
THINK OF IT LIKE AN ATKINS MEAL.
©2004 Steve Watkins/Dist. by Tribune Media Services, Inc.
www.comicspage.com or www.myhousebroken.com
5-20

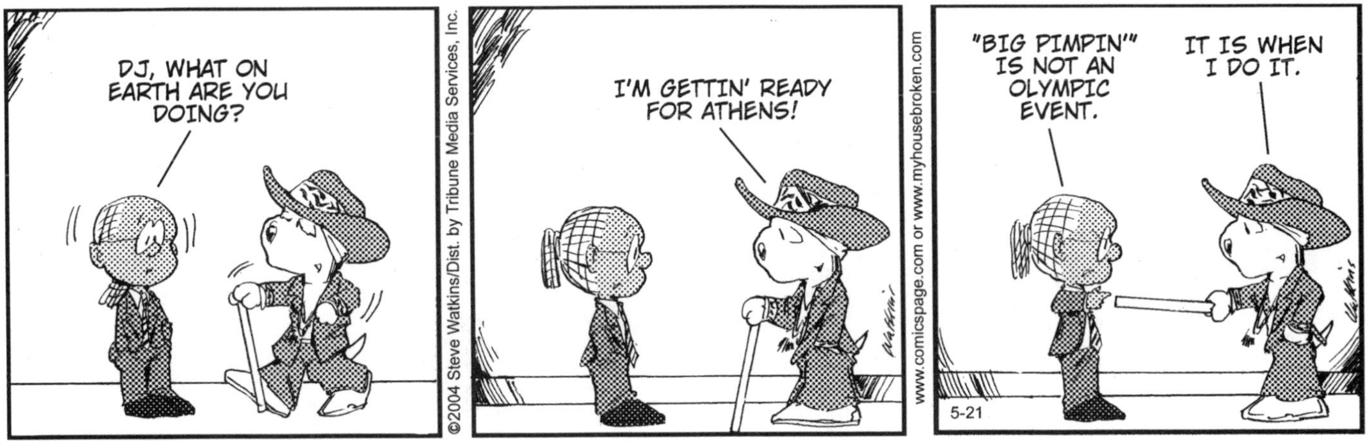
DJ, WHAT ON EARTH ARE YOU DOING?
I'M GETTIN' READY FOR ATHENS!
"BIG PIMPIN'" IS NOT AN OLYMPIC EVENT.
IT IS WHEN I DO IT.
©2004 Steve Watkins/Dist. by Tribune Media Services, Inc.
www.comicspage.com or www.myhousebroken.com
5-21

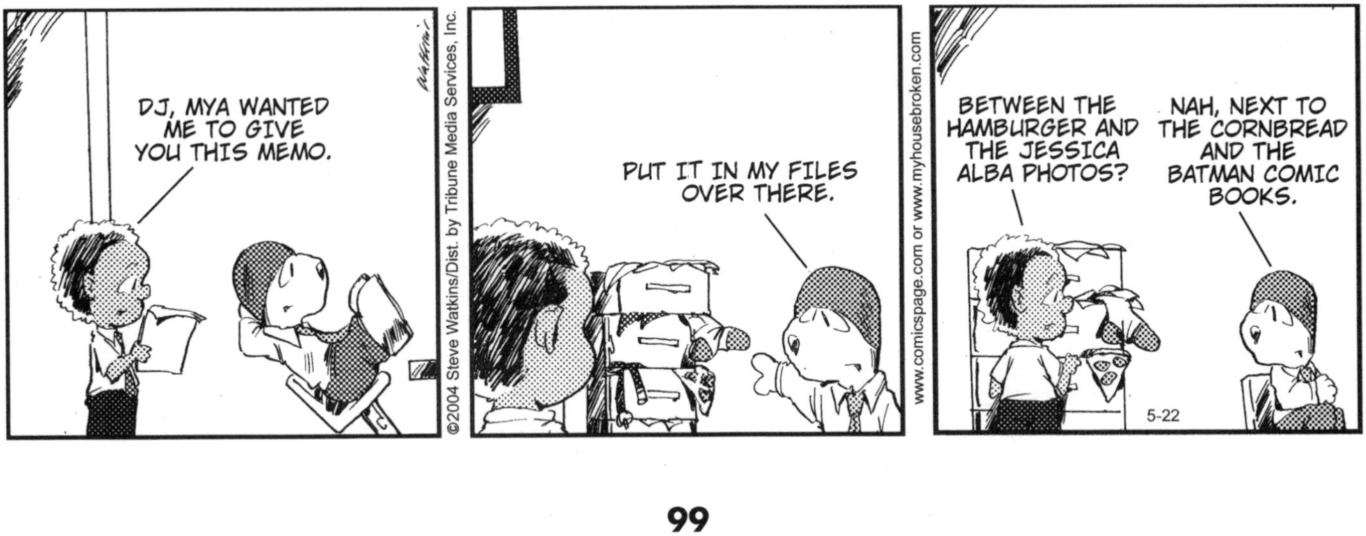
DJ, MYA WANTED ME TO GIVE YOU THIS MEMO.
PUT IT IN MY FILES OVER THERE.
BETWEEN THE HAMBURGER AND THE JESSICA ALBA PHOTOS?
NAH, NEXT TO THE CORNBREAD AND THE BATMAN COMIC BOOKS.
©2004 Steve Watkins/Dist. by Tribune Media Services, Inc.
www.comicspage.com or www.myhousebroken.com
5-22

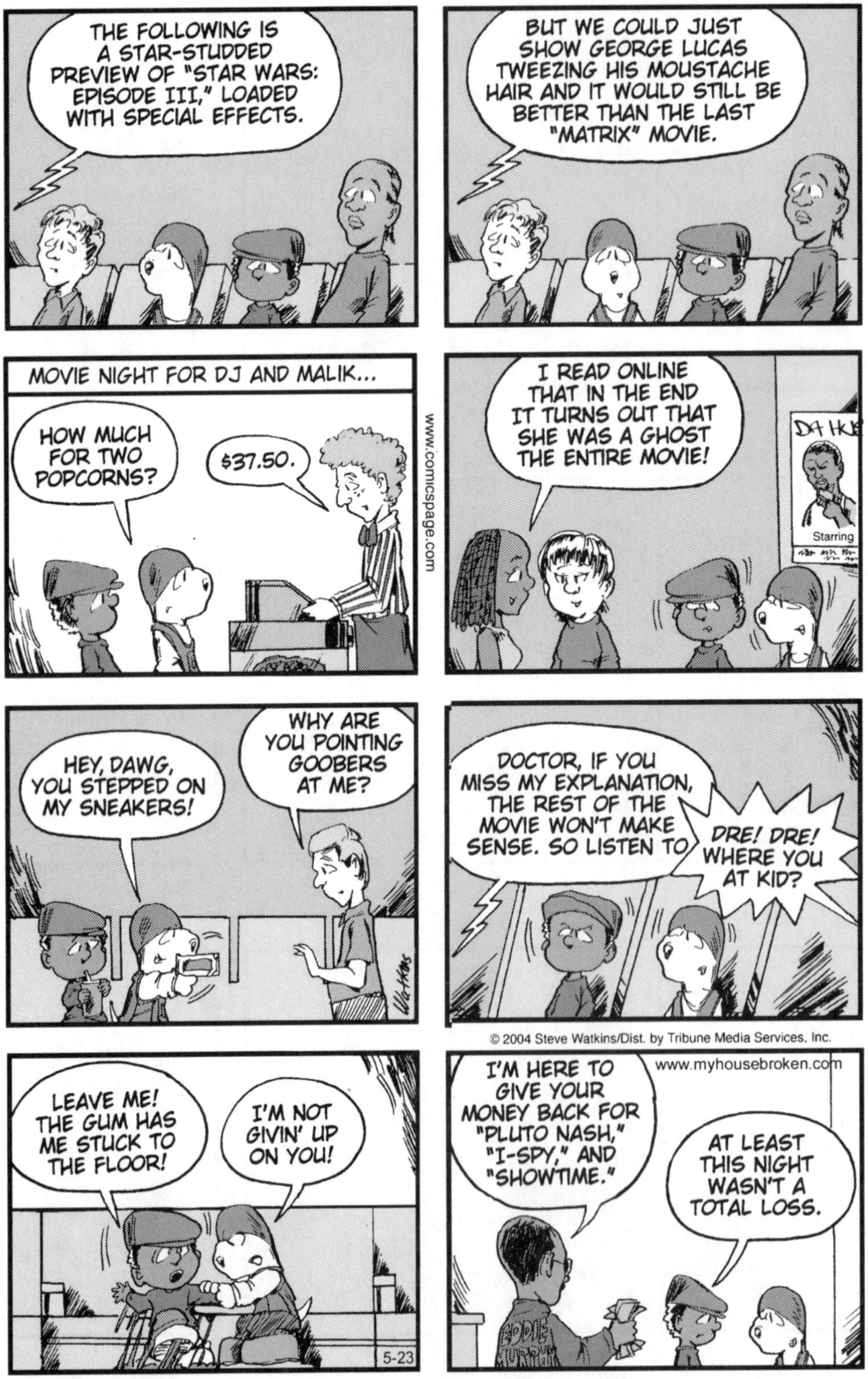
THE FOLLOWING IS A STAR-STUDDED PREVIEW OF "STAR WARS: EPISODE III," LOADED WITH SPECIAL EFFECTS.
BUT WE COULD JUST SHOW GEORGE LUCAS TWEEZING HIS MOUSTACHE HAIR AND IT WOULD STILL BE BETTER THAN THE LAST "MATRIX" MOVIE.
MOVIE NIGHT FOR DJ AND MALIK...
HOW MUCH FOR TWO POPCORNS?
$37.50.
www.comicspage.com
I READ ONLINE THAT IN THE END IT TURNS OUT THAT SHE WAS A GHOST THE ENTIRE MOVIE!
Starring
HEY, DAWG, YOU STEPPED ON MY SNEAKERS!
WHY ARE YOU POINTING GOOBERS AT ME?
DOCTOR, IF YOU MISS MY EXPLANATION, THE REST OF THE MOVIE WON'T MAKE SENSE. SO LISTEN TO
DRE! DRE! WHERE YOU AT KID?
LEAVE ME! THE GUM HAS ME STUCK TO THE FLOOR!
I'M NOT GIVIN' UP ON YOU!
5-23
www.myhousebroken.com
I'M HERE TO GIVE YOUR MONEY BACK FOR "PLUTO NASH," "I-SPY," AND "SHOWTIME."
AT LEAST THIS NIGHT WASN'T A TOTAL LOSS.

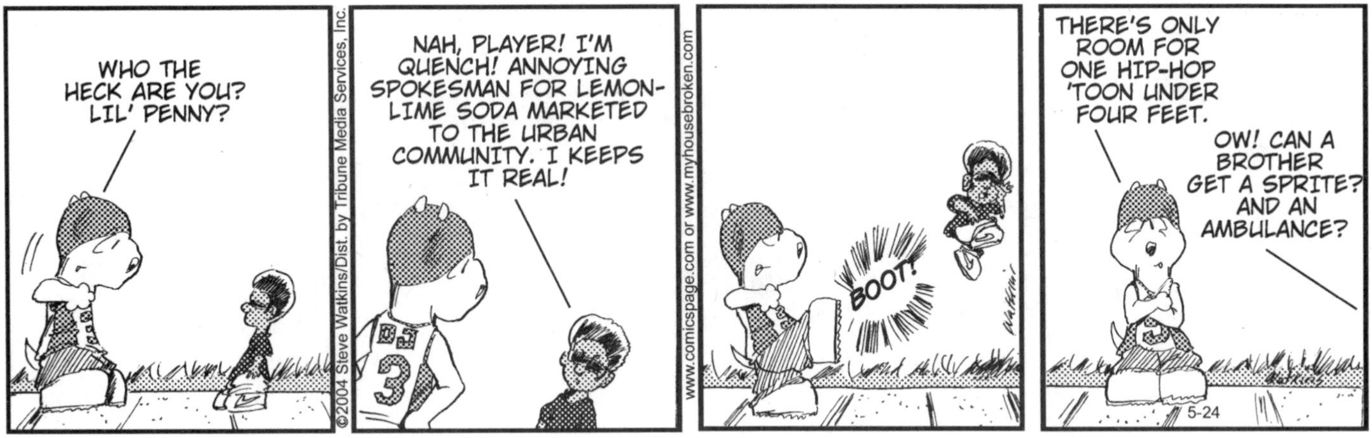
WHO THE HECK ARE YOU? LIL' PENNY?
©2004 Steve Watkins/Dist. by Tribune Media Services, Inc.
NAH, PLAYER! I'M QUENCH! ANNOYING SPOKESMAN FOR LEMON-LIME SODA MARKETED TO THE URBAN COMMUNITY. I KEEPS IT REAL!
www.comicspage.com or www.myhousebroken.com
BOOT!
THERE'S ONLY ROOM FOR ONE HIP-HOP 'TOON UNDER FOUR FEET.
OW! CAN A BROTHER GET A SPRITE? AND AN AMBULANCE?
5-24

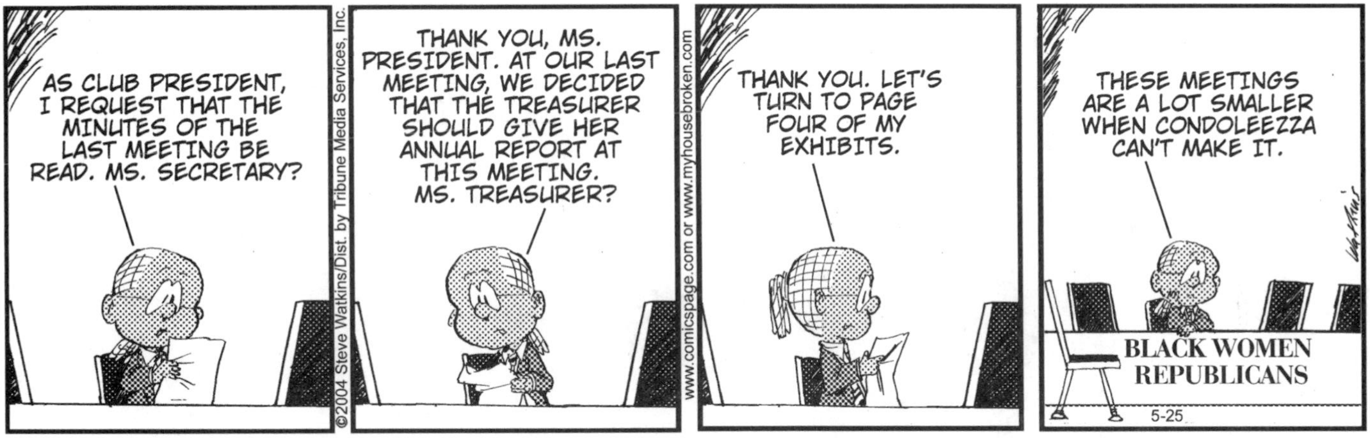
AS CLUB PRESIDENT, I REQUEST THAT THE MINUTES OF THE LAST MEETING BE READ. MS. SECRETARY?
©2004 Steve Watkins/Dist. by Tribune Media Services, Inc.
THANK YOU, MS. PRESIDENT. AT OUR LAST MEETING, WE DECIDED THAT THE TREASURER SHOULD GIVE HER ANNUAL REPORT AT THIS MEETING. MS. TREASURER?
www.comicspage.com or www.myhousebroken.com
THANK YOU. LET'S TURN TO PAGE FOUR OF MY EXHIBITS.
THESE MEETINGS ARE A LOT SMALLER WHEN CONDOLEEZZA CAN'T MAKE IT.
BLACK WOMEN REPUBLICANS
5-25

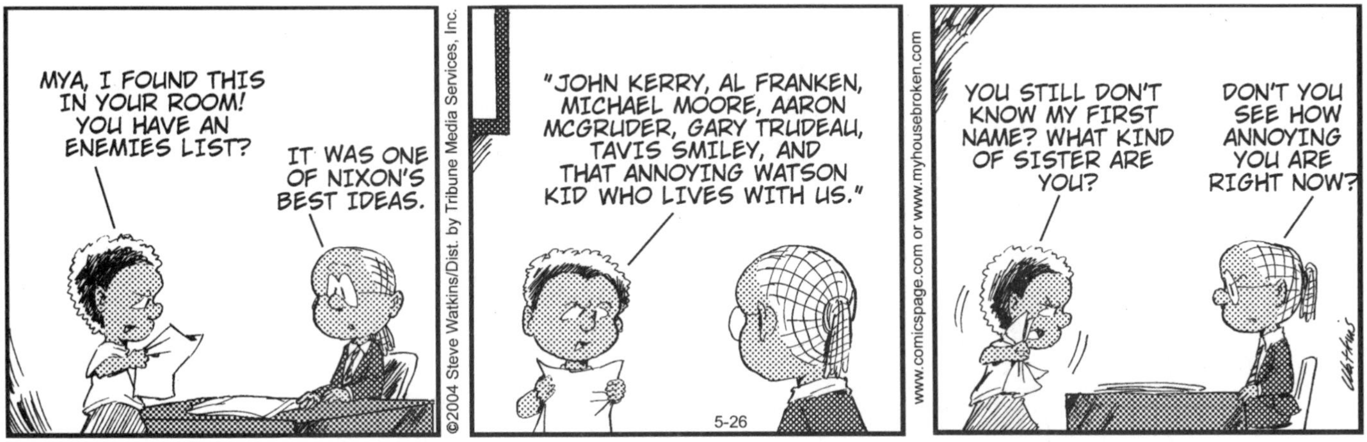
MYA, I FOUND THIS IN YOUR ROOM! YOU HAVE AN ENEMIES LIST?
IT WAS ONE OF NIXON'S BEST IDEAS.
©2004 Steve Watkins/Dist. by Tribune Media Services, Inc.
"JOHN KERRY, AL FRANKEN, MICHAEL MOORE, AARON MCGRUDER, GARY TRUDEAU, TAVIS SMILEY, AND THAT ANNOYING WATSON KID WHO LIVES WITH US."
5-26
www.comicspage.com or www.myhousebroken.com
YOU STILL DON'T KNOW MY FIRST NAME? WHAT KIND OF SISTER ARE YOU?
DON'T YOU SEE HOW ANNOYING YOU ARE RIGHT NOW?

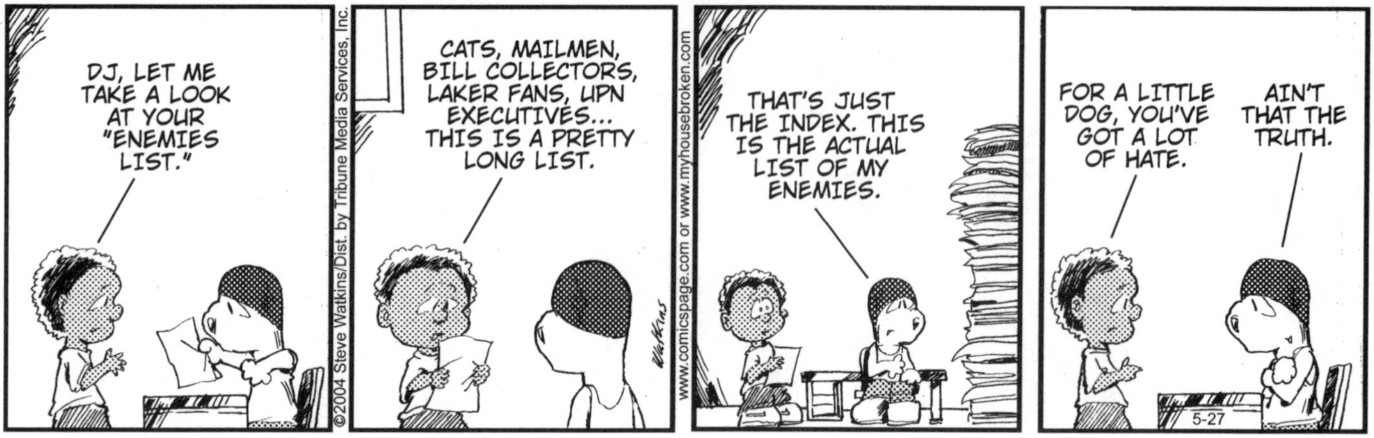
DJ, LET ME TAKE A LOOK AT YOUR "ENEMIES LIST."
©2004 Steve Watkins/Dist. by Tribune Media Services, Inc.
CATS, MAILMEN, BILL COLLECTORS, LAKER FANS, UPN EXECUTIVES... THIS IS A PRETTY LONG LIST.
www.comicspage.com or www.myhousebroken.com
THAT'S JUST THE INDEX. THIS IS THE ACTUAL LIST OF MY ENEMIES.
FOR A LITTLE DOG, YOU'VE GOT A LOT OF HATE.
AIN'T THAT THE TRUTH.
5-27

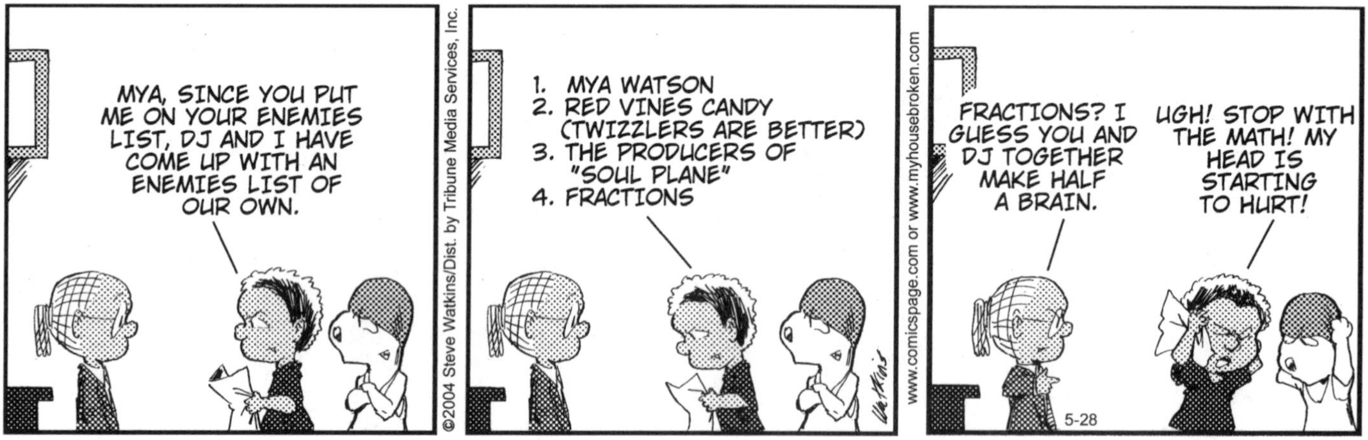
MYA, SINCE YOU PUT ME ON YOUR ENEMIES LIST, DJ AND I HAVE COME UP WITH AN ENEMIES LIST OF OUR OWN.
©2004 Steve Watkins/Dist. by Tribune Media Services, Inc.
1. MYA WATSON
2. RED VINES CANDY (TWIZZLERS ARE BETTER)
3. THE PRODUCERS OF "SOUL PLANE"
4. FRACTIONS
www.comicspage.com or www.myhousebroken.com
FRACTIONS? I GUESS YOU AND DJ TOGETHER MAKE HALF A BRAIN.
UGH! STOP WITH THE MATH! MY HEAD IS STARTING TO HURT!
5-28

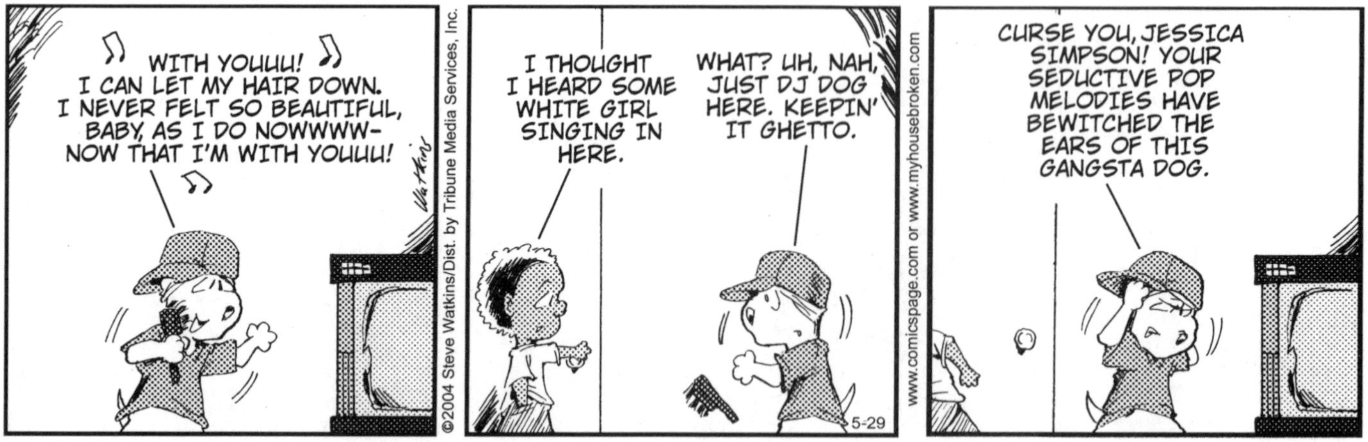
WITH YOUUU! I CAN LET MY HAIR DOWN. I NEVER FELT SO BEAUTIFUL, BABY, AS I DO NOWWWW- NOW THAT I'M WITH YOUUU!
©2004 Steve Watkins/Dist. by Tribune Media Services, Inc.
I THOUGHT I HEARD SOME WHITE GIRL SINGING IN HERE.
WHAT? UH, NAH, JUST DJ DOG HERE. KEEPIN' IT GHETTO.
5-29
www.comicspage.com or www.myhousebroken.com
CURSE YOU, JESSICA SIMPSON! YOUR SEDUCTIVE POP MELODIES HAVE BEWITCHED THE EARS OF THIS GANGSTA DOG.

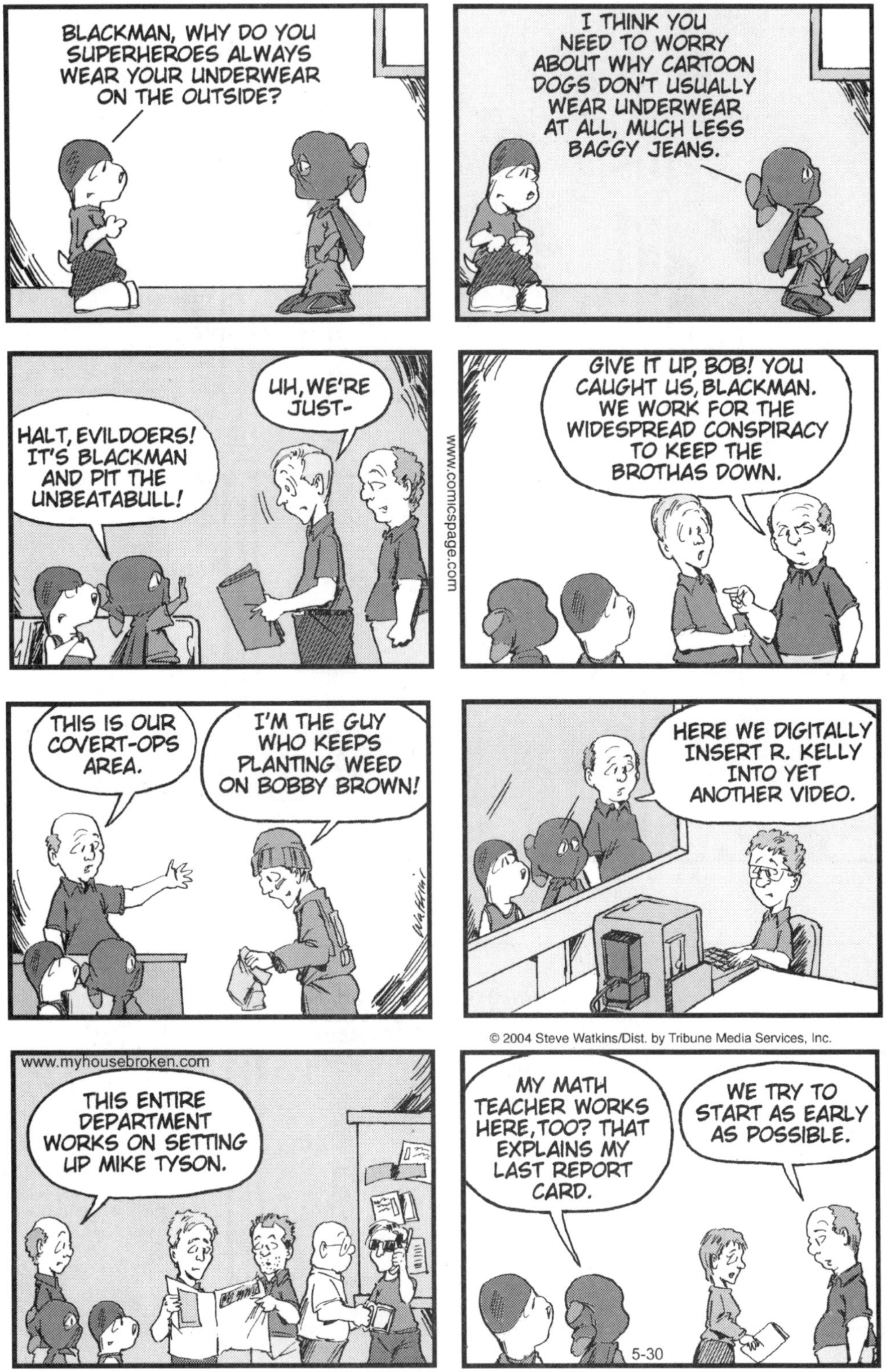
BLACKMAN, WHY DO YOU SUPERHEROES ALWAYS WEAR YOUR UNDERWEAR ON THE OUTSIDE?
I THINK YOU NEED TO WORRY ABOUT WHY CARTOON DOGS DON'T USUALLY WEAR UNDERWEAR AT ALL, MUCH LESS BAGGY JEANS.
HALT, EVILDOERS! IT'S BLACKMAN AND PIT THE UNBEATABULL!
UH, WE'RE JUST-
www.comicspage.com
GIVE IT UP, BOB! YOU CAUGHT US, BLACKMAN. WE WORK FOR THE WIDESPREAD CONSPIRACY TO KEEP THE BROTHAS DOWN.
THIS IS OUR COVERT-OPS AREA.
I'M THE GUY WHO KEEPS PLANTING WEED ON BOBBY BROWN!
HERE WE DIGITALLY INSERT R. KELLY INTO YET ANOTHER VIDEO.
© 2004 Steve Watkins/Dist. by Tribune Media Services, Inc.
www.myhousebroken.com
THIS ENTIRE DEPARTMENT WORKS ON SETTING UP MIKE TYSON.
MY MATH TEACHER WORKS HERE, TOO? THAT EXPLAINS MY LAST REPORT CARD.
WE TRY TO START AS EARLY AS POSSIBLE.
5-30

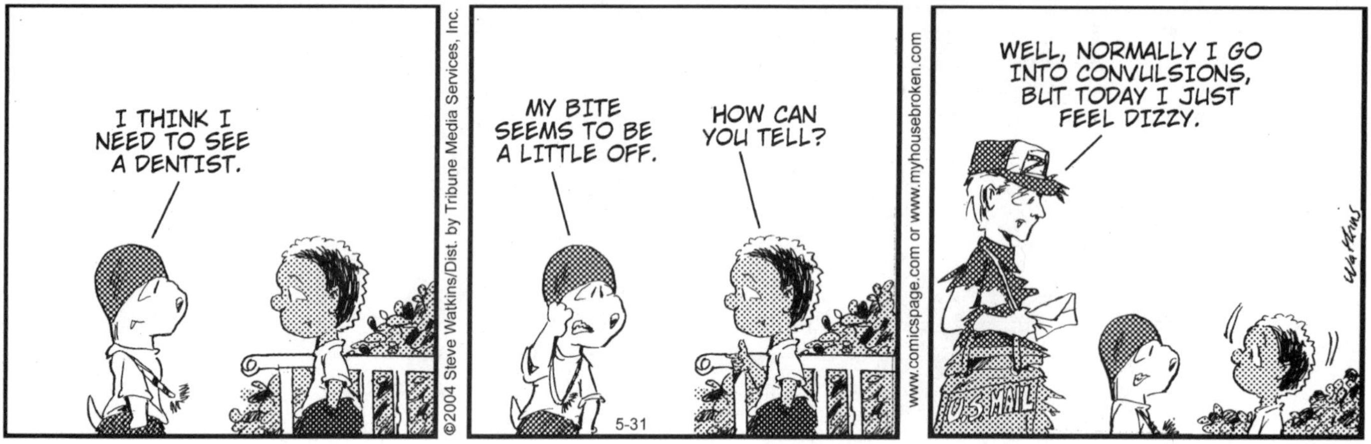
I THINK I NEED TO SEE A DENTIST.
©2004 Steve Watkins/Dist. by Tribune Media Services, Inc.
MY BITE SEEMS TO BE A LITTLE OFF.
HOW CAN YOU TELL?
5-31
www.comicspage.com or www.myhousebroken.com
WELL, NORMALLY I GO INTO CONVULSIONS, BUT TODAY I JUST FEEL DIZZY.
U.S. MAIL

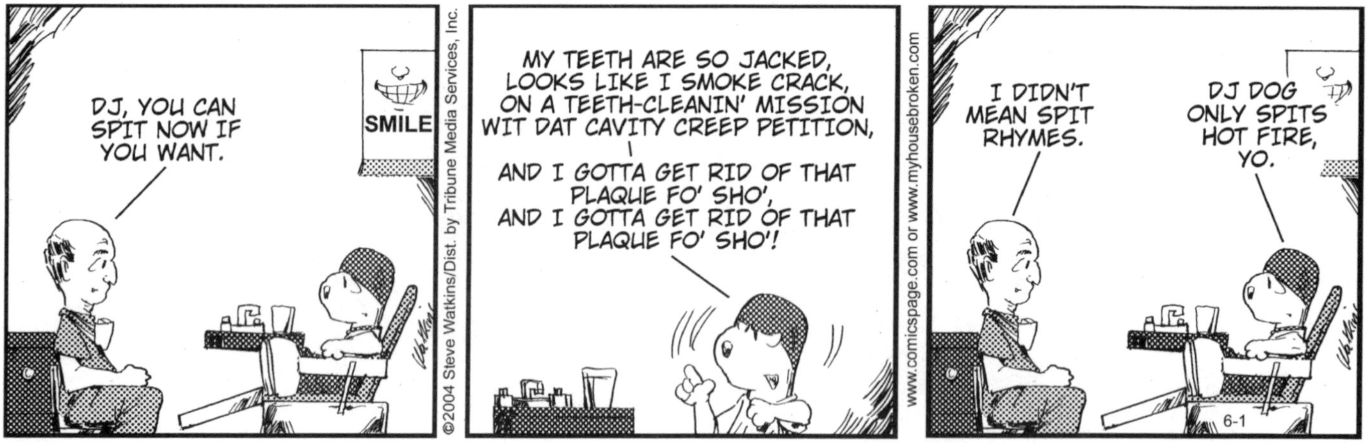
DJ, YOU CAN SPIT NOW IF YOU WANT.
SMILE
©2004 Steve Watkins/Dist. by Tribune Media Services, Inc.
MY TEETH ARE SO JACKED, LOOKS LIKE I SMOKE CRACK, ON A TEETH-CLEANIN' MISSION WIT DAT CAVITY CREEP PETITION,
AND I GOTTA GET RID OF THAT PLAQUE FO' SHO', AND I GOTTA GET RID OF THAT PLAQUE FO' SHO'!
www.comicspage.com or www.myhousebroken.com
I DIDN'T MEAN SPIT RHYMES.
DJ DOG ONLY SPITS HOT FIRE, YO.
6-1

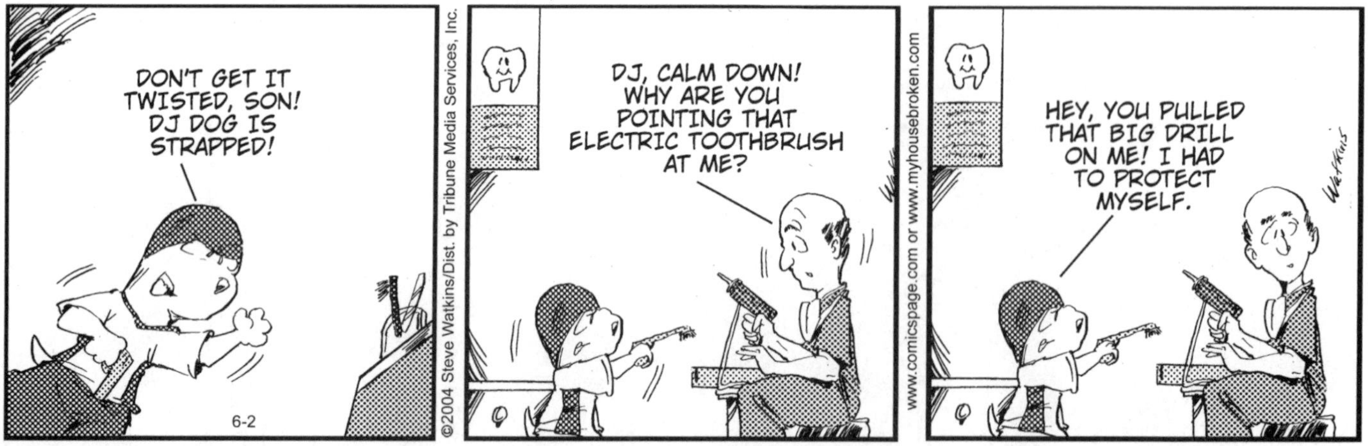
DON'T GET IT TWISTED, SON! DJ DOG IS STRAPPED!
6-2
©2004 Steve Watkins/Dist. by Tribune Media Services, Inc.
DJ, CALM DOWN! WHY ARE YOU POINTING THAT ELECTRIC TOOTHBRUSH AT ME?
www.comicspage.com or www.myhousebroken.com
HEY, YOU PULLED THAT BIG DRILL ON ME! I HAD TO PROTECT MYSELF.

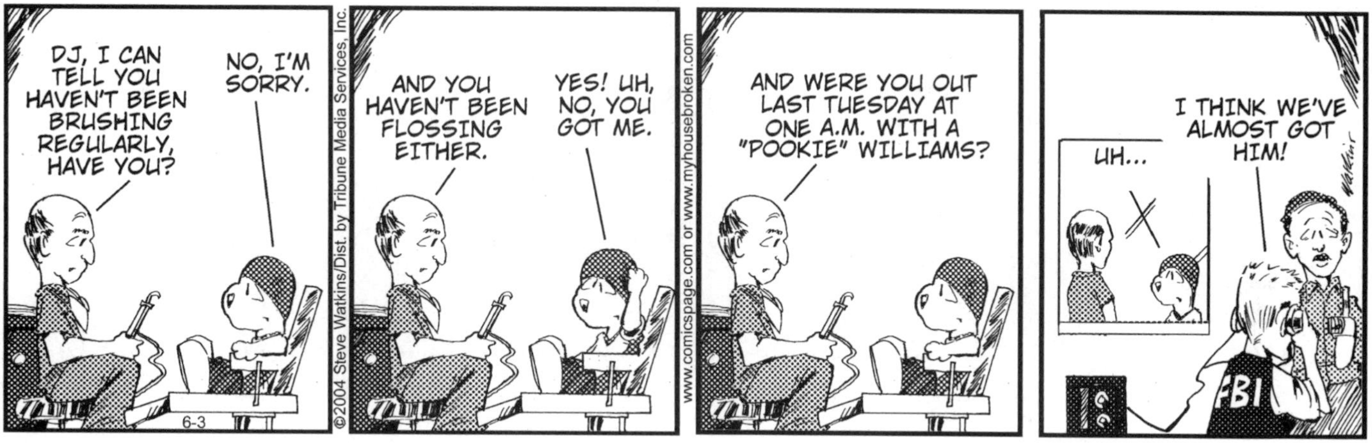
DJ, I CAN TELL YOU HAVEN'T BEEN BRUSHING REGULARLY, HAVE YOU?
NO, I'M SORRY.
AND YOU HAVEN'T BEEN FLOSSING EITHER.
YES! UH, NO, YOU GOT ME.
AND WERE YOU OUT LAST TUESDAY AT ONE A.M. WITH A "POOKIE" WILLIAMS?
UH...
I THINK WE'VE ALMOST GOT HIM!
FBI
6-3
©2004 Steve Watkins/Dist. by Tribune Media Services, Inc.
www.comicspage.com or www.myhousebroken.com

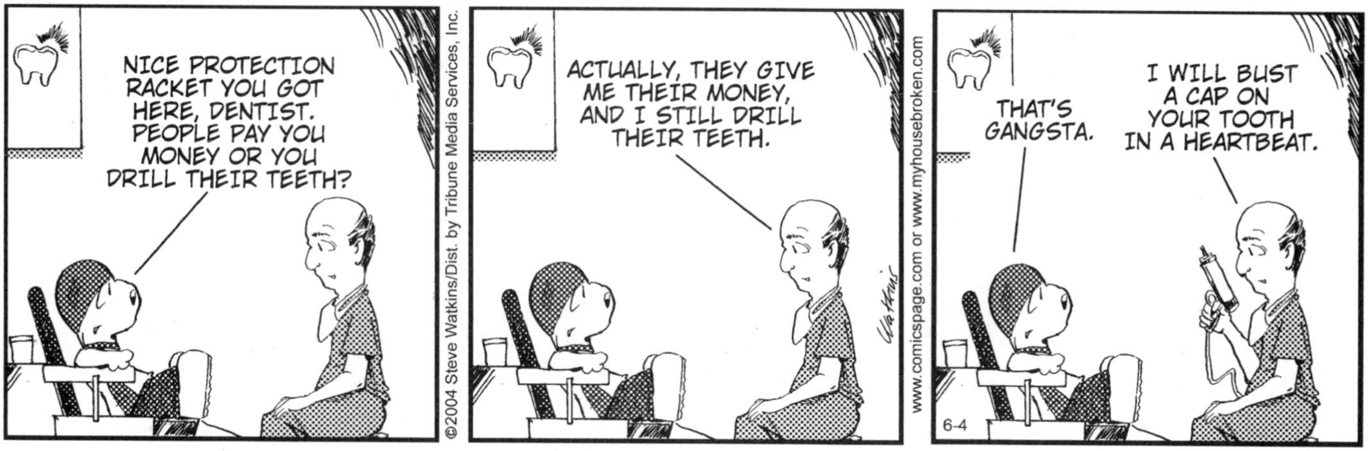
NICE PROTECTION RACKET YOU GOT HERE, DENTIST. PEOPLE PAY YOU MONEY OR YOU DRILL THEIR TEETH?
ACTUALLY, THEY GIVE ME THEIR MONEY, AND I STILL DRILL THEIR TEETH.
THAT'S GANGSTA.
I WILL BUST A CAP ON YOUR TOOTH IN A HEARTBEAT.
6-4
©2004 Steve Watkins/Dist. by Tribune Media Services, Inc.
www.comicspage.com or www.myhousebroken.com

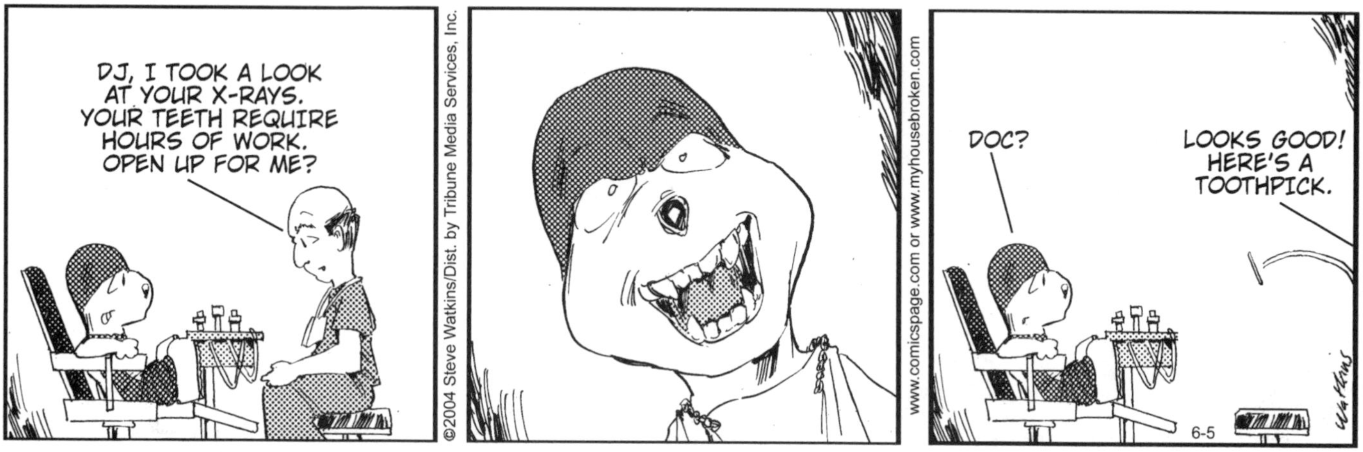
DJ, I TOOK A LOOK AT YOUR X-RAYS. YOUR TEETH REQUIRE HOURS OF WORK. OPEN UP FOR ME?
DOC?
LOOKS GOOD! HERE'S A TOOTHPICK.
6-5
©2004 Steve Watkins/Dist. by Tribune Media Services, Inc.
www.comicspage.com or www.myhousebroken.com

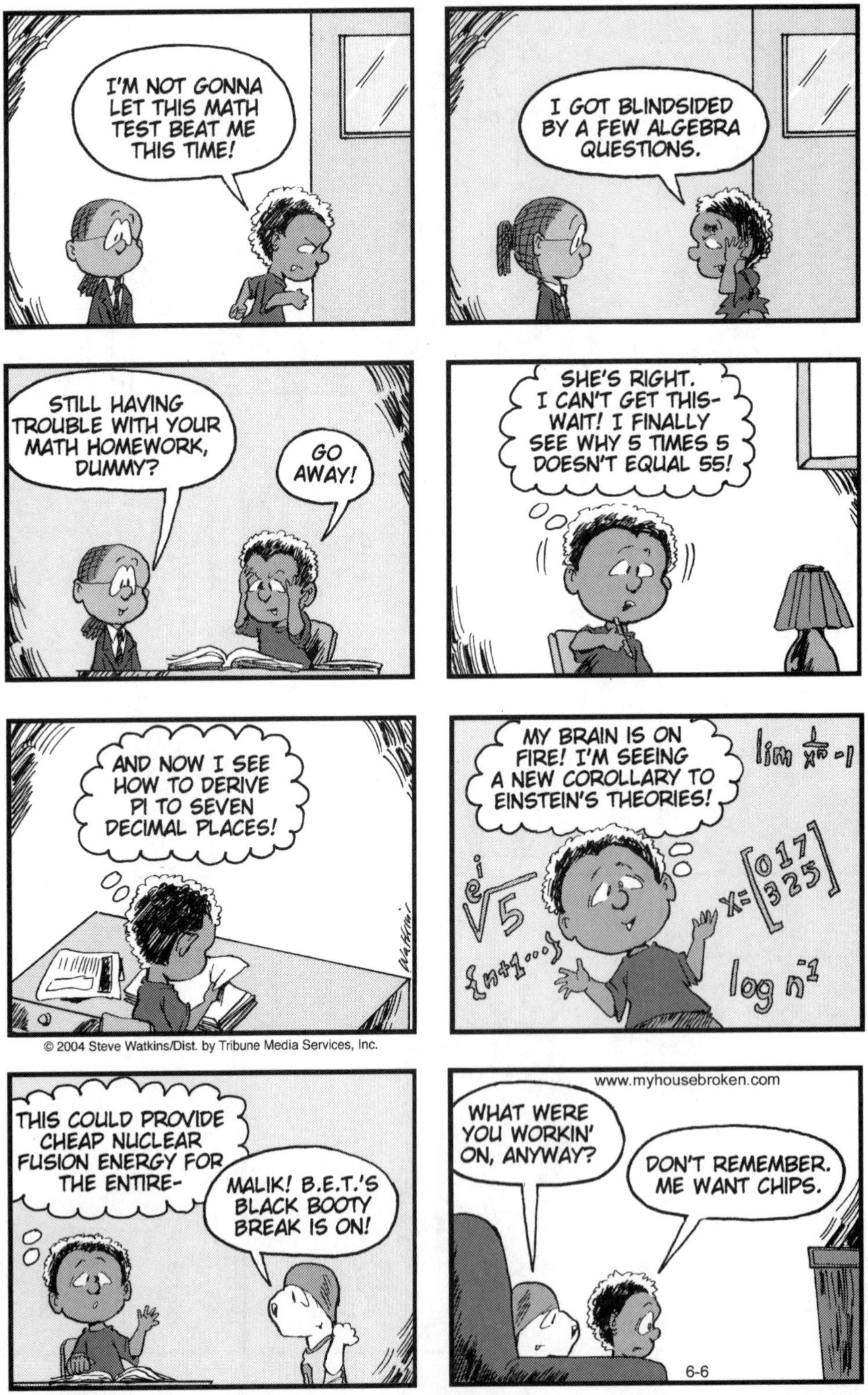

I'M NOT GONNA LET THIS MATH TEST BEAT ME THIS TIME!
I GOT BLINDSIDED BY A FEW ALGEBRA QUESTIONS.
STILL HAVING TROUBLE WITH YOUR MATH HOMEWORK, DUMMY?
GO AWAY!
SHE'S RIGHT. I CAN'T GET THIS- WAIT! I FINALLY SEE WHY 5 TIMES 5 DOESN'T EQUAL 55!
AND NOW I SEE HOW TO DERIVE PI TO SEVEN DECIMAL PLACES!
MY BRAIN IS ON FIRE! I'M SEEING A NEW COROLLARY TO EINSTEIN'S THEORIES!
THIS COULD PROVIDE CHEAP NUCLEAR FUSION ENERGY FOR THE ENTIRE-
MALIK! B.E.T.'S BLACK BOOTY BREAK IS ON!
www.myhousebroken.com
WHAT WERE YOU WORKIN' ON, ANYWAY?
DON'T REMEMBER. ME WANT CHIPS.
6-6

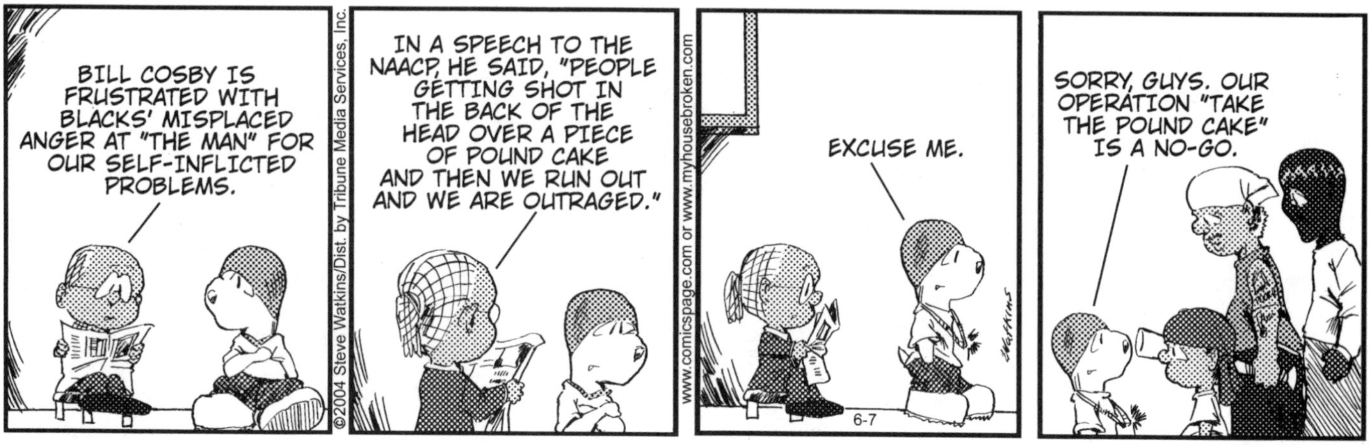
BILL COSBY IS FRUSTRATED WITH BLACKS' MISPLACED ANGER AT "THE MAN" FOR OUR SELF-INFLICTED PROBLEMS.
©2004 Steve Watkins/Dist. by Tribune Media Services, Inc.
IN A SPEECH TO THE NAACP, HE SAID, "PEOPLE GETTING SHOT IN THE BACK OF THE HEAD OVER A PIECE OF POUND CAKE AND THEN WE RUN OUT AND WE ARE OUTRAGED."
www.comicspage.com or www.myhousebroken.com
EXCUSE ME.
6-7
SORRY, GUYS. OUR OPERATION "TAKE THE POUND CAKE" IS A NO-GO.

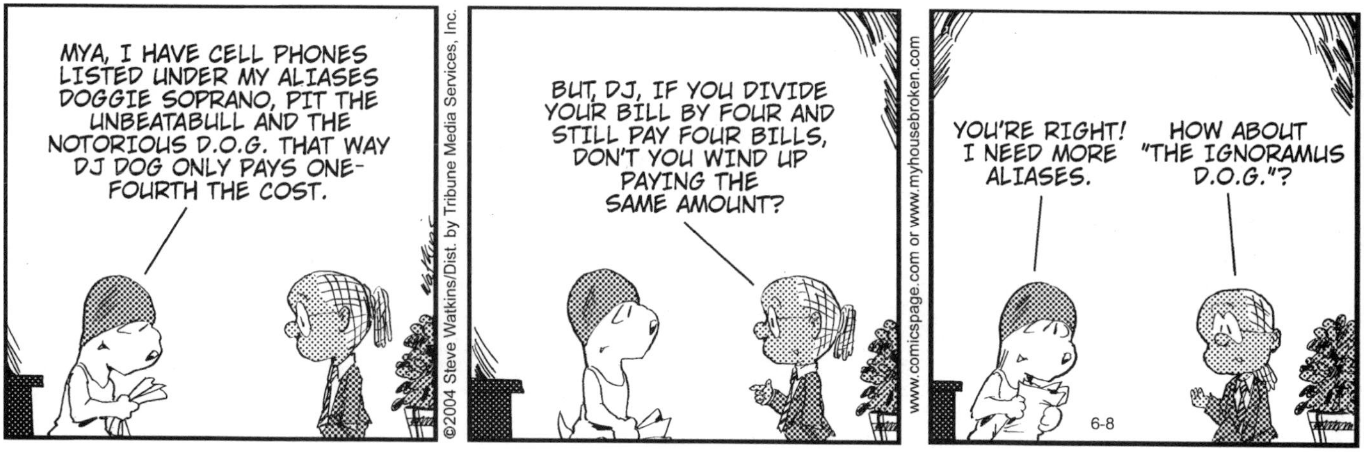
MYA, I HAVE CELL PHONES LISTED UNDER MY ALIASES DOGGIE SOPRANO, PIT THE UNBEATABULL AND THE NOTORIOUS D.O.G. THAT WAY DJ DOG ONLY PAYS ONE-FOURTH THE COST.
©2004 Steve Watkins/Dist. by Tribune Media Services, Inc.
BUT, DJ, IF YOU DIVIDE YOUR BILL BY FOUR AND STILL PAY FOUR BILLS, DON'T YOU WIND UP PAYING THE SAME AMOUNT?
www.comicspage.com or www.myhousebroken.com
YOU'RE RIGHT! I NEED MORE ALIASES.
HOW ABOUT "THE IGNORAMUS D.O.G."?
6-8

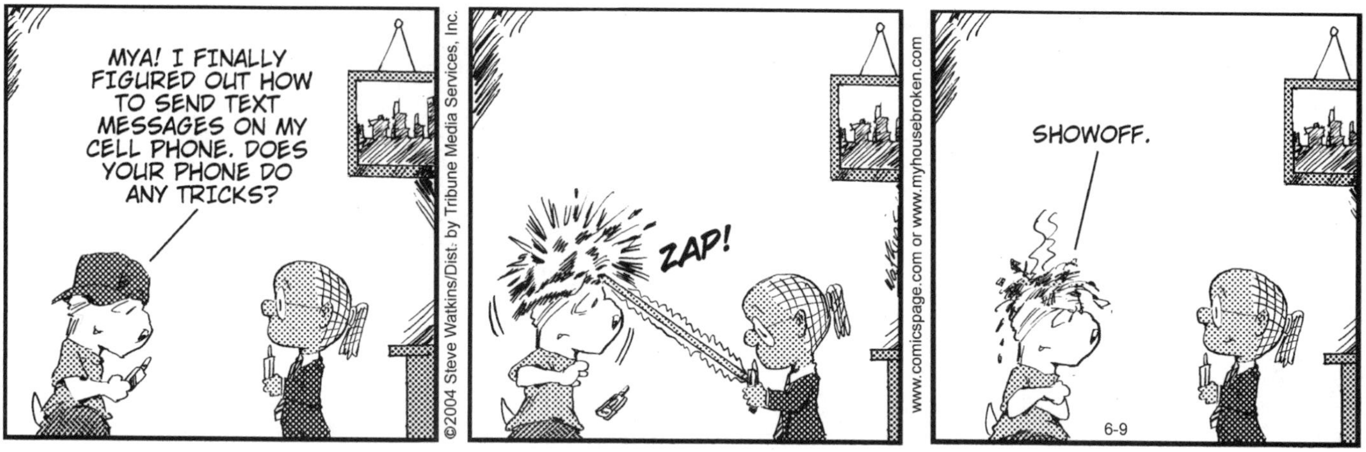
MYA! I FINALLY FIGURED OUT HOW TO SEND TEXT MESSAGES ON MY CELL PHONE. DOES YOUR PHONE DO ANY TRICKS?
©2004 Steve Watkins/Dist. by Tribune Media Services, Inc.
ZAP!
www.comicspage.com or www.myhousebroken.com
SHOWOFF.
6-9

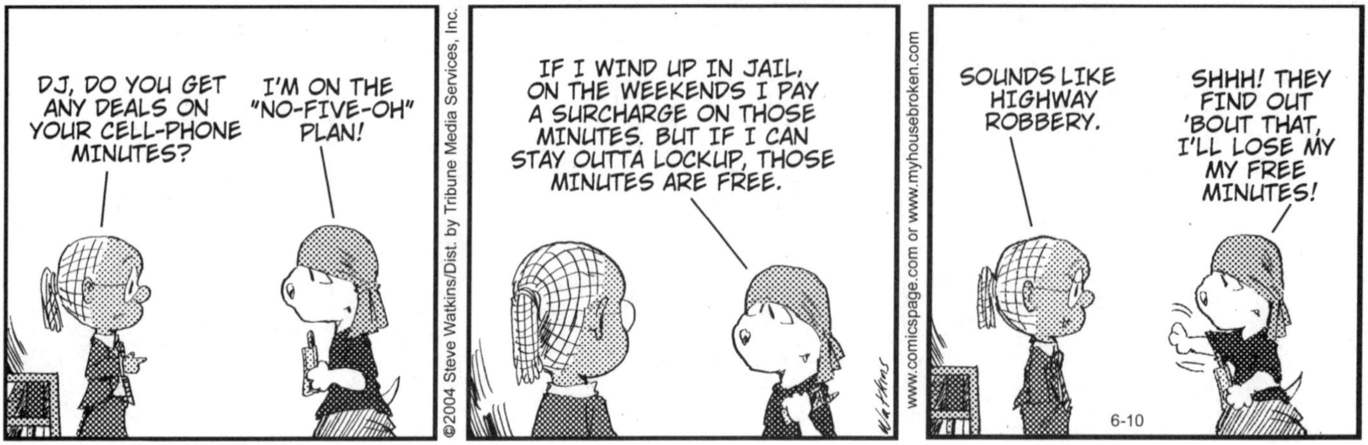
DJ, DO YOU GET ANY DEALS ON YOUR CELL-PHONE MINUTES?
I'M ON THE "NO-FIVE-OH" PLAN!
©2004 Steve Watkins/Dist. by Tribune Media Services, Inc.
IF I WIND UP IN JAIL, ON THE WEEKENDS I PAY A SURCHARGE ON THOSE MINUTES. BUT IF I CAN STAY OUTTA LOCKUP, THOSE MINUTES ARE FREE.
www.comicspage.com or www.myhousebroken.com
SOUNDS LIKE HIGHWAY ROBBERY.
SHHH! THEY FIND OUT 'BOUT THAT, I'LL LOSE MY MY FREE MINUTES!
6-10

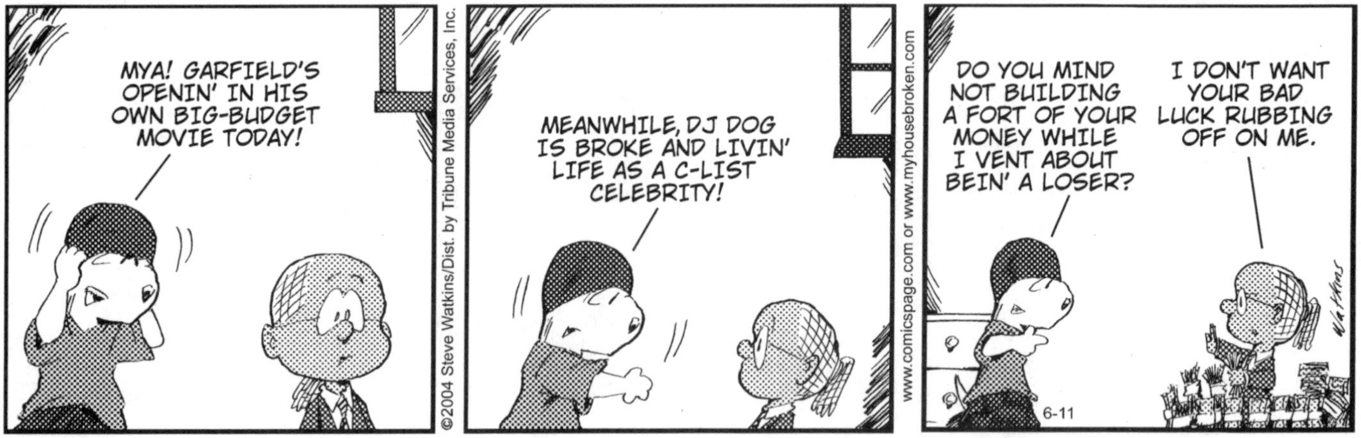
MYA! GARFIELD'S OPENIN' IN HIS OWN BIG-BUDGET MOVIE TODAY!
©2004 Steve Watkins/Dist. by Tribune Media Services, Inc.
MEANWHILE, DJ DOG IS BROKE AND LIVIN' LIFE AS A C-LIST CELEBRITY!
www.comicspage.com or www.myhousebroken.com
DO YOU MIND NOT BUILDING A FORT OF YOUR MONEY WHILE I VENT ABOUT BEIN' A LOSER?
I DON'T WANT YOUR BAD LUCK RUBBING OFF ON ME.
6-11

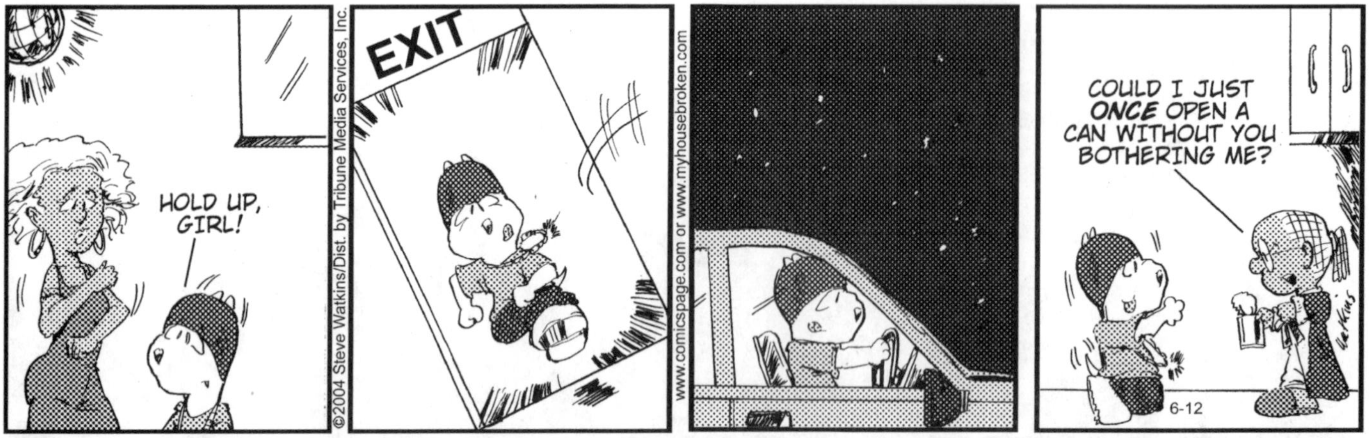
HOLD UP, GIRL!
©2004 Steve Watkins/Dist. by Tribune Media Services, Inc.
EXIT
www.comicspage.com or www.myhousebroken.com
COULD I JUST ONCE OPEN A CAN WITHOUT YOU BOTHERING ME?
6-12

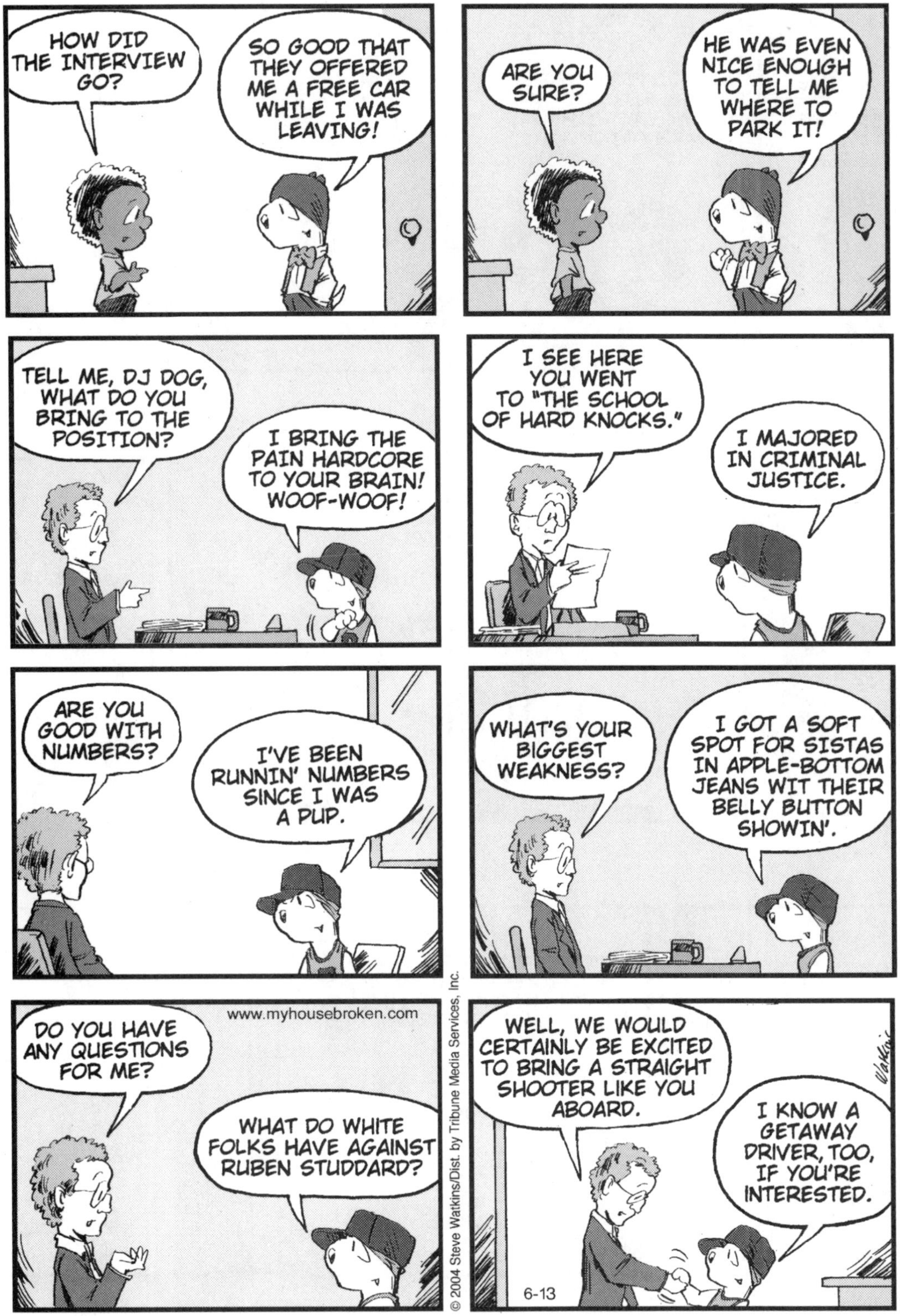
HOW DID THE INTERVIEW GO?
SO GOOD THAT THEY OFFERED ME A FREE CAR WHILE I WAS LEAVING!
ARE YOU SURE?
HE WAS EVEN NICE ENOUGH TO TELL ME WHERE TO PARK IT!
TELL ME, DJ DOG, WHAT DO YOU BRING TO THE POSITION?
I BRING THE PAIN HARDCORE TO YOUR BRAIN! WOOF-WOOF!
I SEE HERE YOU WENT TO "THE SCHOOL OF HARD KNOCKS."
I MAJORED IN CRIMINAL JUSTICE.
ARE YOU GOOD WITH NUMBERS?
I'VE BEEN RUNNIN' NUMBERS SINCE I WAS A PUP.
WHAT'S YOUR BIGGEST WEAKNESS?
I GOT A SOFT SPOT FOR SISTAS IN APPLE-BOTTOM JEANS WIT THEIR BELLY BUTTON SHOWIN'.
DO YOU HAVE ANY QUESTIONS FOR ME?
www.myhousebroken.com
WHAT DO WHITE FOLKS HAVE AGAINST RUBEN STUDDARD?
© 2004 Steve Watkins/Dist. by Tribune Media Services, Inc.
WELL, WE WOULD CERTAINLY BE EXCITED TO BRING A STRAIGHT SHOOTER LIKE YOU ABOARD.
I KNOW A GETAWAY DRIVER, TOO, IF YOU'RE INTERESTED.
6-13
Watkins

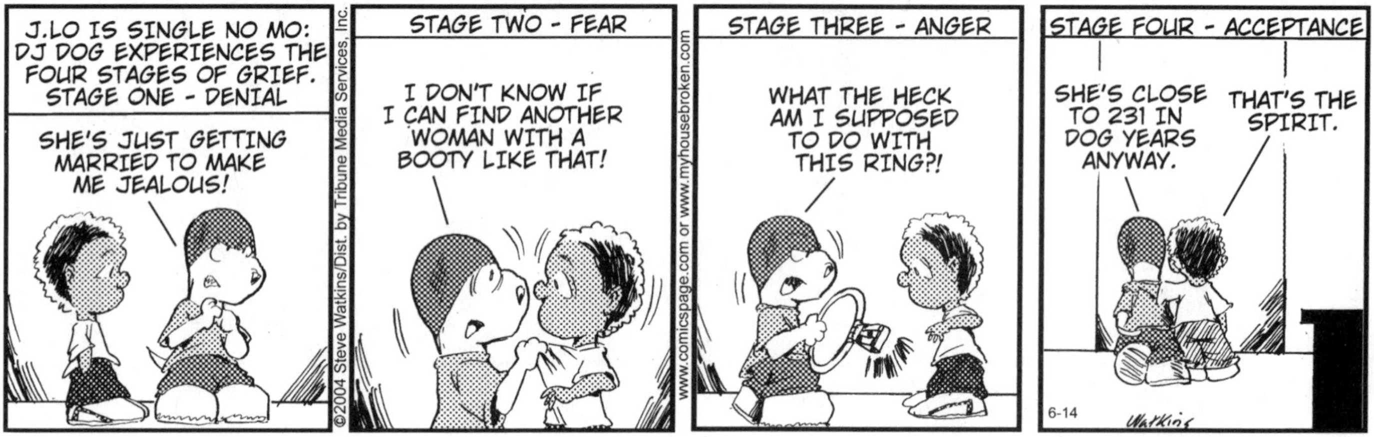
J.LO IS SINGLE NO MO: DJ DOG EXPERIENCES THE FOUR STAGES OF GRIEF. STAGE ONE - DENIAL
SHE'S JUST GETTING MARRIED TO MAKE ME JEALOUS!
©2004 Steve Watkins/Dist. by Tribune Media Services, Inc.
STAGE TWO - FEAR
I DON'T KNOW IF I CAN FIND ANOTHER WOMAN WITH A BOOTY LIKE THAT!
www.comicspage.com or www.myhousebroken.com
STAGE THREE - ANGER
WHAT THE HECK AM I SUPPOSED TO DO WITH THIS RING?!
STAGE FOUR - ACCEPTANCE
SHE'S CLOSE TO 231 IN DOG YEARS ANYWAY.
THAT'S THE SPIRIT.
6-14
Watkins

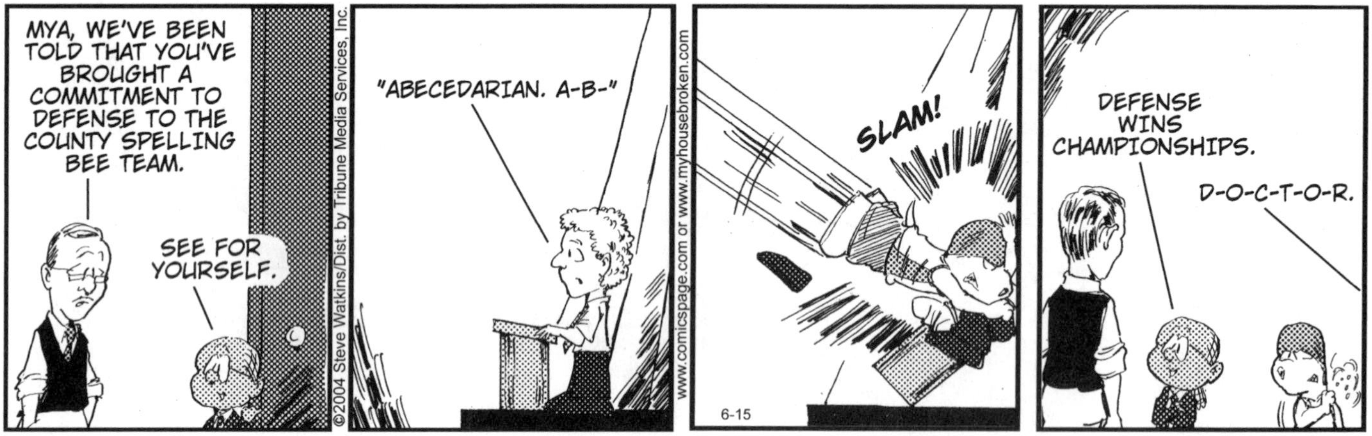
MYA, WE'VE BEEN TOLD THAT YOU'VE BROUGHT A COMMITMENT TO DEFENSE TO THE COUNTY SPELLING BEE TEAM.
SEE FOR YOURSELF.
©2004 Steve Watkins/Dist. by Tribune Media Services, Inc.
"ABECEDARIAN. A-B-"
www.comicspage.com or www.myhousebroken.com
6-15
SLAM!
DEFENSE WINS CHAMPIONSHIPS.
D-O-C-T-O-R.

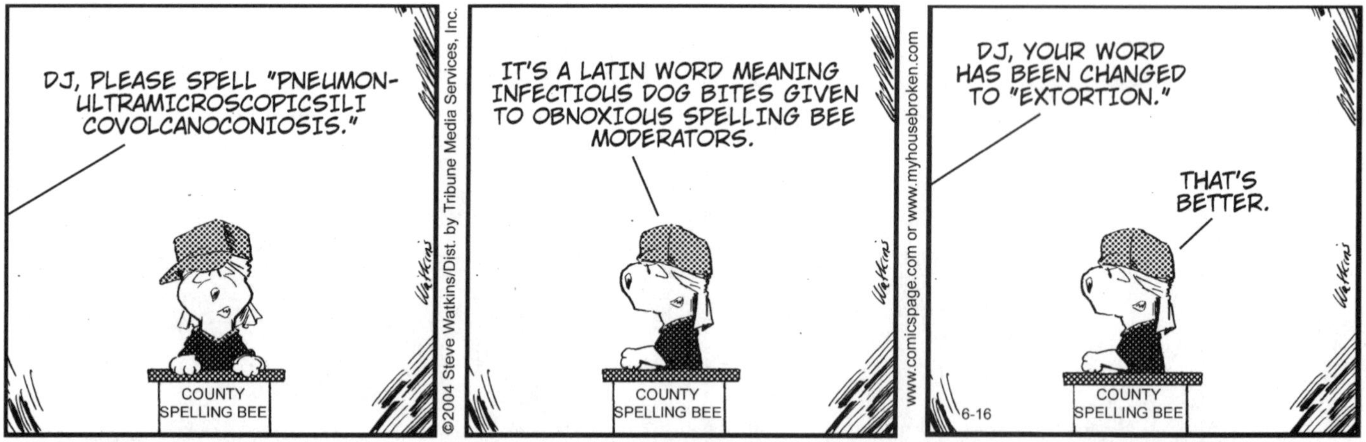
DJ, PLEASE SPELL "PNEUMON-ULTRAMICROSCOPICSILI COVOLCANOCONIOSIS."
COUNTY SPELLING BEE
Watkins
©2004 Steve Watkins/Dist. by Tribune Media Services, Inc.
IT'S A LATIN WORD MEANING INFECTIOUS DOG BITES GIVEN TO OBNOXIOUS SPELLING BEE MODERATORS.
COUNTY SPELLING BEE
Watkins
www.comicspage.com or www.myhousebroken.com
DJ, YOUR WORD HAS BEEN CHANGED TO "EXTORTION."
THAT'S BETTER.
6-16
COUNTY SPELLING BEE
Watkins

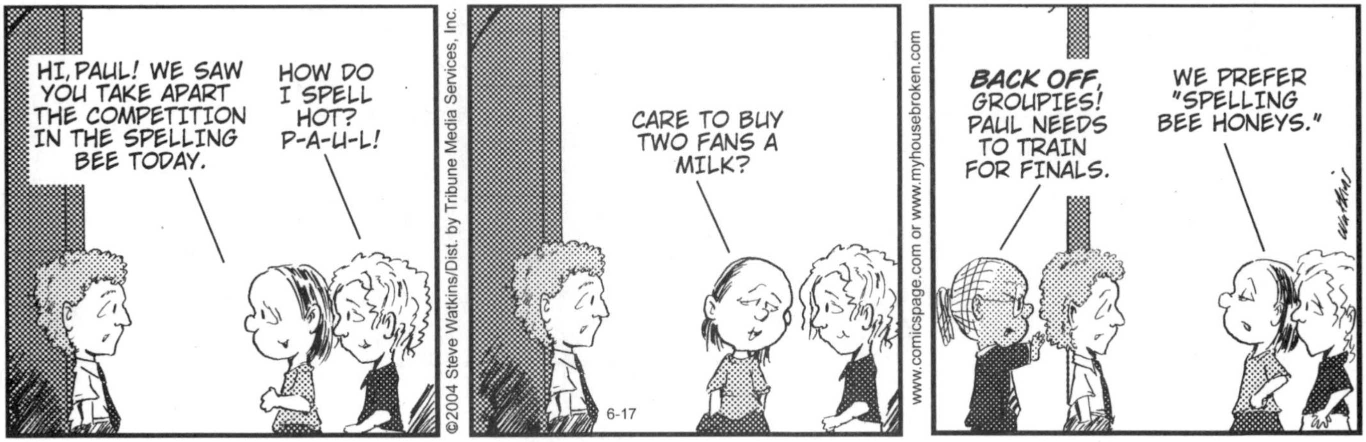
HI, PAUL! WE SAW YOU TAKE APART THE COMPETITION IN THE SPELLING BEE TODAY.
HOW DO I SPELL HOT? P-A-U-L!
©2004 Steve Watkins/Dist. by Tribune Media Services, Inc.
CARE TO BUY TWO FANS A MILK?
6-17
www.comicspage.com or www.myhousebroken.com
BACK OFF, GROUPIES! PAUL NEEDS TO TRAIN FOR FINALS.
WE PREFER "SPELLING BEE HONEYS."

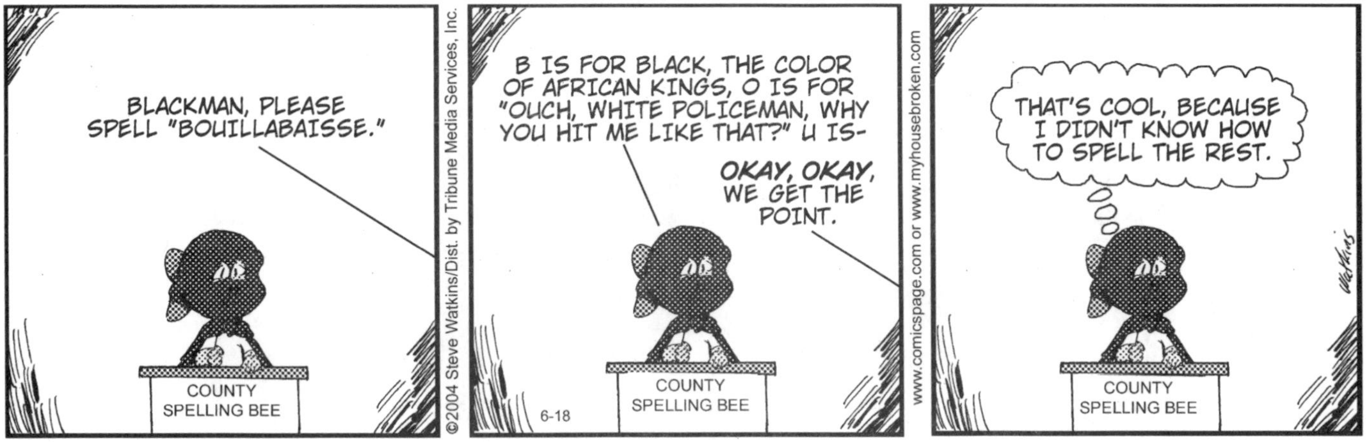
BLACKMAN, PLEASE SPELL "BOUILLABAISSE."
COUNTY SPELLING BEE
©2004 Steve Watkins/Dist. by Tribune Media Services, Inc.
B IS FOR BLACK, THE COLOR OF AFRICAN KINGS, O IS FOR "OUCH, WHITE POLICEMAN, WHY YOU HIT ME LIKE THAT?" U IS-
OKAY, OKAY, WE GET THE POINT.
COUNTY SPELLING BEE
6-18
www.comicspage.com or www.myhousebroken.com
THAT'S COOL, BECAUSE I DIDN'T KNOW HOW TO SPELL THE REST.
COUNTY SPELLING BEE

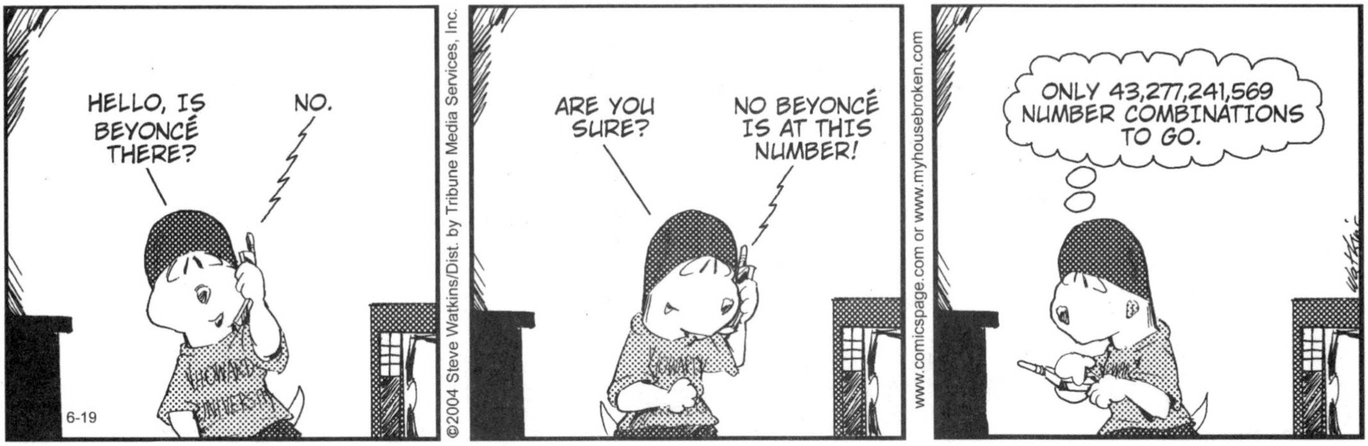
HELLO, IS BEYONCÉ THERE?
NO.
6-19
©2004 Steve Watkins/Dist. by Tribune Media Services, Inc.
ARE YOU SURE?
NO BEYONCÉ IS AT THIS NUMBER!
www.comicspage.com or www.myhousebroken.com
ONLY 43,277,241,569 NUMBER COMBINATIONS TO GO.

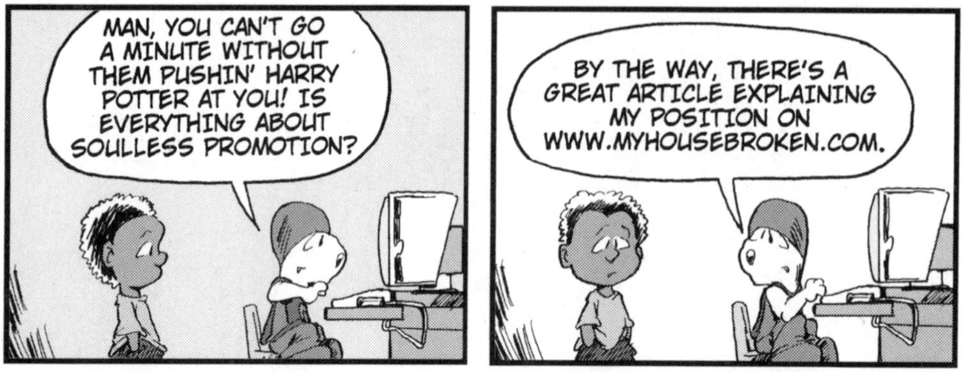
MAN, YOU CAN'T GO A MINUTE WITHOUT THEM PUSHIN' HARRY POTTER AT YOU! IS EVERYTHING ABOUT SOULLESS PROMOTION?
BY THE WAY, THERE'S A GREAT ARTICLE EXPLAINING MY POSITION ON WWW.MYHOUSEBROKEN.COM.

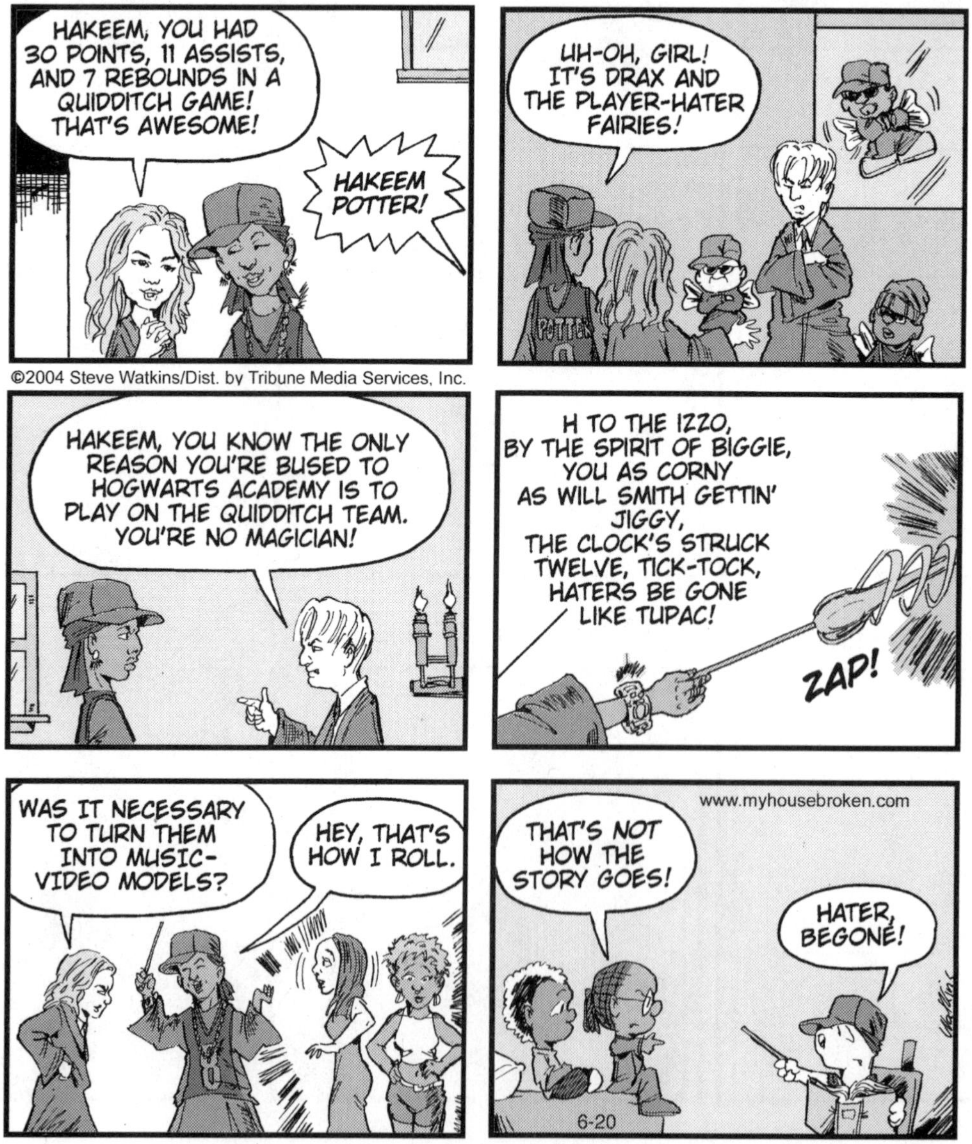
HAKEEM, YOU HAD 30 POINTS, 11 ASSISTS, AND 7 REBOUNDS IN A QUIDDITCH GAME! THAT'S AWESOME!
HAKEEM POTTER!
UH-OH, GIRL! IT'S DRAX AND THE PLAYER-HATER FAIRIES!
HAKEEM, YOU KNOW THE ONLY REASON YOU'RE BUSED TO HOGWARTS ACADEMY IS TO PLAY ON THE QUIDDITCH TEAM. YOU'RE NO MAGICIAN!
H TO THE IZZO, BY THE SPIRIT OF BIGGIE, YOU AS CORNY AS WILL SMITH GETTIN' JIGGY, THE CLOCK'S STRUCK TWELVE, TICK-TOCK, HATERS BE GONE LIKE TUPAC!
ZAP!
WAS IT NECESSARY TO TURN THEM INTO MUSIC-VIDEO MODELS?
HEY, THAT'S HOW I ROLL.
www.myhousebroken.com
THAT'S NOT HOW THE STORY GOES!
HATER, BEGONE!
6-20

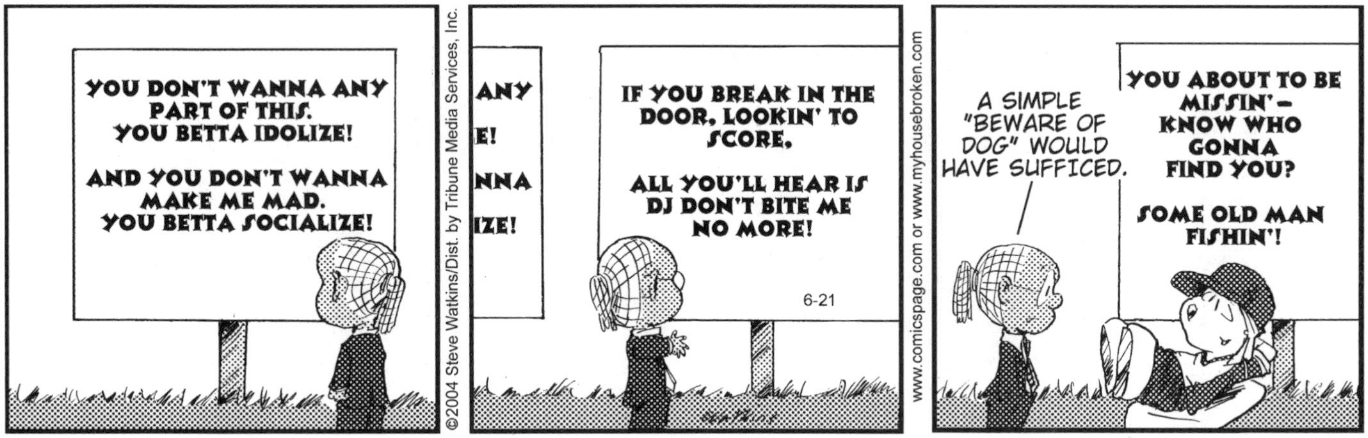
YOU DON'T WANNA ANY PART OF THIS. YOU BETTA IDOLIZE!
AND YOU DON'T WANNA MAKE ME MAD. YOU BETTA SOCIALIZE!
IF YOU BREAK IN THE DOOR, LOOKIN' TO SCORE,
ALL YOU'LL HEAR IS DJ DON'T BITE ME NO MORE!
6-21
A SIMPLE "BEWARE OF DOG" WOULD HAVE SUFFICED.
YOU ABOUT TO BE MISSIN' – KNOW WHO GONNA FIND YOU?
SOME OLD MAN FISHIN'!

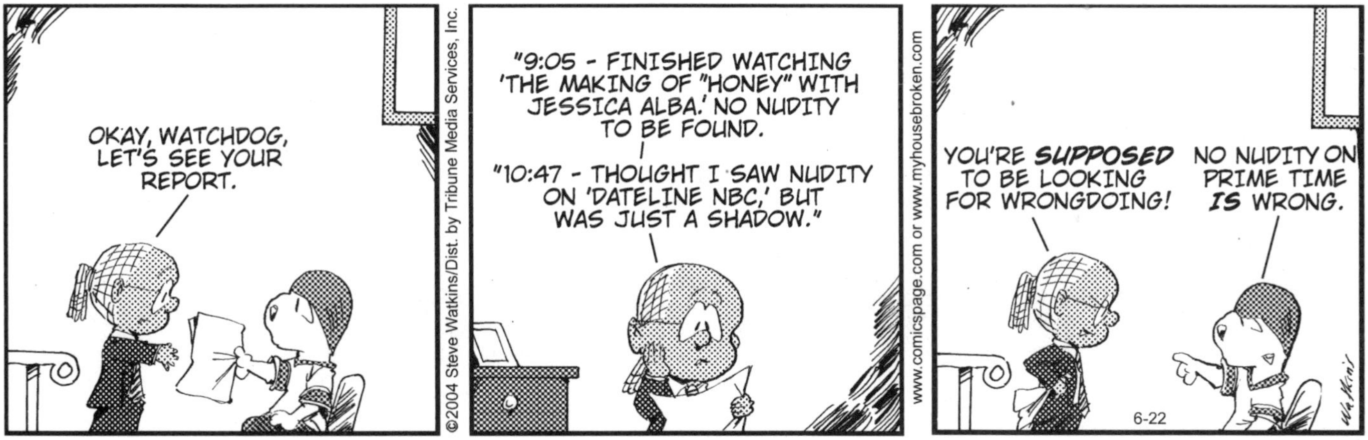
OKAY, WATCHDOG, LET'S SEE YOUR REPORT.
"9:05 - FINISHED WATCHING 'THE MAKING OF "HONEY" WITH JESSICA ALBA.' NO NUDITY TO BE FOUND.
"10:47 - THOUGHT I SAW NUDITY ON 'DATELINE NBC,' BUT WAS JUST A SHADOW."
YOU'RE ***SUPPOSED*** TO BE LOOKING FOR WRONGDOING!
NO NUDITY ON PRIME TIME ***IS*** WRONG.
6-22

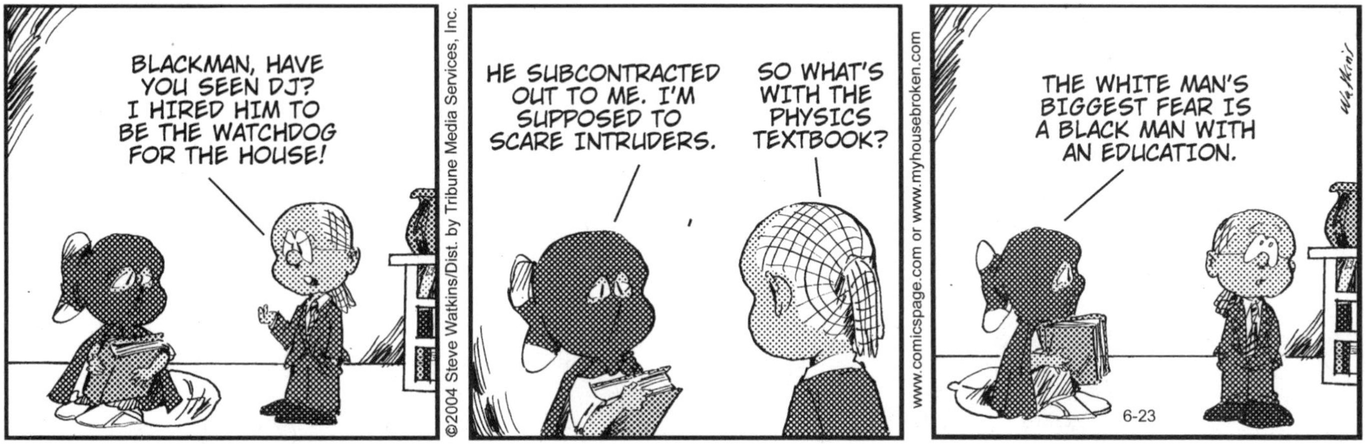
BLACKMAN, HAVE YOU SEEN DJ? I HIRED HIM TO BE THE WATCHDOG FOR THE HOUSE!
HE SUBCONTRACTED OUT TO ME. I'M SUPPOSED TO SCARE INTRUDERS.
SO WHAT'S WITH THE PHYSICS TEXTBOOK?
THE WHITE MAN'S BIGGEST FEAR IS A BLACK MAN WITH AN EDUCATION.
6-23

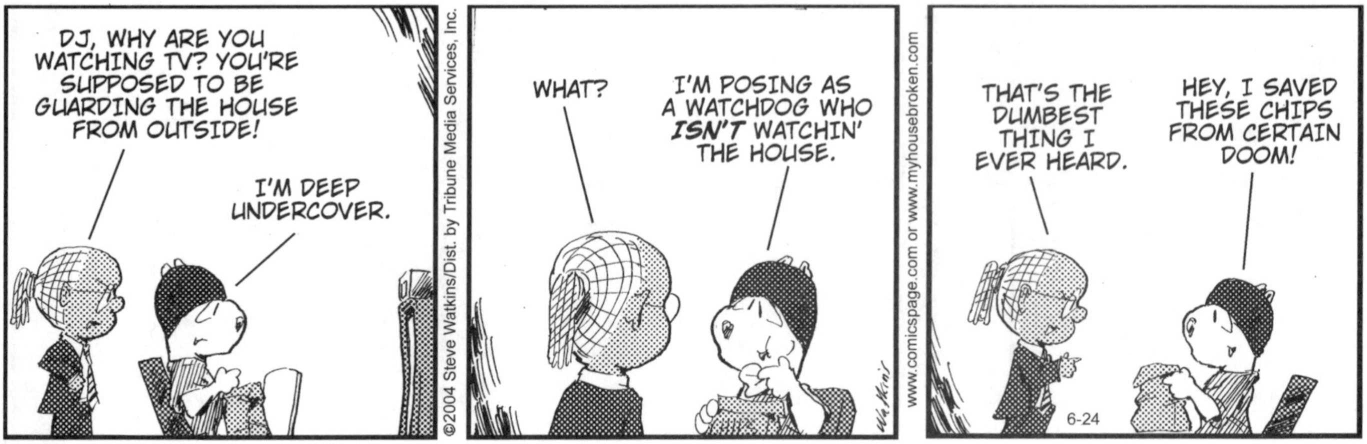

DJ, WHY ARE YOU WATCHING TV? YOU'RE SUPPOSED TO BE GUARDING THE HOUSE FROM OUTSIDE!
I'M DEEP UNDERCOVER.
©2004 Steve Watkins/Dist. by Tribune Media Services, Inc.
WHAT?
I'M POSING AS A WATCHDOG WHO *ISN'T* WATCHIN' THE HOUSE.
www.comicspage.com or www.myhousebroken.com
THAT'S THE DUMBEST THING I EVER HEARD.
HEY, I SAVED THESE CHIPS FROM CERTAIN DOOM!
6-24

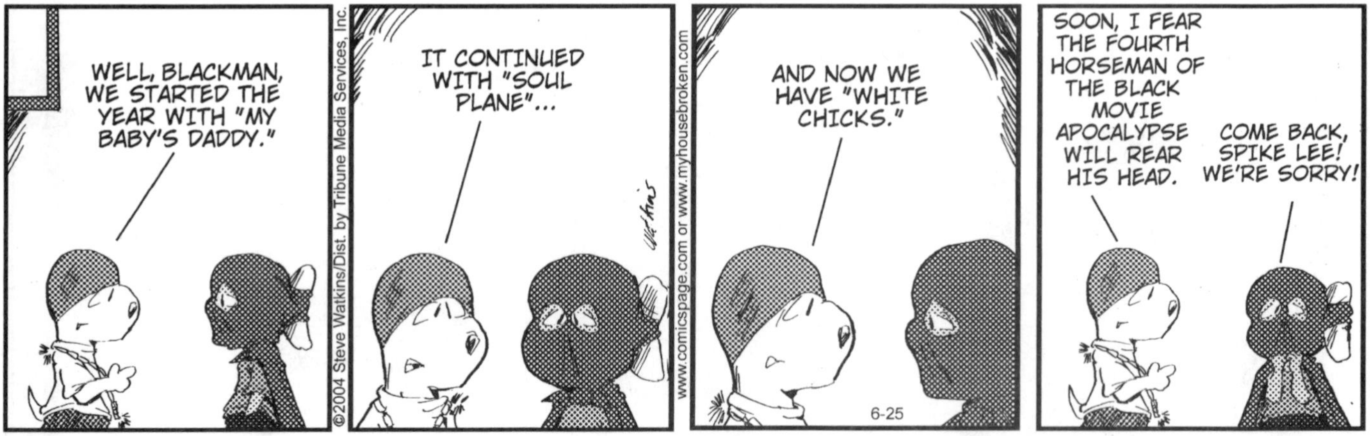

WELL, BLACKMAN, WE STARTED THE YEAR WITH "MY BABY'S DADDY."
©2004 Steve Watkins/Dist. by Tribune Media Services, Inc.
IT CONTINUED WITH "SOUL PLANE"...
www.comicspage.com or www.myhousebroken.com
AND NOW WE HAVE "WHITE CHICKS."
6-25
SOON, I FEAR THE FOURTH HORSEMAN OF THE BLACK MOVIE APOCALYPSE WILL REAR HIS HEAD.
COME BACK, SPIKE LEE! WE'RE SORRY!

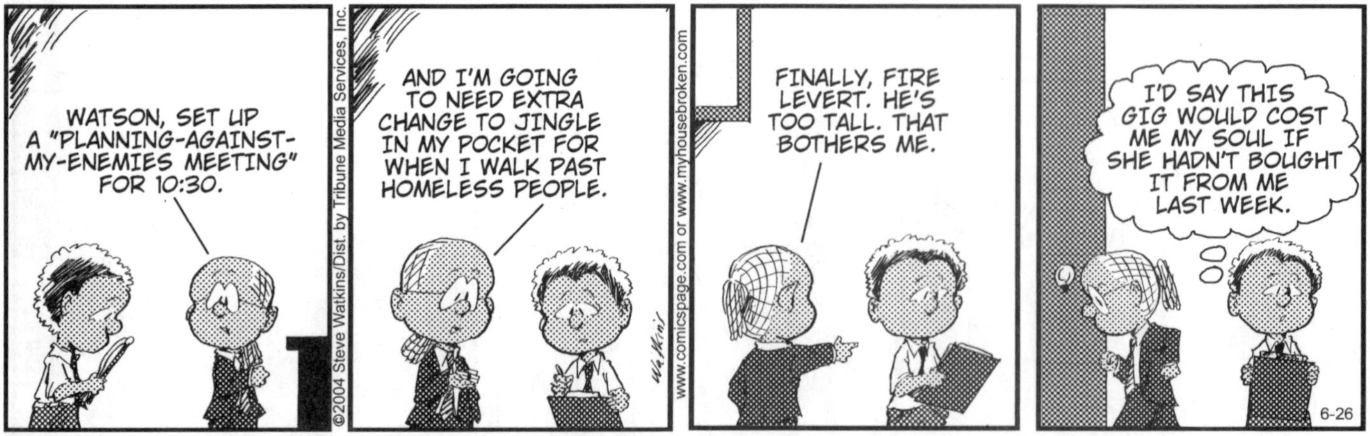

WATSON, SET UP A "PLANNING-AGAINST-MY-ENEMIES MEETING" FOR 10:30.
©2004 Steve Watkins/Dist. by Tribune Media Services, Inc.
AND I'M GOING TO NEED EXTRA CHANGE TO JINGLE IN MY POCKET FOR WHEN I WALK PAST HOMELESS PEOPLE.
www.comicspage.com or www.myhousebroken.com
FINALLY, FIRE LEVERT. HE'S TOO TALL. THAT BOTHERS ME.
I'D SAY THIS GIG WOULD COST ME MY SOUL IF SHE HADN'T BOUGHT IT FROM ME LAST WEEK.
6-26

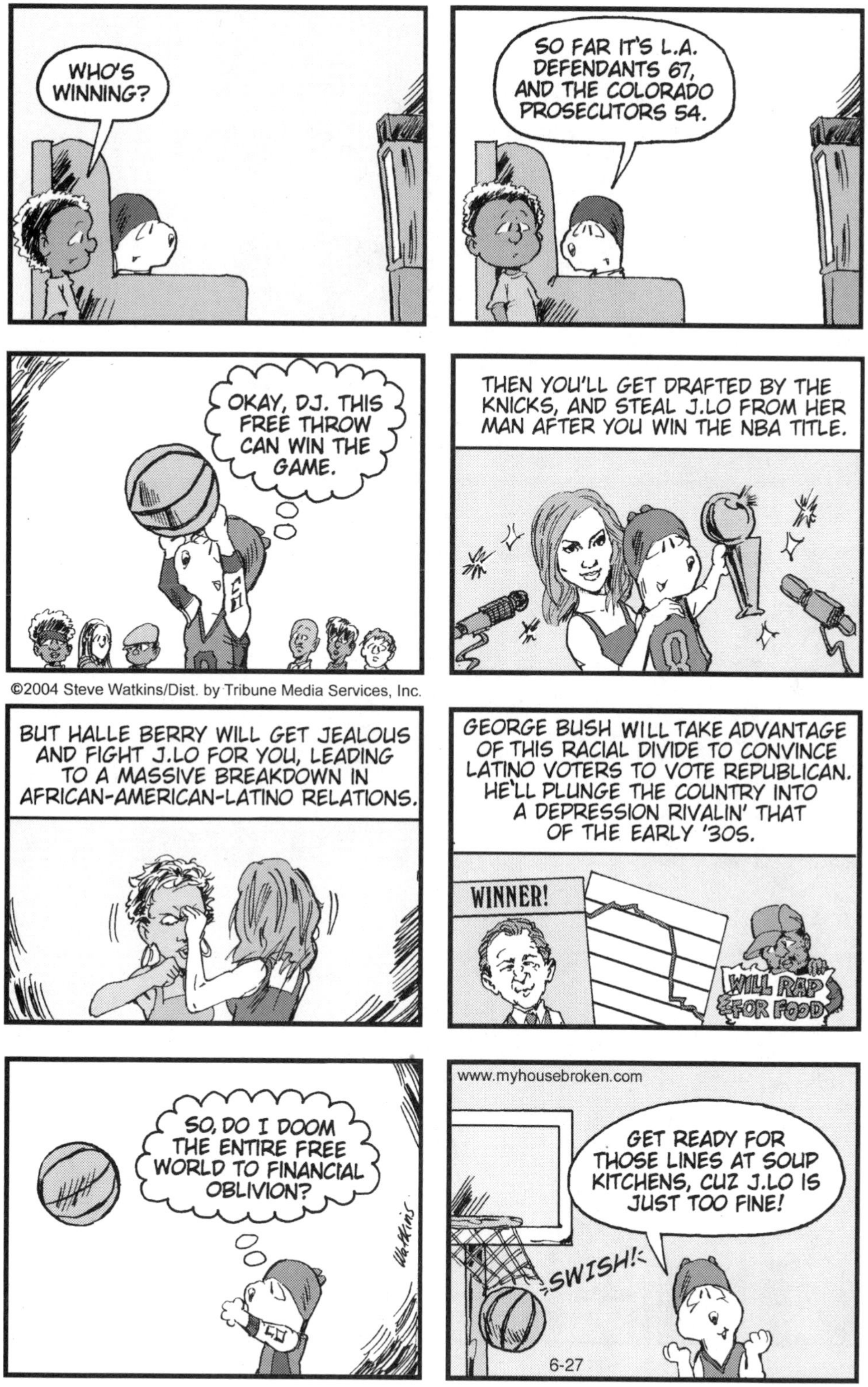
WHO'S WINNING?
SO FAR IT'S L.A. DEFENDANTS 67, AND THE COLORADO PROSECUTORS 54.
OKAY, DJ. THIS FREE THROW CAN WIN THE GAME.
THEN YOU'LL GET DRAFTED BY THE KNICKS, AND STEAL J.LO FROM HER MAN AFTER YOU WIN THE NBA TITLE.
BUT HALLE BERRY WILL GET JEALOUS AND FIGHT J.LO FOR YOU, LEADING TO A MASSIVE BREAKDOWN IN AFRICAN-AMERICAN-LATINO RELATIONS.
GEORGE BUSH WILL TAKE ADVANTAGE OF THIS RACIAL DIVIDE TO CONVINCE LATINO VOTERS TO VOTE REPUBLICAN. HE'LL PLUNGE THE COUNTRY INTO A DEPRESSION RIVALIN' THAT OF THE EARLY '30S.
WINNER!
WILL RAP FOR FOOD
SO, DO I DOOM THE ENTIRE FREE WORLD TO FINANCIAL OBLIVION?
Watkins
www.myhousebroken.com
GET READY FOR THOSE LINES AT SOUP KITCHENS, CUZ J.LO IS JUST TOO FINE!
SWISH!
6-27

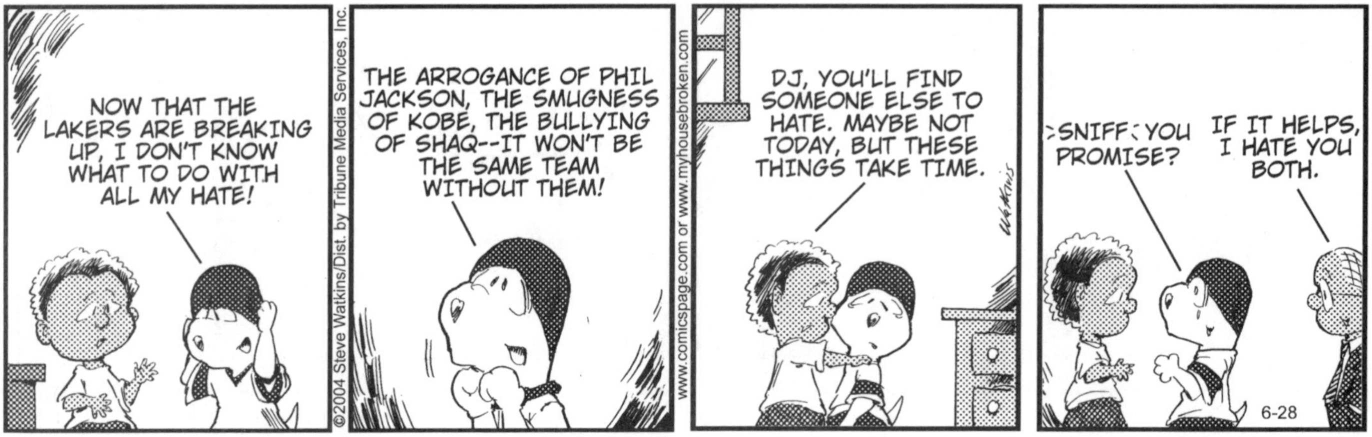
NOW THAT THE LAKERS ARE BREAKING UP, I DON'T KNOW WHAT TO DO WITH ALL MY HATE!
©2004 Steve Watkins/Dist. by Tribune Media Services, Inc.
THE ARROGANCE OF PHIL JACKSON, THE SMUGNESS OF KOBE, THE BULLYING OF SHAQ--IT WON'T BE THE SAME TEAM WITHOUT THEM!
www.comicspage.com or www.myhousebroken.com
DJ, YOU'LL FIND SOMEONE ELSE TO HATE. MAYBE NOT TODAY, BUT THESE THINGS TAKE TIME.
>SNIFF< YOU PROMISE?
IF IT HELPS, I HATE YOU BOTH.
6-28

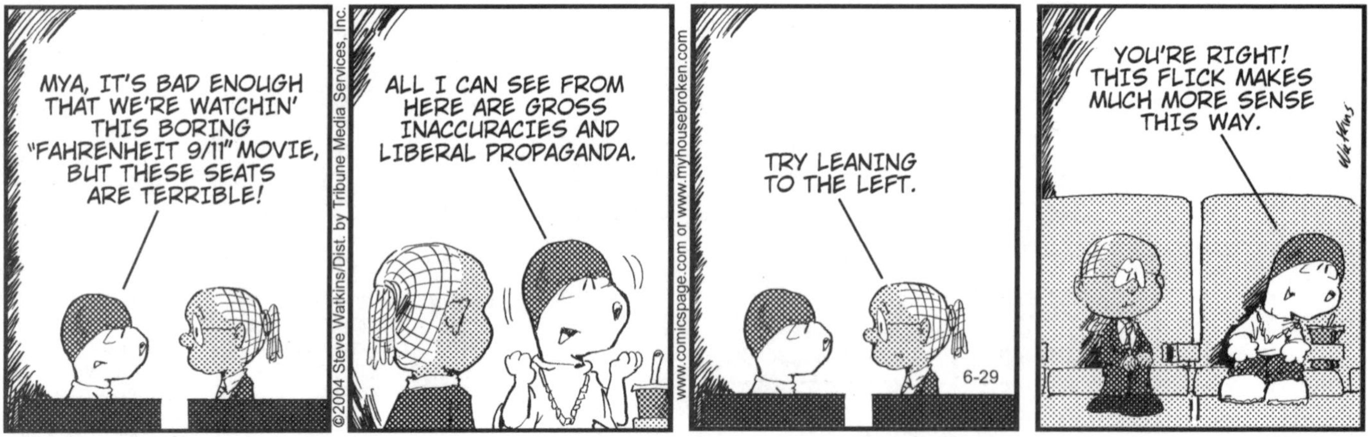
MYA, IT'S BAD ENOUGH THAT WE'RE WATCHIN' THIS BORING "FAHRENHEIT 9/11" MOVIE, BUT THESE SEATS ARE TERRIBLE!
©2004 Steve Watkins/Dist. by Tribune Media Services, Inc.
ALL I CAN SEE FROM HERE ARE GROSS INACCURACIES AND LIBERAL PROPAGANDA.
www.comicspage.com or www.myhousebroken.com
TRY LEANING TO THE LEFT.
6-29
YOU'RE RIGHT! THIS FLICK MAKES MUCH MORE SENSE THIS WAY.

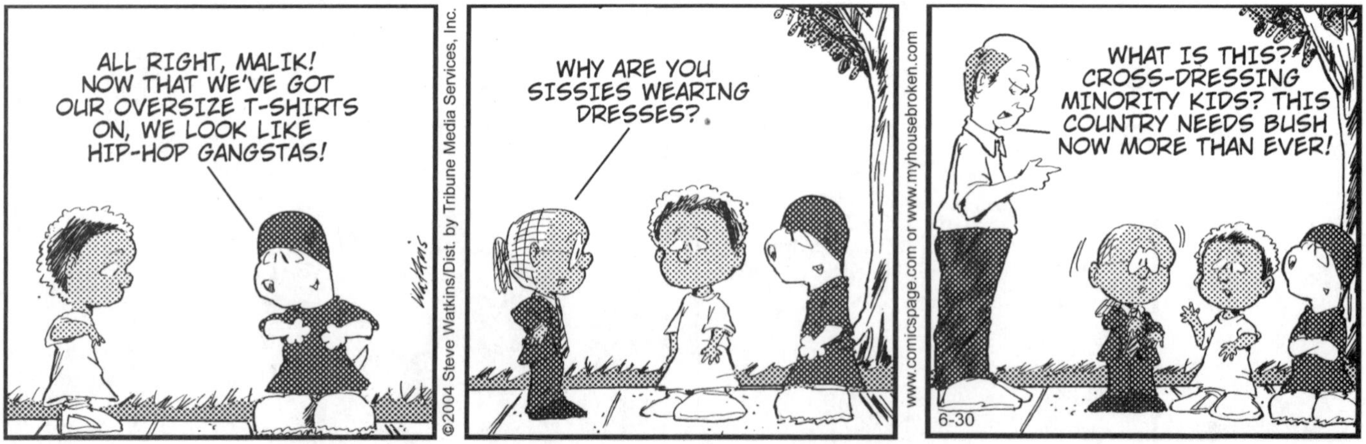
ALL RIGHT, MALIK! NOW THAT WE'VE GOT OUR OVERSIZE T-SHIRTS ON, WE LOOK LIKE HIP-HOP GANGSTAS!
©2004 Steve Watkins/Dist. by Tribune Media Services, Inc.
WHY ARE YOU SISSIES WEARING DRESSES?
www.comicspage.com or www.myhousebroken.com
WHAT IS THIS? CROSS-DRESSING MINORITY KIDS? THIS COUNTRY NEEDS BUSH NOW MORE THAN EVER!
6-30

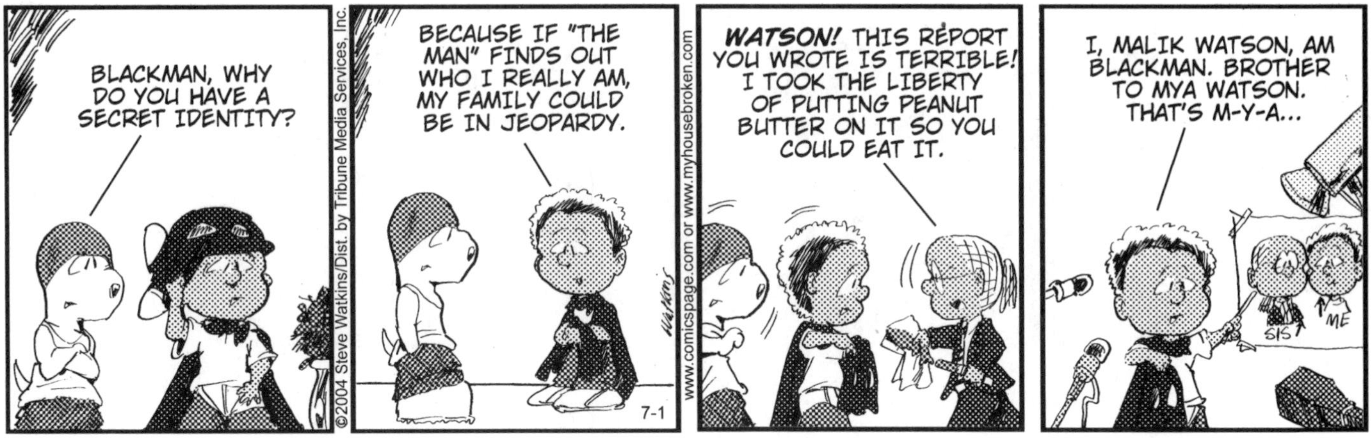
BLACKMAN, WHY DO YOU HAVE A SECRET IDENTITY?
©2004 Steve Watkins/Dist. by Tribune Media Services, Inc.
BECAUSE IF "THE MAN" FINDS OUT WHO I REALLY AM, MY FAMILY COULD BE IN JEOPARDY.
7-1
www.comicspage.com or www.myhousebroken.com
WATSON! THIS REPORT YOU WROTE IS TERRIBLE! I TOOK THE LIBERTY OF PUTTING PEANUT BUTTER ON IT SO YOU COULD EAT IT.
I, MALIK WATSON, AM BLACKMAN. BROTHER TO MYA WATSON. THAT'S M-Y-A...
SIS
ME

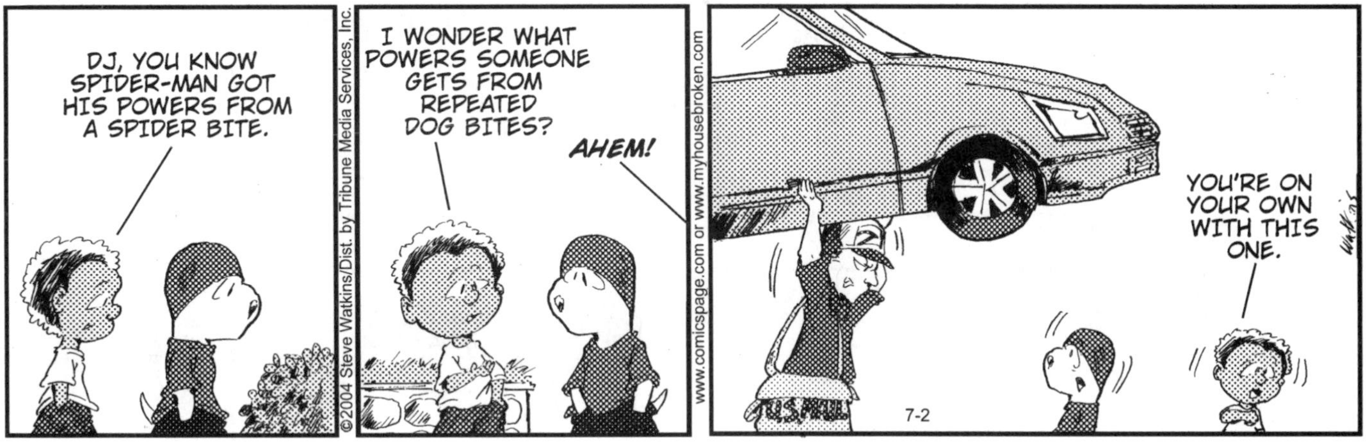
DJ, YOU KNOW SPIDER-MAN GOT HIS POWERS FROM A SPIDER BITE.
©2004 Steve Watkins/Dist. by Tribune Media Services, Inc.
I WONDER WHAT POWERS SOMEONE GETS FROM REPEATED DOG BITES?
AHEM!
www.comicspage.com or www.myhousebroken.com
YOU'RE ON YOUR OWN WITH THIS ONE.
7-2

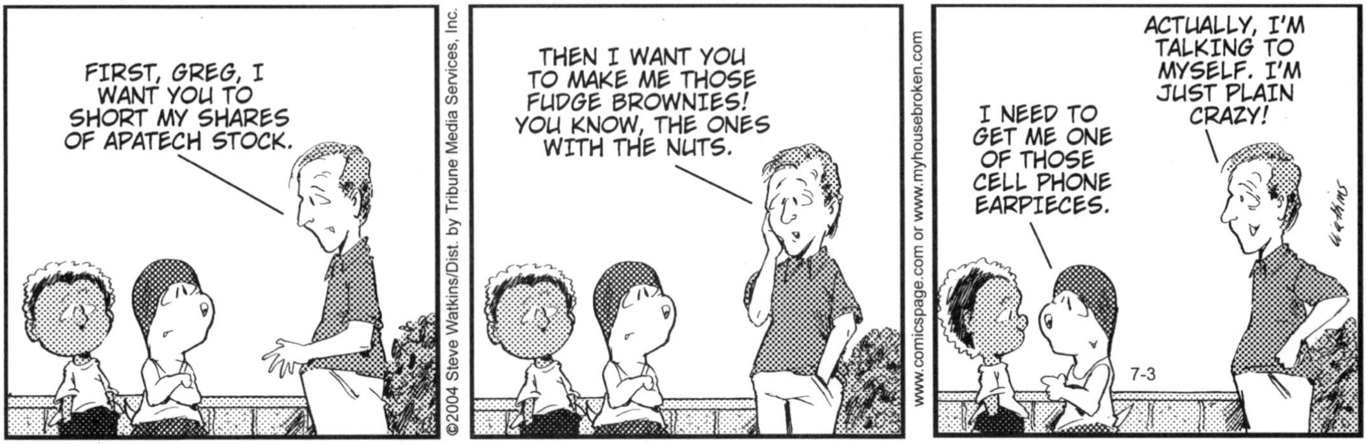
FIRST, GREG, I WANT YOU TO SHORT MY SHARES OF APATECH STOCK.
©2004 Steve Watkins/Dist. by Tribune Media Services, Inc.
THEN I WANT YOU TO MAKE ME THOSE FUDGE BROWNIES! YOU KNOW, THE ONES WITH THE NUTS.
www.comicspage.com or www.myhousebroken.com
I NEED TO GET ME ONE OF THOSE CELL PHONE EARPIECES.
ACTUALLY, I'M TALKING TO MYSELF. I'M JUST PLAIN CRAZY!
7-3

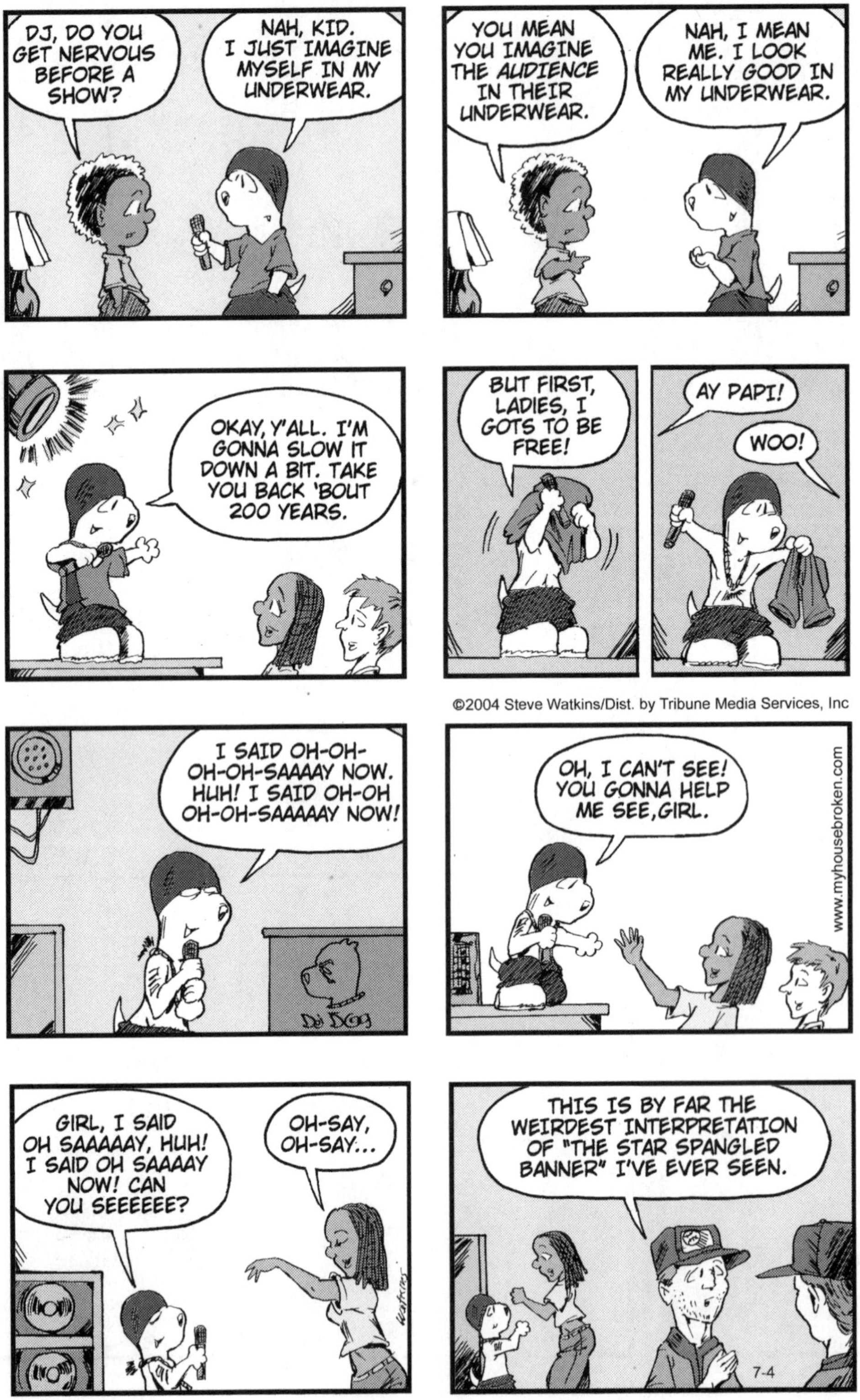
DJ, DO YOU GET NERVOUS BEFORE A SHOW?
NAH, KID. I JUST IMAGINE MYSELF IN MY UNDERWEAR.
YOU MEAN YOU IMAGINE THE *AUDIENCE* IN THEIR UNDERWEAR.
NAH, I MEAN ME. I LOOK REALLY GOOD IN MY UNDERWEAR.
OKAY, Y'ALL. I'M GONNA SLOW IT DOWN A BIT. TAKE YOU BACK 'BOUT 200 YEARS.
BUT FIRST, LADIES, I GOTS TO BE FREE!
AY PAPI!
WOO!
©2004 Steve Watkins/Dist. by Tribune Media Services, Inc
I SAID OH-OH-OH-OH-SAAAAY NOW. HUH! I SAID OH-OH OH-OH-SAAAAAY NOW!
DJ DOG
OH, I CAN'T SEE! YOU GONNA HELP ME SEE,GIRL.
www.myhousebroken.com
GIRL, I SAID OH SAAAAAY, HUH! I SAID OH SAAAAY NOW! CAN YOU SEEEEEEE?
OH-SAY, OH-SAY...
THIS IS BY FAR THE WEIRDEST INTERPRETATION OF "THE STAR SPANGLED BANNER" I'VE EVER SEEN.
7-4

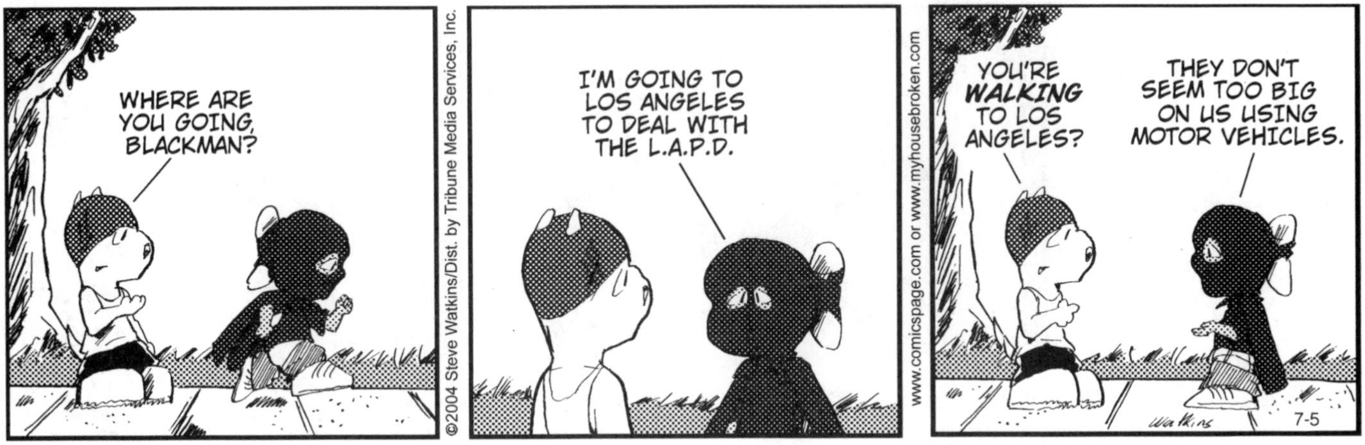
WHERE ARE YOU GOING, BLACKMAN?
©2004 Steve Watkins/Dist. by Tribune Media Services, Inc.
I'M GOING TO LOS ANGELES TO DEAL WITH THE L.A.P.D.
www.comicspage.com or www.myhousebroken.com
YOU'RE **WALKING** TO LOS ANGELES?
THEY DON'T SEEM TOO BIG ON US USING MOTOR VEHICLES.
Watkins
7-5

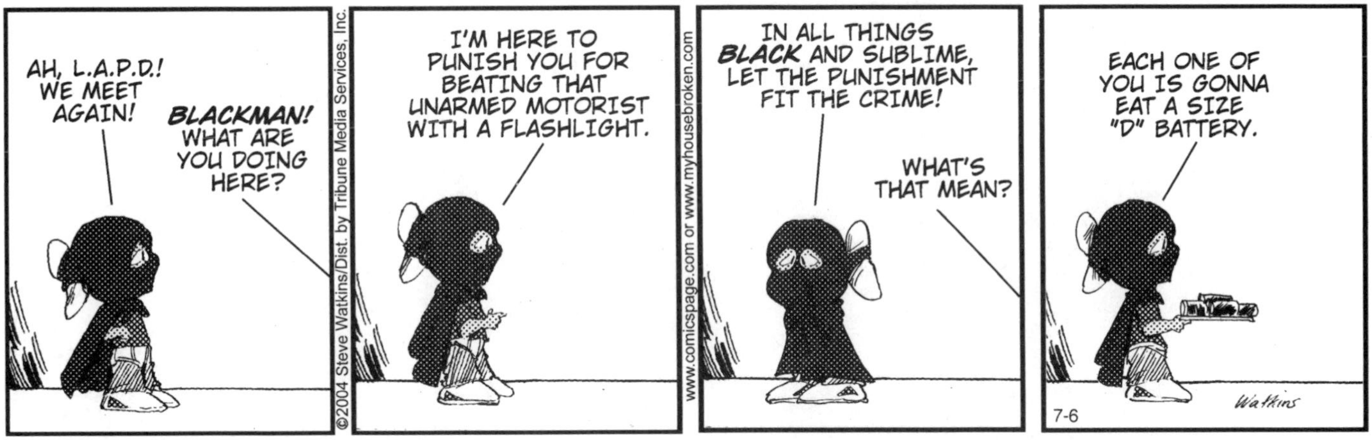
AH, L.A.P.D.! WE MEET AGAIN!
BLACKMAN! WHAT ARE YOU DOING HERE?
©2004 Steve Watkins/Dist. by Tribune Media Services, Inc.
I'M HERE TO PUNISH YOU FOR BEATING THAT UNARMED MOTORIST WITH A FLASHLIGHT.
www.comicspage.com or www.myhousebroken.com
IN ALL THINGS **BLACK** AND SUBLIME, LET THE PUNISHMENT FIT THE CRIME!
WHAT'S THAT MEAN?
EACH ONE OF YOU IS GONNA EAT A SIZE "D" BATTERY.
7-6
Watkins

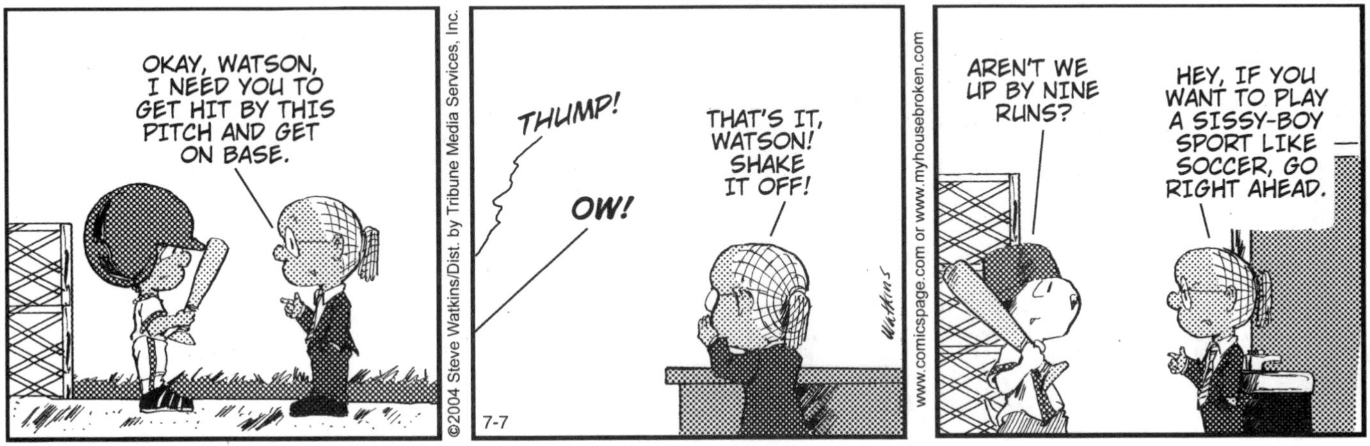
OKAY, WATSON, I NEED YOU TO GET HIT BY THIS PITCH AND GET ON BASE.
©2004 Steve Watkins/Dist. by Tribune Media Services, Inc.
THUMP!
OW!
THAT'S IT, WATSON! SHAKE IT OFF!
Watkins
7-7
www.comicspage.com or www.myhousebroken.com
AREN'T WE UP BY NINE RUNS?
HEY, IF YOU WANT TO PLAY A SISSY-BOY SPORT LIKE SOCCER, GO RIGHT AHEAD.

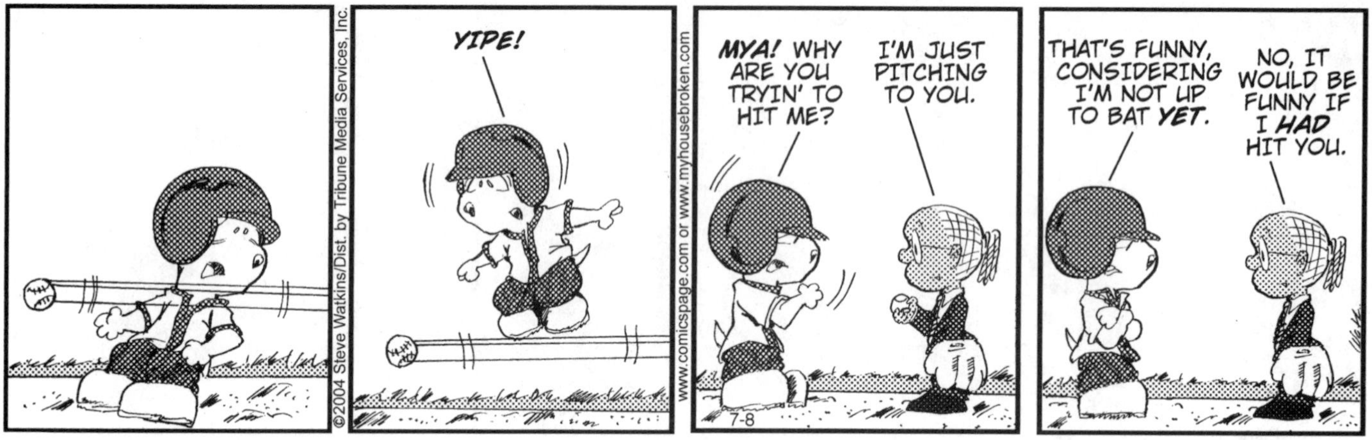
YIPE!
©2004 Steve Watkins/Dist. by Tribune Media Services, Inc.
MYA! WHY ARE YOU TRYIN' TO HIT ME?
I'M JUST PITCHING TO YOU.
www.comicspage.com or www.myhousebroken.com
7-8
THAT'S FUNNY, CONSIDERING I'M NOT UP TO BAT YET.
NO, IT WOULD BE FUNNY IF I HAD HIT YOU.

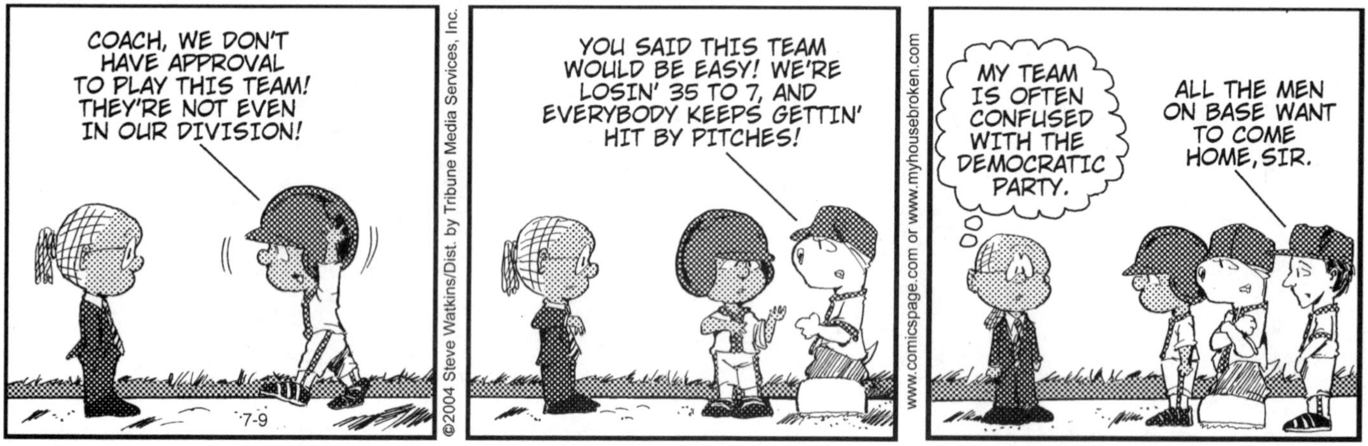
COACH, WE DON'T HAVE APPROVAL TO PLAY THIS TEAM! THEY'RE NOT EVEN IN OUR DIVISION!
7-9
©2004 Steve Watkins/Dist. by Tribune Media Services, Inc.
YOU SAID THIS TEAM WOULD BE EASY! WE'RE LOSIN' 35 TO 7, AND EVERYBODY KEEPS GETTIN' HIT BY PITCHES!
www.comicspage.com or www.myhousebroken.com
MY TEAM IS OFTEN CONFUSED WITH THE DEMOCRATIC PARTY.
ALL THE MEN ON BASE WANT TO COME HOME, SIR.

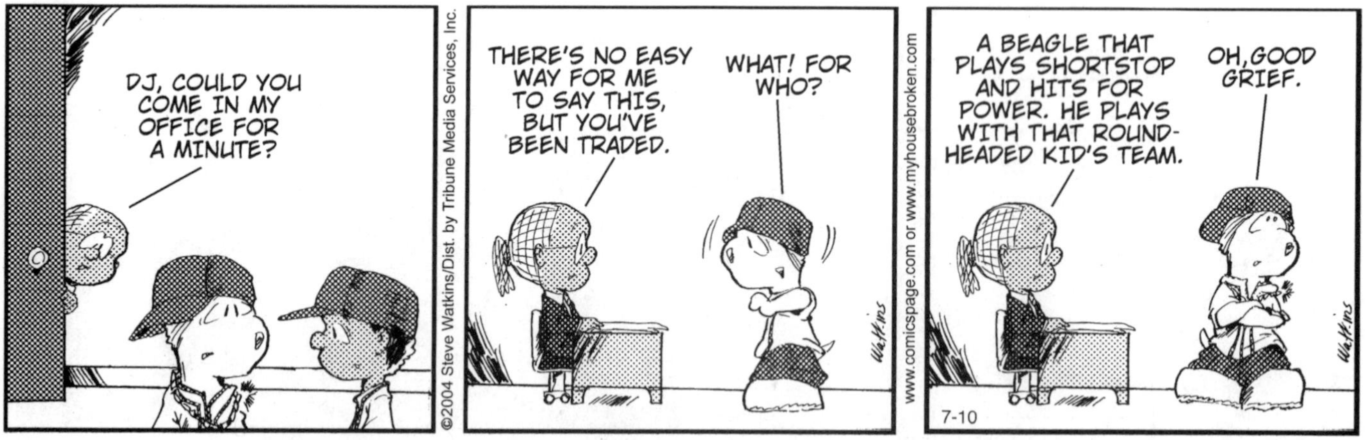
DJ, COULD YOU COME IN MY OFFICE FOR A MINUTE?
©2004 Steve Watkins/Dist. by Tribune Media Services, Inc.
THERE'S NO EASY WAY FOR ME TO SAY THIS, BUT YOU'VE BEEN TRADED.
WHAT! FOR WHO?
Watkins
www.comicspage.com or www.myhousebroken.com
A BEAGLE THAT PLAYS SHORTSTOP AND HITS FOR POWER. HE PLAYS WITH THAT ROUND-HEADED KID'S TEAM.
OH, GOOD GRIEF.
7-10
Watkins

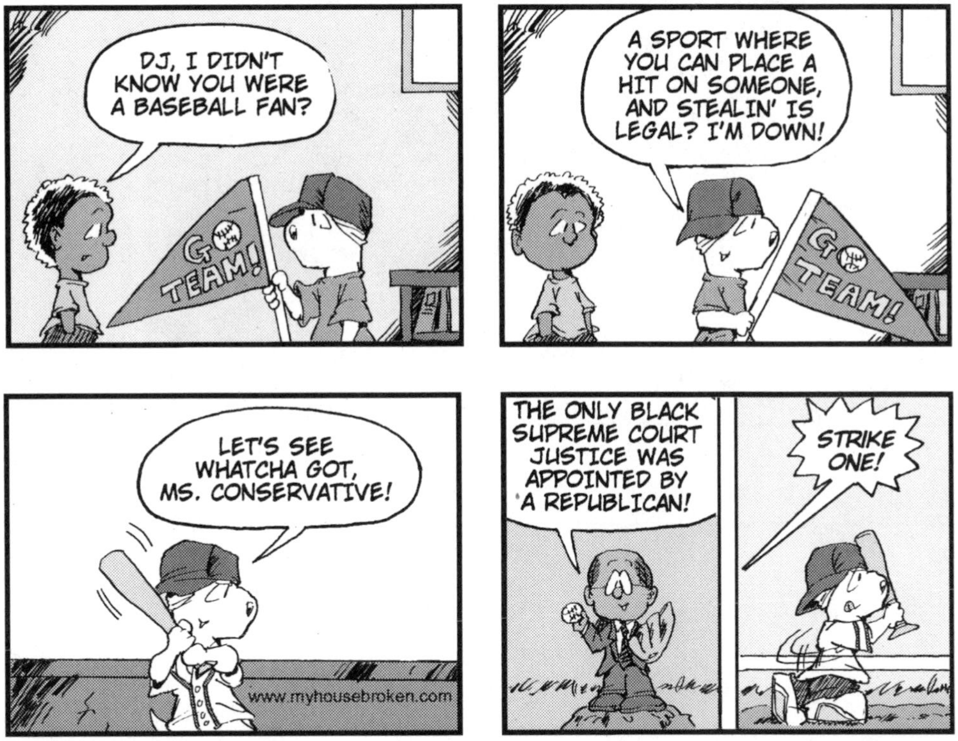
DJ, I DIDN'T KNOW YOU WERE A BASEBALL FAN?
GO TEAM!
A SPORT WHERE YOU CAN PLACE A HIT ON SOMEONE, AND STEALIN' IS LEGAL? I'M DOWN!
GO TEAM!
LET'S SEE WHATCHA GOT, MS. CONSERVATIVE!
www.myhousebroken.com
THE ONLY BLACK SUPREME COURT JUSTICE WAS APPOINTED BY A REPUBLICAN!
STRIKE ONE!

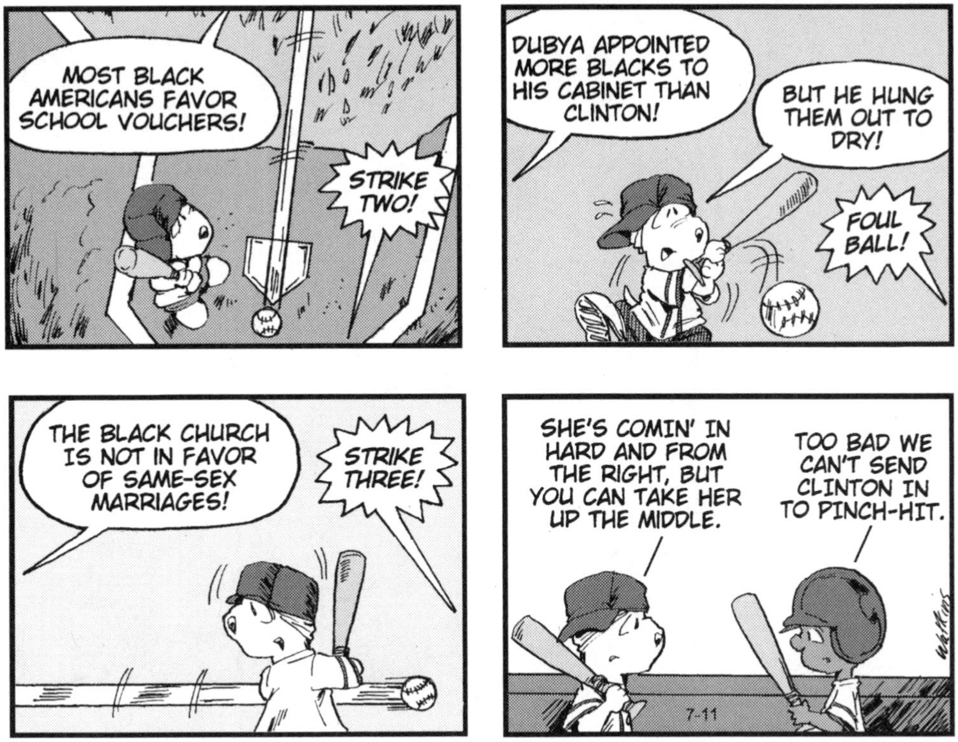
MOST BLACK AMERICANS FAVOR SCHOOL VOUCHERS!
STRIKE TWO!
DUBYA APPOINTED MORE BLACKS TO HIS CABINET THAN CLINTON!
BUT HE HUNG THEM OUT TO DRY!
FOUL BALL!
THE BLACK CHURCH IS NOT IN FAVOR OF SAME-SEX MARRIAGES!
STRIKE THREE!
SHE'S COMIN' IN HARD AND FROM THE RIGHT, BUT YOU CAN TAKE HER UP THE MIDDLE.
TOO BAD WE CAN'T SEND CLINTON IN TO PINCH-HIT.
7-11

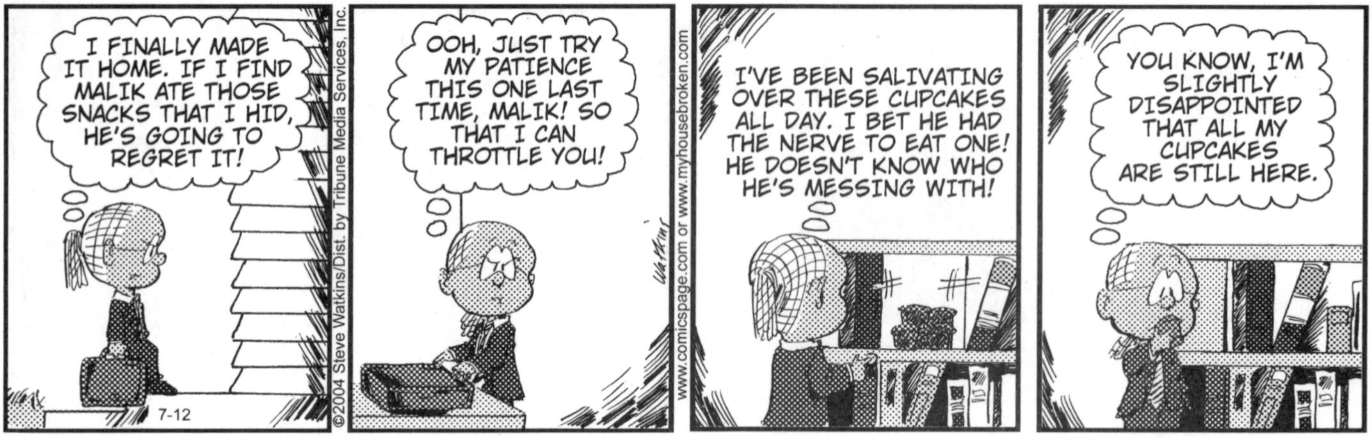
I FINALLY MADE IT HOME. IF I FIND MALIK ATE THOSE SNACKS THAT I HID, HE'S GOING TO REGRET IT!
7-12
©2004 Steve Watkins/Dist. by Tribune Media Services, Inc.
OOH, JUST TRY MY PATIENCE THIS ONE LAST TIME, MALIK! SO THAT I CAN THROTTLE YOU!
www.comicspage.com or www.myhousebroken.com
I'VE BEEN SALIVATING OVER THESE CUPCAKES ALL DAY. I BET HE HAD THE NERVE TO EAT ONE! HE DOESN'T KNOW WHO HE'S MESSING WITH!
YOU KNOW, I'M SLIGHTLY DISAPPOINTED THAT ALL MY CUPCAKES ARE STILL HERE.

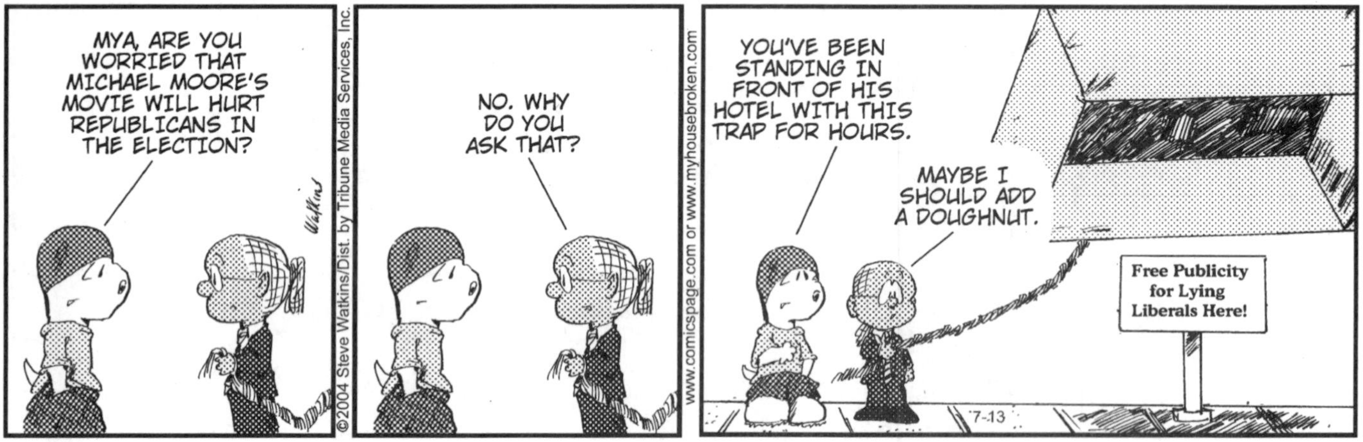
MYA, ARE YOU WORRIED THAT MICHAEL MOORE'S MOVIE WILL HURT REPUBLICANS IN THE ELECTION?
©2004 Steve Watkins/Dist. by Tribune Media Services, Inc.
NO. WHY DO YOU ASK THAT?
www.comicspage.com or www.myhousebroken.com
YOU'VE BEEN STANDING IN FRONT OF HIS HOTEL WITH THIS TRAP FOR HOURS.
MAYBE I SHOULD ADD A DOUGHNUT.
Free Publicity for Lying Liberals Here!
7-13

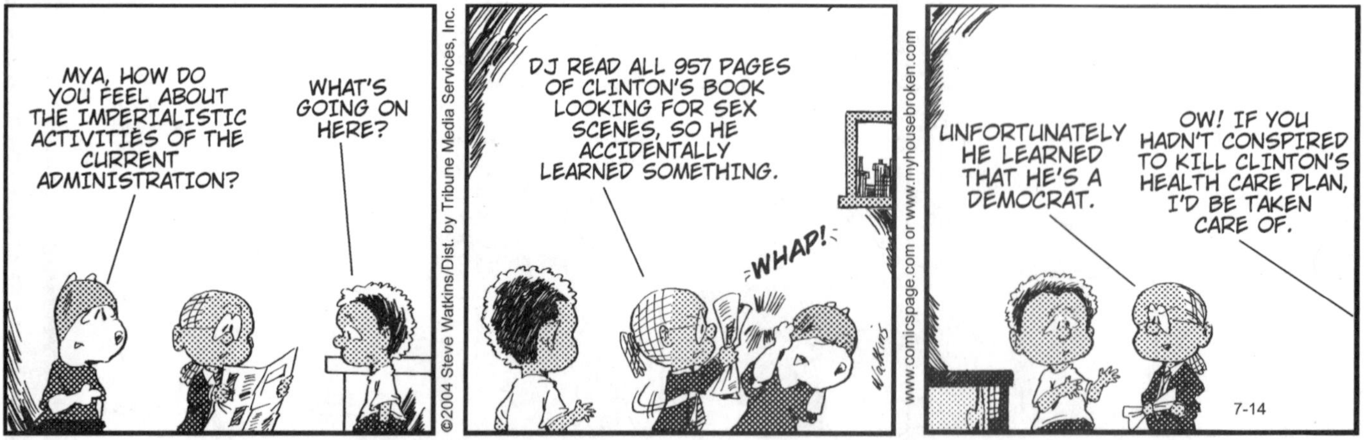
MYA, HOW DO YOU FEEL ABOUT THE IMPERIALISTIC ACTIVITIES OF THE CURRENT ADMINISTRATION?
WHAT'S GOING ON HERE?
©2004 Steve Watkins/Dist. by Tribune Media Services, Inc.
DJ READ ALL 957 PAGES OF CLINTON'S BOOK LOOKING FOR SEX SCENES, SO HE ACCIDENTALLY LEARNED SOMETHING.
WHAP!
www.comicspage.com or www.myhousebroken.com
UNFORTUNATELY HE LEARNED THAT HE'S A DEMOCRAT.
OW! IF YOU HADN'T CONSPIRED TO KILL CLINTON'S HEALTH CARE PLAN, I'D BE TAKEN CARE OF.
7-14

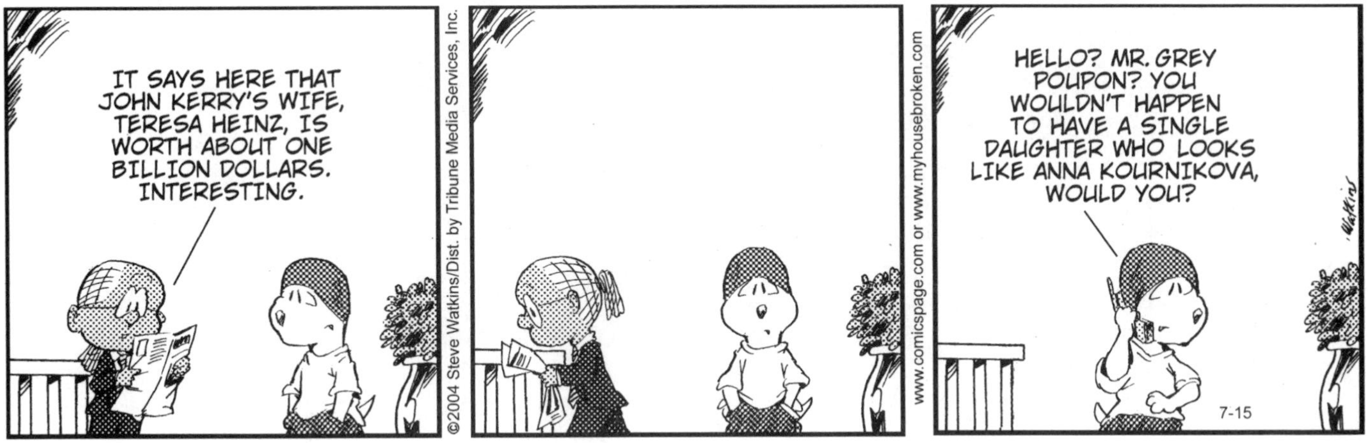
IT SAYS HERE THAT JOHN KERRY'S WIFE, TERESA HEINZ, IS WORTH ABOUT ONE BILLION DOLLARS. INTERESTING.
©2004 Steve Watkins/Dist. by Tribune Media Services, Inc.
www.comicspage.com or www.myhousebroken.com
HELLO? MR. GREY POUPON? YOU WOULDN'T HAPPEN TO HAVE A SINGLE DAUGHTER WHO LOOKS LIKE ANNA KOURNIKOVA, WOULD YOU?
7-15

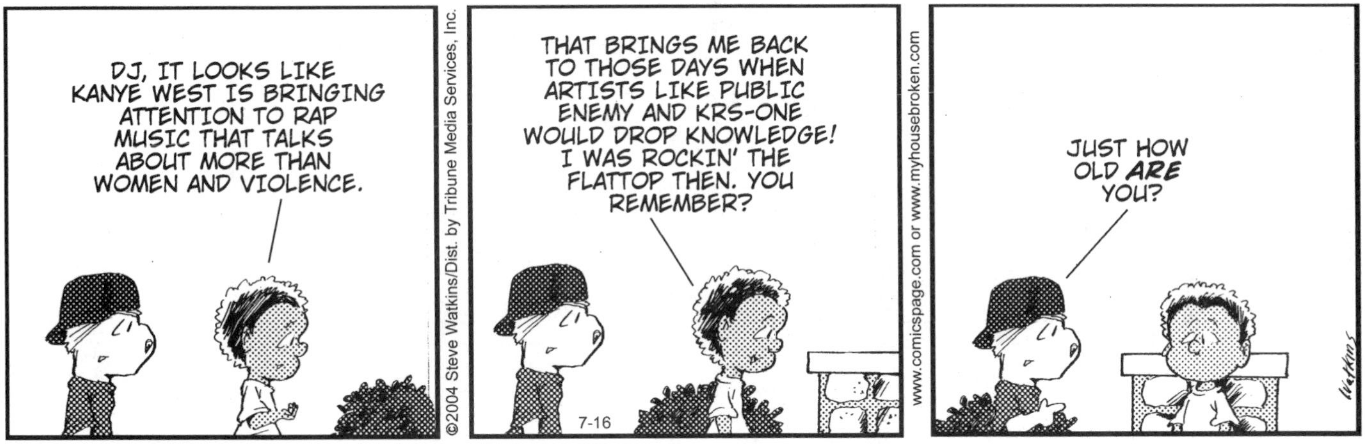
DJ, IT LOOKS LIKE KANYE WEST IS BRINGING ATTENTION TO RAP MUSIC THAT TALKS ABOUT MORE THAN WOMEN AND VIOLENCE.
©2004 Steve Watkins/Dist. by Tribune Media Services, Inc.
THAT BRINGS ME BACK TO THOSE DAYS WHEN ARTISTS LIKE PUBLIC ENEMY AND KRS-ONE WOULD DROP KNOWLEDGE! I WAS ROCKIN' THE FLATTOP THEN. YOU REMEMBER?
7-16
www.comicspage.com or www.myhousebroken.com
JUST HOW OLD ARE YOU?

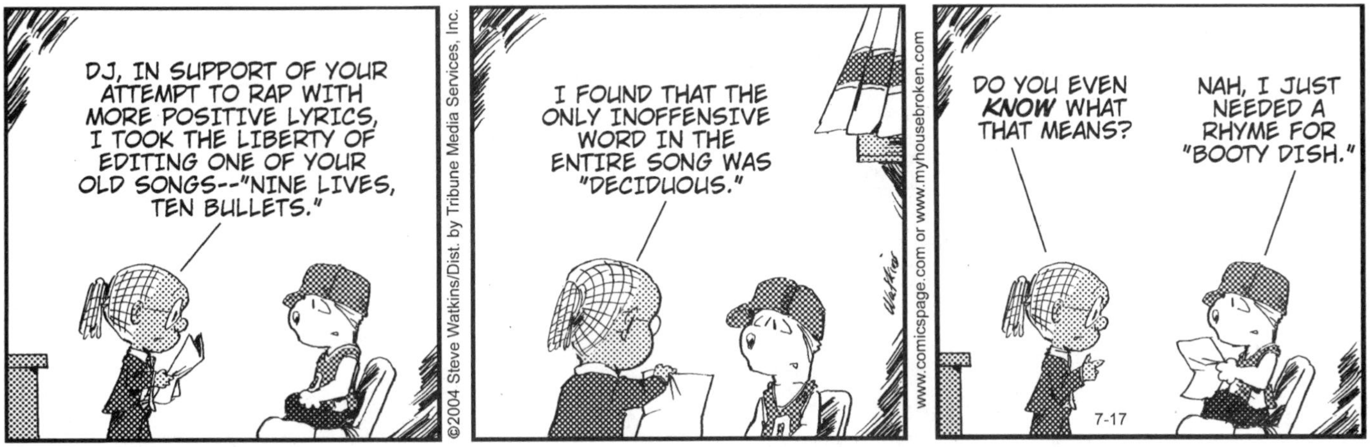
DJ, IN SUPPORT OF YOUR ATTEMPT TO RAP WITH MORE POSITIVE LYRICS, I TOOK THE LIBERTY OF EDITING ONE OF YOUR OLD SONGS--"NINE LIVES, TEN BULLETS."
©2004 Steve Watkins/Dist. by Tribune Media Services, Inc.
I FOUND THAT THE ONLY INOFFENSIVE WORD IN THE ENTIRE SONG WAS "DECIDUOUS."
www.comicspage.com or www.myhousebroken.com
DO YOU EVEN KNOW WHAT THAT MEANS?
NAH, I JUST NEEDED A RHYME FOR "BOOTY DISH."
7-17

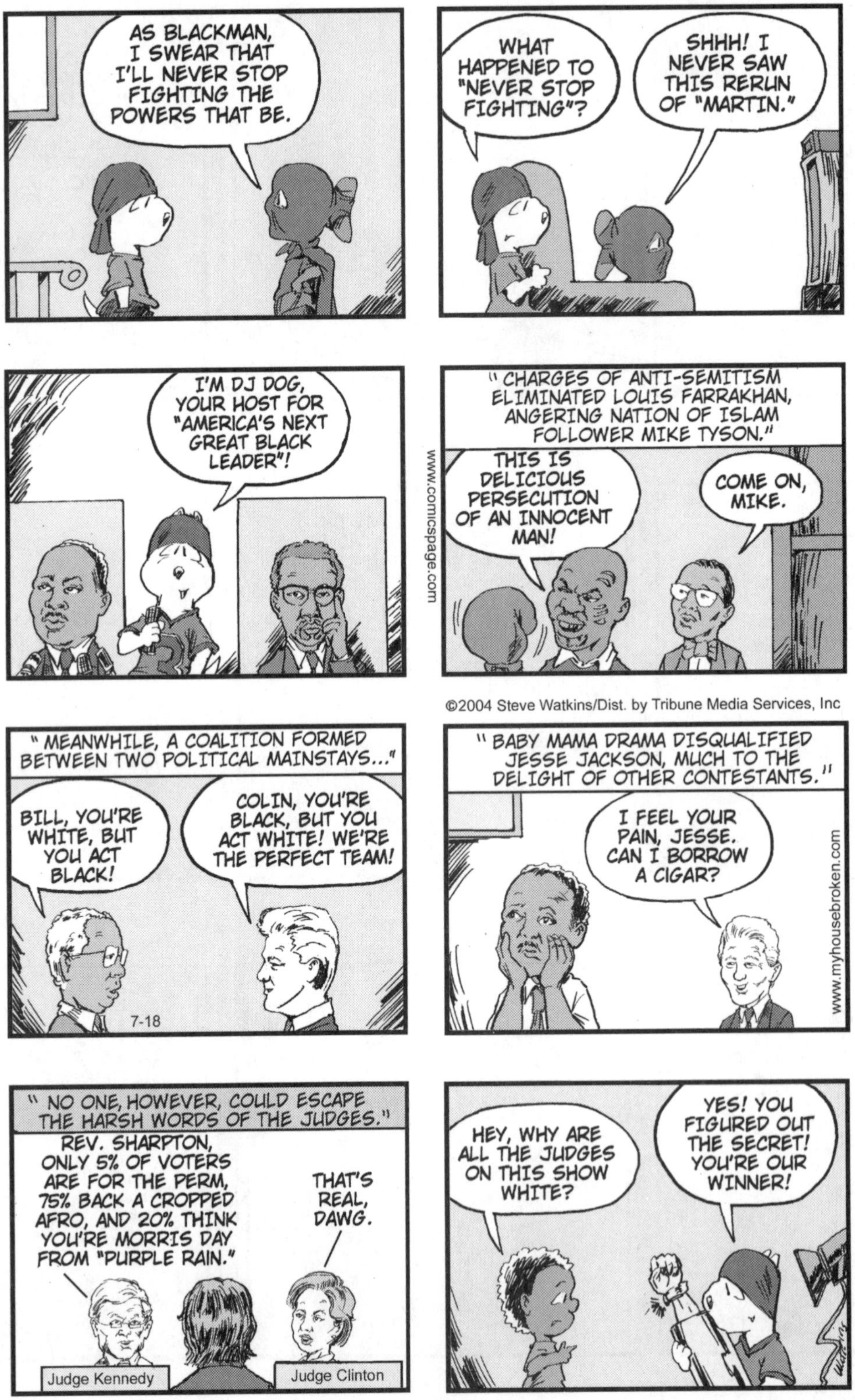

AS BLACKMAN, I SWEAR THAT I'LL NEVER STOP FIGHTING THE POWERS THAT BE.
WHAT HAPPENED TO "NEVER STOP FIGHTING"?
SHHH! I NEVER SAW THIS RERUN OF "MARTIN."
I'M DJ DOG, YOUR HOST FOR "AMERICA'S NEXT GREAT BLACK LEADER"!
www.comicspage.com
" CHARGES OF ANTI-SEMITISM ELIMINATED LOUIS FARRAKHAN, ANGERING NATION OF ISLAM FOLLOWER MIKE TYSON."
THIS IS DELICIOUS PERSECUTION OF AN INNOCENT MAN!
COME ON, MIKE.
©2004 Steve Watkins/Dist. by Tribune Media Services, Inc
" MEANWHILE, A COALITION FORMED BETWEEN TWO POLITICAL MAINSTAYS..."
BILL, YOU'RE WHITE, BUT YOU ACT BLACK!
COLIN, YOU'RE BLACK, BUT YOU ACT WHITE! WE'RE THE PERFECT TEAM!
7-18
" BABY MAMA DRAMA DISQUALIFIED JESSE JACKSON, MUCH TO THE DELIGHT OF OTHER CONTESTANTS."
I FEEL YOUR PAIN, JESSE. CAN I BORROW A CIGAR?
www.myhousebroken.com
" NO ONE, HOWEVER, COULD ESCAPE THE HARSH WORDS OF THE JUDGES."
REV. SHARPTON, ONLY 5% OF VOTERS ARE FOR THE PERM, 75% BACK A CROPPED AFRO, AND 20% THINK YOU'RE MORRIS DAY FROM "PURPLE RAIN."
THAT'S REAL, DAWG.
Judge Kennedy
Judge Clinton
HEY, WHY ARE ALL THE JUDGES ON THIS SHOW WHITE?
YES! YOU FIGURED OUT THE SECRET! YOU'RE OUR WINNER!

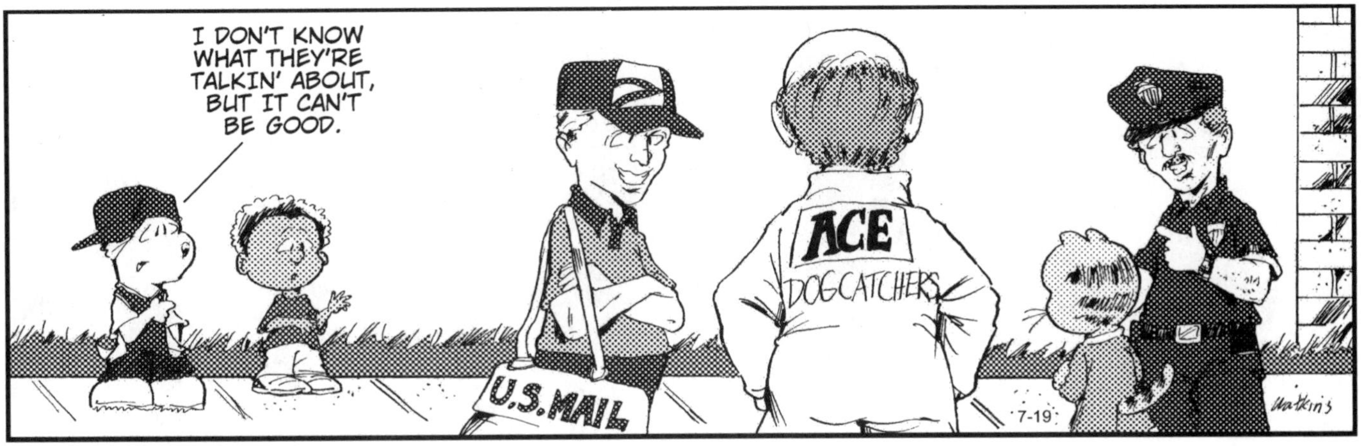
I DON'T KNOW WHAT THEY'RE TALKIN' ABOUT, BUT IT CAN'T BE GOOD.
ACE
DOGCATCHERS
U.S. MAIL
7-19
Watkins

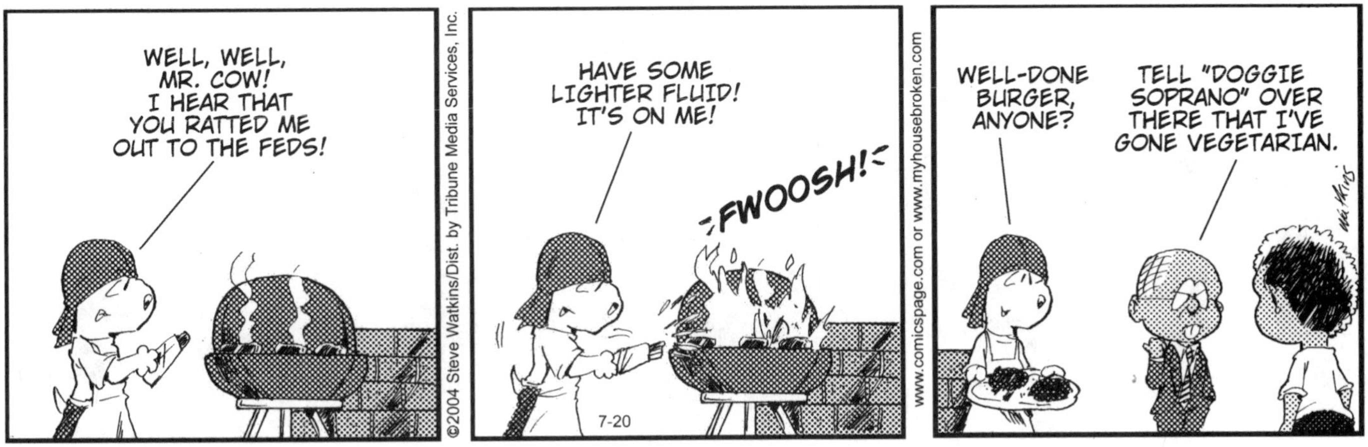
WELL, WELL, MR. COW! I HEAR THAT YOU RATTED ME OUT TO THE FEDS!
HAVE SOME LIGHTER FLUID! IT'S ON ME!
FWOOSH!
7-20
WELL-DONE BURGER, ANYONE?
TELL "DOGGIE SOPRANO" OVER THERE THAT I'VE GONE VEGETARIAN.
Watkins

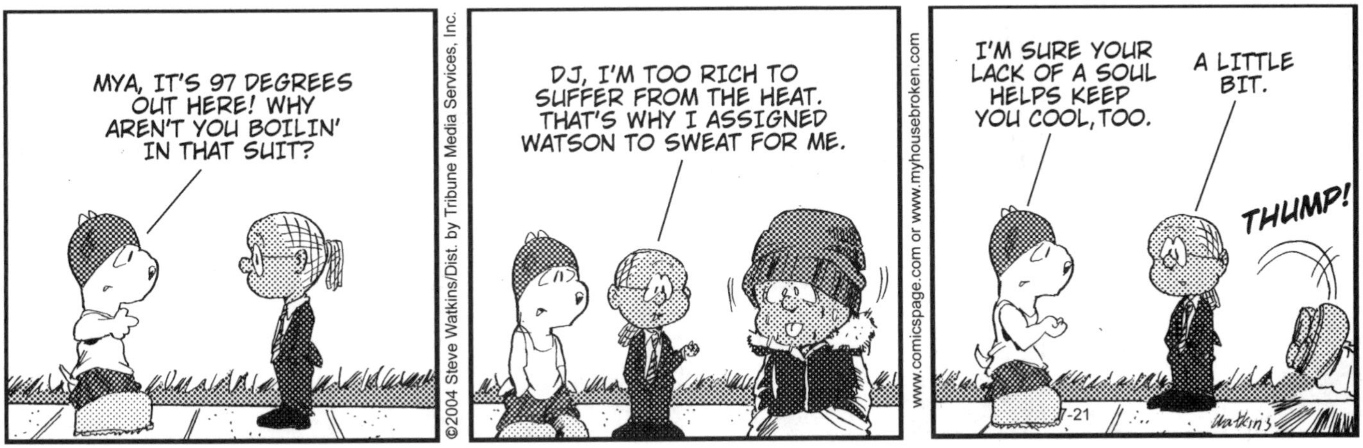
MYA, IT'S 97 DEGREES OUT HERE! WHY AREN'T YOU BOILIN' IN THAT SUIT?
DJ, I'M TOO RICH TO SUFFER FROM THE HEAT. THAT'S WHY I ASSIGNED WATSON TO SWEAT FOR ME.
I'M SURE YOUR LACK OF A SOUL HELPS KEEP YOU COOL, TOO.
A LITTLE BIT.
THUMP!
7-21
Watkins

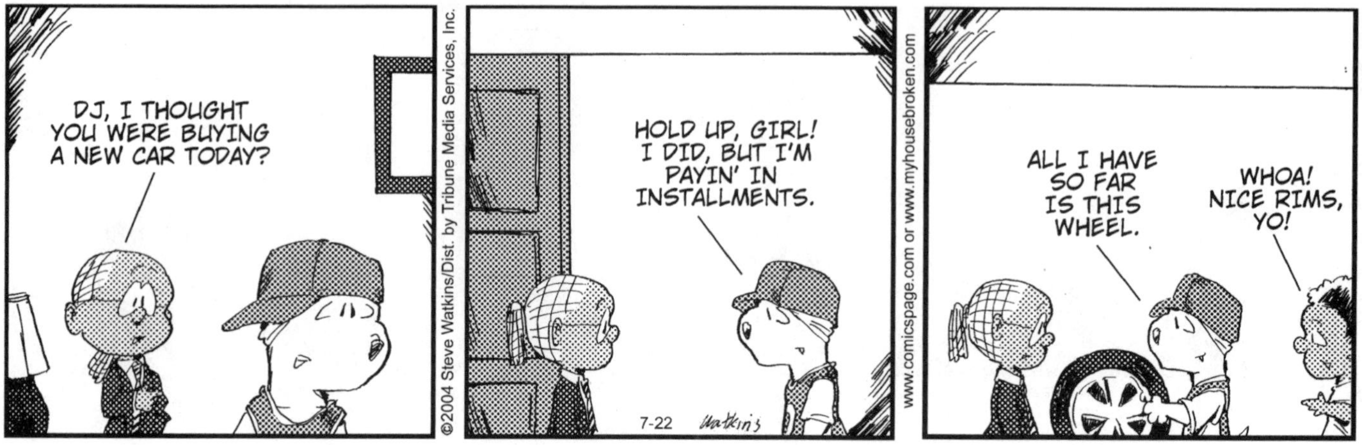
DJ, I THOUGHT YOU WERE BUYING A NEW CAR TODAY?
©2004 Steve Watkins/Dist. by Tribune Media Services, Inc.
HOLD UP, GIRL! I DID, BUT I'M PAYIN' IN INSTALLMENTS.
7-22
www.comicspage.com or www.myhousebroken.com
ALL I HAVE SO FAR IS THIS WHEEL.
WHOA! NICE RIMS, YO!

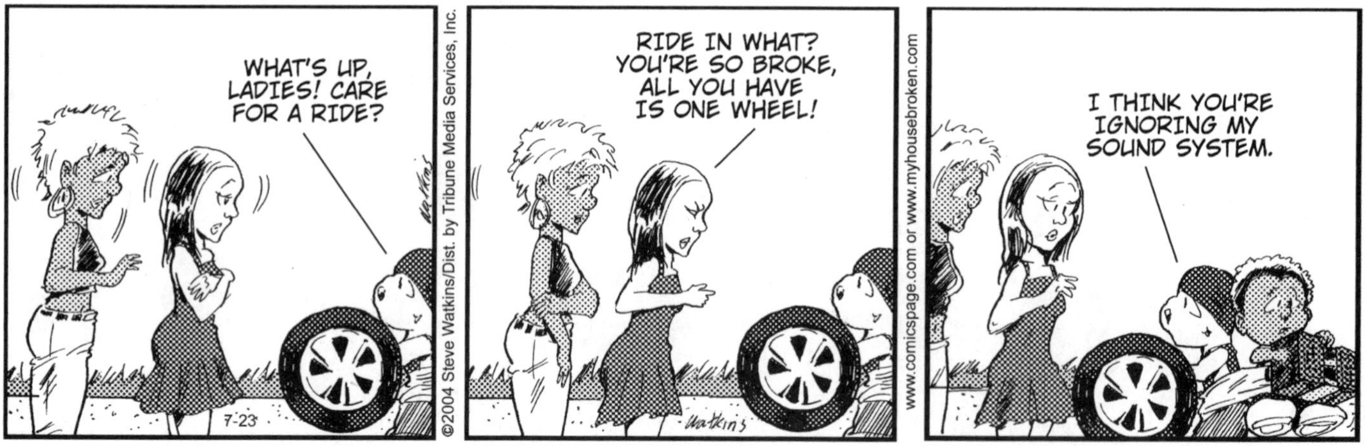
WHAT'S UP, LADIES! CARE FOR A RIDE?
7-23
©2004 Steve Watkins/Dist. by Tribune Media Services, Inc.
RIDE IN WHAT? YOU'RE SO BROKE, ALL YOU HAVE IS ONE WHEEL!
www.comicspage.com or www.myhousebroken.com
I THINK YOU'RE IGNORING MY SOUND SYSTEM.

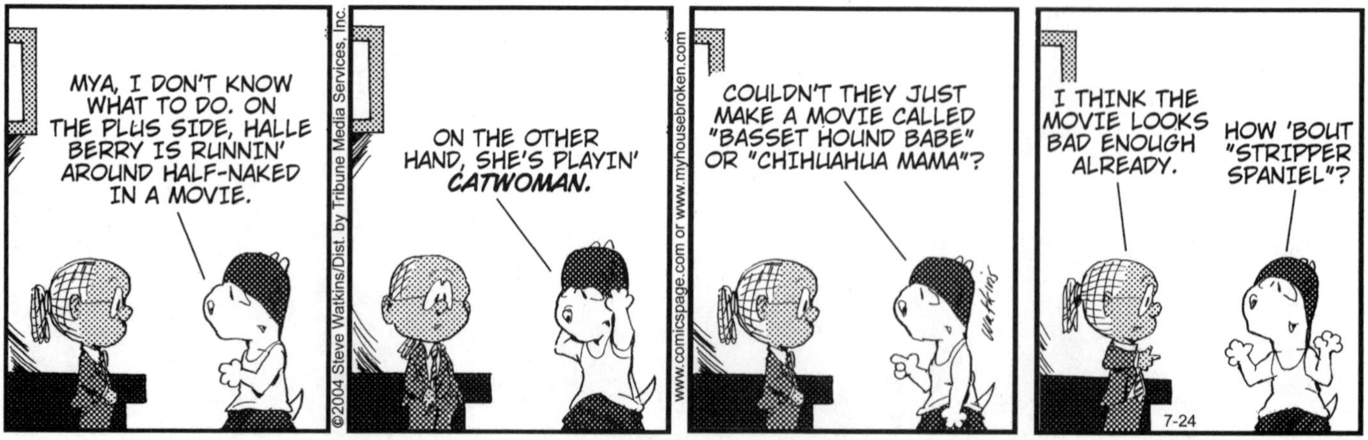
MYA, I DON'T KNOW WHAT TO DO. ON THE PLUS SIDE, HALLE BERRY IS RUNNIN' AROUND HALF-NAKED IN A MOVIE.
©2004 Steve Watkins/Dist. by Tribune Media Services, Inc.
ON THE OTHER HAND, SHE'S PLAYIN' ***CATWOMAN.***
www.comicspage.com or www.myhousebroken.com
COULDN'T THEY JUST MAKE A MOVIE CALLED "BASSET HOUND BABE" OR "CHIHUAHUA MAMA"?
I THINK THE MOVIE LOOKS BAD ENOUGH ALREADY.
HOW 'BOUT "STRIPPER SPANIEL"?
7-24

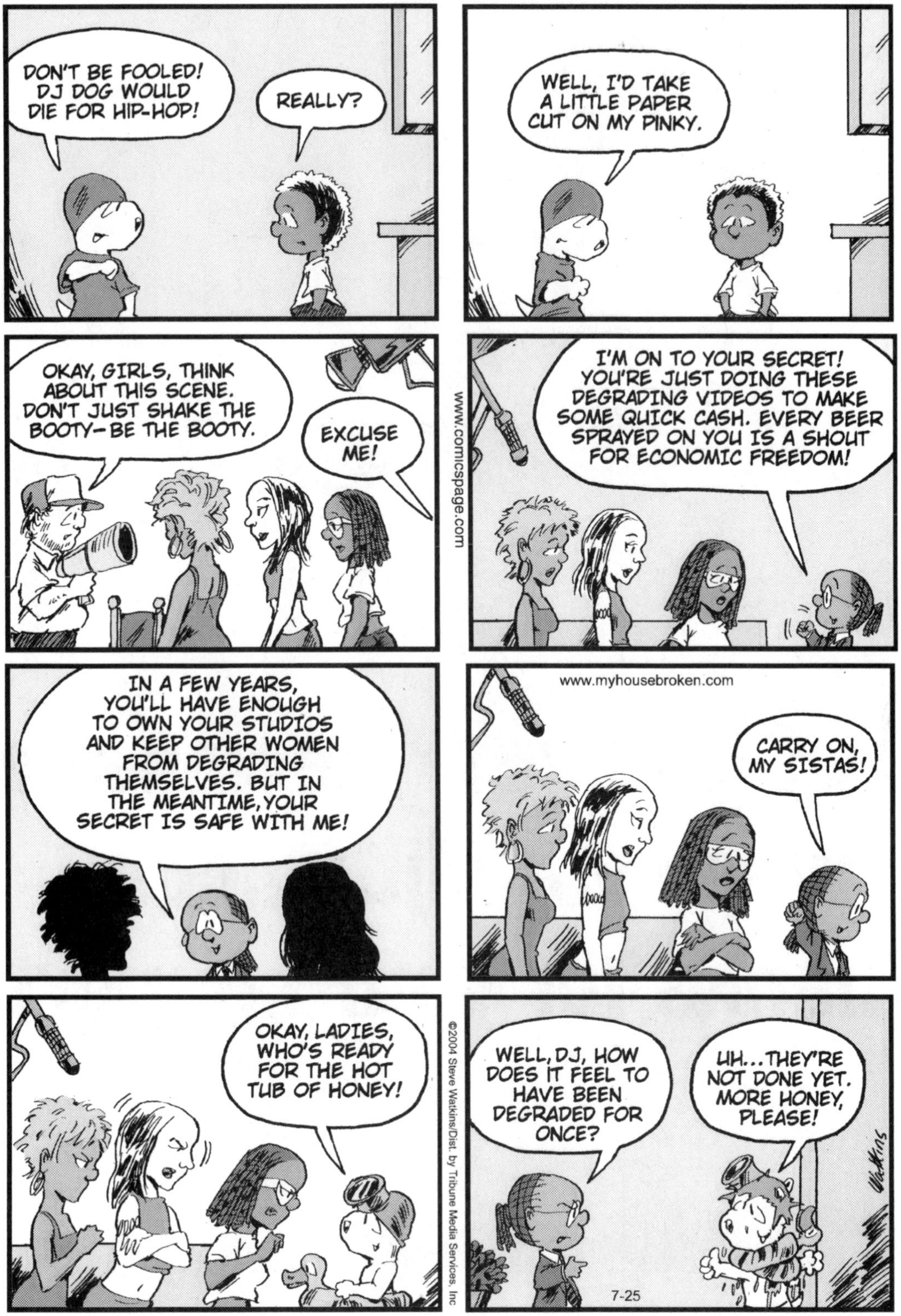
DON'T BE FOOLED! DJ DOG WOULD DIE FOR HIP-HOP!
REALLY?
WELL, I'D TAKE A LITTLE PAPER CUT ON MY PINKY.
OKAY, GIRLS, THINK ABOUT THIS SCENE. DON'T JUST SHAKE THE BOOTY–BE THE BOOTY.
EXCUSE ME!
www.comicspage.com
I'M ON TO YOUR SECRET! YOU'RE JUST DOING THESE DEGRADING VIDEOS TO MAKE SOME QUICK CASH. EVERY BEER SPRAYED ON YOU IS A SHOUT FOR ECONOMIC FREEDOM!
IN A FEW YEARS, YOU'LL HAVE ENOUGH TO OWN YOUR STUDIOS AND KEEP OTHER WOMEN FROM DEGRADING THEMSELVES. BUT IN THE MEANTIME, YOUR SECRET IS SAFE WITH ME!
www.myhousebroken.com
CARRY ON, MY SISTAS!
OKAY, LADIES, WHO'S READY FOR THE HOT TUB OF HONEY!
©2004 Steve Watkins/Dist. by Tribune Media Services, Inc
WELL, DJ, HOW DOES IT FEEL TO HAVE BEEN DEGRADED FOR ONCE?
UH...THEY'RE NOT DONE YET. MORE HONEY, PLEASE!
Watkins
7-25

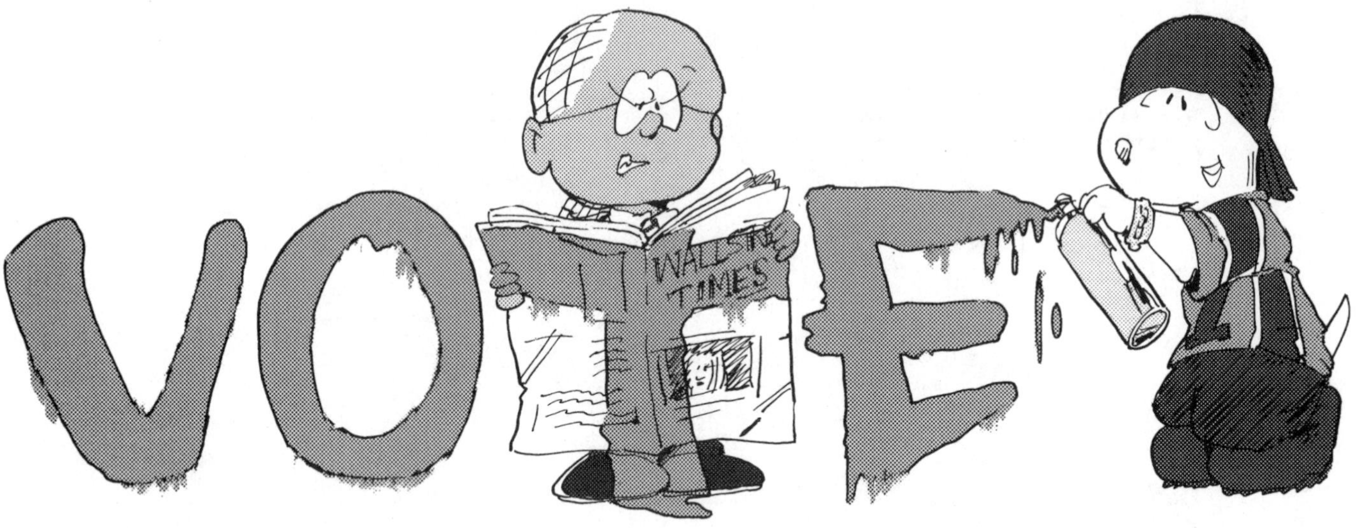
VOTE
TIMES

DJ Dog into your newspaper at www.votedjdog.com! Thanks for your support!